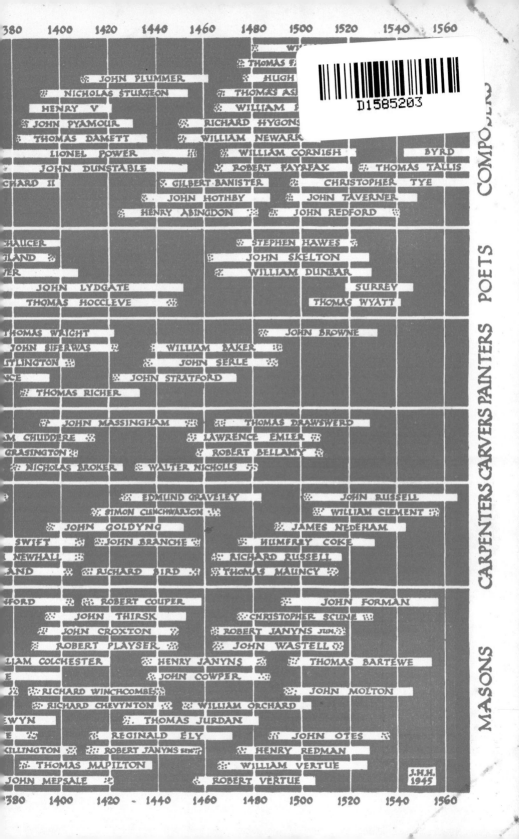

Darwin.
1950.

GOTHIC ENGLAND

(1948)
2nd Et

£16

GB Al͞

1   Westminster Abbey: Henry VII's Chapel, 1503-19.
From the colour plate in Ackermann's *Westminster Abbey*

GOTHIC ENGLAND

A Survey of National Culture
1300–1550

BY

JOHN HARVEY

Second Edition, Revised

B. T. BATSFORD LTD.
LONDON   ★   NEW YORK
TORONTO   SYDNEY

First published, Spring 1947
Second Edition, Summer 1948

MADE AND PRINTED IN GREAT BRITAIN
BY JARROLD AND SONS LTD., NORWICH, FOR THE PUBLISHERS B. T. BATSFORD LTD.
LONDON: 15 NORTH AUDLEY STREET, W.I AND MALVERN WELLS, WORCESTERSHIRE
NEW YORK: 122 EAST 55TH STREET   TORONTO: 480–6 UNIVERSITY AVENUE
SYDNEY: 156 CASTLEREAGH STREET

CONTENTS

PREFACE

ENGLISH art between the Black Death and the Reformation has suffered
an unjust neglect: detested by Ruskin and the champions of the "purer"
productions of the age of faith, it has seemed merely contemptible to the
Classicists. This holds true not only of architecture, sculpture, and
painting, but in a somewhat less degree of music and poetry. Shakespeare
and the great Elizabethans have been allowed, as Chesterton put it, to
throw "a gigantic shadow back" upon all that went before. Chaucer,
essentially greater as a poet than Shakespeare (who was primarily a
dramatist), and Dunstable, a more outstanding composer than Byrd, have
receded until they are seen as dim and distorted figures, if at all. As for
architects and artists, their very existence is denied, and even when it is
admitted, as in the *Cambridge Medieval History*,[1] we are told that "the
individual artists through whose hands Gothic art took shape are for the
most part unknown . . . to connect the names (of known individuals) with
surviving work is rarely possible, and so the artistic personality of their
owners remains obscure". An even more recent authority goes so far as
to say that "the history of mediæval architecture is bound to remain
essentially anonymous".[2]

So far as England is concerned, these statements are singularly inappro-
priate, and they do much less than justice to the impressive array of facts
gathered by Wyatt Papworth between one hundred and fifty years ago,
and published in the *Dictionary* of the Architectural Publication Society,
to say nothing of the wide sweep of Lethaby's researches, and the specialized work of many other students, past and present. The facts already in
print are quite sufficient to give a clue to the chief individuals responsible
for the trends of our architecture from 1300 onwards, while there is every
reason to think that equivalent knowledge of painters and sculptors awaits
only a more thorough investigation of manuscript sources. The current
view can be easily explained: the whole subject of the Middle Ages is
badly handicapped in the matter of publicity—it is not regarded as
"straight" history as are the days of Tutankhamen or Themistocles,
Caesar or Constantine, Cromwell or Castlereagh. "Ye Olden Time" has
been labelled "quaint" and no one expects that it will be taken seriously.

Besides this, another English preconception rules that art and its
practitioners (poets, musicians, architects, or artists) are definitely
eccentric, and they too need not be taken seriously, any more than the
Middle Ages. Fortunately the march of invention, while engaged in
extinguishing a large section of the human race and taking a terrible toll
of its cultural monuments, has, by means of the camera, the cinema, the
gramophone, and colour-reproduction processes, made it possible for every
educable person to take an interest in art, so that ancient prepossessions
and prejudices are gradually being pushed back towards the last ditch.

Almost all sane people agree that two world wars in a quarter of a
century, prosecuted with the aid of modern science, are two too many,

[1] Vol. VIII (1936), p. 720.
[2] Dr. Nikolaus Pevsner in *Journal* of Warburg Inst., V, 1942, 232.

but there is no general agreement as to the means to be adopted to secure peace. Such means are only likely to be found by people exceptionally gifted with human understanding, but some degree of understanding of the present can undoubtedly be achieved by the study of the past, which contains the causes of present effects. Everyone who is concerned with the destiny of his children should thus give some thought to history, and of all branches of history that which gives least scope to bias and blind prejudice is the history of the forms of art. Personal taste in painting or poetry is rarely so intense that its possessor will exterminate those who disagree with him, and the many shades of opinion are less amenable to stampede than in the sphere of politics. An enthusiastic presentment of the High Middle Ages must not be taken as disparaging the work of other times, but simply as an attempt to restore to a worthy position the output of a neglected period.

Similarly, no jingoistic patriotism is to be inferred from the concentration of interest upon England; the first commandment in the case is Solon's "Know thyself". It will be seen that there are particular reasons for studying this cultural epoch, not merely for its own sake, but for the light which it throws upon all periods of national emergence and development. Much that is fundamental in English character and temperament was then essentially what it is now, while remoteness in date may make

"This used to be Perpendicular."

By kind permission of the proprietors of "Punch"

it easier to attain to an external point of view, embracing our vices and our follies in equal measure with our more pleasing qualities.

This book is largely concerned with the course of development taken by our mature architectural style, commonly known as Perpendicular. It will be noticed that I make no attempt to find a verbal definition of this phase of art; indeed, I am doubtful of the value of all such attempts to pin down the elusive outlines of tradition and fashion which go to make up "style". Luckily, I am not faced with the point-blank demand, rhetorical or otherwise: "What is Perpendicular?" The reader whose main interest lies in the answer to this question, is advised to concentrate upon the illustrations, and to study the buildings themselves. Later on I shall have occasion to enlarge upon the fact that it was this period which saw English architecture transformed into an organic unity, greater than the sum of its parts; it is then as the ripened perfection of English Gothic that the works of this period are advanced.

The consideration of the art of any place or time must necessarily be founded largely upon personal opinion, for art appeals directly to the emotions rather than to reason. All that can be done is to advance reason to the support of the emotional claims of a masterpiece, or to define specific causes which may have operated in a given case to produce a failure to secure the desired effect. In referring to an effect as "desired" by the artist, I am aware that I am on dangerous ground; we cannot tell just how far the aesthetic concepts of the originator tallied with those current at the present day; but it is abundantly clear from the descriptions of chroniclers and the mutual emulation of parishioners that on the whole the art of the fourteenth and fifteenth centuries was considered beautiful, and that it fulfilled a definite demand made by patrons of greatly differing rank and station. Of artificially cultivated taste, in architecture at least, there is little evidence, but there is a striking parallel between the stilted "aureate diction" cultivated by Lydgate and his successors, and the overworked panelling and decoration of contemporary buildings; both are in marked contrast to the genuine subtlety of the age of Chaucer.

It may occasion surprise that comparatively little reference is made to the classic historical studies of the period, notably Huizinga's *Waning of the Middle Ages*. The omission is intentional; while I have tried to acquaint myself with the results of relevant research in cognate fields, my principal concern has been to gather significant facts from original sources, both published and manuscript, and to relate these facts to the surviving buildings and works of art. In the same way, I have avoided for the most part reference to the course of events abroad; England was not of course sealed off from foreign intercourse, and I shall refer to specific instances of the flow of ideas across the Channel, but compared with other nations, England may be said to have lived in a vacuum, only broken by the sweep of some far-reaching calamity: the famine of 1315, for instance, or the plague of 1348.

In view of the persisting paper shortage, the problem of references presented some difficulty, and since the book is intended for general reading it was decided that the pages ought not to be disfigured with either frequent footnotes or numbers referring to them. I therefore decided to adopt the method used by Mr. David Lack in his *Life of the Robin*, that of printing the notes at the end, page by page, with sufficient clues to avoid ambiguity. Further to save space, the authorities are expressed by abbreviations; the list of these serves as a supplement to the classified bibliography, which, though very far from complete, contains a large number of valuable works and a few references to periodical literature. To have given full references for the details of individual careers of architects and building craftsmen would have swollen the book to limits now impossible, and for this reason the bibliography for "Architectural Personalities" is exceptionally full. A comprehensive biographical dictionary of English architects who practised before 1550 is at present in course of compilation, and I shall be glad to supply references to any serious student who will be at the trouble of writing for them. I shall also be greatly obliged by the communication of corrections and relevant additions to the material included here.

The materials for this book have been gathered in many places, and I have to record my warm appreciation of the kindness and help received at the British Museum, the Public Record Office, the Corporation of London Records Office, Somerset House, and several local Probate Registries; the Bodleian Library, the Cambridge University Library, and several libraries in the provinces; also the libraries of the Society of Antiquaries, the Royal Historical Society, the Royal Institute of British Architects, the Courtauld Institute of Art, the Society of Genealogists, and the London Library; to the National Buildings Record; and to Mr. H. C. F. M. Fillmore, Town Clerk of Warwick, who gave me admirable facilities for reading the unique MS. accounts of Richard Beauchamp, Earl of Warwick.

The list of personal indebtedness is a long one, and I regret that in many cases this bare mention forms the only record of very substantial assistance and the willing expenditure of valuable time. To Mr. Herbert Chitty, Mr. T. D. Atkinson, and Mr. E. A. Greening Lamborn, I owe a long-standing debt for their unflagging kindness and enthusiastic help, while for advice or information on particular points I have to thank the following:

Mr. H. E. Balch, Miss M. J. Becker, Mr. G. H. Blore, Mr. W. P. Blore, Mr. P. B. Chatwin, Mr. H. R. Creswick, Mr. S. Phillips Dales, Mrs. K. A. Esdaile, the Rev. S. J. A. Evans, Sir Kaye Le Fleming, Mrs. Dorothy Gardiner, Mr. Walter H. Godfrey, Dr. Rose Graham, Mr. A. M. Hind, Mr. F. R. Hiorns, Mr. H. L. Honeyman, Mr. G. P. Jones, Mr. E. M. Jope, Professor Douglas Knoop, Mr. C. E. Lugard, Mr. Herbert Menges, Mr. E. G. Millar, Sir John Myres, Mr. B. H. St. J. O'Neil, Dr. N. Pevsner, the Rev. Angelo Raine, Mr. R. W. Ramsey, Miss L. J. Redstone, Professor A. E. Richardson, Dr. H. E. Salter, Mr. L. F. Salzman, Dr. H. W. Saunders, Mr. F. Shenton, Dr. W. Douglas Simpson, Mr. R. Somerville, Mr. John Summerson, Mr. Lawrence E. Tanner, Mr. E. G. Tibbitts, Mr. A. R. Wagner, Mr. F. Williamson, and Mr. Francis Wormald.

To Mr. Philip Henderson I owe a special debt, for not content with giving me permission to quote from his version of Skelton, he has most generously sent me revised texts in advance of the publication of his second edition.

During the writing of the book I have also enjoyed the benefit of discussion with my friends Arthur Oswald and Ralph Davis, and the patient textual criticism of my father, William Harvey, who has twice read through the copy. My wife has, as on previous occasions, doubled the parts of inspiration and experimental control. Lastly, let me record that Mr. Harry Batsford and Charles Fry not only suggested the book, but bore with fortitude its metamorphosis into something quite other than they had hoped, and yet maintained their constant, much abused, but cheerful energy in its production.

JOHN HARVEY

Half Moon Cottage,
Little Bookham, Surrey
31 October 1945

THE ILLUSTRATIONS

[*Actual or approximate dates of construction are given wherever possible, but approximate* single *dates (thus:* c. 1500) *must be accepted with caution, as they are generally based on stylistic evidence. Names of designers and craftsmen are given from documentary sources. The captions are included in the general index.*]

THE illustrations are intended to present a picture of the culture of the period complementary to, and to some extent separate from, that given in the text. Mostly architectural, they include examples of painting, sculpture, music, and the decorative arts, chosen for their outstanding value or typical character. In general, the main line of development is represented, rather than regional or local peculiarities.

The endpapers give a general view of the important artists of each class; the names included are restricted to Englishmen, with the exception of a few men of presumably foreign origin who practised their art in England. There is one exception to this rule: the inclusion among the poets of the Scot, William Dunbar. This can only be justified on the ground of his intrinsic importance in the development of English verse, and no discourtesy to the sister nation is intended thereby.

The cartoon on page vii is reproduced by permission of the proprietors of *Punch*, from the issue of 2 May 1945.

The frontispiece is reproduced from a colour print in Ackermann's *History of Westminster Abbey*, vol. II; comparison with Fig. 147 well shows how much has been lost, as well as gained, by the invention of photography.

The music of Figs. 8, 9, 105 is from J. Stainer: *Early Bodleian Music*, vol. II.

Fig. 19 is from a photograph by the late Dr. F. J. Allen, and reproduced from his book, *The Great Church Towers of England*, by permission of the Cambridge University Press.

Fig. 25 is from a drawing by J. C. Buckler in the British Museum.

Figs. 61, 62 are from engravings in the brothers Bucks' *Antiquities*, vols. I and II; they show rather better than any but aerial photographs the standardized form taken by the fortified residence in the fourteenth century.

Fig. 66 is reproduced from Dr. Herbert Read's *English Stained Glass*, by permission of the author and Messrs. Putnam & Co., Ltd.

Fig. 68 is from Professor E. W. Tristram's reconstructed copy (in Canterbury Cathedral) of the original painting on the tester of the Black Prince's tomb. The reproduction has been made by permission of the Dean and Chapter of Canterbury and Professor Tristram, and with the kind assistance of Miss Margaret Babington, O.B.E., Mr. Colin W. Walker, and the Chief Vesturer of the Cathedral.

Figs. 69, 139 take their material from standard works of reference, somewhat amplified; the roads shown are those of the fourteenth-century Gough Map, with additions chiefly based on the positions of important bridges.

Figs. 72, 73 are from R. W. Billings: *Durham Cathedral*, 1843, and from *Persian Art*, 1938 (edited by Dr. A. U. Pope) respectively, the latter by permission of the Oxford University Press.

Fig. 77 is from R. Richards: *Old Cheshire Churches*, by permission of the author. Published by B. T. Batsford, Ltd.

Figs. 85, 86 are reproduced from the standard work *English Mediæval Painting*, by Dr. Tancred Borenius and Professor E. W. Tristram, by permission of the authors. Published by Pantheon Casa Editrice, Florence.

Fig. 90 is from the original in the Department of British and Mediæval Antiquities, by permission of the Trustees of the British Museum.

Fig. 92 is from M. Symonds and L. Preece: *Needlework through the Ages*, 1928, by permission of the author and Messrs. Hodder & Stoughton. The original is in the Musée de Cluny, Paris.

Fig. 93 is from W. G. Thomson: *Tapestry Weaving in England*, published by B. T. Batsford, Ltd., 1903.

Fig. 94 is from the Inventory of Historical Monuments, *West London*, by permission of the Controller of H.M. Stationery Office.

Fig. 96 is from Dr. E. G. Millar's *English Illuminated Manuscripts of the Fourteenth and Fifteenth Centuries*, 1928, by permission of the Trustees of the British Museum and Dr. Millar. Special thanks are due to the Society of Antiquaries of London, who generously lent a copy of the book for reproduction.

Fig. 97 is from the late Maurice Drake's *A History of English Glass-Painting*, 1912, after a drawing by Mr. Wilfred Drake, by permission of Messrs. Werner Laurie Ltd. and Mrs. Maurice Drake.

Fig. 99 is from Mr. Frank Kendon's *Mural Paintings in English Churches during the Middle Ages*, 1923, by permission of Messrs. John Lane the Bodley Head Ltd.

Fig. 106 is from the late Aymer Vallance's *The Old Colleges of Oxford*, 1912, published by B. T. Batsford, Ltd.

Figs. 108, 135, 148 are from *Westminster Abbey and St. Margaret's Church*, by permission of Messrs. John Tiranti Ltd.

Fig. 112 is by the Kunstgeschichtliches Seminar, Marburg, and Fig. 113 from Uhde's *Cathedrals*.

Fig. 142 is from an engraving in John Britton: *Architectural Antiquities*, vol. II, after a drawing by F. Mackenzie, 1809.

Fig. 159 is from the Society of Antiquaries' *Historical Print No. 1*, by permission of the Society of Antiquaries and of the Trustees of the British Museum, from whose copy the reproduction has been made.

Fig. 169 is from an engraving in E. W. Brayley & J. Britton: *History of the Ancient Palace . . . at Westminster*, 1836, after R. W. Billings.

Fig. 172 shows, not the total amount of building work in progress, but the amount of new work *begun* in each period of five years. The sources are necessarily incomplete, but are adequate for royal buildings, works at cathedrals, university colleges, and guildhalls, and the largest private castles and manor-houses, while important works at large parish churches are also included. There is no reason to suppose that the relative numbers of dated works at different periods are not fairly representative.

Figs. 175, 176 are from the originals in the Victoria and Albert Museum, by permission of the Trustees.

ACKNOWLEDGMENT

The author and publishers here express their indebtedness to the following persons for the illustrations mentioned: The Trustees of the British Museum for Figs. 25, 90, 152, 159; Mr. H. Munro Cautley, F.S.A., A.R.I.B.A., for Fig. 5; Mr. Gerald Cobb and the Trustees of the British Museum for Fig. 115; Country Life Ltd. for Fig. 29; Mr. F. H. Crossley, F.S.A., for Figs. 2, 36, 38, 65, 82, 103, 119, 151; Mr. J. Dixon-Scott and the British Council for Figs. 54, 110, 128, 132, 150, 162; Mr. G. C. Druce for Fig. 173; Mr. Herbert Felton, F.R.P.S., for Figs. 7, 22, 51, 84, 102, 104, 111, 114, 125, 130, 147, 154, 156; Messrs. F. Frith & Co., Reigate, for Fig. 13; Messrs. Jarrold & Sons Ltd. for Fig. 121; Mr. A. F. Kersting for Figs. 6, 10, 14, 33, 44, 45, 50, 71, 76, 101, 118, 134, 137, 164; Mr. Walter Marshall for Fig. 116; the National Buildings Record for Figs. 30, 43, 47, 80, 100, 129, 145, 167, 168; Messrs. Photochrom Ltd. for Fig. 136; Mr. Sydney Pitcher, F.R.P.S., for Fig. 23; Mr. G. H. Salmon for Figs. 88, 160; Mr. S. Smith, Lincoln, for Fig. 81; Mr. John H. Stone for Figs. 21, 32; Mr. Will F. Taylor for Figs. 3, 4, 18, 24, 27, 28, 48, 74, 75, 107, 122, 127, 143, 157, 158, 163, 166; Messrs. J. Valentine & Sons Ltd. for Fig. 155; Mr. A. E. Walsham for Figs. 15, 89, 109, 140; and Mr. W. Watson for Fig. 117.

Figs. 12, 20, 31, 34, 35, 37, 39, 40, 41, 42, 46, 49, 52, 53, 55, 56, 57, 59, 60, 63, 64, 67, 78, 91, 95, 120, 123, 133, 141, 144, 146, 149, 161, 165, 170, 171, 174 are from photographs by the late Brian C. Clayton; Fig. 11 from a photograph by the late Frank E. Howard; these and Figs. 58, 79, 83, 87, 88, 124, 131, 138, 153 are in the publishers' collection. Figs. 8, 9, 16, 17, 26, 69, 70, 98, 105, 126, 139, 172 are from line-drawings by the author.

2   Warwick, Beauchamp Chapel: Saint and Angel, 1447–50.
Sculptor: John Massingham

3 Canterbury Cathedral : Nave and Central Tower, 1378–1497.
Designer : Henry Yevele ; of Tower, John Wastell

INTRODUCTION

As far back as records go, there have been seekers for a past golden age where justice and truth reigned over a happy breed of men. Sober historians point out that while records of this fortunate age are lacking, there is plenty of evidence for the existence of the same corruption and selfishness which still mar the chronicles of the nations. Nearly five thousand years ago Uruka-gina, king of Lagash, set down the reforms whereby he substituted free justice for bondage to officialdom—our hearts are wrung by his picture of the wrongs done to his subjects, those sufferers of a hundred and fifty generations back—within their land "were inspectors as far as the sea". The officials were removed and the burden lightened, but in the intervening centuries the trouble has crept back and the clash between the material and the ideal repeats itself again and again.

So the sceptic will look dubious when he hears a D. H. Lawrence singing—"Before Plato told the great lie of ideals men slimly went like fishes, and didn't care". There is something in Lawrence's vision, all the same. Idealism, of course, had existed for centuries before Plato, but no one thought of making ideals into a shibboleth or a strait-jacket. Plato was born in 427 B.C., two years after the death of Pericles and a couple of generations too late to take part in the culmination of Greek literature and Greek art. The creative artists and their patrons were dead, and the glory of Greece on the wane; it still remained for the philosophers to arrive and to talk "about it and about". Plato showed them how, and they are still at it, but the success of philosophy as a career derives at best from a misconception.

It is to the artistic triumphs upon the Acropolis of Athens and to the Parthenon above all that Greek thought owes its power, and by means of this magical trade-mark Plato and his followers have gripped the world's attention. A philosophy cannot shape history purely by its own merits, for to the reasonable man in the street nothing succeeds like success, and a policy is judged by its fruits. The simple facts that the Parthenon was built before Plato's birth, and that his teaching did much to destroy the cultural outlook of which the Parthenon was the tangible symbol, remain ungrasped. Plato sought perfection by the path of human wisdom and this theoretical approach to life led him in the end to formulate laws for an ideal state; laws breathing the fiercest intolerance known to history. Thus logic lynches life by the attempt to make men good by Act of Parliament, and to form that perfect community "where everyone shall do as he likes, and those who won't shall be made".

The world before Plato was at least fortunate in lacking this ferment, and in its self-absorption which made proselytism and religious persecution unimaginable. Herodotus could begin the study of comparative religion and lay the foundations of the diffusionist hypothesis without the frenzy of the fanatic or the smug complacency of the tourist. The tranquil life of the ethnic religions was first seriously challenged by the Old

Testament Hebrews, within whose own tribal cult there grew up a violently exclusive school, seeking to exalt the prestige of Jahweh by preaching the devastation of all other gods and their worshippers.

To the age of tolerance succeeded the epoch of missionary fervour, exemplified by the work of Plato in the West and that of Gautama Buddha in the East. The early Christians, the Sassanian "reformers" of Zoroastrianism, and finally Islam, added to the doctrines of conversion and mutual exclusion, and one and all were ready to

> . . . prove their Doctrine Orthodox
> With Apostolick Blows and Knocks.

Men could no longer go slimly like fishes, nor even lead reasonably unmolested lives, except in China where the national worship proved strong enough to reconcile the exclusive pretensions of Tao and Buddhism; and in remote backwaters such as the islands of the Pacific and deep valleys of Himalaya, where small groups of men equipped with relics of a cultural tradition have lived happy lives while century gave place to century, "the world forgetting, by the world forgot".

Such seclusion leads to stagnation and eliminates impulses towards change; cultural characteristics are perpetuated religiously in all their details and in a fossilized condition from generation to generation, and the social fabric is regulated by the sanctions imposed by hereditary priest-kings. That such sanctions are (or at least were before the impact of Europe) effective, and a great deal more suited to human needs than most Model By-Laws, can be read in the sympathetic study of tabu in Stevenson's *In the South Seas.*

In the larger communities of the pre-Platonic world, such institutions not only perpetuated existing culture, but called forth new artistic efforts in response to definite problems set by the monarch, in whose person the whole well-being of the people centred. Such a ruler was Gudea of Lagash, who sent expeditions over the whole of the Middle East to bring back stone, marble, and cedarwood, gold, silver, and porphyry, with which to build a temple more glorious than any yet set up by men's hands; and this was in the twenty-fourth century B.C., as far distant from the Parthenon in time as the Parthenon is from us. Nor was this an exception; for three thousand years before Pericles the nations of the ancient world vied with each other in producing for their rulers palaces and temples, statues and paintings, utensils and jewellery, all of a beauty, a refinement of taste, and excellent workmanship rarely if ever surpassed since. In spite of wars and invasions, and the natural and inevitable rise and fall of taste in a relative sense, the long periods over which a high level of positive achievement was maintained, in Mesopotamia, in Egypt, in Asia Minor, and later in China, are remarkable witnesses to the practical success of the principles of pre-Platonic government.

In sharp contrast are the rapid fluctuations of culture and comparative barbarism during the last two thousand years; a restless discontent with tradition and a constant search for those "new things" which to the older and more balanced of the Romans spelt revolution. Revolution rather than evolution, and the violent destruction of the old tradition at each replacement, have become symptomatic of this newer order of things. The quest of ideals (one's own), laudable in itself, has been linked with bitter persecution of all those whose ideals or tastes happen to differ; in such a persecution it is always the outstanding personalities, with marked individuality, who suffer the most, with dreadful results to the common stock of knowledge and of beauty achieved. This is the tragic fallacy of "humanism".

Humanism, which should be the father of humanity and of the humanities is, by a paradox, only too often their most inveterate foe. It is said that Victorian copybooks declared "the sheep was given to Man for food and clothing", and while this may be the reason for the sheep's existence, it is doubtful whether man should dwell overlong on his own pre-eminence in the world of nature. By insisting on the primacy of human reason we are drawn immediately into the dilemma of conflicting authorities, for strangely enough, while a collection of the "reasonable men" of the English common law will often be found to agree in substance upon normal problems of common sense, hardly any two professional reasoners can be found to agree with each other. Confusion is worse confounded when, as in the Christian world, there is superadded a conflict between the civil authority of the Head of State (who is divinely appointed either by conquest, or heredity, or by the Providential finger of a vote) and the ecclesiastical authority of the Church, which too claims divine appointment as the basis of its claim to obedience.

Darwin and the evolutionists attempted to show man's kinship to the rest of the creation by appealing to similarities of structure and function, and by postulating a potential intellect and capacity for education in the animal kingdom. Fabre, after a long lifetime of patient experiment, and many other critics of the evolutionary hypothesis, as for instance Professor R. A. Wilson in *The Miraculous Birth of Language*, deny Darwin's postulate as being contrary to the observed facts, and claim that the animal creation lacks the capacity to reason, or at least the central unifying faculty of reason. When we consider the record of human history over a period of some fifty or sixty centuries, with its constantly repeated lessons of cause and effect, would it not be equally plausible to argue man's community with the brutes, on the ground of his obvious lack of real reasoning power, or capacity to profit by the lessons of past failure?

Man's vaunted reason, in the light reflected by the actions of the wisest individuals, is but a poor argument for the pre-eminent position of humanity, and for a positive demonstration of man's separateness in kind it is necessary to study the arts: that is to say the various means by which man can demonstrate to the senses his individual skill and his conscious ability to form a pattern which is indissolubly his own, and framed by his own choice. His choice can never be free in the widest sense, for time and space exert their limitations, but within those bounds, and the frontiers set by his own personality, the artist is the freest creature that lives on this terrestrial sphere.

The emergence of the human artist is actually identical with the rise of civilization itself; the artist is truly the craftsman, and even at this present time differs from the more usually understood type of "craftsman" in degree only, not in kind. No hard and fast dividing line can ever be drawn between the blacksmith and the "art metal worker", between the freestone mason and the sculptor, between the carpenter and the wood-carver, or between the two species of painters. More conclusive still, in the jealously guarded realm of verse, the very word poet means in Greek precisely what is connoted by its now obsolete English, but current Scots counterpart, "maker". In the modern ages of "refinement" we have become accustomed to artificial social divisions which imply more than real identity of function, but the fundamental truth was still recognized in our own Middle Ages, for we find in the *Red Book of Hergest* that the porter tells Kilhwch: "The knife is in the meat, and the drink is in the horn, and there is revelry in Arthur's hall, and none may enter therein but the son of a privileged country or a craftsman bringing his craft." As late as the mid-fifteenth century John Russell, usher in chamber and marshal in hall to Humfrey, Duke of Gloucester, "Good Duke Humfrey", gives a table of precedence from Knight down to "Childe" by the steps of Squire, yeoman of the crown, groom, and page, and then expressly states "hit rebuketh not a knyght the kynges grome to sytte at his table". Royal craftsmen, such as the minstrels and versifiers, masons, carpenters, painters, glaziers, smiths, plumbers, shipwrights, and members of other skilled callings, were ranked in the degrees from esquire to page according to their standing. Consequently it was no unusual thing for such a man as Henry Yevele, Master Mason to Richard II, to be sitting at the table of William of Wykeham, Bishop of Winchester, in company with peers of the realm and chief justices of the two benches.

The decline in the status of the craftsman has been very gradual: it was the skill of the craftsman, developed in some way which we do not understand, which caused civilization itself, but modern archaeology has at least reached the point where it is possible to arrive at a close approximation to when and where the great change took place. According to H. Peake and H. J. Fleure in *Peasants and Potters*, "A number of converging lines of evidence . . . lead us to suspect that most of the essential elements of civilization developed before 5000 B.C. in some region within 200 miles of Aleppo" and the epochal discoveries are characterized as "the cultivation of wheat and barley, the shaping of stone implements by grinding, the making of pottery, the invention of spinning and weaving, and the discovery that the ores of metal could be melted and cast into a mould. It seems likely, too, that the erection of permanent houses dates from about the same time."

Imhotep, designer of the step-pyramid of Saqqara for his royal master, Zoser of the Third Dynasty of Egypt, and of many other important works, somewhere in the third millennium B.C. was held in such reverence that he ultimately became deified; the Greeks recorded carefully the names of architects and other artists, and most of the important works of Islamic

4   York Minster: West Front and Towers. Designer: probably Master Simon
(front, 1291–1338); Central Tower (1407–23): William Colchester; West Towers
(1432–72): Thomas Pak

5   Wetherden Church: Nave roof, *c.* 1500

art are accurately dated and signed by their designers. In China and Japan detailed records and signatures form a continuous record of artists and their work up to the present day, and even when journeying eastwards from Europe proper into Turkey, one notices the proud interest taken by even comparatively uneducated Turks in the great buildings designed by Sinan, the Albanian architect of the sixteenth century, whose last and greatest is the Selimié Mosque in Adrianople, dating from A.D. 1571, a work of outstanding nobility and delicacy of execution. Certainly the Englishman of the twentieth century has a far slighter interest in the works of Wren, and of other architects he knows little or nothing.

The reason for our lack of interest in the artists of the past is to be found in the great failing of the modern world, that it has allowed itself to become divorced from life, which implies divorce from our past, both as cause and as effect. Dr. Coulton quotes very appositely the *Punch* cartoon of the London suburban boy who, after a fortnight in the country, came home and complained: "Here, we get our milk from clean brass cans; and there they get it from a nasty dirty cow." Apart from sentimental dairy-farming of the kind indulged in by poor Marie Antoinette, there does seem to be room for hope in the strong reaction towards the land, towards craftsmanship, and towards a greater community of interest between different types and classes, as opposed to the nonsense vapourings about theoretical "equality" indulged in by the encyclopedists of the eighteenth and socialists of the nineteenth centuries.

Artists, and indeed all highly skilled craftsmen, tend to be anarchists, in the strict sense of the word, for their overpowering need is the expression of their individuality through their work, and all forms of outside interference are objectionable. To quote Lawrence again: "If I have to choose between the bourgeois and the bolshevist I choose the bourgeois, he will interfere with me less", but he goes on to show that one is impaled on the horns of a dilemma, for the bourgeois will lead to the bolshevist "as a half-lie causes the immediate contradiction of the half-lie". In truth the modern world, like the voter at a parliamentary election, has only the choice between being hanged and being shot, and is unable to break the spell, as Fabre's processionary caterpillars, to save their lives, could not leave the silken circle they were laying round the flower-pot rim.

The older world under its emperors, kings, and tribal chiefs, even under bad ones, was better placed than we, so far as artistic expression is concerned, and this could be demonstrated graphically by plotting on the same sheet the incidence of outstanding works of art, and of great autocratic rulers. History gives us some grounds for believing that the minimal levels of human existence are gradually being raised, but it is at least equally important to be sure that the maximal levels of true cultural humanity are not being lowered. I have said before, and would stress again, that it is in art in its widest sense that we find the truest index of human values, and the position of the artist should be the first consideration of government, not a shamefaced afterthought.

The greatest periods in art will then be found, *ceteris paribus*, where there is strong and well-rooted government by an individual of exquisite taste, and an atmosphere of relative toleration. In Britain we have no adequate records of our pre-Platonic period, and the destruction of documents renders the art history (as distinct from archaeology) of the time before the eleventh century A.D. a closed book. Strange cross-currents from Gaul and Byzantium and the farther East and North went to the making of the older English art destroyed by the Danes. Alfred and his successors had to build up a new tradition, and by the eleventh century a distinctive national style had evolved, based largely upon timber constructional elements. Finally with Norman influence at the court of Edward the Confessor, England entered the main stream of Romanesque art. Saxon England was a wealthy and luxurious country, but with the failing energy of the old dynasty the creative impulse was already dying when the national life was snapped off near Hastings on the evening of 14 October 1066.

The Conquest hastened the movement towards Continental art, and notwithstanding William's earnest endeavour to govern through the Saxon nobles and by the native laws, at the end of his reign the English were a depressed class with a barbarous language exiled from the court. This question of language is crucial, for cultural development largely depends on a vernacular poetry. The tide began to turn when Henry I married the heiress of the Saxon line, but only about 1350 did French give place to English in the grammar schools, and not until 1362 in the courts of law.

This is not to say that England had to make a fresh start in the fourteenth century; on the contrary, our language, literature, music, and all forms of art have their roots deep in the past and draw their vitality from the matured memory of long-past seasons and above all from the fresh Gothic spring of the thirteenth century. Throughout western Europe the tenth and eleventh centuries had been a dark and turbulent time, but the recapture of Jerusalem in 1099 spread a new wave of hope, unjustified it is true on the score of the Crusades themselves, but prophetic all the same of a new warmth, a new richness of culture which was to be carried from out of the southern and eastern lands across and around Europe and up to the Arctic Circle. Another cycle in the history of man had begun.

Each such cycle grows out of the last, or upon its ruins; its course may be run faster or more slowly, but whatever its duration, whether the three thousand years of ancient Egypt or the three hundred of the Renaissance, it will be found to exhibit to a marked degree the vicissitudes of life, and to reflect on a larger scale the unity and proportion of those greater art-forms which spring from man's own inner consciousness. The closest analogy will be with such a form as the musical symphony, expressed purely in time, and upon a highly developed plan, admitting of equally detailed arrangement in its subdivisions, and all in accord with the principles of sonata-form from which it grows.

We must not push such a comparison too far, but it may assist our grasp of the universality of phenomena; the fact that all art-forms, just as all epochs in history, are in series. When the understanding of cultural history has been thoroughly assimilated and systematized it should be possible to sketch in the lost sections of the record with the same certainty that Mendeléeff predicted from the gaps in the atomic series the discovery of new elements with given characteristics, a prediction triumphantly vindicated by the march of discovery within the scientist's own lifetime. Similarly, the whole future lies within men's imagination, for there is the root of creative art. Mozart could write concerning his method of composition: "When I am . . . completely myself, entirely alone, and of good cheer . . . my ideas flow best and most abundantly. *Whence* and *how* they come, I know not; nor can I force them. Those ideas that please me I retain in memory . . . provided I am not disturbed, my subject enlarges itself, becomes methodized and defined, and the whole, though it be long, stands almost complete and finished in my mind, so that I can survey it, like a fine picture or a beautiful statue, at a glance. Nor do I hear in my imagination the parts *successively*, but I hear them, as it were, all at once. What a delight this is I cannot tell! All this inventing, this producing, takes place in a pleasing lively dream. Still the actual hearing of the *tout ensemble* is after all the best. What has been thus produced I do not easily forget, and this is perhaps the best gift I have my Divine Maker to thank for."

In a greater or less degree something of this sort takes place with every artist, and the process is highly individual. Occasionally genuine collaboration is found, as when Villard de Honnecourt worked out a church plan by discussion with Pierre de Corbie, but this is the rare exception, and though extempore verses may be added to a song by members of a feast-day crowd, it is a fantastic misconception of the facts of artistic creation to suggest that the mediæval cathedrals, the mural paintings, the poems, and the songs and dances are the work of the community acting as a whole.

For every great work of art, for every work possessed of a unity of conception, we must posit a personal creator, a single human artist in whose imagination the form appeared before it was wrought with hands. That the names of these persons may be lost does not alter the facts, and so far as the European High Middle Ages are concerned, the period from 1250 to 1550, a vast number of names survive. It would be no exaggeration to say that the men responsible for all the major developments of art in this period are already known to us by name;[1] due allowance has to be

---

[1] In some cases we do not yet understand the exact share of each artist, but to suppose that relatively less is known of mediæval than of Renaissance personalities is a fallacy. How much do we know of Shakespeare? In spite of our vast knowledge of Sir Christopher Wren's public career, hardly more than a love-letter has survived from his personal life. From the four centuries 1150–1550, in England alone, the names of some eighty architectural designers of the first class are already known, and of lesser men there are well over six hundred. Many of the significant careers can be traced in considerable detail. These figures, amounting on an average to some half-dozen leaders and over fifty minor and provincial designers in every generation, must form a substantial proportion of the real totals, when set against a population of perhaps three millions. In 1944 the total number of architects registered in the United Kingdom (population over 45 millions) was 15,093, but of these many were in practice overseas, and a large proportion assistants in government and municipal offices.

c

made for the skilful imitations of a master's work by his pupils, but we may fairly count ourselves quit of the plague of anonymity providing attribution is correctly made to the given master's school.

Once a fair bulk of material is available for the whole period, and a number of key examples can be dated with accuracy, the manifold details will be seen to fall into their place on the great waves of development. Speaking generally, all ages of art have in common an early crudity coupled with spontaneity, growing later into sophistication by means of systematized refinement. So from the solemn and even crude character of Cimabue's work, Giotto drew the thread of a pure clarity of outline and colour; direction once given, Italian painting climbed to the toppling heights of Leonardo and the Bellinis; then the curling wave-crest overturned and in the froth of Raphael ran swiftly downhill. German music tells a similar tale: from the savage strength of the early choirmasters there grew the sublime culmination of John Sebastian Bach; not content with this, his own sons turned the flowing tide into a new channel and a second peak was reached in Haydn and Mozart; the titanic figure of Beethoven strove to add yet a third summit to the group, but only half succeeding, opened the way to the frivolities and mock solemnities of the last century.

So is it with the English Gothic, which found its truest expression in architecture and in music, arts abstract by nature and thus giving the fullest expression to a fundamental mysticism which lies beneath the surface rawness of the English temperament; ideas hardly to be spoken in words or drawn in clear outline, but which reflect an inner world peopled with strange fantasies, sometimes monstrous, sometimes noble. This extraordinary national spirit is not confined to the Gothic age, it is found before and since: in it there is a warm geniality, most marked perhaps in Chaucer, which contains elements of the grotesque and of the gross, but which refuses to be bound by these elements. This indefinable quality runs through all the truly English artists like a golden thread; now woven under, now brought out and emphasized. In recent years it has wellnigh run out; there was a splendid revival of this spirit by Blake, but the Jerusalem which he and Cobbett, from their different points of view, saw arising in England, failed to materialize, and such an atavist as Sir Richard Burton had to seek it in Araby. In destroying Burton's manuscripts, and thus earning the monument of Dowson's envenomed outburst, Lady Burton was but the daughter of her age; across England's green and pleasant land had fallen a dark shadow, and in the shadow there moved such sinister figures as that of Matthew Arnold. Chaucer, held Arnold, could not be one of the great classics because he lacked "high seriousness" (Arnold learnedly quotes the authority of Aristotle for the necessity of this σπουδαιότης to great poetry); this convenient means of belittling greater men could also of course be applied to Aristophanes, to Villon and Rabelais, the great classics of France, and to many another. The case of Shakespeare however would have been mighty inconvenient, and Arnold blandly claims for Shakespeare this high seriousness which

6   Maidstone Church, 1395–c. 1405.   School of Henry Yevele

7 Beverley Minster: West Front, *c.* 1390–1420.
Designer: perhaps William Rolston

Chaucer and the rest are denied. Can Arnold have ever read Shakespeare with understanding, or the slightest trace of a sense of humour?

No; at the tragic climax of Hamlet, Shakespeare could bring the house down with a vulgar pun: "The king shall drink to Hamlet's *better breath*; And in the cup an union [onion] shall he throw . . .", and the haunting song in Cymbeline has its broken-hearted little joke: "Golden lads and girls all must, *As chimney-sweepers*, come to dust." The mingling of laughter and comic incidents with tears and breathless agonizing suspense is essentially true to life, and it is in these descents from the plane of high seriousness that Shakespeare excels Marlowe. The age that was determined on its pure high-minded literary pabulum was also resolved to exalt Raphael and Beethoven on unnatural pedestals, and to shy away from the real teeming life which it had thrust into the slums and workhouses.

This utter lack of the old English spirit foredoomed the Gothic revival to still-birth. Victorian England was horrified by the "coarseness" and "indecency" of a large proportion of the grotesque carvings to be found in genuine medieval churches; the nearest to humour in church which might be admitted (with some scandalized dissentients even then) were mildly funny caricatures of contemporary politicians outside Chester Cathedral. Likewise the clear lilt of such early tunes as were unearthed by eager musical antiquaries was promptly overlaid with a rich syrup of nineteenth-century harmonies. No wonder that Europe, and eventually England itself, became sick of the very name of Gothic!

The spontaneity of the first age of Gothic is perhaps best realized from some of the few pieces of secular music which have survived; not to mention the famous Reading rota printed in all the histories, we may quote a delightful little piece from the Bodleian, "Mirie it is", whose words

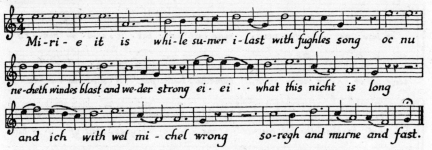

Mi-ri - e it is whi-le su-mer i-last with fughles song oc nu

ne-cheth windes blast and we-der strong ei - ei - - what this nicht is long

and ich with wel mi - chel wrong so-regh and murne and fast.

FIG. 8. *Mirie it is*, song of the early thirteenth century.

and music echo just that warp and woof of jollity and suffering that make up life as it is lived in a northern country with a changeable climate and a hard-won livelihood. "Foweles in the frith" and several other charming little pieces are well worth the trouble of copying out and performing, for they provide a far more truly human picture of thirteenth-century English manners than an immense array of quotations from chronicles and official records.

The search for organic unity in art can be traced in an upward swelling curve onwards from 1200 to 1400, after which there was a melancholy depression which will be discussed later. Through this period of depression lived John Dunstable, the greatest of mediæval composers, and almost certainly from him comes one of the loveliest songs ever written—"Alas departynge". Unlike most of the earlier music, that of Dunstable has a "singing" melody in every part; there is here no question of an air harmonized, nor of a *canto fermo* supported by additional parts descanting

FIG. 9.   *Alas departynge*, song of the first half of the fifteenth century.

upon it. Both the parts in this song are of equal beauty, and the interwoven harmonies and points of imitation are extraordinarily rich in effect, yet maintaining all the while a strong reserved simplicity. For those who find the Middle Ages hard to understand nothing would be more helpful than the repeated playing or singing of "Alas departynge" and some other of Dunstable's known works, such as "O Rosabella" and "Quam pulchra es", which last, to the Latin words of part of the Song of Songs, betrays a gloriously secular and thoroughly English spirit.

The nature and extent of secular influences in the Middle Ages seem to have been altogether misunderstood by the two main schools of mediævalists. Both the Roman Catholic apologists and their most bitter opponents take it for granted that the Church, rightly or wrongly, was the controlling factor in life, and that because higher education was largely confined to men in holy orders, the leadership of society was almost exclusively a clerical prerogative. If life were indeed conditioned by scholastic philosophy, this might have been true, but it is in the forms of art rather than in the schools of philosophy that we must seek the vital truths which illumine mankind's pilgrimage from age to age. The artist and craftsman, though he certainly owed much to clerical schools and to ecclesiastical patronage, was himself usually a layman.

The ancient ethnic religions one and all encouraged art in every form, and it might be said that art itself is fundamentally the outward and visible form of the spiritual one-ness with the Creator and the Creation which is the avowed object of such cults. Plato on the contrary viewed the arts with grave suspicion, and this was the attitude of the Jahwist Hebrews, of the early Christians, and of primitive Islam. Iconoclasm of a very far-reaching character was the unfortunate consequence, and it is well established that Muslim fanatics systematically destroyed prehistoric high places and sculptured stones all over the Near East, while equally fervent Christians were bidden by the Edict of Nantes of A.D. 658 to carry out a similar work of destruction, and practically all the pagan writings of northern Europe were burnt as an *auto-da-fé* at the conversions of the tribes. When the Spaniards reached Mexico and Central America in the sixteenth century they presided over similar bonfires, and in both cases the loss to mankind has been catastrophic.

The writings destroyed in Britain would have provided solid evidence of that pre-Christian and also pre-Roman culture, whose existence can now only be presumed from the material finds and from the scanty notices left by the surviving writers of Mediterranean Europe. Even after the destruction of the native literature, much of its contents was undoubtedly preserved by oral tradition, as the Kalevala was in Finland until the nineteenth century. In England the new Christian culture was too pervasive to permit of such a wholesale survival, but our folk-lore, songs, carols, and local customs even to-day bear witness to the inherent strength of the displaced tradition. All through the dark age and the age of faith the Church was attempting to stamp out the remains of this older cult, more especially such features as dances and feasts held in the churches, which were regarded, and quite correctly regarded, as the successors of the old temples, whose sites they often usurped. Fortunately, there existed within the Church, side by side with the fanatics, another school of thought, which held that wherever possible the old beliefs, the old temples, the old festivals, should be reconsecrated to the service of Christ. In this way the mediæval Church acted as a museum of folk-lore, and its calendar tended to incorporate the seasonal observances of its predecessors.[1]

The total of pagan influences upon secular thought and practice must have been considerable, and shows itself in a vast and widespread array of grotesques bearing no relation to the churches in which they are found. The places best fitted for display were monopolized by the official exhibitions of sacred subjects, but in the nooks and crannies, under the seats, in the odd corners of stock patternwork and spandrels of minor arches, on the parapets and under the gutters, a whole secular encyclopedia of life ran riot. That this was tolerated by the clergy, monastic, collegiate, and parochial, shows pretty clearly that they did not dare, or did not wish, to press matters against their semi-pagan brethren too far. The parish priest often was in actual fact, as in Chaucer, the ploughman's brother, while the higher clergy came of well-to-do families whose other members might be baron, knight, or country squire, either indifferent to Church affairs or positively on the side of the lay craftsmen.

Outside of the sphere of public attacks on Church dogma or the verbal expression of heresy, the authorities were content with the *status quo*, and so long as lay knowledge of the Bible was restricted to the synoptic Gospels and to a series of retold scriptural stories, it was comparatively easy to maintain this attitude of *laissez-faire*. There must have been many churchmen between the fifth and the fifteenth centuries who recognized only too well the difficulty of their position if once the Bible as a whole lay open. Whatever may be the case with the theologian, it is not possible for the ordinary layman to reconcile the "Forgive them, Father" of Jesus with the psalmist's benediction of him that taketh the children of Babylon and dasheth them against the stones. The Church was heavily handicapped by being irrevocably committed in theory to the whole Bible; in the days of its greatest power it could have made its position practically impregnable had it been able without loss of face to jettison the Old Testament. But the acceptance by the Fathers of the Jewish scriptures in bulk in order to have the benefit of their prophecies of the Messiah, put the later Church at a disadvantage as soon as the Bible came into the hands of any large mass of human beings reading it in the light of normal human reason.

That the Church should have done its best to conceal the Bible during

[1] There seems also to have been a witch-cult with devotees not exclusively ignorant. See the demonstration of "Satanist" symbolism in the fifteenth-century "Triptych of Aix" in *Illustrated London News*, CLXXX (2 and 30 January 1932), 13,180. England's highest society was involved in 1441 in the trial of Eleanor, Duchess of Gloucester, for sorcery directed against the King.

10 Canterbury Cathedral: Nave and Crossing, 1391–1405.
Designer: Henry Yevele; of strainer arch: John Wastell

11 Saffron Walden Church: Nave, *c.* 1490–1520

12 Cirencester Church: Nave, 1515–30

Late Perpendicular, East and West

the Middle Ages is not particularly discreditable; it was only by this means that the machine could be kept turning, and while it is perfectly true that the savage doctrines of sin and predestination long antedated Calvin, as Dr. Coulton has made clear, it was only after the Reformation that the fanatics were able to have it all their own way. The fanatics of the earlier ages may have held the same identical doctrines as did the sixteenth and seventeenth century iconoclasts who did their worst in the attempt to wreck European civilization, but the heavy hand of the cautious body of the Church restrained their frenzy. Bitterly as we may regret the destruction caused by the first impact of Christianity upon our earlier culture, we have to thank the common sense and even the natural sloth of the Roman Church that so much has survived. The busy hand of the Reformers respected nothing save the ability to amass worldly goods of him who can.

What is astonishing in the Roman Catholic apologists is that instead of countering the accusation that they kept the Bible closed with the frank statement that they did so because it was essential to salvation that the scriptures should be expounded by the doctors only, they have wasted much breath on futile attempts to prove that the Bible was widely taught in the Middle Ages, and that non-heretical translations were permitted. The whole point is that to all intents and purposes, there were no non-heretical translations into the common tongue. The English Authorized Version is a masterpiece of such a character that the task of the hostile critic is an invidious one; yet is it not permissible to wonder whether more harm than good was done when its magnificent prose rendered open to everyman the world's choicest records of cruelty, intolerance, and vice? Was it not this apotheosis of English prose that throttled our tradition of epic poetry?

For better or for worse, the Middle Ages knew it not, though they knew its edifying and amusing stories, retold and mingled with apocrypha and legends. This, with the partly pagan character of the Church itself, and the almost wholly pagan forms of its ceremonies and vestments, joined with the secular traditions to make of England a close approximation in many respects to the national ideal of ancient times. This ideal was all the closer for the fact that, long before Henry VIII insisted on the name of Supreme Head of the Church of England, his predecessors had taken repeated steps to curb the alien power of Rome, and exercised a very real authority over the English Church. From the unification of English law and administration by Edward I to the acceptance of the unwholesome first-fruits of the Renaissance by Henry VIII, a period of over two hundred years, England developed within herself, an ideal unit. The whole history of Europe can offer no parallel to the fruitfulness of this period of enlightened nationalism.

I

THE NATIONAL STYLE OF ENGLAND

WHEN Thomas Rickman coined the term "Perpendicular" to describe the architecture of the mature Gothic in England, he made the task of the learner easy, but at the same time he put the style itself into a coffin. Sharpe's substitution of "Rectilinear" screwed down the lid, and the greatest achievements of England had to await the coming of Frank Howard before their true significance was pointed out.[1] Howard died before his task was half done, and a good deal of the old Ruskinian contempt for our "decadent" art has crept back, so little does the public see or think for itself. For who in England can escape for long from the ever-present marvels of our artistic summer?

How many of those who pay their lip-service to Chaucer and Malory realize that the nave of Canterbury is the counterpart and contemporary of the Tales, or that the *Morte d'Arthur* was written just in time to be read by Edward IV in his new hall at Eltham, and to spur him on to the refounding of St. George's Chapel? English art is a unity transcending the sum of its parts, and we have to look at architecture and painting and the dainty products of craftsmanship to understand the magnificent world in which Chaucer moved and the sunset splendour of Malory's tragic prose.

Here at our very doors lies a new world to explore—a world with which we rub elbows daily and fail to recognize on our walks—a world built up in these same surroundings we know so well by men of our own kind, our very ancestors. In this it differs from the other great periods of our art: the Norman Romanesque was a direct importation from France, and so in its essentials was the Gothic of the twelfth and thirteenth centuries. After 1500 our art borrowed from Italy and from Flanders to form the cross-bred Elizabethan and Jacobean styles; Inigo Jones brought home Palladio's revised Italian tenets, Wren and Vanbrugh infused new French influences, while in the next century the Italian styles were revived, the old of Palladio, and the new rococo of the stucco-workers.

All these importations were naturalized, but they did not grow internally in organic continuity with the past: for three hundred years England was to be a battle-ground for contending styles—surface fashions which cloaked from view the skeleton remains of a great tradition. That tradition, truly representative of England at its best, had grown up with the unifying of the nation under Edward I and later took its place as the native response to the cultural impulses radiating from his successors.

---

[1] J. D. Sedding had anticipated him, but apparently to little purpose.

Photo: F. Frith & Co.

13 Coventry Cathedral: Tower and Spire, 1373–1433.
Designer: possibly Robert Skillyngton

15　Oxford, Magdalen College: Great Tower, 1490–1509.
Designer: William Orchard

14　Oxford, Merton College: Tower, 1448–50.
Designer: Robert Janyns, senior

For the art of this distinctively national period we have no adequate name, and are forced to adopt that of "Perpendicular" to avoid misunderstanding. It is simply "English", as distinct in its character as Ancient Egyptian, Chinese, or Mayan art, but we cannot apply the national adjective without ambiguity. What were the characteristics of this national art; what underlying theories or beliefs did it represent; of what material circumstances was it the outcome? These are questions which we now have to answer.

Like English work of all periods, it was first and foremost an art of line, not an art of mass. This is the fundamental distinction proclaimed by Blake, and insisted on by foreign observers. Norman architecture, like Roman, with great surfaces of wall and pier and vault, had been an art of mass, and as such could hardly take its place in the apostolic succession of native art. When Gothic forms appeared in Europe, doubtless influenced by Eastern geometers, they were transformed by the North into the basis of a fundamentally new style. Eastern geometric forms and pointed arches appear as masses of coloured light and shade, and colour is the key to their beauty. In Europe north of the Alps, a chromatic architecture was impossible, and the new emphasis developed the dominance of the vertical line. All through the thirteenth century this upthrust of pillars and arches was being exploited by the logical minds of northern France, and translated into material fact. The French Gothic cathedrals excel in actual height: their bay design touches the limits of practicable attenuation, and at Beauvais even exceeded them. This was while the Gothic style itself was still young and its forms immature and overmuch influenced by Romanesque survivals. Structural daring outran its aesthetic.

France never fully adopted the vault or the steeple as ends in themselves, in contrast to England, Flanders, Germany, and Spain, where both forms exercised the ingenuity of generation after generation of Gothic masters. It was England that achieved a perfect synthesis of structural and aesthetic elements in the Perpendicular style, for in England alone was there a truly national life during the Middle Ages. Until England had been given back to the English by Edward I, such an artistic synthesis was impossible: now it sprang into being as a genuine expression of the English spirit, evoked by the taste of great kings, nobles, and prelates. It was not, nor could it be, a uniform, unchanging and uninspired style, as might be supposed from the cavilling of its detractors. Through the two centuries of its free existence it exhibits marked changes, in common with the other arts, and parallel to the phases of our national life. While its vices and its ultimate decadence were symptoms of a disease in the body politic, its great virtues exemplify the fundamental strength of the English folk.

It was the first, and for that matter the last, thoroughly English outpouring of ideas, and was intimately bound up with our everyday life; it was inevitable that it should be affected to a notable extent by political and social changes affecting England, and that the difference which severed it from the contemporary art of foreign countries should be an index of the separateness and intense individuality of England's historic destiny.

D

That this is the case is merely the recognition that in a special respect England is unique among European countries: being an island she has developed as an integral unit without serious interruption or change of frontiers. France and Spain until the Renaissance, Germany, Italy, and Scandinavia up to modern times, have been in a state of flux, loose geographical concepts rather than living organisms. The same is even more true of the east European nations, Poland, Russia, Greece; only Hungary, gifted with a natural mountain frontier almost as protective as

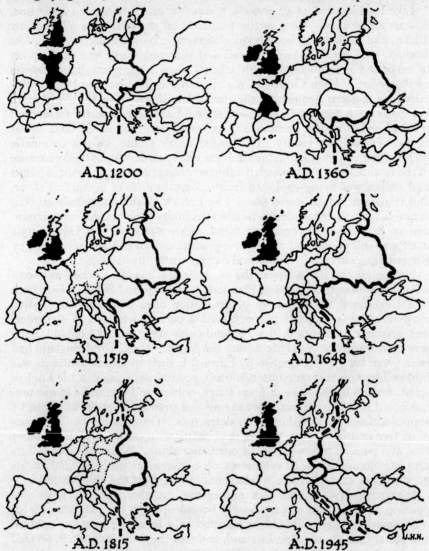

A.D. 1200

A.D. 1360

A.D. 1519

A.D. 1648

A.D. 1815

A.D. 1945

FIG. 16.　Europe's fluid frontiers.　The thick line indicates the political eastern boundary of western Europe.

England's moat, preserved throughout the Middle Ages her natural unity, and developed on lines closely parallel to our own.

In contrast to these fluid entities of the Continent, divided against themselves or frequently subject to changing foreign rule, England in her sequestered corner has been able to crystallize internally upon a natural pattern formed by the various elements already contained within her boundaries, or brought in from the outer world by deliberate choice. This gives to the study of English culture a quite especial value; owing to the lesser degree of complication arising from national and political cross-currents, the resultant in England is in a sense purer and less liable to misinterpretation, and so offers a yard-stick by which to measure the

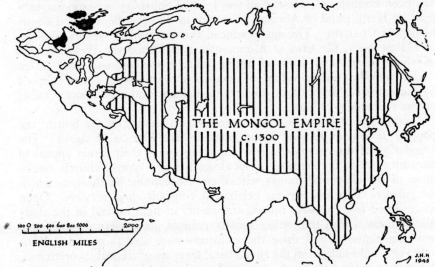

FIG. 17. The Mongol Empire and divided Europe.

fluctuations elsewhere. That England should be set up as an art standard may astonish foreign critics, but it must be realized that our achievements in architecture and craftsmanship were rendered possible by the combination of stable government with commercial prosperity. London so predominated over the cities of the northern world that even in Saxon times its wealth and magnificence amazed the Normans, and it remained the centre of Celtic romance for centuries after the retreat of the Britons to Wales. To the Scots and Norwegians it was a metropolis almost equal to Rome, its importance admitted even by the grudging assent of the envious and the enemy.[1]

Circumstances conspired to favour the new style; during the thirteenth century the Asiatic Empire of the Mongol Tartars had established itself as successor to the world empires of antiquity, and opened the Orient to travellers from Europe. There was a Catholic cathedral in Peking, and

[1] It was a Scot (almost certainly William Dunbar) who wrote the splendid poetic tribute, "London, thou art the flower of cities all!"

Western settlers in most of the great cities of Asia. With Persia contacts were particularly frequent, and in company with Genoese and Venetian merchants went English ambassadors and travellers. These predecessors of Sir Thomas Herbert, of Burton, Doughty, and T. E. Lawrence are almost unknown to history, but many curious correspondences in art motives prove the reality of this source of influence upon the forms of ornament and even of structure. Silks, spices, and Eastern mercery arrived every year in the trading galleys of Genoa and Venice.

In Europe itself equally strong and more direct forces were operating. Through the troubled twelfth century there had been a great revival of literary humanism, and of this revival many of the most prominent figures had been English. Greatest of all was John of Salisbury, a Saxon Englishman by birth, pupil of Abelard, secretary to Thomas Becket, and finally bishop of Chartres. The age produced the outstanding writers, William of Malmesbury, Geoffrey of Monmouth, and Gerald the Welshman, all of whom contributed works of lasting value to the common stock. This "false dawn" of human values in literature and art was for a time eclipsed by the excessive devotion of scholars to dialectic and a philosophy based on the refinement of logic.

A new type of humanism was to follow, originating in the South: the popular revival of religion inaugurated by St. Francis of Assisi. The foundation of the orders of preaching friars, with their direct appeal to humanity, led to the demand for an altogether new type of church, unlike those of the cloistered monks with their processions, or those in which the colleges of secular priests celebrated constant choir services. Open space, freed from massive pillars, and plenty of light instead of the shot-silk dimness within the earlier heavily painted glass, were the principal new requirements, and these the architects were able to provide. With only very slight help from the geometrical treatises of clerical theoreticians, the master craftsmen by a process of empiric trial and error extending over several centuries had reached a point where they were able to reduce the masonry supports of a church to the absolute minimum, and at the same time to roof a great space with a vault whose thrust was counterpoised by an elaborate system of flying buttresses and pinnacles. Between the slender piers and buttresses were great windows, letting in a flood of light, and a new type of internal wall decoration by means of carved panelling was devised to break up this light and prevent its glare from becoming objectionable. The wall-surfaces themselves tended to disappear, and the elaboration of panelling found its last refuge in the vault.

Unlike the simple ribbed vaults of the Continent (except Spain, where Moorish patternwork was suggestive, and to a slighter extent Germany), England developed a highly articulated system of vaulting in many subdivisions, and in the end a type entirely her own, the fan-vault, which was the logical outcome of the multiplied detail that had gone before. While these structural devices were being explored, a great aesthetic development was in progress towards the suavity of line and perfection of detail which distinguish the later English work. Not only in masoncraft

19   Derby Cathedral: Tower, 1510–32.
Designer: John Otes

18   Hedon Church: Tower, 1427–37.
Designer: Robert Playser

21 Worcester Cathedral: Tower, *c.* 1365–74.
Designer: John Clyve

20 Wells, St. Cuthbert's Church: Tower, *c.* 1410–30

23 Gloucester Cathedral: South Transept, Presbytery, and Tower, 1332–1460. Designer: probably William Ramsey; of Tower, perhaps John Hobbs

22 Canterbury Cathedral: Central Tower, 1490–97. Designer: John Wastell

24 Lavenham Church, 1485–1525

25 Tattershall Church, *c.* 1465–85. Designer: probably John Cowper.
From a drawing by J. C. Buckler

did England excel at this time; her older craft of carpentry brought itself up to date, and even outpaced work in stone. English timber construction within our period is absolutely without rival; not even among the mast-churches of Norway or the great cloth-halls of the Low Countries can anything approaching English work in ingenious construction or finished detail be discovered.

In all the arts England was making enormous strides, and the clue to this lay in the amazing vitality of the Plantagenet Royal Line: more

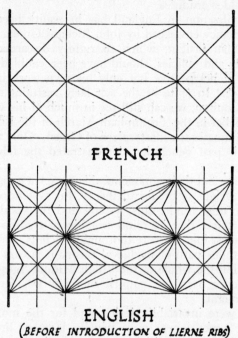

FRENCH

ENGLISH
(*BEFORE INTRODUCTION OF LIERNE RIBS*)

FIG. 26.   The Vault Rib in England developed for the sake of pattern, *c*.1300.

brilliant and less calculating than the House of France, the Angevin Kings of England burnt themselves out in the three hundred years of their reign. All were men of uncommon stamp: even the vices of John or Edward II and the piety of Henry VI far transcended the humdrum normality of our punier age. The active patronage of art by such a series of rulers was bound to have far-reaching effects, and in several cases personal genius was actively employed. Richard Cœur-de-Lion and Richard II were composer-poets; Henry V a musician of fine quality; his son almost a professional architect; Edward I an orator who in each of three languages could move his audience to tears. Clearly, these sovereigns seen as artists and connoisseurs, will appear in a different light from that in which they are commonly viewed.

European royalties were linked to the ancient cultures of the East by closer ties of blood than those which bound them to their own subjects.

Under their patronage the Gothic era dawned, and Europe left the dim light of semi-barbarism for the brilliance of civilization. The Norman and Frankish Crusaders had been regarded by their Muslim opponents as hardly better than half-grown children, for in the eleventh and twelfth centuries it was the world of Byzantium and Islam that carried a torch. Yet little by little, better blood and refined manners moved westward together, and in the persons of Eleanor of Aquitaine and Eleanor of Provence, the highest culture impinged on English life and began to sweep away the older crudities.

The rise of civilization in England has in reality been far from the Progress of Democracy envisaged by John Richard Green. It is a tragedy that Green's human insight, which so rightly discarded the grinding machinery of wars and policies, should have been coupled to a fixed idea that twisted out of perspective not only his own work but all that has been written since. In spite of the scholarly restraint and intellectual integrity of Dr. Coulton, we can still see in much of his work something of that pathetic belief in the Triumphant March of the English People to Freedom which animates the masterpiece of Green. Only too clearly have the events of this past generation demonstrated the falsity of Green's hypothesis.[1]

Green's followers and their opponents alike attach a great, and probably disproportionate weight to mediæval theory, the system of the scholastic Churchmen. We may admire this system, and the good which accompanied it, and yet feel that its blind worship of tradition and its cruel persecution of honest inquiry were thoroughly vicious. But in attempting to follow the tortuous path of mediæval theory it is easy to lose sight of the fact that during the whole of the "high Middle Ages" from 1250 to 1550, actual practice based on empiric methods was far in advance of contemporary thought.

The theorists were invariably clerics, and for the most part actually ecclesiastics; the practitioners were usually laymen, brought up in a tradition it is true, but a tradition not of authority but of experimental research. Hence, while the scholars were ignorant of perspective, and very few even of the clerical illuminators could draw a recognizable portrait, lay craftsmen were drawing from living models and carving lifelike heads of their companions and of public figures. While the writers of musical

---

[1] The facts have of course been driven home with great skill and literary brilliance by Mr. Belloc and his colleagues, but it is a pity that their scholarship on points of detail should be so open to question. Dr. Coulton has been able to refute a great many of the arguments of the "Catholic Historians" and Mr. John A. Knowles has dispelled a great deal of the romantic halo that has been painted round the mediæval Guilds. It is necessary to read both sides with equal care, and to eschew allegations of religious bias. Mr. Belloc's propensity for brilliant but somewhat reckless generalization appears at its best and worst in his book *The Stane Street*, where no religious issue is involved. Captain W. A. Grant shows in *The Topography of Stane Street*, 1922, that Mr. Belloc's whole topographical thesis is vitiated by his ignorance of the geodetic facts of the case. I think this deserves careful consideration on the part of Dr. Coulton and the "anti-Roman" school, if I may so describe them, with all due respect.

treatises expounded the Greek Modes at third and fourth hand, minstrels and harpers and the members of royal and noble bands were developing secular part-song and instrumental music into living harmony with their ear as a touchstone and a keen spirit of emulation to spur them on.

The real progress of the period, quite inexplicable if its origins are sought in scholastic philosophy and science, took place in virtue of painstaking trial and error on the part of the masters of the various crafts. To meet the demand for grander buildings, more sumptuous clothing, tastier meals, more lifelike and colourful portraits, the men whose life it was to supply these things were constantly engaged in keen experiment, and it is for this reason that Gothic art is almost always so fresh and seldom wears the jaded look which comes when the periods of experiment are over and stereotype copying takes their place. Every great work of Gothic art (and most of the minor works) is an experiment, often a successful experiment, but in any case vital and leading on to the next link in the chain.

Among these works it is possible to discern great individuality of treatment, enough of itself to give the lie to the strange theory of artistic anonymity in the Middle Ages. That little is known of the personalities of the masters concerned is hardly surprising, when we consider the scanty information which has survived regarding Chaucer, Shakespeare, and Spenser. It was seldom that the monkish chronicler regarded the craftsman as worthy of mention, for his own especial task was the glorification of the superiors of his house. Lay servants were sometimes mentioned, however, for Gervase of Canterbury gives a detailed account of the coming of William of Sens to Canterbury in 1174, and of the works then carried out, while the St. Albans annalist of the fourteenth century mentioned the important carpenter, Geoffrey, and Henry Wy, a mason.

In a recent critical edition of the album of Villard de Honnecourt, H. R. Hahnloser has shown that that famous work was compiled as a practical encyclopedia for the building lodge of which Honnecourt was master, probably that of the collegiate church of St. Quentin; further, that not only Honnecourt himself, but two of his thirteenth-century successors, who made additions to the book, were literate, and in Latin as well as French. From the technical character of a great part of the work it is abundantly clear that Honnecourt was a lay architect, and in the caption to his drawing of a lion with its keeper he carefully states that it was portrayed from the life.

Most cathedrals and important churches, as well as royal palaces and castles, must have had permanent works establishments under the control of masters comparable to Honnecourt, and on the Continent there are considerable remains of the graphic archives of such lodges. In England there is very little left from the pre-Tudor period, but documentary allusions and the survival of a fourteenth-century sketch- or pattern-book in the Pepysian Collection at Magdalene College, Cambridge, prove that the lack is due to the unkind accidents of time. Probably a very large proportion of the lay masters who could draw could also write, and while signatures occur from the fifteenth century onwards, there are much earlier instances of graffiti scratched into the stonework by masons, and clearly not set out for them by clerics. Elementary education was always available for the boy who really wanted to learn, and the guilds and other bodies of artists and building craftsmen normally stipulated that only freemen's sons should be admitted, while the handing on of craft tradition in families was so general that the son might often benefit from educational facilities at his father's place of work, perhaps one of the secular cathedrals, a monastery, or the royal court.

As early as the mid-thirteenth century, architects, painters, sculptors, and other artists, were ranked as esquires, and when accounts began to be kept in English in the fifteenth century they were often termed gentlemen. So far as social conditions can be paralleled in modern times, the status of the mediæval architect seems to have been analogous to that of his present-day counterpart. He was to be found at the tables of important clients, doubtless an interesting guest, but found himself more at home among the merchant citizens and well-to-do yeomanry. In country districts many of the profession commonly engaged in farming land, and we find Elizabeth, wife of Robert Janyns, the master mason of the Merton College bell-tower, engaged for four days in carting straw for thatching the lodge in 1448.

The chief craftsmen were often very much in the sovereign's confidence, as Henry III's instructions and the state papers of the Tudors show; relations were sometimes of a surprising nature, as when Jack of St. Albans, painter to Edward II, was given fifty shillings by the king's own hand for having danced on a table before the king "and made him laugh beyond measure". John Thirsk, who was called into Henry VI's presence to mark out the king's tomb in Westminster Abbey, soon afterwards became the royal master mason at Windsor Castle, when the post fell vacant.

Royalty was generally fortunate in securing competent as well as talented artists, but monasteries and private clients were not always so lucky. About 1200, the Abbot of St. Albans engaged a gang of masons to build the west front of the abbey church, under the supervision of Master Hugh of Goldcliff, "a clever but deceitful craftsman", who is alleged by the chronicler to have shown "stealth, fraud, impertinence, and above all, extravagance" and into the bargain so designed the work that when it was covered up for the winter in a partly finished state "the walls became fractured and fell with their own weight, so that the wreck of images and flowers became the laughing stock of beholders. The workmen therefore quitted in despair, nor did any wages reward their labours." Legal proceedings by private clients were not uncommon, in cases where the master mason was also the contractor, as was Roger Denys, who got into difficulties over his contracts for extensive rebuilding at the churches of Surfleet and Wyberton, Lincolnshire, in 1418; a carpenter, John of Bytham, was in 1317 charged in the Fair Court of St. Ives with breach of warranty for having built a house for the plaintiff, Roger of Moulton,

27 Bath Abbey, 1501–39.
Designers: Robert and William Vertue

28 Totnes Church: Tower, 1449–52.
Designer: Roger Growdon

30 Yeovil Church: Nave, *c.* 1380–90.
Designer: possibly William Wynford

"Country Life"

29 Oxford, New College: Antechapel, 1380–83.
Designer: William Wynford

with willow instead of oak, and in 1395 Thomas Aylmer, mason, was sued by Sir John Hende, a prominent London citizen and twice Lord Mayor, for failure to perform his contract of six years before to reconstruct a large window in the church of Bradwell-juxta-Coggeshall in Essex.

It is time to consider the problem of the material circumstances which gave rise to the development of English art in the fourteenth century and which determined, in some measure, the outcome of the period of change. England's insular position decided in favour of an independent local style, owing little to contemporary work on the Continent, while motives of security coupled with growing luxury and ostentation made stone the dominant material until the great spread of brick-making in the fifteenth and sixteenth centuries. On the other hand, the demand for larger and wider halls and churches necessarily restricted the use of stone vaults and gave new opportunities to the structural carpenter, who rose to the occasion by inventing trusses capable of spanning any desired space with members cut from oaks of large size. In a few instances the provision of exceptionally large timbers caused long and tedious searches to be made, but so prolific of good oaks was fourteenth-century England that a plentiful supply was forthcoming for the normal requirements of several thousand monasteries, churches, and manor-houses.

In the absence of contemporary works of art criticism, it is for the most part necessary to judge of the aims of the designers from an analysis of their works. That there was deliberate design in the Middle Ages, as distinct from the unconscious moulding of tradition, is clear from many obvious tricks of detail of a geometrical character, the result of experimental playing with a pair of compasses, or with the properties of numbers.[1] None the less, it is satisfactory to find that the idea of such deliberation was formulated as a mediæval commonplace: Geoffrey of Vinsauf, writing his *Poetria Nova* about 1200 (see Appendix I), declared that no less care was required in poetic composition than in the building of a house:

> Si quis habet fundare domum, non currit ad actum
> Impetuosa manus; intrinseca linea cordis
> Praemetitur opus. . . .

Chaucer in his *Troilus* repeats this almost word for word:

> For every wight that hath an hous to founde
> Ne renneth nought the werk for to biginne
> With rakel hond, but he wol byde a stounde,
> And sende his hertes lyne out fro with-inne
> Alderfirst his purpos for to winne.

The pages of Honnecourt bristle with phrases such as "if you want to see a good light roof"; "here is one of the windows of Reims Cathedral . . . I was on my way to obey a call to the land of Hungary when I drew this window, because it pleased me best of all windows"; "I was once in Hungary, where I dwelt a long time, and there I saw a church paved in

---

[1] For the practical use of the 3 : 4 : 5 triangle, see W. Harvey: "Westminster Hall Roof and the Woodman" in *The Builder*, CXXI, 19 August 1921, pp. 220–1.

E

this fashion". Architects of all ages have made use of ideas which appealed
to them on their travels, and many offices, like Honnecourt's lodge,
compile exemplars of useful details, generally suitable for adaptation to
the requirements of each new job, rather than for slavish imitation. Even
the common fifteenth-century contracts for church towers, taverns, and
shops, drawn up by churchwardens and the like, frequently insist on
discriminating imitation: the windows shall be copied from those of
another church from that which is to form the model of the tower itself;
the two faces of a rood-screen shall follow two different exemplars; the
ornamental timberwork of a gable shall answer to such an house, but the
main framing to such another. As now, both the client and the designer
exercised personal taste and a greater or less degree of originality.

Taste varies from century to century, and even markedly in shorter
periods of time; thus we may only discern the preferences of the Middle
Ages upon the assumption that the works which survive, especially those
for important patrons, do represent something close to the aim of the
architect and his client. By means of this one assumption (surely a
reasonable one), it is possible to trace the response of the times to particular
problems, and the special goals set for themselves by the leaders of artistic
fashion. At the opening of the fourteenth century the wave of enthusiasm
for natural form had just passed its peak, and was giving way to mannerism
based on nature. Sprays of leaves, which had been as exact as casts, now
took on undulations which were increasingly a distortion of the original.
Similarly, ingenuity was expended upon the designs of window tracery,
which became more and more involved, more difficult to set out and to
work, and consequently far more costly.

It was the very ingenuity of this period that was its undoing; not only
did it outrun the constable, it also forgot the real purpose of this extravagance of tracery, namely the display to proper advantage of storied windows
of coloured glass. The more involved the stone tracery became, the more
difficult became the task of the glass-painter, and the less effective was the
result viewed, as glass must be, from within. Law and administration had
been codified under Edward I; in spite of backsliding into political chaos
under his son (see Appendix II), the whole tendency of the age was
towards unification and better organization; what is now termed
rationalization or planning. Such influences soon found their reflection
in art, and the major problem which confronted the architects and artists
of the time was so to correlate the parts of their buildings that they should
best contribute to the success of the whole. The casual juxtaposition of
features, beautiful in themselves, but irrelevant in composition, gave place
to carefully devised schemes in which the only unit was the sum total,
and every part was subordinated with meticulous accuracy in a graded
hierarchy of importance.

Thus the interior of a great church, from a collection of exquisite
specimens—window, pier, arch, triforium gallery, vault severy—grew into
an organism endowed with a higher degree of "life" and articulate
members adequately fashioned for their respective purposes. Each

32 Canterbury Cathedral: Cloister vault, 1397–1412.
    Designers: Henry Yevele and Stephen Lote

31 Worcester Cathedral: Cloister vault, c. 1372.
    Designer: John Clyve

34   Croyland Abbey: North Aisle, 1392–1427.
Designer: William Croyland

33   Worcester Cathedral: Cloister, c. 1372.
Designer: John Clyve

window, each arch and pier, each severy of vaulting, contributed towards the effect of the bay to which they belonged; the bays were linked together to form the majestic sweep of nave or choir; the building as a whole might focus upon the well of light flooding down through a central lantern Externally, the proportions of aisles and nave, of wall to roof, of porch to front, and of buttress and pinnacle to plain ashlar became more and more the object of special study. The splendid possibilities of towers and spires increasingly forced themselves upon the attention, while in castles and mansions their dominant position was commonly taken by the gate-house, no longer a mere weapon of defence, but an opportunity for the display of pomp as well as power.

None but the most rudimentary glimpses of all this are to be found before the fourteenth century: Salisbury Cathedral, so often cited as an example of perfect thirteenth-century composition loses more than half its effect if the tower and spire are removed, and, they were not begun until the fourteenth century had run a third of its course. Further, the subordination of parts at Salisbury is markedly at fault; the aisle windows are too large, the triforium too small and cramped, the buttresses disfigured by heavy suites of horizontal mouldings. That these imperfections meet with as little attention as they do is the highest of tributes to Richard of Farleigh, whose unparalleled steeple crowns and glorifies the whole work.

It is in the design of towers and spires that we can most easily discern a very important factor: the conscious evocation by the architect of an emotional response from the observer. No other features lend themselves so well to the expression of strength, power, endurance, majesty, aspiration, and the reality of the spiritual world beyond the material and earthly. That England could produce so many masterpieces of this kind with but the rarest lapses into sentimentality or bathos, is possibly her greatest positive achievement, for this is something more than the mere expression of prosperity or of organized religion, more even than the neutral perfection of exquisite aesthetic taste. The just rendering of the sublime in emotion as well as in pure art, is typical of the highest flights alone of human genius; in music we shall associate it with sections of Bach's Matthew Passion, for instance, or the best of Mozart's Requiem.

What is so astonishing in the cognate expression of emotion through architecture, is not that it should exist, but that in English Gothic art it should occur so abundantly. We know, for instance, that many important steeples have been destroyed, and yet there are remaining quite a dozen examples of first-class size hardly to be matched in grandeur throughout the globe. The multitude of specimens less only in scale defies exact computation, but a moderate estimate of fifty would include nothing but superlative excellence. In some cases we know, and in many others strongly suspect, the identity of the master's hand. At a later stage some of these masters will be discussed in detail, but for the present I would discuss rather the psychological background which made the masterpieces possible, and range among the works themselves.

National temperament is notoriously difficult to define, and epigram-
matic descriptions of the English, like Napoleon's "nation of shopkeepers"
are not immediately suggestive of those qualities with which we are here
concerned, and which so discerning a critic as Boney could not have
failed to notice had he ever lived in this country. The brilliant paradox
of a Chesterton could demonstrate the quintessential mystic of shop-
keeping, and the exquisite shades of value which only the soul of a shop-
keeper could assess, but in seriousness we must seek further for the springs
of action which link together successful trade and inspired and inspiring
art. By the compulsion of historical geography our search will lead us to
contrast the English with their neighbours and kinsfolk: the Germans on
the east, the French to the south, and the "Celts" to the west. From
such a series of contrasts we may see what we are not, and perhaps catch
a glimpse of what we truly are.

The German, in the grip of a mental emotion, is capable of greater
thoroughness than we in his pursuit of the ideal, but combines with this
great sentimentality; his details are so painstakingly, microscopically,
drawn in, that the whole composition refuses to be grasped. Sometimes
the result is crude, often gigantic with the immensity of more and ever
more minutiae heaped upon one another: the crudeness and the sentimental realism appear in the paintings of Matthias Grünewald; the
overpowering scale in Cologne Cathedral.

The Frenchman has a reputation for logic, and will follow pertinaciously
to the appointed end the veriest germ of an idea; his emotion is bodily,
and requires no sentimentality, and sometimes so little sentiment that one
recoils. His realism is cerebral, seizing impressionistically on salient
features so that an exact portrait appears through the mists of elusive
detail. Couperin's silvery *agréments*, the surge of Debussy's waves,
Fragonard's foliage and lighting, and the work of the modern painters all
conform to this temper. If exact detail be demanded of the French,
possibly because of their logic, they are unable to supply it. Where detail
of a precise character occurs in French art, as in much mediæval
sculpture, painting, and illumination, the masters are found to have
derived from the Netherlands and the border provinces: from these
districts were de Honnecourt, André Beauneveu, and Jacquemart de
Hesdin.

Far more difficult is the definition of our western neighbours; the
so-called Celt excels in mystical atmosphere and faint nuances of suggestion, traces of the things just beyond the frontier of the physical universe.
He still lives in an Homeric age where the appreciation of nature and the
capacity to translate it into the metaphor of fleeting words is yet normal.
Modern political life has not encouraged the preservation in permanent
form of this Celtic genius, and we have to go back to illuminated manuscripts produced in that Holy Ireland which tended and rekindled the
dying flame of Western life, or to the magical harp music of Wales
reanimated by Arnold Dolmetsch.

By racial descent, as well as by cultural contact, the English partake of the qualities of all their neighbours, and this may be tested by comparison with the history and art of Flanders. The Flemings, sandwiched between the great Teutonic folk on one hand, and the French on the other, developed an architecture, a school of painting, and an exquisite music, wherein French and German virtues were blended and their vices eschewed. In all these arts the approximation between Flanders and England is very close, yet the difference is plainly marked. It consists in the presence in English work of a *tertium quid*, a quality neither French nor German, betrayed by a warmth of imagination, an almost intangible bloom which is enough to change the colour harmony of the result. It is through this admixture of Celtic fantasy with the strength of Germany and the refinement of France that the best English work can exercise a magic which is entirely its own.

Beyond this are other contributions, not Western nor even European. The adventurous English mind snatches at strange visions of the East and distant scenes; it has always loved the sailorman's parrot and the curiosities collected while "a-roving the Lord knows where". The arrival of an elephant in 1254, presented by St. Louis to Henry III, caused scenes such as we now associate with royalty and famous aviators, and afforded Matthew Paris, who made several drawings of the beast, with one of the few journalistic "scoops" of the Middle Ages. England, of course, was not alone in accepting Eastern motives; the rebuilding of western Europe depended upon the gradual assimilation from the Near and Middle East of the elements of culture lost during the Dark Ages. World culture itself had first sprung from that region, and from it wave after wave has spread, covering the surface of the globe.

Long before recorded history, Britain was the goal of strangers who were moved by the spirit of adventure, conquest, trade, or fear. Having reached the island, last outpost of the great continental mass, they could go no farther. Thus we are the inheritors of greater riches than we know. Gothic elements from Sicily and Provence met others, likewise Eastern in origin but long domiciled in the North, which may have come from Scythia and Siberia to the Vikings and thus in their long-ships to the West. The pointed arch, descendant of the parabolic arch and vault employed by the Hittites and Sassanian Persians, met its counterpart in the timber building of the northerners, where the technique of the house was closely allied to the shipwright's craft. For many centuries, and especially in Saxon times, timber construction dominated England, and the most ancient form of English house, built upon pairs of crucks or elbowed timbers set archwise in the ground, bears a striking resemblance to an upturned boat, such a vessel as the great ship of Sutton Hoo. A few of these houses without walls, and a larger number of similar barns and out-buildings, survive here, while high-pitched huts of this type are still commonly employed in the Pacific Islands. Hocart considered that both the high pitch of the roof and the absence of walls had a ritual significance, but at least in the North the form may be due to the necessity of guarding against the collection of a crushing weight of snow.

By a natural organic development the hut on crucks became a barn-like hall with additional posts in rows supporting longer rafters, and it is by no means impossible that there may be a vestige of truth in the once ridiculed suggestion that the vaulted Gothic church contained a reminiscence of the branching trees of heathen groves. An analogous theory is current orthodoxy concerning the temple-ziggurats of Sumeria, which are considered proof that the Sumerians had come from a mountainous country where their ceremonies had been held on high places. The high place and the grove are the two classic sites for pagan ritual, and the discovery in Britain of temples and sanctuaries of wooden posts, possibly of earlier date than the stone circles, lends colour to the theory of Northern temples in the form of artificial groves.

It is not necessary to postulate any direct derivation of forms in order to accept the principle of cultural imitation and influence. The Christian church, though it derives from Roman forms, took on a markedly different shape in the North, and influences there must have been which determined the separate course taken by the Gothic cathedrals of France and Britain, from that of their Southern counterparts in Italy, Provence, and Aquitaine. Latent paganism was strong in England until the Puritan seventeenth and agnostic eighteenth centuries. Even modern indifference has not stamped out the last of the ancient customs, and it is highly improbable that the bureaucratic car of Juggernaut or the impersonal interference of parsons and police ever will do so.

To all appearance we have wandered far from the church-towers of Gothic England, but it is probable that great part of that emotion which they so feelingly convey results from the fusion of conscious technical invention and artistic genius with subconscious memory of a past tradition, still lingering on though far beyond the craftsman's knowledge. More than this, we ourselves can still establish to our own satisfaction our spiritual kinship by contemplation and investigation of the works and methods of our forerunners. We may find it south of Dorchester, where Maiden Castle looms up, a city of refuge, above the coastal plain; far away on the northern moors, where Long Meg leads her daughters in strange dance; or around Avebury and Stonehenge, where cluster those still more sacred stones, guardians of the age-old dead.

All this we may feel, yet need something more complete, more mature, more sophisticated, though at the same time fully and wholly English. We shall find it in a thousand places, up and down the shires, in cathedral, ruined abbey, frowning castle, village church, and dreaming manor; the accomplishment of the greatest, the most typical two centuries of our life as a nation, the age of the Edwards, of Richard II, of the two Roses, and of their grafting upon the House of Tudor. As if we were travellers in a strange land, instead of our own, we shall need to take our time and let the details of this past existence sink into our consciousness. Time and a little patience are all that is required; soon the characteristics of the regions and those which mark subdivisions of time will become familiar, and we shall find ourselves no longer seeing Gothic buildings as a flock

35   Needham Market Church: roof, *c.* 1460

36   Walsoken Church: roof of South Chapel, *c.* 1520?

38   Framlingham Church: nave roof, c. 1500

37   Swaffham Church: nave roof, c. 1500

of sheep or crowd of Chinese, all alike, but will begin the fascinating game of seeking and recognizing the features of individuality.

Each of the features of this national art deserves to be traced in the course of an extended tour among surviving examples. Let us begin with the tower, or rather the tower and spired steeple, for it is impossible to make a hard-and-fast distinction. Most towers, even Perpendicular towers, were intended to be crowned by a spire, even if it were only to be of timber. In many cases such timber spires as once existed have been burnt or pulled down as dangerous structures. Many square-topped towers, apparently complete in themselves, are yet provided with squinch-arches for a stone spire never built or, as at Shepton Mallet, begun but never carried on. At Durham Cathedral, first a central tower of one stage was built, then a second stage added, and finally preparations were made for a stone spire, when the dissolution of the Priory stopped the work for ever.

First of the great Gothic steeples was that of St. Paul's in London, built early in the thirteenth century, but this had only a timber spire covered with lead. Of those still in existence, the series starts with the central tower of Lincoln, built by Richard of Stow between 1307 and 1311; here some of the vertical emphasis of the coming Perpendicular made its appearance, and the corners of the tower carry up the octagonal buttresses of the Early English substructure, and thus foreshadow one of the most characteristic patterns of the best later work, found also at Salisbury a quarter-century afterwards, and in a modified form at Worcester, the earliest of the great Perpendicular towers. In the fifteenth century this type appeared in towers of important parish churches, such as that of St. Laurence, Reading, completed in 1458, and in several of the great flint towers of East Anglia: that of Wymondham, built by the parishioners to rival the monastic central tower, is dated 1473. Finally it gave us what are perhaps the three finest of all our towers, William Orchard's at Magdalen College, Oxford, and John Wastell's Bell Harry at Canterbury, both begun about 1490, and the Vertues' tower at Bath Abbey, where work began about the turn of the century. This last tower, upon an oblong plan, is a magnificent achievement, though it has been sadly altered by repeated attempts at completion and restoration (3, 15, 27).

This device of the octagonal corner-buttress not only gave direct vertical emphasis, but also simplified the task of achieving unity in the composition of wall and window. Elsewhere, gradual experiment with other methods reached different but perhaps equally distinguished results. At Lincoln only one main story was attempted; at Salisbury there were two, and it is in the repetition of the lower story's features that Salisbury falls a little short of perfection. The lesson of Perpendicular was still to learn: the lesson that a building cannot be constructed out of units possessed of individualities of their own. At Wells, four-square and unbuttressed, William Joy had more nearly achieved the ideal, but unlike Farleigh, he made no attempt to carry the tower beyond a single stage

Fortunately so, for as it was, collapse of the crossing was only averted by the insertion of the immense St. Andrew's arches in the openings of nave and transepts. A generation later, John Clyve at Worcester produced a really satisfying tower, whose two stories are of completely differing, yet complementary designs, while subsidiary buttresses prop the hexagonal clasping turrets (21). Here, unified by Perpendicular detail, was a truly successful tower, which not only possessed unity of its own, but conferred unity upon the building below, as does that of Salisbury, though with slightly marred effect.

Cathedrals, by their nature, allowed little scope except for a central steeple rising above the roofs, or twin western towers of lesser scale. Parish churches, however, offered an ideal position at the west end of the nave for a single tower designed from the ground upwards as a giant finger pointing towards the sky. At Coventry, the church of St. Michael was provided with the greatest and in some ways the most successful of such steeples, rising in four square stages, surmounted by an octagonal lantern with flying buttresses and a three-tiered spire. The tower was completed after some twenty years' work in 1394, and the spire added a generation later. Here there is no repetition, no fumbling; immense square buttresses diminish according to an exquisitely graded curve to the summit, flanking the great west window; above this come three stages containing windows increasing in size and accompanied by added enrichment towards the parapet. The actual weight of masonry, and still more its apparent weight, is thus lightened progressively, in preparation for the pinnacles with their arches leaping at the delicately poised lantern. Lastly, the spire is itself most subtly contoured and traceried in its two lower stages, the second being distinguished by stepped ribs like miniature buttresses upon alternate faces and flanking narrow windows, while the last and tallest stage rises straight to the weathercock, pierced by a window in each of its eight faces at about one-quarter of its height above the middle tier (13).

Neither the directness of Giotto's famous campanile nor the complexities of Ulm can be ranked above the steeple of Coventry, which deserves mention as one of the wonders of the world. Once, travelling in an express train between Nuneaton and Rugby, I glanced out to the west, and by some accident which had cleared the atmosphere, Coventry appeared like a crystal city in the brilliant sunshine, set upon its hill, and dominating it, above its two attendant spires, soared the 300 feet of St. Michael, portentous as its namesake's sword. It has never been my fortune to see it thus again, but the memory remains to prove that the possession of one masterpiece can make even Coventry glorious as the New Jerusalem.

With Coventry St. Michael we come into the most brilliant period of our art, which I for one would rank as not second even to the Athens of Pericles in supreme beauty. The modern critics tell us to avoid the terms of beauty and ugliness, but surely this is to dehumanize humanity. Man ever has, and ever must, respond to beauty, whether he analyse it or no. So I shall make no apology for referring upon occasion to the loveliness of this work and of that, the gracious suitability which is beautiful because fitting to its purpose and its surroundings. We need only look at the portraits, statues, and effigies of past times to see that in many cases they actually had a higher standard of personal human beauty than have we; and if it is objected that the portraits and the effigies are imaginary and ideal, then all the more did the *standard* exist, if not the reality. The clear-cut refinement and sparkling quality of the faces of kings and angels in the Wilton Diptych mark out this last decade of the fourteenth century as one of the most exalted of all.

While Worcester and Coventry built their towers, so did Wells, where William Wynford had to encompass the exceedingly difficult task of adding Perpendicular towers to the great Early English west face of the Cathedral without awkwardness or incongruity. The work was done with such accomplished skill and ingenuity that it is as though the towers had grown by some natural process out of what had gone before. The deep buttresses of the front are carried upwards, to die back against the angles of twin diagonal buttresses at each corner of a tower, and the design of the outward buttresses is ever so slightly different, and more solid, than that of the inner pairs. This brings the composition together towards the centre, and averts any sense of the towers overturning outwards, split apart by a duality of interest and focus. While working at Wells, Wynford may have been approached by one of the canons, Robert Samborne, who was rector of Yeovil and about to undertake the rebuilding of the church. At any rate, the whole of Yeovil church, which was already begun when Samborne died in 1382, bears a resemblance to Wynford's style, the arcades being reminiscent of the ante-chapel of New College, and the tower and its parapet profit from the lessons of Wells (**29, 30**). It is thanks to the towers that the front of Wells is the most nearly perfect of any among the English cathedrals. Its contemporary at Beverley Minster is probably the greatest front of all, for it is in one style, designed at one time, and carried out within a few years. Beverley lacks some of the subtlety of Coventry and Wells, for the diminution of its buttresses is managed somewhat clumsily, and there is rather too much surface decoration, but if it were in some foreign land it would share the fame of a Chartres, a Rheims, or a Cologne (**7**).

Less satisfactory are the towers of the first half of the fifteenth century, though there are a few notable exceptions. William Colchester's great four-square lantern at York has great merit from without, and is the best of all central towers in its interior effect (**4**). Among churches of non-cathedral rank the finest tower is that of Hedon, close to Hull. This, built by Robert Playser between 1427 and 1437, is of admirable proportions, and though it owes little to ornament beyond the tracery of its windows, can hardly be surpassed for the surety of its proportions. As at Coventry, the tower is lightened towards the top, and rather as Worcester allows a hexagonal buttress to rise through supporting claspers, so at Hedon the paired buttresses of the lower stage give place to a single diagonal buttress above. Here, too, the addition of the tower has given unity to a church of several earlier periods (**18**).

In the middle of the century a few fine towers were produced, before the civil wars brought work to a stop. The best of them is Robert Janyns's bell-tower at Merton College Oxford, no large work, but drawn with an assured hand and certainty, of design. Much less happy is the more ambitious tower of Gloucester Cathedral, where the attempt was made to double the success of Worcester by superimposing two stories of paired windows and blind tracery (**14, 23**). This was to go back to the cardinal error of Salisbury, and to make matters worse, buttresses and tracery are wiry and the tower looks far more like an iron construction than do the iron spires of Cologne. Gloucester met with some contemporary approval, but the smaller version carried out at Great Malvern Priory vastly improves upon the original. Elsewhere, it was for the most part the parapet and pinnacles of Gloucester, the "Gloucester coronet" that were imitated; the feature reached Bristol and Dundry, Somerset, and as far as Cardiff in Wales; in a much modified form, some fifty years later, it reappeared at Wrexham.

Somerset, following upon the successful towers of Wells Cathedral, had been specializing in towers since the last quarter of the fourteenth century. Yeovil, begun about 1380 by its rector, who was also a Canon of Wells, may owe the excellence of its design to consultation with Wynford, while another remarkable tower, designed for spire, was built at Shepton Mallet, five miles from Wells, about the same time. The parish church of St. Cuthbert, Wells, built its western tower, a noble one, about 1410, and thereafter Somerset did not lack for towers in progress until the Reformation (**20**). The highly elaborate examples, such as Taunton St. Mary Magdalene, are of late date, mostly begun after the coming of Henry Tudor in 1485. The more restrained designs, for example Mells, in progress in 1446, are usually of earlier date, and are often to be preferred in composition.

Tall and very simple towers were being built in Devon between 1400 and 1450; one of the most remarkable is that of Ashburton, which was chosen as one of four examples to be imitated at Totnes when its tower was determined upon in 1449 (**28**). Totnes is far more elaborate than Ashburton but not unduly so, and is certainly one of the finest parochial towers in the country.. In the Midlands also design had reached a high pitch of accomplishment, one of the best of the early period being that of St. Margaret, Leicester, begun about 1448, while St. Mary, Nottingham, has a distinguished central tower dating from the closing years of the century. By far the finest of the Midland towers is that of All Saints, Derby, begun about 1510 and designed by John Otes, a pupil of Wastell (**19**).

This last period of English tower design was the richest of all; besides the important works already mentioned, were Lavenham, Suffolk, hardly to be rivalled among parish towers, and built at two periods between 1486 and 1525, largely from monies given by the De Veres, Earls of Oxford,

39   Ditcheat Church: Nave roof, *c.* 1470–90

40   Somerton Church: Nave roof, *c.* 1490

41   East Dereham Church: roof of North Transept

42   Llanegryn Church: Roodloft, *c.* 1520

and the Spring family, the richest clothiers of the town (24). Other grand towers are those of St. Neots, Huntingdonshire (*c.* 1493–1530); Beaminster, Dorset (*c.* 1499); Probus, Cornwall (1514–47); Cullompton, Devon (*c.* 1540 and later); and the Abbey bell-tower at Evesham (1528–38), still unfinished at the dissolution. The fashion of tower-building had spread all over the country, and even the Cistercians, to whom towers were strictly forbidden by their rule, joined in the work, and as at Fountains in Yorkshire, were in the forefront of successful patrons. It is easy to sneer at the wealthy men who thought to purchase worldly fame and eternal salvation by means of one and the same bequest, but, seeing the glorious results, how can we doubt the substantial sincerity of the age which produced such fruits? Sad and disillusioned by previous poverty and war it may have been, but it rose triumphant over its weaknesses in its swan-song, wherein God was glorified by means of works seldom equalled and never surpassed by men's hands.

If the Perpendicular towers are the most spectacular of our national glories, they are intrinsically no more wonderful than the vaults, the roofs, the cloisters, the gatehouses, or the brilliantly planned colleges and domestic buildings. We saw that it was the special achievement of Perpendicular that throughout all parts of the work it infused a spirit of unity, as J. D. Sedding wrote of it: "the Perpendicular takes up all that was incomplete in former phases, adding thereto the abler disposition of lines and masses, and a higher range of carving and colour decoration, and, in brief, gives every architectural resource its highest and fullest expression", and again: "it is the harvest-time of all our mediæval endeavour." It is this completeness of the style, its capacity for producing the best of everything, and all at once, that makes for less immediate appreciation than falls to simpler and more primitive art.

Planning itself became broader and more comprehensive; the cathedral and the parish church alike became as it were four-dimensional. To the three material dimensions was added another: aesthetic space. Norman architecture had dealt in mass; the early Gothic in line; now at last came space defined by line. The beauty of space simply defined is nowhere better seen than in Westminster Hall: the trefoil arches of the great roof, the plain lines of walls and floor with their long focus, produce an unparalleled magnificence, undreamed of in post-Gothic times. If we turn into a parish church of the period, such as St. Thomas, Salisbury, even bereft of its glass and of most of its colour, there is an immediate impression of space and light, coupled with a grand sense of repose. There is nothing restless, agitated, or obscure. The men who built these works had lost the childlike religion of the earlier age of faith; they were passing through a period of doubt and depression—but they were still able to find God through their own exertions.

Perpendicular churches are so numerous that one may scarcely do more than express personal preferences in naming individual buildings. Among the greater churches the naves of Canterbury and Winchester take pride of place; Yevele and Wynford were the greatest masters of their art that this country has seen, and here are the fruits of their mature experience. Among later works, the rebuilding of Sherborne Abbey, with its magnificent fan-vaulting, ranks very high, though choir and nave are more than a generation apart. So too is King's College Chapel the work of several hands; begun by Reginald Ely, continued by several other masters, and brought to completion by John Wastell, master of the Canterbury Bell Harry. Then we have Christopher Scune's nave of Ripon, an assured work of simple detail but excellent proportion; St. Mary Redcliffe, Bristol, a cathedral in size though but a parish church, and St. George's Chapel in Windsor Castle. Bath Abbey is the only complete Perpendicular cathedral, and exhibits several deceptive subtleties of composition: the asymmetrical tower already mentioned, the confident and engaging simplicity of the west front, and the contrasts between two-centred and four-centred arches, while refinements of detail are displayed against large spaces of plain walling.

The parish churches offer a rich harvest: Maidstone is a good and unspoilt specimen of the school of Yevele, and Yeovil of that of Wynford, while at a later date there are the magnificent woolmen's churches of the Cotswolds and East Anglia: glories such as those of Northleach (53) and Chipping Norton, with its arcades reminiscent of Canterbury; Lavenham and Long Melford, so close together yet so different in detail; Swaffham with its roof (37); Needham Market with another still more remarkable (35); the two great parish churches at Bury St. Edmunds and the many at Norwich and Ipswich. In the marshland are Lynn St. Nicholas, Terrington St. Clement, Walpole St. Peter, Moulton with its noble nave and spire; farther north the grand collegiate church of Tattershall, and Louth, with steeple second (if that) only to Coventry. As at Norwich, so again at York is there an embarrassment of parishes, each with its special attractions. Most outstanding, to my mind, is the graceful lantern of All Saints, Pavement. Yorkshire provides us also with Holy Trinity, Hull, the first parish church of Perpendicular type, and Wakefield, now a cathedral, Halifax with a noble tower, black with soot but comely, and a multitude of great village churches.

Manchester Collegiate Church is one of the best examples of the style, with its spreading array of chapels, its grand tower, and exquisitely carved stalls. Much of Chester Cathedral is of closely related style, and both may owe their design to the Palatine master masons of Chester; Chester too had its official master carpenters, who doubtless produced the cathedral stalls, whose details follow Westminster work of the same period, that of the Herlands. At Chester used to be the simple but excellently designed tower of St. John's Abbey, but it fell during the last century and has not been rebuilt, though drawings and photographs exist. This book is not a catalogue of local styles, and I must desist, but before leaving the parish churches I would say a word for a personal favourite, St. Margaret's Westminster, one of the happiest and most charmingly designed of all, a sanctuary in which one may rest after the strenuous task of appreciating the glories of the Abbey.

What of the cloisters? Where in England, or in the world, can lovelier vaults and pierced screens be found than at Canterbury, Worcester, Gloucester, Wells, Chester, or Lacock Abbey? (31-3). And were it not desecrated by Parliamentary uses, St. Stephen's Cloister in the Ancient Palace of Westminster? From the cloisters it is a natural transition to the colleges with their courts and quadrangles, and except for buildings and rebuildings of post-Gothic style, here the whole output is Perpendicular. From New College and Winchester College with their exquisite detail and glass, through All Souls, Oxford, with John Massingham's sculptures, and Queens' College, Cambridge, type of the Cambridge plan, to King's College, Magdalen College, Oxford, the dignified simplicity of Corpus Christi, Oxford, and the magnificent consummation of Christ Church, all is Perpendicular, the work of the great masters of the style. The fame of Oxford and Cambridge is not due entirely to their academic achievements; architecturally they possess a finer background than perhaps any other towns in Europe, and of this background the greater and by far the more significant part is Perpendicular Gothic. All that is now implied by the terms university and college really springs from the work of Wykeham and of Henry VI, and the buildings which they required for the accomplishment of their educational schemes.

It is in the college plans that the unity of Perpendicular design is seen at its best; here is a clear-cut solution of the problem of providing accommodation for a body of persons assembled together for the double purpose of the service of God in chapel and the carrying on of cultural life in library and chambers. The plan of the closed quadrangle, adopted almost simultaneously at both universities, was the outcome of assimilation between the normal designs of the large house, the college of chantry priests, and the Carthusian monastery with its separate cells grouped about a cloister. In the new residential castles also, as at Hertford and Herstmonceux, cloister-courts became a feature of the plan, with the result that by the end of the period almost all buildings could be designed as variants of the same all-purpose skeleton. Not that this led to monotony; differences of disposition, treatment, and materials gave endless variety and charm to the multitude of late Gothic and Tudor buildings, as the inquirer may see from a glance through the pages of Garner and Stratton's famous work.

For any given problem there will be in all probability only one ideal solution; that is, when one speaks in general terms. The details may differ infinitely, but it was one of the signal triumphs of English art that it should have seized on the essentials and held to them, steadily refusing to waste time upon further experiment and the production of freaks. True everywhere, this is especially noticeable in the case of roof construction. Until the fourteenth century, any large hall had had to resort to the ancient aisled form, with its roof supported upon ranges of wooden posts or stone columns. The structural experiment of the master carpenters overcame the problem of doing away with the posts. William Hurley, called to Ely in 1334, was able to devise a timber roof for the octagon, 65 feet across, and some fifteen years later Philip of Lincoln spanned the nave of York Minster with a timber vault, 45 feet in span and over 200 in length. Finally, in 1394 Hugh Herland had so far developed the principle of the hammer-beam and the timber arch in combination, that he could make confident preparations for the new roof of Westminster Hall, nearly 240 feet in length and almost 70 in span.

The problem once solved, the solution was applied and adapted to all instances. No radically new problems presented themselves, but there is not the least sign of standardization among the glorious roofs of halls and churches. Sometimes, as at Ely, York Minster, Chester Cathedral, and Winchester College Chapel, the true construction was hidden by a timber vault in imitation of stone. More generally, the timbers themselves were moulded and enriched, and the roof provided with angels upon whose wings it might appear to float in air. Again, there might be coffered panelling filled with exquisitely patterned carving and ornamented with bosses, as at Shepton Mallet, Somerset, or St. Mary's, Chester. Three great centres of woodworking existed in Somerset, Cheshire, and the eastern counties, while in London the King's craftsmen produced the most ambitious roofs incorporating features derived from all the local schools. Church roofs are perhaps at their richest in Suffolk, where angel roofs of wonderful and finished craftsmanship are found at Needham Market, Woolpit, Rattlesden, Earl Stonham, Bury St. Mary, and in many other places besides (5, 35-40).

While roofs provided the main opportunity for structural timberwork, the carpenters and carvers were kept busy upon the provision of ritual and purely ornamental features for churches, and fittings and furniture required by the growing luxury of the rich and the desire for comfort among the less well-to-do. In church, the rood-screen, loft, and celure afforded the greatest scope to the operations of carpenter, joiner, carver, and painter. The roods themselves, with their figures of the Christ, have all perished, destroyed by fanaticism, though a few broken fragments remain, chiefly in Wales, and at Kemeys Inferior, Monmouthshire, is the greater part of a fourteenth-century Christ having some artistic pretensions. The remoteness of Wales has also preserved our unique mediæval organ-case, that at Old Radnor, though this is a late example, with linen-fold panelling.

Rood- and parclose-screens exist in comparative plenty, and in such variety that no detailed treatment can here be given. Exquisite vaulted screens are found in many places; rich examples both in Somerset (a particularly fine one at Dunster) and Devon, while the eastern counties are especially famous for screens with painted panelling. The figures at Southwold, Suffolk, and Cawston, Norfolk, give an excellent notion of the colour decoration of a fifteenth-century church, while at Ranworth, Norfolk, are saints of a flamboyant type certainly foreign in inspiration, and for which a Catalan origin has been suggested. The amount of intricate work involved in the making of these screens was enormous; it is not unusual to sneer contemptuously at the "shop-work" of the

43   Dunster Church: Screen, *c.* 1500

44   Halse Church: Screen, *c.* 1500

46 Kingswood Abbey: Gatehouse, c. 1400?

45 Crewkerne Church: West door, c. 1490?

Perpendicular carvers, but when all is said and done, the average standard of execution had risen enormously since the thirteenth century, and if some variety were sacrificed, it was in obedience to that sound instinct in favour of subordination of parts which was the secret of our mature aesthetic (42-4).

Whether in the elaboration of minute parts of a stall-canopy or a font-cover, such as the magnificent examples at Ufford, Suffolk, and Ewelme, Oxfordshire, or in the simpler working of bench-end or panelled pulpit, the craftsman was supreme (45, 95, 151, 170-1, 173-4). Only when the spread of Renaissance details spelt a break with the tradition they understood, did the hands that held the chisel grow careless and clumsy (71). Not in one or two places only, but in centres all over the country from Devon to Yorkshire, were the groups of men who could turn out, year after year and century after century, work of a fine and true finish in unflagging succession.

Church woodwork and painted panels could easily lead to consideration of stained glass and wall-paintings, plate and goldsmith's work, or the reredos and tables of the alabasterman. It is essential to the appreciation of a mediæval church to recall that it was once full of colour in all its parts. There was then no painful contrast between the mellow oak of seating and the sombre figures of saints on the panels of the screen and, on the other hand, whitewashed walls or scraped and garnished masonry. The walls had their own series of paintings, while above the chancel arch or on a wooden tympanum within it was a great Doom, the Last Judgment represented with the blest souls on the one side and the gaping mouth of Hell upon the other, while into it rushed crowds of the wicked, impelled by the halberds and grappling hooks of a horde of demons.

We can still see such a Doom at St. Thomas, Salisbury, and in the south chancel aisle are some charming scenes from the life of the Virgin in oblong panels with a reddish ochre background and a warm olive-green as the predominant colour. At Pickering in Yorkshire is a far more extensive gathering of fourteenth- and mid-fifteenth-century paintings, but they are much poorer than those at Salisbury regarded as art. In the chapel of Haddon Hall also an extensive series has been uncovered. Few and far between as are these existing specimens (there are of course many others not here mentioned), they are enough to give some insight into the colour-scheme which once enlivened the bare fabric of the walls. For the effect of large quantities of stained glass we can go only to York, and to Fairford, Gloucestershire; elsewhere the fanatics and the restorers have had their way, and only single windows and truncated schemes survive. Among the greater churches and colleges we are rather better off, with a fine fifteenth-century range of York glass at Great Malvern, and the splendid fourteenth- and sixteenth-century glazing of New College, Oxford, and King's College Chapel, Cambridge.

Though in a fragmentary state, enough glass remains, eked out by records of former glazing now destroyed, to show that the windows of the Perpendicular period were designed as an integral part of the architectural effect. Just as bands of horizontal moulding are found, as at Canterbury nave and in King's College Chapel, serving to link together into a combined whole the bays of a Perpendicular church, so did similar horizontal ranges of saints form bands linking up the windows of the aisles. In the masonry it was the vertical line that predominated; the glass restored a balance with its rows of figures giving a level emphasis of colour. As in all else, the craftsmen in glass had reached a far higher standard of competence in draughtsmanship and colouring than their predecessors of the thirteenth and earlier centuries. The beginning of the great change in glass, as in architecture, can be seen in the choir of Gloucester, and a generation later, at New College, it was complete.

Almost all the treasures of plate and alabaster are now in museums and private collections. The Victoria and Albert Museum houses an admirably representative collection, including the lovely censer and incense-boat of silver which belonged to Ramsey Abbey, dredged up from the bed of Whittlesey Mere in the middle of the nineteenth century (175-6). Of the alabasters, a number of charming panels or tables are still to be found in churches; one of the Nativity, found beneath the church floor, is at West Horsley in Surrey, and an exquisite panel of the Annunciation occurs on the mid-fifteenth-century tomb of a priest in Wells Cathedral (67).

Not all the best craftsmanship went into objects of religious significance, but comparatively few secular pieces have survived. The British Museum possesses the quadrant of Richard II, engraved with his White Hart badge and with its dial figured with Arabic numerals, and also a large English bronze jug of the same period with inscriptions and badges in relief, which had mysteriously penetrated to the kingdom of Ashanti, whence it was recovered by the British Expedition of 1896 (90). A later work of bronze which has escaped the melting-pot on account of its official character is the great bronze bushel of Henry VII, now in the West Gate Museum at Winchester, together with earlier and later weights and measures.

Something yet remains to be said on the subject of secular building itself: the vast array of town and country houses built between the reign of Edward II and that of Henry VIII. In most parts of the country, the ordinary small house or cottage was built of timber framing, the panels filled with hurdles or wattling, and daubed over with clay, or a composition of clay, lime, and chopped straw. These were the forerunners of the prefabricated building of which we hear so much nowadays: quite frequently houses were framed by the carpenter at his yard, often placed beside a river, then transported in parts by barge and wagon to the site, and there erected in order. Every timber had to be marked at the joints with corresponding (Roman) numerals, to permit of correct assembly. These marks may often be seen quite clearly from the street, as on the Grammar School, Stratford-on-Avon, built by master carpenter John Hasill in 1427, or on a long row on the west side of Cheap Street in Sherborne, where a new addition can easily be distinguished by its lack of marks.

In the greater towns—York, Norwich, Shrewsbury, Gloucester, Bury

St. Edmunds—are many fine street fronts and dwellings on corner sites with bracketed corner-posts of elaborate design and carving. Many such town houses give the lie to the prevalent tradition of mediæval darkness and cramped quarters by their long ranges of continuous window, such as occur at the White Hart Inn, Newark-on-Trent, or in stone at the Prior's Lodging, Much Wenlock (57). Another fine building with large windows is the Tribunal at Glastonbury, described as "newly built" for a sessions house and gaol, in 1517. Here is no attempt at slavish symmetry; the straightforward front of two stories is plain below and broken above by an oriel of slight projection. The door beneath Tudor arms and rose on the left, and four pairs of window-lights, each four-centred beneath a square head, fill the whole of the ground-floor width, while above an oriel of four lights, with a single light in each of its canted faces, separates two-light windows at each end, similar to those below. Above the lower windows runs a string-course, while at the top is a heavier moulded cornice and a plain parapet. A touch of interest is provided by the canted lights of the oriel, running back into the wall, which is pared away obliquely on each side (51).

Farther down the street is the George, originally a monastic hostelry for pilgrims, built by Abbot John Selwood towards the close of the reign of Edward IV. Here the street front is far more elaborate and comprises three stories, but again there is no studied symmetry. The house is flanked by buttresses of unusual hexagonal section, and is divided almost at the centre by the bracket intended to support the sign. All appearance of a duality is avoided by the completely differing treatment of the two halves; on the left a bay window runs the full height, while the right half is left flat and is divided into five parts, three and two divided by a narrow strip of plain wall corresponding to the position of the bracket. The three-light windows are above the main entrance archway, while three stages of paired windows light the rooms on the right. The whole is surmounted by a crenellated parapet of simple design (52).

These two elegant buildings in Glastonbury seem to me more worthy of detailed description than many a larger mansion, for they contain respectively, within small compass, the "penny plain" and the "twopence coloured" of our last Gothic age. Neither pretends to be great architecture, but both are admirably suited for their purposes: the hostel betrays the importance of the shrine visited by its pilgrims, while the Tribunal presents a workday face to the Abbot's tenants and suitors who will throng the courts held within. The trilogy is completed by the great abbey barn on the other side of the town, whose transeptal porches and spacious interior are still in readiness for the vanished tithes of the abbey lands.

These stone houses of Somerset, the timbering of Suffolk or the Midlands, the brick of Buckden Palace or Thorpland Hall, are the true ancestors of our vernacular architecture: those villages and hamlets which seem to grow out of the soil itself. They owe little or nothing to the classic pedantry of the professional architects with their pattern-books; almost

G

all to the forgotten genius of the little masters of the Gothic age, who worked excellent well and most enduringly in imitation of the greater triumphs of Perpendicular. As all good building should be, they are un-self-conscious; they make no parade of their qualities, but if they exert themselves at all it is to be good neighbours with the next houses upon either side. If they set advertisements upon their frontages, they are those of the reigning sovereign, of the local prelate or squire; such badges will be cut in stone or wood and beautiful in form, not printed garishly on paper to become a thing of faded tatters ripe for replacement. Like all the productions of their time, in short, these buildings possessed good manners (46, 58-60).

The greater buildings, works of the masters who formed and developed the style, will be dealt with later, but I would stress again the incomparable richness of this period. There is no form of art unrepresented, religious or secular; no material unused, no type of skill left unemployed. The mason, the carpenter, the bricklayer, the smith, glazier and plumber, carver and painter, goldsmith and alabasterman, all were busy. The production of works of art accounted for a large proportion of the livelihood earned by the population; if a building, an utensil, an article of clothing were necessary, it was also essential that it should be beautifully made, thus a pleasure to use. However much the rich might grind the faces of the poor, those poor were clad in good cloth of excellent weave and colour, and their life could not but be enriched by their physical surroundings. Here was far better hope of progress than in the crazy spread of costly mechanical devices.

It remains to be considered how this vast organization of the arts was achieved and to what extent it was affected by the fluctuations in our national fortunes between 1300 and 1550. We have seen that while a prosperous trade and internal security had been achieved under Edward I, and thus made it possible to spend part of a large income on art and good craftsmanship, the changes which led to the establishment of the Perpendicular style were not material in character, but resulted from the spread of a new attitude to life, as well as from the natural tendency of repeated experiment to end in successful and generally adopted results. Perpendicular was not the outcome of poverty and failure, but of riches and success. Only to a comparatively slight extent was its course changed by the coming of the Black Death, which did but accelerate a movement already in being.

It has been shown within comparatively recent years that the whole procedure of administration in England grew up by force of imitation. The King and his Council and the departments of State which clustered around them formed a pattern which was copied on a smaller scale elsewhere. Forms of law and processes known to the King's Courts were adopted and grafted on to the local procedure of the ancient territorial and seignorial jurisdictions. The King had his Exchequer; so did the bishops have theirs, and so too did some of the great monasteries. Methods of accountancy enrolment and audit, all passed downwards gradually

47 Maidstone College, 1395–*c.* 1405. School of Henry Yevele

48 Ely Priory: Great Gatehouse, 1396–*c.* 1400. Designer: John Mepsale

49   St. Osyth's Priory: Gatehouse, *c.* 1475

50   Colchester, St. John's Abbey: Gatehouse, *c.* 1480

from top to bottom of the social hierarchy. Thus there was in existence a gradual assimilation of forms of administration similar to, and underlying, the assimilation of different building types which we have already seen. If the outward concrete expression of monastery, fortress, or domestic establishment came to resemble each other, it was no accident, but the result of a growing resemblance between the institutions themselves.

The wheel turns full circle; the Roman basilica, a secular building, became prototype of the Christian churches; a thousand years later, changed in form, the churches were being used for all manner of secular purposes, as markets, public halls, occasionally as libraries, sometimes, though in the teeth of ecclesiastical censure, for the holding of dances and feasts. Church and state, layman and cleric, house, convent, castle, and college were becoming more closely integrated when the ferment of the Renaissance disrupted all, and the work was to do once again. Since 1550 religion has in England been a matter of Sundays; it has never again become a part of everyday life; similarly, worldly considerations and above all a sense of humour, have been excluded from the practice of religion.

Like Confucius long before them, and Goethe long after, the leaders of mediæval action sought an all-pervading unity; unlike either Confucius or Goethe, they were able not merely to discover the principle, but to go far in introducing it into their daily life, and that of the whole people. Nowhere was this more true than in England. Unity in art is a more elusive, less obvious thing than unity in law or administration, and one might suppose even more difficult of achievement, but notwithstanding this it was attained, and by the same process of imitation. The artistic centre of the country was at the Court, where were artists and master craftsmen of all types. The force of court fashion was sufficient to carry their work to the greater centres of the land, the cities, and the chief castles and mansions of the nobility, and of course to the sees of the bishops and the houses of those mitred abbots who sat in Parliament.

All these nobles, courtiers, and prelates set up their own smaller establishments to deal with the production of buildings and works of art, and by virtue of inviting the king's specialists to advise them and of employing their pupils, they secured their position in the forefront of fashion. Beyond this came the mere copying of church from church, painting from painting, or sculptured group from group, which produced eminently satisfactory results in the smaller towns and more remote parts of the countryside. Bearing in mind this graded scale of art, the all-pervading achievement of Perpendicular explains itself and is seen to be, as great art must be, the outcome of a natural process.

Another factor greatly assisted this unification: the exercise by the Crown of its power of impressing workmen and others for various purposes. Even without impressment, there was a steady flow of enterprising artists to the Court, where there were golden opportunities for men of talent. Pressed men were less likely to be of hand-picked quality, and many of them deserted and slipped back to their home districts, but even so they would be likely to carry back with them some knowledge acquired at London, Windsor, or the other centres of royal undertakings. The King and his Court were also in constant motion about the country, and this too tended to communicate a common quality to the various local schools.

At the end of the thirteenth century, and leading symptom of the change which the earlier Gothic was undergoing, the ogee curve made its appearance and was to remain characteristic of the whole maturity of Gothic art. Sedding, in his brilliant essay, showed the falsity of Ruskin's assumption that the ogee was an "unnatural" form, and further, that by means of the introduction of ogee curves into detail such as cusping, the hard lines of Perpendicular were softened without loss of their ruling strength and cohesion. The first consequence of the coming of the ogee was the rise of Curvilinear tracery, that form which, abandoned in England, was to become the Flamboyant of France in the fifteenth century. "The Frenchman," said Sedding, "never knows when to cry 'Enough'", and here was the ultimate demonstration: for beautiful as are a few Curvilinear and Flamboyant traceries, they are in the mass sadly deficient in that power which is essential to a great and living art.

It is not the ogee curve in itself which is faulty, but its application to the wrong purposes. As in nature, straightness and sturdiness are needful qualities in supporting members; flowing curves may characterize detail and unessential forms. In England this was perceived almost at once, and by 1300 a reaction against the meandering ogee line had set in with the appearance of the first "split" tracery of so-called Kentish type. In this form, cusps and foiled patterns were prevented from becoming a mere endless reversed curve by the interposition of sharp spikes or tongues issuing in the reverse direction. Further, this motive was applied to quatrefoils, and these were set in groups in the head of large windows, thus giving a foretaste of the crystalline patterns of the earliest Perpendicular. Other variations from current curvilinear practice, likewise foreshadowing Perpendicular treatment, were also introduced, and the whole of these specialized developments occurred within the area of the Canterbury and Kent school of masons. It does not follow that their origin was purely local, for two reasons: first, Kent was nearest to the Continent, and more subject to outside influences than the rest of England, and it was besides exceptionally prosperous and had carried its emancipation from the feudal land system beyond that of other counties; secondly, the principal Court masons of the time belonged to this school and resided for at least a great part of their careers in London.

Between 1290 and 1335, Masters Michael, Walter, and Thomas of Canterbury were chief masons to the King, while Richard and Roger of Crundale and John of Battle probably derived from the same region. Responsible for the Eleanor crosses and tomb, for several other remarkable monuments, and for St. Stephen's Chapel in Westminster Palace, this group of masters laid the foundations of a national style. The unfinished

51 Glastonbury: the Tribunal, c. 1515

52 Glastonbury: the George Inn, c. 1480

54   Launceston Church: Porch, 1511–24
Cotswold stone and Cornish granite

53   Northleach Church: Porch, c. 1410

56 Feering Church: Porch, c. 1505

55 Ardleigh Church: Porch, c. 1500

Essex flint and brickwork

57   Much Wenlock: Prior's House, *c.* 1480

58   Wickhambrook, Gifford's Hall: the Solar, *c.* 1500

church of St. Thomas at Winchelsea, and St. Augustine's Abbey gatehouse at Canterbury, in course of erection in 1308, forerunner of all the turreted gatehouses of later England, marked out in tentative fashion the course which was to be followed. The building of St. Stephen's Chapel, with its great windows and the introduction of verticality and straight-line tracery about 1330 by William of Ramsey, one of the King's Masons, stood on each side of the frontier of Perpendicular; finally, the new transept and choir of Gloucester Abbey, costly memorial to the murdered Edward II, exhibited the new style itself, tentative as yet but sharply recognizable.

Just at this moment, when the artistic revolution had begun and was swiftly proceeding, it received a check from the opening of the war with France, coupled with more obscure economic difficulties which had already caused a marked set-back to national prosperity before the coming of the Black Death. The plague dislocated the old European society, though not to the extent which was believed a generation ago; but in England and particularly at London it was at its worst. Recovery was swift, perhaps owing to the courage which is born of disaster, or to a recrudescence of genuine personal religion: both these elements may have played a part in the outburst of artistic creation witnessed by the second half of the fourteenth century. The pent-up energy generated before the French War and the Plague was suddenly released, and a spate of works of the greatest splendour was the result; the harmonious strands of architecture, music, poetry, sculpture, and painting, formed the majestic first movement of an immense symphony.

To extend the metaphor, few countries have ever boasted two such conductors in succession as were Edward III and Richard II; both keenly alive to the ultimate refinements of aesthetic perception, the palm must probably be awarded to Richard II as a superlative connoisseur of all that was noblest in art. Not limited by the two senses of sight and hearing, he surrounded himself with exquisitely woven fabrics pleasant to the touch, and rare perfumes, while on his table were displayed dishes representing the highest point ever reached in the fine art of cookery. Outside the Court of China at its greatest and most enlightened moments, and possibly the supreme reigns of Minoan Crete, the world can never have seen the equal of Westminster under Richard II.

This perfect equilibrium of the arts endured only for a few brief years, the child of the King's policy of peace with France, close relations with other states, and encouragement of the two artistic circles which centred round his uncle John of Gaunt and the great and benevolent prelate Wykeham, an ecclesiastical despot of the best sort. Notwithstanding the opposition between the semi-heretical adherents of Gaunt and the clerical civil service led by Wykeham, the King's will proved for the time a universal solvent, and Chaucer and the great artists such as Henry Yevele and Hugh Herland found favour in both camps. Political rivalries were for a short time placed second to artistic emulation, with wonderful results for England; had it not been for the bitter legacy of the years of

Richard's minority, all might have been well. Richard, as a boy of fourteen, had quelled the Peasants' Revolt, and had in intention fulfilled the ideal of a patriot king bearing impartial justice which we find in *Piers Plowman*.

The entrenched politicians were over-strong for his youth, and his promised clemency to the rebels was overborne; after this not even the vast scale of his charity to the thousands who freely thronged the Court to eat the scraps from his table could altogether overcome the whispered criticisms of his "extravagance". Worse, the same politicians in 1388 had proscribed and hunted down Richard's personal friends, including the aged and beloved Sir Simon Burley, knight of the Garter; and this, though under cover of retrenchment, for the sole purpose of keeping power in their own hands. Richard never brought himself to forgive this, and after the death of his first queen, Anne of Bohemia, gave way to a carefully planned and executed revenge. Probably this temporary loss of a sense of proportion was his fatal error, but whatever the cause, the treason of Henry Bolingbroke his cousin, and the more disgusting treachery of several lesser figures, effectually laid an axe to the root of the English monarchy and wellnigh cut short English art at the same time.

Everywhere the fifteenth century was heralded by unrest and by anxious questioning in men's minds; Wyclif and Hus had set light to the train of religious revolt which was to end in the Reformation, and the recurrent plagues and tempests of the previous fifty years made men wonder uneasily whether they had in some manner merited the wrath of God. To all this England superadded a constitutional cataclysm. The old system was being forcibly broken up and the old security was stripped away. Insecurity breeds fear, and fear brings panic measures in its train. The Church, which had long had the power to burn heretics, but had prudently made little use of this weapon, took fright, and a dreadful era of persecution was ushered in. England under Henry IV passed a statute to this end, and the spectacle of sincerity proved by martyrdom begins: a spectacle rendered all the more terrible to us who know the sequel, that the persecuted made equally embittered persecutors when their turn came.

Henry IV was smitten by disease, and the death of Richard II, of which he was at least morally guilty, lay heavy on his soul; his son, Henry V, carried Puritan Catholicism a step farther, and was relentless in his outlook towards heretics. Between the upper and the nether millstones of persecution and heresy, men began to seek escape in pietism. In place of the jovial religion of Chaucer and the nature-loving piety of Langland, there grew up the morbid religion centred upon the dead Christ, bleeding on the Cross, a sacrifice for pain-racked wretched man, and his only hope. The mellowness of the great artists of the fourteenth century is displaced by a querulous outlook, by long-winded and pointless dissertations, and by sheer poverty of ideas. In architecture, vain repetitions of decorative panelling and uninspired window tracery fill up the space somehow, and this in turn allowed of increased shopwork, leading to mass-production at the expense of individual design.

The political leaders of the country were now barons of the "buff-coat

59 Lacock Village, fifteenth century

60 Burford: Almshouses, *c.* 1456–70

61, 62   The fortified Mansion: (*above*) Wingfield, Suffolk, *c.* 1384; (*below*) Maxstoke, *c.* 1345. From the engravings by S. and N. Buck

and spur"s chool, if we may so term it; men with notably less interest in art than the refined entourage of Richard II. Their open-air interests are typified in the fine book of the chase, *The Master of Game*, written by the Duke of York, killed at Agincourt in 1415; on the other hand, Henry V did something to encourage architecture and music (and was probably a composer himself), while his brother Humfrey, Duke of Gloucester, was a noted patron of art and letters and gave to Oxford University the nucleus of its famous library including, it is interesting to note, a copy of Vitruvius on Architecture.

Notwithstanding the very unfavourable circumstances, there was some survival of the older artistic traditions, handed on by the personal pupils of the fourteenth-century masters, as Hoccleve was of Chaucer and Stephen Lote of Yevele. During the minority of Henry VI, the Dukes of Gloucester and Bedford did a good deal to keep a current of art flowing in Court circles, and Henry himself, when he reached years of discretion, showed a marked delight in architecture and in education. As a patron of architects he succeeded in gathering together what was left of the older traditions and moulding them to serve his requirements at Eton and Cambridge, and took the trouble to master a great deal of the technicalities of planning and design.

Henry VI was far too unworldly to make a successful king, and the nobility were able to bring into the open those quarrels which they had been nursing ever since the Lancastrian usurpation; the baronial support of Henry Bolingbroke had been largely in the hope that he would prove an amenable puppet, but both he and Henry V had signally disappointed this expectation, and it was only after death had removed the Duke of Bedford that the unsatisfactory state of affairs in France and the lack of policy at home gave them their opportunity. The ensuing civil war meant of course another slump in art, and the accession of Edward IV in 1461 did nothing to relieve it; on the contrary the poverty resulting from the French and civil wars forced further retrenchment, and there was also dismissal of civil servants, including architects, who had served under Henry VI.

A second civil war led to the short-lived restoration of Henry VI as a puppet in the hands of Warwick the Kingmaker, then to Edward's return, this time to stay. Feeling himself secure, he began to spend money, and new impetus was given to architecture and to music. The great hall of Eltham Palace, by no means equal to Westminster Hall either in size or in constructional skill, was built, and the new invention of printing was introduced by Master William Caxton, whose work was soon to revolutionize the world of knowledge and education.

The short reign of Richard III continued the artistic progress of the end of Edward IV's, but Bosworth Field brought in the House of Tudor, and with it the beginning of a new outlook. Strange horizons were becoming visible: Columbus was studying Marco Polo with a view to discovering a new route to the wealth of the Indies by way of the West; the Portuguese seamen, fulfilling the policy of exploration laid down for them by Prince Henry the Navigator, half-English grandson of John of Gaunt, were finding another such route round Africa; the morbid introspection of gloom and doubt gave way before a renewed hope and expectation. The King of England, trained in the hard school of exile, was a thrifty saver, but could spend where he deemed it necessary, and was no poor judge of art. He likewise redeemed his cold exterior by little acts of kindness and generosity to the poor and outcast, for whom he may have had a fellow feeling.

The last vestiges of monastic austerity began to break down, except among the Carthusians, and though few houses were so flagrantly immoral as Protestant historians would like to believe, most showed a complete disregard of the rules of their orders in indulging in costly domestic buildings in which to live like petty noblemen, and in embellishing their churches with towers and great windows intended for outward show. To them flocked wandering minstrels and clowns, who could be sure of their patronage, and likewise troupes of itinerant players. Clowning and music, verse recitations, an altogether sprightlier outlook on life, became normal both for castle and cloister.

The great tower houses in which the nobles of the Wars of the Roses had immured themselves, not so much against the enemy as against their own unruly mercenaries, gave way to mansions modelled on the royal palaces and parallel in development to the quadrangular college-plans of the universities. Early forms of the spinet and harpsichord became popular, and gay and tuneful keyboard pieces began to be composed by Hugh Ashton and others. Flighty new fashions at Court, and the filigree elaboration of architectural decoration signalized a Rococo age, in which the stronger and more enduring qualities of the older England formed a ground-bass above which ran a descant of eager fretted and broken notes, touches of humour and grotesquerie; the sonorous strength of the Chaucerian tradition is found in the noble poems of the Scots Dunbar, while in England Chaucer's ribald but manly humour also found an exponent in Skelton. But while the Scot worked over Chaucer's old metres, Skelton, though of slighter power, exhibited greater imagination in devising for himself a new stanza of short lines, eager and jerky, racing on swiftly, and now brought up short, symbolic of the age.

Yet beneath this wind-flawed surface a stronger, more sullen and subdued, yet perhaps more truly English current flowed on: architecturally this found its expression in the nobly proportioned church towers, some of them almost devoid of adventitious ornament, but secure in the qualities of endurance and majesty. Here was a reaction from frivolity back to the simple and the straightforward, with their direct appeal, their assurance that beneath the troubled vanities of the everyday world lies a deep and abiding calm. Tye and Tallis and a whole school of church composers matched this architecture in grandeur of musical expression, which, more fortunate than the sister art, was to undergo a steady organic development through the century, closing in our last great composers of the Catholic tradition, Byrd and Morley.

64   Great Malvern Priory: Tiles, 1453

63   Monmouth: Heraldic Tile

67 Wells Cathedral: tomb of priest, c. 1440

66 Battlefield Church, c. 1440?
Fragment of Glazing

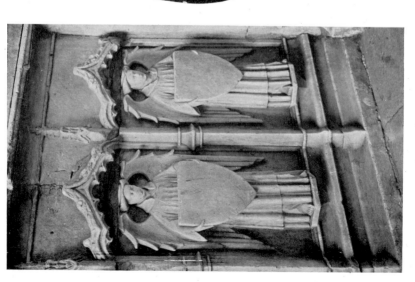

65 Lowick Church: tomb of Ralph Greene,
1418–20. Designer: Thomas Prentys

What might have been the companion culmination of English architecture we shall never know; before the movement of simple proportions and noble outline was properly begun, all was over; the invasion from overseas of new and incompatible motives, motives derived from the utterly unsuitable ornament of ancient Rome seen through Italian eyes, overwhelmed the whole of the old tradition, except its bony skeleton, in a flood of new notions and new men. Thrust from the Court, where it had been so assiduously fostered since the days of Henry III, architecture and the minor arts took refuge at the University of Oxford, where, though they found no abiding home, yet they maintained themselves in some honourable estate for another century. Here and there in the countryside we stumble across some hidden backwater where a school of masons or carpenters went on using its old patterns even longer; casual flotsam and jetsam from the great wreck litter the wide spreading shires of England, and, tenuous as they are, form an essential link binding the past to successive ages and to the present. Plan, construction, and the handling of local materials: these were the legacy of Gothic art to what came after. Like many a great line, the House of Gothic architecture left no male heir; yet in the warmth and cheerful proportions of the brick houses of Anne and the Georges we may recognize the lineaments of Tudor Gothic's bastard son.

H

II

THE GOLDEN AGE OF GOTHIC GENIUS

THE unity of law and administration given to England by the genius of
Edward I expressed a growing unity of life and thought, and this rapidly
discovered forms of outward expression in architecture. The adventurous
but undisciplined experiments of the first wave of naturalism were soon
seen to lack this unity of conception which gave the keynote to the period.
Even before Curvilinear experimentation with the compasses had produced its Flamboyant outcome, it had itself been discarded by the keener
taste of the Kentish masters working at Court. Several methods of pre-
venting the lush monotony of the repeated ogee-curve were devised:
foremost of these was the "Kentish" split or forked cusp, which separated
the ogee foils. The use, with or without this device, of geometrically
disposed trefoils, quatrefoils, and cinquefoils, and of intersecting instead
of branching lines of tracery-mould were other methods adopted to secure
the effect.

The decorative aspects of the new art of the period show remarkable
likenesses to Eastern arabesque and geometric strap-work, and, as in the
case of the four-centred arch, a connexion of some kind seems almost
certain. Diapering and then panelling of wall-surfaces were adopted as
ancillary means of unifying the contrasting elements of wall and window,
and provided opportunities for the sculptor and the painter. All these
ideas of pattern were brought to their highest pitch at Westminster, where
the resumption of work upon St. Stephen's Chapel in 1331 was a first-
fruit of Edward III's personal government. The plan of the chapel had
been settled in 1292 by Master Michael of Canterbury, but owing to the
fire of 1298, which rendered much of the Palace uninhabitable, only the
undercroft or Lower Chapel had been completed at the end of Edward II's
reign, though considerable stocks of material had been brought together
for the continuation of the work.

Master Thomas of Canterbury, who was designing the details of the
Upper Chapel in 1331, had worked in the Palace since 1324 and perhaps
earlier, at first as assistant to Master Walter of Canterbury, who may
perhaps have been his father. About 1326 he took charge of work at the
new chapel of the London Guildhall, while at the same time the Westminster accounts allowed him £1 for a robe and thus demonstrate his
responsible position. He presumably continued to supervise the Guildhall
Chapel during the chaotic rule of Mortimer, and was able to come back to
St. Stephen's as soon as Edward III was able to resume work in the spring
of 1331. He is last heard of in 1335, and probably died in that year or

68 Canterbury Cathedral: tester of the Black Prince's tomb, *c.* 1377.
Painter: probably Gilbert Prince.
From the reconstruction by Professor E. W. Tristram

early in the next, but during this short period of five years he had completed the whole of the lower story of the chapel, with its traceried windows and exquisite western porch.

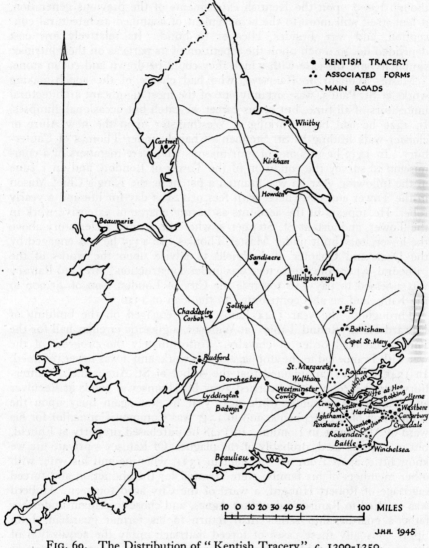

● KENTISH TRACERY
∴ ASSOCIATED FORMS
⌒ MAIN ROADS

Whitby

Cartmel

Kirkham

Howden

Beaumaris

Sandiacre

Billingborough

Chaddesley
Corbet
Solihull

Ely

Bottisham
Capel St. Mary

Rudford

St. Margarets
Waltham
Westminster
Cowley
Dorchester
Lyddington
Bedwyn

Royden

Cliffe at Hoo
Bobbing
Herne
Cray
Rochester
Harbledown
Ightham
Westbere
Canterbury
Penshurst
Ulcombe
Chartham
Crundale
Rolvenden
Battle
Winchelsea

Beaulieu

10 0 10 20 30 40 50   100 MILES

J.H.H. 1945

FIG. 69. The Distribution of "Kentish Tracery", c. 1300-1350.

Notwithstanding the advanced fashion of this work, it was still thoroughly Kentish in style, and showed hardly more than the germs of those stiffer characteristics which were to become typical of Perpendicular at Gloucester within the next few years, and to remain with it thenceforward. But at St. Paul's Cathedral a new Chapter House and surrounding

Cloister were begun in 1332, and contained all the elements of the new style: tracery comprising straight lines and vertical members; window mullions extended downwards to form wall-panelling; the four-centred arch; and the broad casement moulding. Here was a new departure—though based upon the Kentish experiments of the previous generation, it lent itself still more to the achievement of a unified architectural conception, and was, besides, cheaper to build. Its relatively low cost depended not so much upon the repetition of its parts as on their intrinsic simplicity and the ease with which they could be drawn and cut in stone.

Master William de Ramseye, who had charge of the epoch-making works at St. Paul's, was certainly one of the most significant architectural innovators of all time, but of his career we catch but occasional glimpses. In 1326 he had been working at Westminster upon the new Alure or cloister-walk leading to St. Stephen's Chapel, under Thomas of Canterbury. In 1335 he was one of four masons who were members of a commission to survey the condition of the Tower of London, and on 1 June in the following year he was granted a patent as the King's Chief Mason in the Tower and elsewhere, with fees of 12*d.* a day for life and a yearly robe. He appears in the accounts as having charge of extensive work in the Tower, and also at St. Stephen's, where he erected a clerestory above the lower story built under Master Thomas. In 1337 he was engaged by the Dean and Chapter of Lichfield to advise upon the works of the cathedral, where the presbytery was under construction. In 1340 Ramsey · was assessed to pay £10 towards the City of London loan of £5,000 to the King, and he also contributed to the loan of 1346.

Throughout the year 1344 Ramsey was engaged on the building of Edward III's "Round Table" at Windsor, a gigantic circular hall for the King's intended order of chivalry. Unfortunately the progress of the war with France led to the stoppage of this work, and it was never resumed. In 1345 Ramsey complained that the Abbot of St. Augustine's, Canterbury, and his retinue, had carried away his (Ramsey's) goods at Reculver and beaten his servants, while next year he was again busy upon the completion of St. Stephen's, and in 1347 was Common Councillor for his ward of Aldersgate in London. In 1348 he purchased property at Enfield, but in 1349 he died, probably of the plague. Of Ramsey's private life we know little, apart from one incident in 1331, when he and his wife, with other members of his family, were arrested for the abduction and forced marriage of Robert Huberd, a ward of the City aged fourteen. Huberd was married to Ramsey's daughter Agnes, and chose to remain under her father's guardianship rather than return to his former guardian, John Spray. Usually these cases of forced marriage imply the acquisition of the ward's considerable fortune, but in this case the "victim" seems at least to have been a willing one.

The antecedents of the Ramsey family provide a genealogical puzzle, for it is clear that there were at least two Williams and three Johns during the period under consideration. William, the King's Mason, had a brother John, who also died in 1349, and a second brother, Nicholas. Another

John, marbler of the parish of St. Botolph, Aldersgate, died in 1371, leaving bequests for the maintenance of chantries in that church for the souls of Master William de Rameseye (our mason), Christiana, wife of William, and others; while an earlier John had been warden of the masons at Westminster in 1325. Master William de Ramseye senior had been involved in the abduction of Robert Huberd, but could not be found by the City authorities. It is at least possible that he was identical with the master mason of Norwich Cathedral of that name, who was working there in 1327 and 1330, while at Norwich an earlier John de Rameseye had been master mason about 1305, and appears in deeds until 1321 or later.

It seems on the whole probable that the London Ramseys had been trained at Norwich Cathedral, then the centre of the great school of East Anglian illumination. That Norwich was far from being isolated is shown by the case of William Lyngwode, a carpenter from the Bishop's manor of Blofield, seven miles east of Norwich, who travelled to Winchester in 1308 and spent two years there on the making of the glorious choir stalls of the cathedral. Lyngwode was excused from doing suit at the manor court of Blofield at the special request of the Bishop of Winchester, and it is evident that he must have become a famous craftsman before he was called to undertake work so far distant from his home. Instances such as this demonstrate the weakness of the evidence for a backward East Anglian "island".[1]

Ramsey and his colleagues not only established a new decorative style, but also profoundly modified constructional usage. The transom, which in the thirteenth century had been adopted in domestic windows to separate the hinged shutters from the fixed lights above, was now seen to be a more satisfactory stiffener than iron bars for the great windows of churches. It appears, for example, in the south transept of Gloucester before 1337, and again in the choir reconstruction after that date. The Gloucester work, adjacent to a royal castle in Ramsey's charge, and built around the tomb of the martyred Edward II, is too closely akin to the design of St. Paul's Chapter House and cloister arcades for this to be a matter of coincidence.

In carpentry, the hammer-beam roof-truss solved the problem of spans over thirty feet; a primitive truss of the type occurs in Villard de Honnecourt's album of c. 1240, as a "good light roof" for placing above a stone vault. If any direct developments followed from this, they seem to have disappeared, for structural carpentry received little attention in France, and in England the earliest existing roof of hammer-beam character appears to be that of the Pilgrim's Hall at Winchester. This is, however, of small span, and its date cannot be fixed with accuracy from the internal evidence, as the work is of crude type. Winchester and its district were not productive of great carpenters, and Mr. T. D. Atkinson suggests East

[1] Bond, in his *Gothic Architecture in England*, p. 501, becomes fantastic when he states that in the fourteenth and even into the fifteenth century "Norfolk and Suffolk ... were hardly an integral part of England; but severed from the mainland by rivers and fens more completely than Ireland is now from England".

Anglian influence; if (as the late Nathaniel Lloyd believed) the roof belongs to the early years of the century, this influence can be found in the person of William Lyngwode. An alternative possibility must be faced: that the roof is of considerably later date, and owes its design directly or indirectly to the presence in Winchester of Hugh Herland, the designer of Westminster Hall roof, the first datable hammer-beam construction, designed in 1393. Herland was certainly working for William of Wykeham in Hampshire as early as 1387, and quite possibly from the time of Wykeham's accession to the see twenty years before.

Yet another far-reaching structural change was taking place in the design of vaulting; since the early thirteenth century English vaults had been increasing the number of ribs until at Exeter, about 1288, Master Roger was designing a vault comprising five ribs between the wall and the

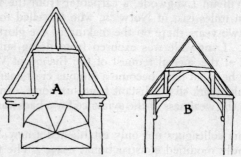

FIG. 70. The Hammer-beam roof-truss: A—Villard de Honnecourt, *c.* 1240; B—Pilgrims' Hall, Winchester, mid-fourteenth century.

cross-arch from each springing. In addition to these curving ribs were the level ridge-ribs which ran longitudinally from end to end of the vault and transversely across the middle of each bay. Now, there came a further development: still more ribs, neither arched nor level, were introduced; these additional ribs are known in English as liernes. So far as can be ascertained, the earliest use of real liernes was in the vault of the crypt of St. Stephen's Chapel, Westminster, built between 1319 and 1327, probably to the design of Master Walter of Canterbury. Within a few years high vaults of large size were being built on the same principles: at Bristol before 1332, in the Wells Lady Chapel by 1325, and in Gloucester south transept about ten years later.

Besides dividing the surface of the vault up into small panels which could be bridged with single stones, the new device opened up an entirely new field to the ingenuity of the designer. Up to this time most architects had been content to work by rule-of-thumb methods, for their knowledge of solid geometry was rudimentary; now, architectural education leapt forward until, by 1400, clumsy effects such as those of the Wells retrochoir vault were of the greatest rarity, while in many cases the power of foreseeing an effect in perspective was carried to a pitch of perfection rarely equalled.

England was experiencing a revolutionary change in outlook and habits:

to the austerity of Edward I succeeded the effeminate aestheticism of his son which, after an interval of anarchy, gave place to the cultured luxury of Edward III and his grandson. In an artistic sense the thirteenth century had been the age of the single-minded and the pure in heart, a springtime in which English life took deep root; but the fourteenth, like the heat of summer, brought the plant to its full growth and into bud and blossom. When Edward III, in the first flush of his youth and fatherhood, overthrew Roger Mortimer in the autumn of 1330, he flung open the portal of a new age; even so was a new age inaugurated, five centuries later almost to the day, by the opening of a railroad from Liverpool to Manchester.

This sensation of living in a new age was typified by the appearance in Paris of the famous "Ars Nova" of Philippe de Vitri (1291–1361): a system of music of free and lyric melody; unlike the "Art Nouveau" of the late nineteenth century, this was not the forlorn hope of uttermost despair, but the vanguard of a fresh cultural life: Europe's greatest contribution to the common fund since Athens ran its course from Solon to Pericles. In the study of the fourteenth century we must above all guard against the thought of things ancient and outworn, for here more than anywhere in the history of Europe all was bright and new and vigorous with life.

In England the spiritual godfather of the movement was Richard Aungerville, better known as Richard de Bury (1287–1345), lord chancellor, Bishop of Durham, and friend of Edward III. In 1330 he visited the pope, John XXII, at Avignon, and at the papal court met Petrarch, who was impressed by his learning and eagerly asked for information concerning the distant North. Again, in 1338, he was on the Continent, having meanwhile paid another visit to Avignon in 1333; on the last of his journeys he accompanied Edward III to Cologne and Coblenz to meet the Emperor Louis IV. But travel and the society of cultured men were not Bury's chief delight, which was the passionate acquisition and care of books. His Latin *Philobiblon*, the first and greatest of all book-collectors' books, shows how universal in outlook was the spirit of his time. We no longer peer at grotesque figures through a glass darkly, but as in the plays of Aristophanes or the letters of Cicero, so in the pages of Bury, of Froissart, of Chaucer, do we meet them face to face.

Not long after the general awakening came the resurgence of English as a national literary language; used for political skits and lampoons by many anonymous writers, and for religious purposes by Richard Rolle, Robert Mannyng, and others, the vulgar speech soon became recognized as a vehicle for general literature. Mannyng composed a rhyming chronicle of England, and from 1333 to 1352 the warlike deeds of Edward III were sung by Laurence Minot, in some respects the Kipling of the day. The great age of English, however, opens with Chaucer's Book of the Duchesse in 1369, and closes with his death in 1400: besides Chaucer's mature output this period includes William Langland's *Piers Plowman* and John Gower's one long English poem, *Confessio Amantis*. In addition to this remarkable outpouring of English verse within the space of a single generation, we have the fine prose translations of Latin works made by

John Trevisa, including that of Higden's *Polychronicon* finished in 1387, and one of the immense encyclopedia of Bartholomew "de Glanville" finished twelve years later. Here again a remarkable work was brought to triumphant completion only just before the collapse which marked the end of the century.

While it would be idle to seek a detailed commentary on contemporary architecture and the arts in English fourteenth-century literature, many sidelights are found which throw into prominence the great expenditure on building and decoration which typified the age. Towards the close of the century the friar in the *Somnour's Tale* attempts to cadge money for his building fund:

> "Yif me thanne of thy gold, to make our cloistre,"
> Quod he, "for many a muscle and many an oistre,
> Whan other men han ben ful wel at eyse,
> Hath been our fode, our cloistre for to reyse.
> And yet, god woot, unnethe the fundement
> Parfourned is, ne of our pavement
> Nis nat a tyle yet with-inne our wones;
> By god, we owen fourty pound for stones!"

and the anonymous *Peres the Ploughman's Crede* of *c.* 1394 gives a long and often-quoted description of a Dominican convent. An indirect, in fact inverted testimony to the high skill of the masons and carpenters of the period occurs in *Piers Plowman*:

> Ich hadde wonder at whan . and wher that the pye [magpie]
> Lernede legge styckes . that leyen in here neste;
> Ther is no wryght, as ich wene . sholde worche here nest to paye.
> Yf eny mason ther-to . makede a molde
> With alle here wyse castes . wonder me thynketh!

Allusions to popular tunes of the time are also found, such as the well-known reference to *Angelus ad Virginem* and *The Kinges Note* in the Miller's Tale; the "Kinges Note" has been identified with considerable probability as the sequence "Ave rex gentis Anglorum" in honour of St. Edmund King and Martyr.

What is so striking about this English writing only just burst from its swaddling bands is its individuality; Chaucer, Gower, Langland, Trevisa, even Minot, have all their own styles; the fantastic attempts to split the personality of Langland have been decisively refuted after thirty years of patient research by Professor R. W. Chambers and his collaborators. Textual criticism has at last proved to scholars what was always a flaming truth to the common-sense reader: in *Piers Plowman* "one man unlocks his heart. Five men do not unlock the hearts of five men." Other students have pieced together the few hints we are given as to Langland's personality and career, and he stands now as an historical figure, no longer a problematical myth. Another great stylist yet remains anonymous: the author of *Pearl*, *Sir Gawayne and the Grene Knight*, *Patience*, and *Purity*. Dated close to 1370, *Sir Gawayne* must have been written by someone in close touch with the Court, and *Pearl* may well be an elegy for the infant

71   Brent Knoll Church: Bench-end. (The Geese hang the Fox)

72   Durham Cathedral Priory: Kitchen vault, 1366.   Designer: John Lewyn.
An engraving from Billings's *Durham Cathedral*

73   Persian brick vault, Isfahan: Masjid-i-Jami.
Perhaps twelfth to thirteenth century A.D.

Margaret, granddaughter of Edward III. Much the strongest claim to authorship is that of Ralph Strode, fellow of Merton College and a known poet of distinction, whose works (if they are not represented by these poems) have most unaccountably disappeared. The elaborate diction of *Sir Gawayne* at any rate is strongly suggestive of a deeply erudite and accomplished writer, precisely the reputation Strode has left behind.

The architectural triumphs are too numerous even to catalogue, but a few of the greatest provincial masters must be mentioned: Richard of Farleigh, whose masterpiece was the steeple of Salisbury Cathedral, apparently began his career as master mason to Bath Abbey, where he was granted a corrody in 1335. He also worked at Reading Abbey,[1] and was probably designer of the tower of Pershore Abbey and the choir vault there, one of the best of the early works in the lierne method; he was still living, at Keynsham, near Bath, in 1363. William Joy was the transformer of Wells Cathedral, builder of its retrochoir and central tower; perhaps also of the new work at Malmesbury Abbey. Like Farleigh, he was a candidate for a corrody at Bath Abbey, but in the end he failed to secure it; he had apparently done good service for the King before this time, 1336, but in what respect is not known.

Later in the century Philip of Lincoln, a carpenter, vaulted in timber the 45-foot nave of York Minster; he first worked at York in 1346, and was still there, greatly increased in wealth and dignity, thirty years later. From Yorkshire came a family of masons and stone-carvers, the Patringtons; William worked on the imagery of St. Stephen's Chapel between 1351 and 1358; Robert senior became a freeman of York in 1353 and master mason of the Minster in 1369; while Ralph and a younger Robert, also of York, died in 1391 and 1430 respectively. Other important men whose work lay outside the Home Counties were John Sponlee, who from 1350 was in charge of the works at Windsor Castle, having probably been called thither from Winchcombe Abbey; Thomas of Cambridge, in charge of the Chapter House of Hereford Cathedral, in course of erection 1364–70; John Lewyn, mason to the Bishop of Durham, who had an immense northern practice (which included the building of Bolton Castle) from 1364 to his death in 1398—and incidentally produced one of the most outstanding vaults in England, that of the Prior's Kitchen at Durham, exactly (though doubtless unconsciously) copying the forms of Persian brick vaults of some centuries earlier (72-3); John Clyve, designer of the glorious tower of Worcester Cathedral (21); Robert Lesyngham, master at Exeter Cathedral from 1376 to 1390 during the erection of the screen of the west front and the great east window; and Nicholas Waleys, of Bristol, already famous in 1366 when he was called to Bridgwater to superintend the building of the church spire and who died in 1403, the wealthy owner of extensive properties.

All these men were affected by the revolution in design which had been produced by the Canterbury-London school, but worked for the most

[1] He may well have been the Master Richard of Reading who in 1333 made two images by task-work for the gable of St. Stephen's Chapel, Westminster.

I

part outside its immediate orbit. Of the Royal School itself the chief exponents were Henry Yevele, who worked in London from 1355 to his death in 1400—designer of royal tombs and fortresses, and of the splendid naves of Westminster Abbey (following the lines of the thirteenth-century design), and Canterbury Cathedral, where he brought the new style to its triumphant apotheosis; William Wynford, associate of William of Wykeham, architect of the Wells western towers, of Wykeham's colleges, of the Winchester nave (74), and perhaps of Wardour Castle, begun for John Lord Lovel about 1393; and Hugh Herland, greatest of carpenters, who collaborated with Yevele in London and with Wynford at Winchester College. It is worthy of note in passing that Herland and his father William must be regarded as originators of the fully developed type of canopied quire-stall; the famous series at Lincoln, dating from c. 1370, and the even more exquisite set at Chester, bear in almost every part unmistakable traces of the Herland touch. Many individual craftsmen must have carved them, as the uneven execution of the misericords and the vast quantity of work alone would prove, but there are exquisite details which could only have been achieved by a master; in addition to the Herlands a probable collaborator was William Newhall, the King's chief carpenter at Chester from 1377 until his death in 1411 (77, 79, 81).

John of Gaunt, Duke of Lancaster and titular King of Castile, maintained a Court almost as splendid as that of his nephew Richard II, and while he patronized some of the royal artists, such as Yevele and Gilbert Prince the painter, he also employed permanent officers of his own, notably William Wintringham, a Southwark carpenter who had built the great hall roof of Windsor Castle under William Herland's supervision, and who rose to be John of Gaunt's Surveyor-General and a man of property. At Kenilworth Castle, the grand additions of Gaunt were carried out by a mason-contractor in a big way, Robert Skillington, who may also have worked at St. Mary's Church, Warwick, and St. Michael's in Coventry, where important work of closely similar character was being carried out near to the same date, c. 1390 (13).

Like Gaunt, the Black Prince employed his own masons in addition to Yevele, and at Chester and at Vale Royal Abbey not far off, his work was under the supervision of William Helpston, master mason of the county of Chester from 1359 to 1396. Among a host of lesser men of the Court School was John Clavyll who in 1390 carried out very extensive works at Gloucester Castle for the King; like the rather earlier Robert and Thomas of Gloucester, who had been wardens of the royal masons at Windsor and at London, Clavyll was one of the personal links binding London to Gloucester—links which explain the closely contemporaneous appearance of innovations in design at the two centres. Though Gloucester was never so great a centre of masonic activity as has been supposed (for the documentary evidence and that of masons' marks suggests that Gloucester was generally dependent on Bristol, London, Winchcombe, and Oxford), it was of undoubted importance for its continuous output of work, a constant stream of skilled workers came and went, carrying

75 Tattershall Church: Nave, c. 1495–85.
    Designer: probably John Cowper

74 Winchester Cathedral: Nave, 1394–c. 1460.
    Designer: William Wynford

76 Ely Cathedral: Octagon and Lantern from above, 1322–40.
Designers: Master John and John Atte Grene; of Lantern: William Hurley

with them the combined knowledge of the Court School and of the Abbey masters, who were engaged in the fashioning of another innovation, the fan-vault, which itself was at least partly suggested by the timber vaults of the King's Carpenters, William Hurley and Hugh Herland.

Before Henry Yevele brought to Canterbury the fully developed "London Perpendicular", the Kentish style had been carried to an independent peak by John Box, who followed the geometric traditions of Walter and Thomas, the great Canterbury masters of the first half of the century. Box was working for the Prior of Christ Church, Canterbury (the Cathedral Priory) in 1350, immediately after the Black Death, and was one of the masters summoned by the King to fill the gaps which the pestilence had wrought in the ranks of the royal artists. At Canterbury, Box may have been responsible for the tomb of Archbishop Stratford, who died during the plague, and its miniature vaulting is a perfect example of the mason's knowledge of solid geometry, only excelled by Yevele's uncanny patterning in the great vault of the nave. It is a curious coincidence (if it is a coincidence) that Stratford's immediate successor, the short-lived Archbishop Bradwardine, had been before his elevation to the primacy the most learned geometrician ever produced by mediæval England. Bradwardine had been summoned from Merton College to London about 1335 by Richard de Bury, when the latter was made chancellor; with Bury he accompanied Edward III on his journey to the Rhineland in 1338, and on Bradwardine's suggestion the King subscribed a large sum towards the completion of Cologne Cathedral, the plans for which he is said to have seen.

Whether or no John Box profited from the geometrical researches of Bradwardine, he is of interest to us as resident master at the building of Queenborough Castle when Wykeham was clerk of the works and Yevele (*ex officio* as devizer of the King's castles and buildings south of the Trent) almost certainly the architect. A curious legend has grown up in this connexion, apparently launched by the historian Gibbon, to the effect that his ancestor John Gyboun, a "marbler", was granted an *hereditary toll* over the passage between Sandwich and Stoner by Edward III, in reward for his services in building Queenborough Castle. This curious piece of intelligence derives from Hasted's *History of Kent*, but Hasted had made an extraordinary error of dates, besides another still more egregious. Queenborough Castle, it is well known, was in course of building between 1361 and 1369; Hasted's authority, the Patent Rolls, shows that on 1 June 1339, a grant *for life* of all the profits of the passage of the water between the towns of Sandwich and Stonore, *for service done in parts beyond and within the seas*, was made to John Gyboun of Sandwich, the king's *mariner*![1]

Mention has been made above of Master William Hurley, who was Edward III's chief carpenter from 1336 to 1354; with William Ramsey

[1] The distinction between the Latin "marinarius" and "marmorarius" would not be so obvious in the extremely condensed hand of the roll as would appear on the face of it.

his contemporary and colleague, he was the originator of the decorative aspects of the Perpendicular style, and what is of greater significance, of the underlying development in structure. Ten years before Ramsey started to build the new chapter house and cloister of St. Paul's, progenitors of Perpendicular, a great undertaking was begun at Ely Cathedral. After the fall of the Norman central tower in 1322, the sacrist, Alan of Walsingham, busied himself in preparations for an altogether different form of central lantern, which should be completely immune from the risk of collapse. Whether Walsingham himself designed the octagon is a matter of very considerable doubt, and the entry in the accounts for 1323-4 of a payment to a certain person from London who came to "ordain" the new work strongly suggests that one of the royal architects was the real originator of this plan, perhaps inspired by travellers' tales of the great octagons of the East. It is even possible that the Master John who figures in the accounts was John Ramsey senior, father or uncle of William. At the same time the equally mysterious figures of Peter "Quadratarius" and his brother may possibly be identical with the Peter of Titchmarsh who was head of the commission to survey defects in the Tower of London in 1335, and either Henry or Hugh of Titchmarsh, also London masons of the period.

The Ely timberwork was first put into the hands of Master Thomas of Newport, Essex, who was in charge from 1322 to 1326. He can be identified as the Master Thomas Page of Newport who in 1317 had undertaken to make a set of quire-stalls for Hatfield Regis Priory, receiving £30 as well as gentlemanly allowances while working there, consisting of two white loaves daily with a gallon of ale, a dish of cooked meat or fish from the kitchen or else four herrings or six eggs. At Ely he was allowed board of 1s. 3d. a week, and robe and furs worth 15s. 3d. each year.

For some reason, possibly his inability to devise a means of roofing the octagon with its span of 70 feet, Page was superseded between 1326 and 1334 by no less a person than William Hurley, the great London carpenter, already in the royal service and soon to become King's Chief Carpenter on Edward III's reorganization of the Royal Works. Simultaneously, a new mason, John Attegrene, appears: now the masonry work of the octagon can be divided, stylistically, into two parts: below and above the string-course above the great windows. The upper story with its quasi-Perpendicular windows shows a very marked difference of treatment, and it is reasonable to connect this with the change of masons (76). Wherever Attegrene may have come from, he was informed of at least the rudiments of the new style, and rather more advanced "Perpendicular" treatment occurs in Hurley's wooden traceried panelling inside the lantern, and in the canopies for the series of quire-stalls which he began in 1338. The lantern was structurally complete by 1339, and is as revolutionary in its conception as the recased choir of Gloucester, then hardly begun (23).

The Gloucester work is remarkable for the great opportunity given to the glass-painter, and it has often been suggested that the glaziers of the period had a considerable share in the formation of the new style. This

77   Chester Cathedral: Stalls, *c.* 1390. School of Hugh Herland

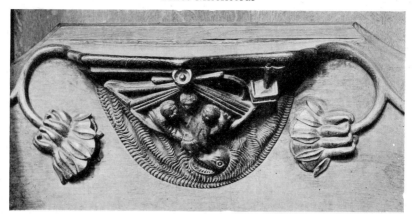

78　Ripon Cathedral: Jonah, 1489–94. Designer: probably William Brownfleet

79　Chester Cathedral, *c.* 1390. School of Hugh Herland

80　Windsor, St. George's Chapel: The Meeting at Picquigny (1475), 1480–83
Designer: John Squyer

81   Lincoln Cathedral: Misericord (The Fall of Pride), *c.* 1375
School of William and Hugh Herland

82   Warwick St. Mary's Church: Effigy of Richard Beauchamp, Earl of Warwick,
1450. Sculptor: John Massingham; founder: William Austen

84 Gainsborough Old Hall, c. 1480

83 Northiam, Great Dixter: Hall, c. 1465–75

is chronologically improbable: it is true that the design of the enormous east window at Gloucester can be approximately dated, since it is a memorial to the battle of Crécy fought in 1346; but the glass itself is probably no earlier than 1360, and even at that date still belongs to a transitional period of glass design. In other words, the glass made as late as 1360 is a great deal less up-to-date than the tracery for which it was made; the tracery on the other hand is quite likely to have been in position before the Black Death, which began towards the end of 1348. On the whole, we may expect that the glaziers, as subsidiary artists, followed the lead of the masons and sculptors, and this is borne out by the much slower transformation in the technique of glass-painting, which only reached the stage of developed "Perpendicular" characteristics about 1380–90, in the hands of the greatest glazier of the age, Thomas of Oxford.

The amazing change in glass-painting covered by the middle years of the century has been shown in graphic form by the juxtaposition of coloured drawings of two figures of St. Catherine from the east window of Exeter Cathedral; one is a survivor of the original window of 1317, by Michael "le Verrer", the other is the work of Robert Lyen in 1389; within the space of one long lifetime, barbaric outlines and strong "garish colour" had given place to excellent draughtsmanship and harmonious colouring combining delicacy with sufficient depth (97). From the time of the glazing of St. Stephen's Chapel (1352 and onwards), the glazier was an artist of assured position: John of Chester and John Geddyng, at St. Stephen's, and their colleague John Attelard, who also worked at mural painting, were men of substance, and John Brampton, appointed King's Glazier in 1378, was jointly with Margery his wife in 1380 left a legacy of a tester ornamented with boars' heads, a fermail of gold made to represent four points of the compass, a pair of paternosters (rosaries) of amber, a silk girdle with imitation roses in silver, a silver cup of Paris workmanship, furred robes, and so forth, clear evidence of good social standing.

In so far as glass-painters contributed to the design of interiors, it was by apt contrast: their long horizontal ranks of figures, making bands of colour formed an admirable counterpoint to the vertical lines of mullions and tracery, and the gracious figures vied with those carved in marble, stone, or wood, and themselves painted, which filled the niches between the windows and in the panelling and screenwork. The craft of the imager was separate, though the master freemasons were often themselves skilled sculptors. In 1365 Edward III paid £50 to John Lindsey for a "table" (presumably a carved retable for an altar) for St. George's Chapel at Windsor, and in the following year William Lindsey (a mistake seems probable, for the description of his work tallies with that of John) a carver of wooden images in London, had 10 marks in reward as well as a former sum paid him. William Patrington's imagery for St. Stephen's Chapel has already been referred to; other specialist carvers later in the century were Peter of Nottingham, who supplied the great alabaster reredos for Windsor, Robert Grasington who carved the oak angels in Westminster

Hall, and William Chuddere, sculptor of stone images for the Hall (89, 94). On the other hand, Walter Walton, Yevele's deputy at Westminster had earlier received sums in payment for sculpture at the Hall, and the impressive statues of kings at the south end may be his work. Yevele and his partner and successor Lote derived a great part of their income from tomb design and manufacture, and it may be supposed that both were first-class carvers of stone and marble; Lote or some other sculptor of real genius survived the turn of the century long enough to produce the haunting face of an old man in the Canterbury cloisters, very possibly a posthumous portrait of Yevele himself.

Also within the orbit of the royal masters are the statues at Wykeham's Winchester College; the finest and best preserved is that of the Virgin and Child above the outer gate; the Virgin is serene and lovely, while the Child, who grasped a bird now lost, is laughing.[1] This laughing Child is one of the miracles of mediæval art, and while it entirely lacks the theatrical character of Claus Sluter's slightly later Burgundian sculptures, possesses a poise and serenity which challenge comparison with the finest figures of Greek, Indian, or French sculpture. This outer tower was begun at the end of 1394, after the rest of the College was complete; the only master's name mentioned in connexion with it is that of William Wynford, and though there is no record of him as a sculptor, his work at Wells and at Winchester (whither in 1151 Bishop Henry of Blois had brought from Rome a number of antique statues) had brought him into contact with the best earlier statuary; it is far from improbable that we have in these figures of the Madonna works from the chisel of Wynford himself (88).

As in the case of the other arts, it was in the adornment of St. Stephen's Chapel that English painting of the early fourteenth century reached its culmination; fragments survive, together with sufficient copies to show the whole of the scheme adopted and to exhibit the style of the work. A very large number of painters were employed during the years following 1350, but the accounts are quite unequivocal in attributing the design to Master Hugh of St. Albans, while John of Coton was associated with him in drawing certain of the images. They were paid 1s. a day each, and were by no means constant in their attendance; they evidently had other works in hand elsewhere. Under them were John Elham, Gilbert Pokerich, and John Pekele, taking 10d. daily; William Walsingham, Richard Norwich, William Maynard, William Somervill, John Oxford, John Exeter, Thomas Ruddok, Gilbert Prince, John Davy, John Cambridge, Lowen Tassyn, Janyn Godmered, and Henry Blithe at 9d. a day each; and a number of assistants and servants at lower rates of pay. In 1355 a certain John Barneby was being paid 2s. a day, but it is not clear why he should have received double the rate allowed to Hugh of St. Albans, who was

---

[1] Doubt has been cast upon the authenticity of the Child's head, but Mr. Herbert Chitty tells me that in company with the late Mr. W. D. Caröe he inspected this Madonna from a scaffolding at close quarters; both were satisfied that the head of the Child formed part of the same block with the rest of the figure. Mr. T. D. Atkinson also informs me that he has examined the statue, and has found no trace of a crack or joint.

85 Portrait of Richard II, Westminster Abbey, *c.* 1395.
Painter: probably André Beauneveu

86 The Wilton Diptych, National Gallery, *c.* 1396. Painter: possibly Thomas Litlyngton

still in charge of the work in 1357, and probably until its substantial completion, for he lived until 1368.

Master Hugh in himself is an interesting figure, for he first appears in 1348 as a groom of the King's chamber, charged with painting the King's ships, flags, and 300 pennons with the arms of St. George for the King's voyage to Gascony, and when he made his will in 1362 he had in his possession a valuable painting of Lombardy in seven pieces; it is quite possible that he went with Edward III to Bordeaux and thence penetrated into Provence and northern Italy. At any rate the St. Stephen's accounts for 1352 show that he was then paid 16s. for 2 lb. of cynopre (cinnabar or native vermilion) from Montpellier, which he may have brought home himself. Hugh must have had at least an artistic, and probably a personal relationship to the earlier St. Albans painters, that John who had caused Edward II to laugh so heartily, and the Masters Walter and Thomas of Edward I's time.

His connexions with the South are of great significance: a recent study of the portrayal of space in mediæval painting remarks (apparently in ignorance of Master Hugh's known contact with Italian work) "the master of the Job scenes (in St. Stephen's Chapel) had some affiliations with the Italian school, perhaps the school established at Avignon, where Matteo Giovinetti da Viterbo was working for Clement VI in 1346 . . . the acceptance of the date 1350–60 would imply that the northern adaptations of Italian spatial forms exemplified by the settings of the donor scenes (the figures of Edward III, his queen, and children) appeared in England before they did in Franco-Flemish painting".

Painters, like other artists, were impressed by Edward III for the work of St. Stephen's Chapel, and the list of names probably includes a large proportion of the country's talent, as well as the two names apparently those of Flemings, Lowen Tassyn and Janyn Godmered; Barneby also may have been a foreigner, and rewarded highly for his trouble in coming to England. William Walsingham was perhaps Hugh's principal assistant in his old age, and John Davy belonged to a family of painters well known in the City of London. The most interesting name is that of Gilbert Prince, who was later on King's Painter and a very wealthy and successful citizen. The London artists' quarter was in Cripplegate Ward, where the fraternity of painters supported a light in honour of St. Luke in the parish church of St. Giles. In this parish a certain John Prince appears in 1340, and in 1349 one Richard, son of Adam Nayler, bequeathed to him certain houses in Grub Street in the parish of St. Giles-without-Cripplegate, and other tenements and rents at Harrow, with remainder to Gilbert de Kyngeston, painter, for his life. It seems not unlikely that this Gilbert was John Prince's pupil, and afterwards took on his name; such a proceeding was then by no means uncommon.

Gilbert Prince was certainly working at Westminster in 1351 and 1352, and in 1364 he was paid £24 for painting banners for the funeral of Joan, Queen of Scotland. Towards the end of Edward III's reign he ornamented a pair of curtains for the King's bed and also painted four banners with the King's Arms for the minstrels' trumpets. Throughout Richard II's reign until his own death early in 1396, Gilbert Prince is the only King's Painter named in the accounts, and had charge of works of great value connected with state funerals and festivities, plays and maskings, and the King's journeys, as well as for other works in his art unspecified. His career as a leading member of his guild can be traced from 1363, and he was a Common Councillor of London in 1376 and from 1384 to 1388; Stow mentions the tomb of "Gilbert Prince, alderman" as having existed in St. Giles Cripplegate before the fire of 1545, but there appears to be no other evidence that he attained this rank. It is just possible that confusion might have arisen from the inscription referring to him as "alderman" of the fraternity of St. Luke.

In addition to his work at Court he was paid considerable sums by John of Gaunt, Duke of Lancaster, in 1375 and 1380, while in 1378 Richard Ashburnham and Gilbert Mayfield acknowledged that they owed him the sum of £712 to be paid by Michaelmas 1382, and the debt was later satisfied. In modern values this represents at least £15,000, and probably very much more—it may have been a Crown debt to Prince secured by indirect means (e.g. Ashburnham and Mayfield, a prominent city merchant, may have been debtors at the Exchequer for a subsidy collected by them), but the very large annual sums allowed to Prince in the Issue Rolls show that he must have had charge of a large and well-organized shop, and the name of his clerk Thomas Litlington, who succeeded him as King's Painter, is known.

When Gilbert died he left £100 each to his second wife Elizabeth and to his three young children Robert, John, and Joan, who later claimed their money from the City Chamberlain upon reaching their majority. Gilbert's own house comprised a hall, chamber, pantry, buttery, and kitchen, and was very richly furnished, while he also owned a number of other properties.

From the outstanding Court Painter of the age, we must turn to the surviving paintings of the London and Court School. Of the first class only five examples remain, and of these all but two have been seriously damaged. The comparatively perfect paintings are the great Westminster Abbey portrait of Richard II and the Wilton Diptych; the others are the painting beneath the tester of the Black Prince's tomb in Canterbury Cathedral, the greatly dilapidated series on the east wall of the Chapter House at Westminster, and the four panels which cover the joint tomb of Richard II and his first Queen, Anne of Bohemia (68, 85-7).

To describe all of these as paintings of the Court School is in fact to beg the question, for there are strong reasons for thinking that two of the five are the work of the great French painter André Beauneveu: namely the portrait of Richard II, and the painted tester of his tomb. The latter is now too far gone for detailed stylistic analysis, but there is documentary evidence of the year 1395 which links it to the great portrait, and makes a common authorship highly probable. A great deal has been written on the subject of the Abbey portrait, and it has been attributed to several distinct

87　The Wilton Diptych, National Gallery, *c.* 1396　(left wing).
Painter : possibly Thomas Litlyngton

national styles, as well as to numerous individuals. The late Professor Lethaby, whose eye for personal characteristics in mediæval art was probably unrivalled, ultimately favoured the ascription to Beauneveu, first suggested by Mr. S. C. Cockerell, and the treatment of the hands and throne and of the arbitrary and stylized folds of the robe is so close to Beauneveu's known work in a manuscript in the Paris Bibliothèque Nationale (MS. franç. 13,091) that one cannot doubt that a very near connexion exists; certainly there is no resemblance to the work of Beauneveu's rival, Jacquemart de Hesdin. The portrait is related in its ideas to French rather than to English antecedents, for example the "Parement de Narbonne" of about 1375. The rather sketchy drawing of accessories and the vagueness of the features sharply define this typically French work from the certain products of the English, the Flemish, and the German schools. Besides, we know from Froissart that some of Beauneveu's work was in England, and his home, Valenciennes, was not in the kingdom of France, but in Hainault, whence had come Edward III's Queen Philippa.

When the Wilton Diptych is considered the problem is very different; instead of the vagueness and broad draughtsmanship of the great portrait we find a minuteness of detail and finished execution which will bear comparison with the work of any miniaturist, and equal if they do not even excel the comparable characteristics of the destroyed pages of the Turin Hours which have been ascribed to Hubert van Eyck. Those pages are attributed to the period 1415–17, and in view of the fact that the Wilton Diptych is exactly twenty years earlier, it would be tempting to suppose it a work of Hubert's middle life, of which so little is known that the higher critics will even deny Hubert's existence altogether![1]

There are, however, noteworthy dissimilarities, and comparison of the beasts and birds in the borders of the Turin Hours with the heraldic harts and lions of the Diptych discloses an altogether different outlook on the portrayal of animal life. The exquisite apes and peacocks of the Flemish master are subordinated to the Low Countries grotesquerie of the foliage in which they stand: Richard II's White Hart Royal is viewed as an heraldic beast in a flowery mead, seen through the eyes of a painter possessed of the English preoccupation with animals for their own sake, also seen in the birds of John Siferwas's Sherborne Missal, and the similar studies in the Pepysian sketchbook at Magdalene College, Cambridge.

Besides, it is in the heraldry of the Wilton Diptych that the clue to its significance lies; Miss M. V. Clarke proved from it that the painting must date from the years 1395–6, on purely historical grounds.[2] I would go

---

[1] Fortunately, common sense is supported by X-ray photography, which proves the existence in the Ghent altarpiece of two distinct techniques, that of Jan van Eyck, and another earlier in date.

[2] *Later* dates have been advanced: the diptych is claimed as an "icon" of the Richard "cult" following upon his death in 1400; or as a memorial picture painted by order of Henry V after his accession in 1413, and the reburial of Richard at Westminster. But neither of these dates can be reconciled with the concurrent evidence of several different kinds brought together by Miss Clarke.

K

further, and say that the style of its heraldry is convincing proof of its English origin; it has neither the over-articulate ferocity of Germanic arms nor the mannered impressionism of the French. While a Rhinelander or a Fleming might have painted the strewn flowers and chaplets of roses, he could never have resisted the temptation to dramatize the beasts; and equally a painter of the school of Paris would never have been at such infinite pains in the details of English coat-armour, English coronets or, for that matter, English faces.

This is not to say that there are not traces of foreign influence: the chaplets of roses aforementioned and a certain clarity of outline probably reflect the contemporary style of Cologne, where Hermann Wynrich von Wesel was the leader of a flourishing school whose ornament, a generation later, would be Stephan Lochner. The wonderful St. Veronica of the Munich Pinacothek witnesses to the greatness of the Cologne painters of Meister Hermann's generation, and it is significant that one Herebrecht of Cologne was painting an altarpiece for St. Paul's Cathedral during the last two years of Richard II. It has been pointed out that some of the Chapter House frescoes at Westminster (not those of the east wall), given by Brother John of Northampton (fl. 1372–1404), are akin to the work of Meister Bertram von Minden, one of whose school is credited with the work. Meister Bertram, who was born in the first half of the century, was working for the Hamburg town council in 1367, and was in Lübeck in 1375; in this same year Lübeck received with great pomp the Emperor Charles IV, father of Richard II's first queen. Herman Scheere, who illuminated a number of very important English manuscripts between 1400 and 1415, was more probably from Flanders than Cologne; he was at any rate quite distinct from the famous Master Herman Wynrich mentioned above; the latter about the year 1378 succeeded to the workshop of Wilhelm von Herle, whose widow Jutta he married; Wynrich died in 1414. Both Scheere and Wynrich must be distinguished from the "Hermann de Coulogne" who in 1403 was working at Champmol by Dijon under Jan Maelweel (Jean Malouel)—this third Hermann was a layer of gold backgrounds; on the other hand, a connexion of the Maelweel group (the three brothers Limbourg, illuminators of the famous Grandes Heures du duc de Berri, seem to have been Maelweel's nephews) with English painting at the time of the Wilton Diptych is intrinsically likely.

The hands in the Diptych are of remarkable beauty and can hardly be paralleled in their individuality of treatment: perhaps the nearest to identity of feeling and convention are in the Pietà in the Louvre attributed to Maelweel. Maelweel came from Guelderland and in 1396 was in the service of Queen Isabeau at Paris; he afterwards worked for the Duke of Burgundy, and died in 1415. His career mingled the same Teutonic and Romance influences that were also current in London, but neither the Pietà nor his "Martyrdom of St. Denis" reflect any of the brightness and calm joyousness so conspicuous in the Wilton Diptych.

The question is: what English painter of the time was capable of such a work? Unfortunately no reference has yet been discovered which can

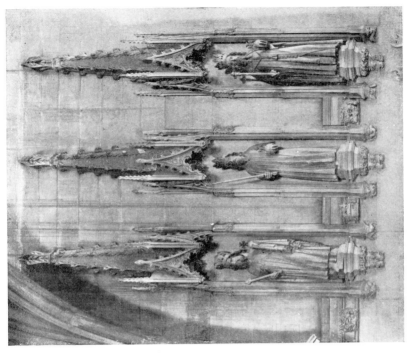
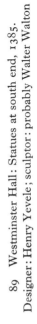

89 Westminster Hall: Statues at south end, 1385.
Designer: Henry Yevele; sculptor: probably Walter Walton

88 Winchester College: Madonna of Outer Gate, 1394– .
Designer: William Wynford

91 Westminster Abbey, Henry VII's Chapel:
Detail of bronze gates, c. 1510

90 Bronze Jug, now in British Museum, c. 1390.
London bellfounder's work

possibly relate to it, and the matter is therefore beyond proof, but the field can probably be reduced to a very narrow orbit indeed. Here the question of date becomes all-important; Miss Clarke showed that the livery of collars of broom-cods sent by Charles VI to Richard could hardly have arrived before the summer of 1395, while the total absence of any positive reference in the painting to a queen seems to preclude a date later than November 1396, when Isabella landed in England, and almost equally the period after the proxy marriage of 12 March in the same year. On the other hand, such a work could not be accomplished in a very short space of time, and if its completion took more than a year, it is the date of starting that must be pushed back. This is quite possible, for the golden collars would probably be among the last details to be added.

In 1395 Gilbert Prince was still the King's Painter, and his immense experience in heraldry and the design of settings and costumes for disguisings would eminently fit him for the type of detail found in the diptych; the conventions of the painting are those of the school of Hugh of St. Albans, in which we know that Prince was trained. But on 22 January 1396 Gilbert was sufficiently infirm to make his will, and within a month he was dead. An alternative author, or possibly a collaborator, must then be sought, and who should this be but Gilbert's clerk, Thomas Litlington? Mention of "Thomas Gibonservant Prynce" (i.e. Thomas the servant of Gibon or Gilbert Prince) occurs as early as the beginning of 1390, and on 12 September 1393 a sum of over £650 was paid to Gilbert by the hands of Thomas his clerk. He is mentioned in Gilbert's will as "Thomas Litlyngton my clerk" while the Issue Rolls for 1394-7 show that a total of just over £700 was paid for divers works, banners, painting, and their pensions, divided between "Gilbert Prince, late the King's Painter, and Thomas Litlyngton, now the King's Painter". In 1396 and 1397 Thomas Lyttlyngton "peyntour" occurs in London, and on 17 June 1399 a protection was issued to "Thomas Litlyngton alias Thomas Prynce, peyntour and citizen of London" going in the company of John, Duke of Exeter, on the King's last ill-fated expedition to Ireland. Lastly, he appears in London in December 1400, but by the beginning of 1403 Thomas Kent seems to have been the royal painter. If we are to consider Thomas rather than Gilbert as the painter of the Diptych, an early death would best account for the lack of any comparable works and for the long oblivion in which his name has slept.

Our steps must now be retraced in order to give brief consideration to the two remaining paintings already referred to: that on the tester of the Black Prince's tomb and the wall paintings in the Chapter House at Westminster. The composition above the Black Prince's tomb is altogether remarkable, both in form and colour: within a cusped panel the Trinity is depicted in the form of God the Father seated on the rainbow and with His feet on the earth, with Christ on the Cross standing between His knees and supported by His upheld arms. In the angles between the cusped panel and the corners of the tester are winged Symbols of the Four Evangelists. The Almighty wears a white tunic covered with black diaper patterns enclosing vermilion badges with the white letters IHS, and a dark blue tunic patterned with yellow flowers; rich red linings contrast with a background of greenish-blue sky, covered with stars. The Evangelistic Symbols are all winged, and here, as in the six-winged Seraphim of the Westminster Chapter House, we are reminded of the angels holding draperies in Master Hugh's work at St. Stephen's Chapel. The wings in all these instances, and also in the Wilton Diptych, are treated with extraordinary sympathy, so that one is uncannily led to feel that the artist has actually seen the angel or winged creature he represents.

All these works possess an inspired sweep of outline and combine sublimity of conception with an intuitive tenderness rare in Northern art. It may well be that this factor derived in part from the Italian paintings studied by Hugh of St. Albans and doubtless by his pupils and assistants, Gilbert Prince among them. The Canterbury Trinity should be Prince's work, and we seem to have examples of the work of three successive generations of this Court School, beginning with Hugh and ending with Thomas Litlington. This half-century was of course that of the "Northern Renaissance" which embraced far more than England, but it was here on the outposts of Europe that saw the most remarkable chain of development arising out of such small beginnings as Simone Martini's journey to Avignon in the summer of 1336.

English art had itself exerted a great influence on parts of the Continent fifty years before; the Cologne painters had learnt much from the England of Edward I and II, and doubtless such occasions as Edward III's visit to the Rhine in 1338 had not been without artistic interchanges. English scholars and artists thronged the Paris of the early fourteenth century; a Johannes Anglicus worked at Avignon in 1345 upon the monument of Pope John XXII, a monument copied from that of Edward II at Gloucester, and another Joannes Anglicus was master of the works of St. Urbain at Troyes. English embroidery was exported to the whole of Europe, and about 1379 John "Aghehe" of London, tapicer, was working in Arras itself, while a Parisian tapestry-maker of the same period was Pierre l'Anglois. National influences were almost inextricably mixed; a large proportion of the Parisian illuminators of the early fourteenth century were probably English, but on the other hand, of six Norwich painters who took up the freedom between 1374 and 1388, three were named John de Frenge, Stephen Frenge, and Edmund Frensshe; and this in Norfolk, which was reputedly one of the least French of English counties. The other three painters were John of Bradewelle, John Leggard, and Thomas of Ocle: among the six it is probable that we have the author of the Norwich Cathedral retable, which dates from the period 1380–1400 (99).

Norfolk had of course been the home of the great English school of illumination in the early years of the fourteenth century, but this gave place to a new style, analogous to the "Perpendicular" developments in architecture, painting, and stained glass. The last of the East Anglian manuscripts is the Luttrell Psalter of about 1340, and well before the

Black Death the new influences were making themselves felt. The history of the English illumination of the reign of Edward III still has to be written,[1] but soon after the accession of Richard II a number of superb works add another lustre to the glories of the time. Among the executants two are outstanding, one of them the nameless illuminator (perhaps a Westminster monk) who produced Abbot Litlyngton's Missal in 1383-4, and the Liber Regalis or Coronation Book of Richard II.

In the crucial ten years of Richard's personal rule, 1389-99, the greatest of English limners is known by name: the Dominican John Siferwas, member of a family of country squires established near Windsor and in Dorset since the thirteenth century. Siferwas was ordained acolyte in 1380, and was still living in 1421, but his two great works were executed in and soon after 1396: a Missal for Sherborne Abbey, Dorset, and a Lectionary for presentation to Salisbury Cathedral, made to the order of John Lord Lovel, whom we have already met as the builder of Wardour Castle. The fine page with portraits of Lord Lovel and Siferwas himself, though somewhat hard in its insistent black-and-scarlet, is important evidence of the influence already exercised by the lay painters upon illumination. No such attempts at genuine portraiture are found in the manuscripts carried out before the Black Death (96). Regarded as art, the delicious studies of wild birds in the Sherborne Missal give Siferwas an even higher claim to recognition. Here, as in the Wilton Diptych, is animal life seen by a loving student of nature, and given a prominence far beyond that of the songsters who twitter in the margins of Jacquemart de Hesdin's Hours executed for the duc de Berri. The Pepysian Sketchbook contains named sketches of birds and animals, closely related to the work of Siferwas, and it is even possible that this section of it may consist of his own private studies; the figure work must be by other hands.

It is impossible here to deal with the multitude of beautiful objects fashioned by the practitioners of the so-called "minor arts", but it is important to recognize that it was during the reign of Edward III that these arts gained official standing at Court. It was only after the Black Death that specialists emerged from the background of the King's Wardrobe. In 1332 John of Cologne, the King's Armourer, had supervision of the royal embroidery—of course because it was employed on heraldic surcoats and horse-trappings. His successor William Glendale seems to have developed into a royal broderer, and from his death in 1368 there is a regular series of office-holders: Thomas Carleton, who retired in 1380 and died 1388; Hans of Strasbourg, who died about the same time; William Sauston; Robert Ashcombe, appointed 1396, who did not die until 1423, but was superseded in 1400 by Peter Swan, who died 1411; and William Tiller, who was living in 1430. We get glimpses of some of

---

[1] Mr. Francis Wormald, in a lecture to the British Archaeological Association on 3 May 1945 demonstrated the growing realism of the new style (or rather styles), and showed the influence of Italian work and iconography. Later in the century, he suggested, English work may have borrowed Eastern elements through Bohemia.

these men from their wills and from other documents: Carleton and Ashcombe both had extensive properties in the parish of St. Alban Woodstreet and in that vicinity; in 1400 Ashcombe complained of the evil odours wafted into his property from his neighbour's sanitary (?) accommodation; Hans of Strasbourg had a pleasant suburban residence with a dovecot and gardens upon Houndsditch; Glendale bequeathed a white horse to the Dean of the King's Chapel. Both Ashcombe and Swan were given commissions to impress within London and its suburbs "broderers, tailors, painters, and workers in that mistery"—the mention of painters providing interesting proof of the interdependence of the arts practised at the Court.

Hardly had the King's Broderer separated himself from the armoury than the entirely new office of King's Tapicer or Tapestry-maker was set up in imitation. The first holder, John Bullok of London, in 1367 received a grant of similar wages to those taken by William Glendale the King's Broderer; Bullok died three years later leaving City property and also a country estate at Halling in Kent; like other tapicers he dwelt in the parish of St. Dionys Backchurch. Bullok was apparently succeeded by Alan Underwood, who from 1370 had been his assistant, and in 1390 John Lettreford received the office for life. Very little English tapestry of the mediæval period has been preserved, but among the embroideries mention must be made of the Black Prince's surcoat at Canterbury, quite possibly the work of Thomas Carleton, and the magnificent horse-trapper worked on Persian velvet about 1330, and now remade as a chasuble and in the Cluny Museum at Paris (92). This horse-trapper is probably the finest heraldic presentation of the leopards of England in existence, and it is tantalizing that there should be no records of the broderers regularly employed at the Court at that period. Of those whose names appear, the chief seems to have been Roesia, daughter of Thomas Romayn, alderman, and wife of John de Burford, citizen and merchant of London. Roesia was perhaps the last to maintain the old tradition of the *opus anglicanum*, which had been made by women, and in 1317 she provided for the sum of 100 marks an embroidered cope which was to be presented by Queen Isabella to the Pope; she was still living in 1348, when Sir John Pulteney remembered her in his will, so that there is no chronological difficulty in ascribing to her the Cluny horse-trapper.

The oldest office by far among the Artists to the King was that of the Goldsmith; in our period we find Walter of Spalding holding the office in 1317, when he made a silver image at the King's command; Richard Grimsby in 1353; Thomas Hessey, who in 1365 made a large series of silver cups as gifts from the King—Hessey died about 1370. Later John Harsey occurs, at whose death early in 1398 Christopher Tildesley was appointed, and held the office into the reign of Henry IV, for whom in 1406 he made a collar of gold worked with the motto "soveignez" and the letter S (the motto "Souviens" or "Souvenez" was probably the origin of the famous collar of SS), with ten annulets garnished with pearls, diamonds, rubies, and sapphires, the whole of which were delivered to

92 Chasuble made from horse-trapper, now in Cluny Museum, Paris, *c.* 1330–40.
Probably London work

93 English verdure tapestry, discovered at Cambridge, mid-sixteenth century

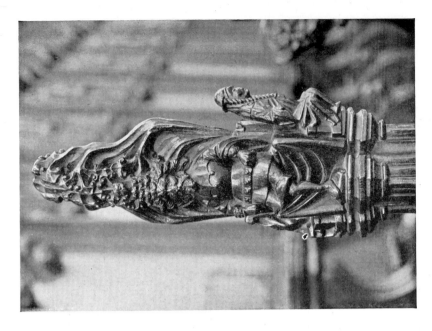

95 Ludlow Church: finial of Stalls, 1447

94 Westminster Hall: angel in roof, 1395–96.
Designer: Hugh Herland; carver: Robert Grasington

the King at Winchester, when Tildesley received £385 6s. 8d. Edward III and Richard II patronized many other London goldsmiths, men such as Nicholas Twyford, who died in 1390, John Bottesham, Drew Barentyn, and Thomas Lamport. Many of these goldsmiths were among the wealthiest and most influential citizens, and their political influence was of such weight as to be worth careful cultivation. The engraving of seals was normally entrusted to a goldsmith, but here also a new office was formed, for in 1381 William Geyton, the King's Engraver in the Tower of London, was altering the Great Seal, and other seals were made in 1392 by Peter Hiltoft, who by that time had succeeded to the same office.

As time goes on and detailed investigation is made of these office-holders and of the contemporary output, more and more definite attributions of works of art become possible, but it is enough for my present purpose if I have made clear the existence of a rich throng of artists who moved in late fourteenth-century London—a galaxy of talent and genius which has perhaps never been seriously rivalled in western Europe. Not only did the King surround himself with an ever-increasing army of specialists, but similar growth was taking place elsewhere: for example, in additional appointments of artists to the Queen, such as Roland Bush, goldsmith to Anne of Bohemia; and in the magnificent state kept by John of Gaunt, titular King of Castile, and the lesser courts of his brothers and of great nobles such as the Earls of Arundel. Never before had there been in England so great a demand for works of the highest quality and price, and only in Henry III can an equally enlightened connoisseur be discovered. But whereas Henry III had had to rely to a great extent on imitations of French art or upon Italian painters and mosaicists, the England of Edward III and his grandson was able to rise to the occasion and show itself equal to the finest work of the Continent. More—in some directions England excelled all her rivals, notable in architecture where Yevele, Wynford, and Herland were laying down an ordered style quite unsurpassed in any clime or age; in poetry, where Chaucer's lyric humour sets ablaze the stilted Court Verse of the day; and in painting, where the walls of St. Stephen's Chapel exceeded in brilliance of composition and execution anything north of the Alps, and the Wilton Diptych reached a pitch of exquisite sensibility hardly ever attained to the west of Constantinople, and but dubiously touched in Italy.

Yet another development of the period which had a profound influence upon art in general was the growth of a regular drama; out of the crude miracles and mummings of twelfth- and thirteenth-century England we find the rudiments of an organized stage appearing in the first year of Richard II, when the scholars of St. Paul's were playing the History of the Old Testament. In 1384, 1391, and 1393 the London parish clerks performed plays lasting for as much as five days together, and Richard II in person attended the performances of 1391, and those of the York Pageants in 1397. The London entertainment consisted of plays of the Passion and Creation of the World, but there is reason to think that just

as in ancient Greece comedies had provided light relief between the
tragedies with their deep religious significance, so here there were
interludes and pastoral comedies interspersed with the serious plays on
scriptural subjects.

Beyond all this, and of even deeper significance, lay England's contribution to music. From a strictly objective viewpoint, much of Europe's
vaunted civilization pales into insignificance beside the immense cultural
achievements of the East. Whatever may be the ultimate value of European science and industrial invention, our art can only rarely be said to
show a clear superiority over that of India or China. To this generalization there is one grand exception: the growth and consummation of
Western music, rooted in harmony. Europe's noblest claim is that she
gave birth to Bach and to Mozart, who carried to almost incredible
perfection the sister arts of counterpoint and chordal harmony; and it is
in England of the age of Richard II that we have to seek for the root of
this well-founded boast. No one nation, still less one individual, can be
given the credit of inventing harmony; harmony is inherent in the physical
properties of sound, and the earliest human appreciation of the fact is
lost in antiquity. It was not, however, until the Christian Middle Ages
that something in the nature of conscious development began to take
place: from the end of the first millennium an obvious forward movement
starts, and definite progress can be traced thenceforward, at any rate to
the period of Mozart and Beethoven. It is extremely probable that the
process was assisted by similar Eastern contacts to those which sowed
the germ of Gothic architecture. The latter is traced to Armenia and the
Caucasus by Strzygowski, and Belaiev advances a parallel claim for the
folk-polyphony of Georgia. Belaiev doubtless goes too far in claiming
that Europe received its polyphony from Georgia ready made, but there
is a striking resemblance to the ear (I can say nothing of structure) between
certain chants in use in the Armenian Church, and the music of some of
the Old Hall MS. composers of the fourteenth and fifteenth centuries,
notably Thomas Damett, Canon of Windsor, who died in 1437, and
"Roy Henry", who is much more likely to have been Henry V than
Henry VI. Unfortunately the relation between ancient and modern
Armenian church music is unknown, for the mediæval manuscripts cannot
now be deciphered.

There is at any rate food for thought in the fact that some of the music
in the Old Hall MS. goes back to the reign of Richard II; that the collection was unquestionably of Royal origin; that Richard himself "*faisoit
balades & chancons, rondeaulx & laix, tres bien & bel*"; and that Leo,
exiled King of Lesser Armenia visited England in 1385, when he received
a present of £1,000. Later, in 1391, Richard granted to Leo an annuity
of £1,000 until such time as he should recover his kingdom. There had
of course been a highly developed polyphony in the West, notably in
France and Italy, before this: in France the great exponents of the *Ars
Nova* were Philippe de Vitri (1291–1361) and Guillaume de Machault
(c. 1300–77), both of them poets; in Italy early in the century were

96 The Lovel Lectionary, British Museum, *c.* 1400.
The painter, John Siferwas, presents the book to John, Lord Lovel of Wardour

Giovanni da Cascia of Florence and Jacopo da Bologna, and a little later the famous blind organist and poet Francesco Landini (1325–97).[1]

What was still lacking in this music was the system of chordal harmony, which from the middle of the fifteenth century was to enable further progress to be made, and was the germ from which all the triumphs of classical music sprang. This system, or at least its principles, was the invention of an Englishman, John Dunstable: he was universally credited with the authorship of the "English style" by the Continental musicians of his own time, and the mystery of what precisely was comprised in this style has recently been resolved by Dr. Manfred Bukofzer, who shows that it was "the new sensation of chordal harmony".

Though some fifty compositions by Dunstable have now been discovered, next to nothing is known of his career: he was in the service of John, Duke of Bedford, apparently while the Duke was Regent of France from 1422 to 1435, and in 1453 he died in London and was buried in St. Stephen's, Walbrook. He was an astronomer and mathematician as well as a composer, and two of his astronomical books survive; beyond this, and the praise of his contemporaries, we as yet know nothing. But this is enough: his youth and upbringing must have been in the Court circles of England's greatest age, and in the history of Western art John Dunstable's career is England's greatest ornament.

[1] Hardly any of this music is given public performance, at any rate not in this country, but a few pieces have been recorded for the gramophone. Most of these records can only be obtained with difficulty, and some have been withdrawn, but there is an almost complete list in Gustave Reese's *Music in the Middle Ages*. English playgoers who recall the charming song sung by Miss Gwen ffrangcon-Davies in *Richard of Bordeaux* may be interested to know that it was an adaptation by Mr. Herbert Menges from Guillaume de Machaut's chanson "Douce dame jolie"; it is included in the recorded suite of Mr. Menges' incidental music on Decca K.727.

III

THE GREAT SLUMP[1]

THE age of Richard II was like to a lofty tower, and such towers must have a broad and sure foundation if they are to stand. This particular tower, a very beacon light of the arts, did not stand; "great was the fall thereof". The source of its weakness certainly did not lie in any incapacity of England to produce a continuous stream of artists and craftsmen; probably the origin of the disaster is to be found not in one, but in several concurrent factors: in a gradually worsening economic situation; in the impoverished disillusionment which followed a half-century of war and pestilence; in the complicated emotional condition of European civilization, no longer accepting implicitly the fundamentals of its official theology; and last, as immediate cause, the personal character and temperament of King Richard himself.

The economic collapse was due to two factors, one native, the other the outcome of foreign relations. Early in the fourteenth century, well before the Black Death, it was found that demesne farming (broadly, farming by means of labour services under an owner-occupier) no longer paid, and various expedients were tried by landowners in the hope of balancing their budget. Economists are not agreed upon the ultimate cause of this agricultural decline, but its main result was the growth of land-leases based on money-payments, in the place of the co-operative services rendered by the peasants to the landowner under the old system of self-contained communities. Landlords, anxious to get their income in hard cash, flooded the market with land, which was leased by the more prosperous members of the labouring classes. The supply of land, however, exceeded the demand, and while the country labourer enjoyed his new-found liberty and his "three acres and a cow", the landlord had large sections of his estate left on his hands, without the labour to cultivate them; in some cases they reverted to waste. Elsewhere, enterprising men purchased flocks of sheep and hired a few shepherds, and for a time prospered on the proceeds of wool exported to the Continent. By the latter part of the fourteenth century the foreign market was declining, but the adverse returns from wool were for a time disguised by a rapid rise in exports of English cloth. The point where a drop in total export value was reached came about the beginning of the fifteenth century.

This already awkward state of affairs greatly deteriorated owing to the loss of our ancient Scandinavian markets to the German Hansa, and later,

[1] "Slump" is no longer slang, and helps to bring home the parallel to the modern reader.

97 Exeter Cathedral, East Window. Figures of St. Catherine: left, 1317,
by Michael le Verrer; right, 1389, by Robert Lyen.
From drawings by Mr. Wilfred Drake

the loss also of the considerable Baltic trade to Poland and Prussia. Chronic war with France closed yet another door, and only the narrow outlet through Calais and the Netherlands was in full use during the greater part of the century.

Even before 1400 the steady reverses of the French war had led to progressive disappointment; war engulfed what was left of the nation's surplus, and the three great plagues of 1349, 1362, and 1369 brought to the whole population horrors even greater than those which the war was carrying into France. Edward III and his sons, brought up in the old convention of war as a gentleman's recreation, did not foresee the ultimate results of their increasing reliance upon the low-bred archer and the engineer with his new-fangled bombard. For the first time in an epoch, European war had become "total".

Richard II, endowed with the same personal courage as the rest of his family, was also graced by a greater insight and a deeper feeling, and was profoundly imbued with the doctrine of his own divine mission to rule over and succour the helpless common folk of his realm. As a boy he had proclaimed himself leader of a rebellious mob, type of all his subjects. Later, when Parliament petitioned against the education of the villein (who by education would gain his freedom and compete with the men who had already arrived), Richard replied "Le roi s'avisera"—in other words, that he had no intention of agreeing to such reactionary nonsense. Richard's much-canvassed extravagance was by no means so exceptional as his opponents claimed at the time, and it was besides not merely for his own personal benefit: while he raised no greater revenue than his predecessors and but little more than his immediate followers, he increased enormously the customary Royal charity. Henry III occasionally fed 500 paupers on one day, and Edward I had provided as many as 100,000 free meals in a year, but Richard is said, doubtless with some exaggeration, to have fed as many as 6,000 or 10,000 persons on a single day. Such extensive doles may have been unwise, but Richard clearly shared with Robin Hood in a propensity to rob the rich to give to the poor.

So revolutionary a policy demanded precautions, such as the famous bodyguard of loyal Cheshire men wearing the badge of the White Hart; it is only too probable that Richard's character became embittered after the cruel proscription of his friends by the Appellants in 1388, and still more after the death of Anne of Bohemia in 1394. John Gower's changed dedication of the *Confessio Amantis*, whose composition was suggested by Richard at a chance meeting on the Thames, shows that between 1390 and 1393 at least one Royalist became estranged from the King. One by one the King disposed of his opponents, until only Henry Bolingbroke was left, and his banishment and that of Archbishop and arch-plotter Arundel seemed to crown the perfected structure of a national monarchy, rendered conterminous with the coasts of England and Wales by the forfeiture of Henry's vast Lancaster estates in 1399. It was the last card, and it brought the house down; it is one of the ironies of history that the union of Lancaster with the Crown should have been accomplished in

L*

inverse sense, and that the verdict of subsequent events has proved that in this respect at least Richard was right.

Unfortunately, the price which Henry paid for his own and Richard's inheritance was too heavy: the sanctity of the kingly office, already compromised by the deposition and murder of Edward II, was now destroyed, the mainspring of government broken. It is not that Henry IV in himself was of so very different a character from Richard, though he was undoubtedly a man of less sensibility and possessed a far slighter degree of cultural inspiration—the power to excite in his servants the supreme flights of genius. What foredoomed the Lancastrians was the profound immorality of their accession; the cupidity and self-seeking of their agents, freed from restraint by an ill example; and the reversal of Richard's cultural alliance with France.

Beneath this English depression ran the vaster wave-trough of the breakdown of mediæval society. Everywhere the new money economy led to the rending of the old feudal ties, which at their best were amicable and secure. Best or worst, the newly rising classes, the classes who bore the brunt of mercenary warfare, would have none of it, and they kicked also against the restraints of the Church. The eager seekers after a panacea believed that they had found it in the jealously guarded Bible, and Wyclif in England and Hus in Bohemia thought to return to the primitive simplicity of the early fathers. Wyclif's programme in the end would have led to the destruction, not only of the monasteries and great church establishment, but of the very universities and of art and science. Like Lavoisier's judges, the reformers "had no need of savants". As soon as this became evident, the sympathy and protection which they had found among such anti-clerical nobles as John of Gaunt were withdrawn, and the Church took fright. In England the outcome of this fear, and of the Church's uneasy conscience, was the infamous statute *de Heretico Comburendo* of 1401, whereby the condemned heretic was handed over to the King's officers to be burned at the stake.

So through the deepening gloom of the fifteenth century we discern a twofold struggle: that of the forces of mercenaries against law and order; that of art-loving Churchmen with conscience qualms against an iconoclastic rabble imbued with the English will to freedom. The house, like the Plantagenet House of England, was divided against itself, and a century of tragic decay had to be endured before in its perishing it gave birth to a new England inspired by new ideals. In the meantime England, like the rest of Europe, was in the grip of "a revival of anarchy in a civilized society". Beyond Europe even stretched a vast area of unrest: the marvellous Asiatic order of the Mongol Empire had crumbled away, and in Asia Minor the Ottoman Turks had been steadily expanding. In 1326 Osman captured Brusa, close to the Sea of Marmora; three years later Nicaea fell; one by one the last bastions of the Eastern Roman Empire went down, until by 1353 the Turkish forces crossed into Europe, taking Gallipoli in the next year and Adrianople in 1357. Meanwhile, the Middle and Far East fell victims to this cyclic turmoil: in 1363 Timur began his conquest of the central Asiatic realms, and his victories continued, spreading desolation for thousands of miles; Bagdad was sacked in 1392, and in 1398 far-off Delhi fell a spoil, while Syria and even part of Asia Minor had been captured before Timur's death in 1405. In China the dynasty of Kublai Khan had been overthrown by the Mings in 1368, and the realms of Cathay were once more closed to foreign travellers, to remain so for over two centuries—such was the sinister ground-bass which muttered on while Plantagenet and Valois fought out their petty squabble for a little patch of land facing the Atlantic; small wonder that with the leaders of Western life so embroiled, the Turks twice defeated the Serbians, and finally crushed Christian resistance at Nicopolis in 1396—only the defeat of Bajazet by Timur in 1402 gave Europe breathing space, promptly employed for civil war in France and Bohemia, and the fostering of senseless national bickerings and religious heresy-hunting.

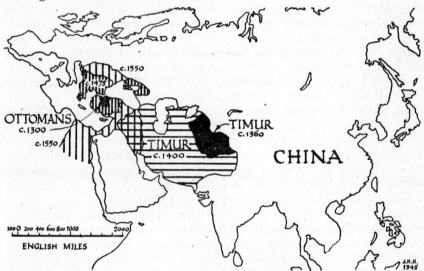

FIG. 98. Ottoman and Timurid expansion.

In such an atmosphere it is hardly surprising that the multiplication of artistic offices at the Court of England gave place to a general falling-off in activity; as the fifteenth century wore on and old office-holders died, some of their places were left unfilled. Broderers, tapicers, painters, were hired for specific jobs, for there was no longer the money to keep an army of specialists at permanent retaining fees. The office of chief carpenter, duplicated under Richard II, had reverted to its old status by the time of Henry V. In almost all directions decline and retrogression are apparent; only Henry V's keen love of music, which seems to have been shared by his brothers John, Duke of Bedford and Humphrey, Duke of Gloucester, led to the formation of a regular musical establishment in the Chapel Royal attached to the King's person.

The change of dynasty in 1399 roughly coincided with the death of a generation of great artists: Geoffrey Chaucer and Henry Yevele both died in 1400, and in poetry and in architecture none could take their place. Wynford and Hugh Herland were old men: so was John Gower; Gilbert Prince the painter had died in 1396. These losses in themselves would have inflicted a serious break with tradition, even in happier circumstances, and as it was their pupils plodded along an imitative course, reproducing much of the form, but little of the spirit, of their predecessors.

In architecture, the opportunities offered by the opening century were of a totally different kind from those which had given rise to the splendid achievements of the past age. The roof of Westminster Hall was hurriedly completed; the naves of Westminster Abbey and Winchester Cathedral dragged on, bit by bit, and later were helped by the generosity of Henry V and his uncle Cardinal Beaufort. Beverley and York Minsters were in any case nearing completion, but John Thornton's glass in the great east window of York has not the power of the works of his exemplar Thomas of Oxford. During Henry IV's reign remarkably little new work was undertaken, and most of the buildings begun in the first forty years of the century were either parish churches or civic buildings: for instance, Norwich, London, Lynn, and York, all undertook new Guildhalls before 1450. With the passing of the age of great cathedral projects, the architect's opportunity in the bigger kinds disappeared, and much of the work done is of small scale as well as mediocre execution. Lack of inspiration led to monotonously repetitive architecture, just as in poetry Hoccleve was toiling painfully and at great length in Chaucer's wake, and Lydgate was embarking on his immense output of moralizing in verse. Nobody would suggest that because Lydgate wrote much and ill, therefore Chaucer's style was at fault; but something of this sort is urged against English Perpendicular art. Because every second parish church was largely or wholly rebuilt in the fifteenth century, specimens of uninspired Perpendicular are far from rare. What must be borne in mind is that even at this lowest ebb of European and English art, some splendid things were produced, and that for the rest, it was not the noble style of Yevele and Herland that was to blame.

Sudden and widespread as was the artistic depression, a degree of continuity was assured by the existence of pupils of the older masters; much as we may lament Lydgate's failure to supply even a passable imitation of Chaucer, it was to Lydgate nevertheless that English poetry looked for guidance. Fortunately, the subtler aspect of Chaucer also had its devotees in James I of Scotland and Charles, Duke of Orleans, both of whom spent many years as captives at the English Court. Through James's "Kingis Quair" derives the later Scots poetry of the Chaucerian school, the verse of Robert Henryson and William Dunbar: but their work belongs to the end of the century. In English the finest of the poems of the early fifteenth century come, ironically enough, from the pen of the French Duke of Orleans, who, both as regards his French and his English output, may be regarded as the last representative of the trouvère outlook, which was to receive its death-blow from the revolutionary work of Villon in mid-century.

During the actual slump, the most important literary works were probably Hoccleve's *Regement of Princes*, completed in 1412, and the roughly contemporary *Reason and Sensuality*, a translation by Lydgate. Lydgate went on to produce the *Troy Book*, the first of his great compilations, between 1412 and 1420. If it were not for the inevitable comparison with Chaucer, these works would occupy a far more important place in our literary history than they do—one cannot always remain on the peaks, and what John Fletcher was to Shakespeare, Hoccleve was to Chaucer, though one might hardly cast Lydgate for the part of Ben Jonson. Prolixity was Lydgate's curse; in his shorter pieces he could call up delightful scenes to the mind—witness his description of St. Valentine's morning:

> The same tyme, I herde a larke synge
>   Ful lustely, agayne the morowe gray:
> "Awake, ye louers, out of your slombringe,
>   This glade morowe, in al the haste ye may;
>   Some obseruaunce dothe vnto this day,
> Your choyse ayen of herte to renewe,
> In confyrmyng for euer to be trewe. . . ."

which compares not unfavourably with the Duke of Orleans' treatment of the same subject:

> Whan fresshe phebus day of seynt valentyne
> Had whirlid vp his golden chare aloft
> The burnyd bemys of it gan to shyne
> In at my chambre where y slepid soft
> Of which the light that he had with him brought
> He wook me of the slepe of heuynes
> Wherin forslepid y alle the nyght dowtles
> Vpon my bed so hard of newous thought. . . .

The rich argosy of the fourteenth century had run aground, and that so much was saved from the wreck was due to the loving care of a band of men who had been the pupils or friends of the masters of the preceding generation. Hoccleve bewailed his own incapacity to continue where Chaucer and Gower left off:

> O, maister deere, and fadir reuerent!
> Mi maister Chaucer, flour of eloquence,
> Mirour of fructuous entendëment,
> O, vniuersel fadir in science!
> Allas! that thou thyn excellent prudence,
>   In thi bed mortel mightist naght by-qwethe;
>   What eiled deth? allas! whi wolde he sle the?
>
> O deth! thou didest naght harme singuleer,
>   In slaghtere of him; but al this land it smertith;
> But nathëlees, yit hast thou no power
>   His namë sle; his hy vertu astertith
>   Vnslayn fro the, which ay vs lyfly hertyth,
> With bookës of his ornat éndytyng,
> That is to al this land enlumynyng.

Hast thou nat eeke my maister Gower slayn,
Whos vertu I am insufficient
ffor to descreyue? . . .

Architecture practically ceased, except for what was already in progress;
at Canterbury the works begun by Yevele were carried on by his partner
Stephen Lote, and something was done at York, but not done well, for
it was owing to a collapse that William Colchester, master mason of
Westminster Abbey, was sent to York by Henry IV in 1407 to take charge
of the rebuilding. The northern city, so long the leader of a school of art,
had been hard hit by recurrent pestilence, and had already had to go as
far as Coventry to find in John Thornton a glass-painter sufficiently
accomplished to be entrusted with the new east window of the Minster.
The new style in glazed windows, like the new style in building, was a
product of the South, and only overcame York prejudices by sheer force
of circumstances. That the introduction of southern craftsmen was
violently resented is proved by the murderous assault upon Colchester
and his assistant, outcome of a conspiracy among some of the local stone-
masons who felt themselves aggrieved. There may, however, have been
contributory causes to the resentment felt, for Henry IV's execution of
Archbishop Scrope only two years before was regarded by the Yorkshire-
men as a martyrdom, and the King's interference in the affairs of the
Minster, of which he was nominally patron, was unlikely to soothe
provincial susceptibilities.

John Clifford, like Stephen Lote, had been closely associated with
Yevele, and as the permanent master mason of London Bridge had considerable standing in the City. Clifford's pupil Richard Beke succeeded
to the same post in 1417, and finally left in 1435 to become master at
Canterbury Cathedral; he died on 16 November 1458, almost fifty years
after he began to work at London Bridge. Clifford lived until 1417, and
Lote and Walter Walton (whom we saw as Yevele's deputy in the 1390's)
until the next year. Through Walton too passed a line of direct influence,
for he bequeathed his best compass to John Croxton, mason, evidently a
close friend or associate. Now Croxton was the master at the building of
the new Guildhall of London, a work which went slowly on from 1411
to 1446; next to Westminster, the Guildhall was the largest of the immense
halls made possible by the new science of timber roofing. At Norwich a
new hall had been begun in 1407, under a local mason, John Marwe,
while Lynn rebuilt its guildhall after a fire in 1423. These were works of
no great inspiration, but excellent workmanship, and show that there
was no lack of good craftsmen in the main centres of population. By
means of such work men possessed of ideas were able to give them
expression, even if it were only in matters of routine; the events of 1399
had been a grave shock to the nervous system of the country, but wherever
life is able to sustain such a shock, the necessary business of every day
provides an anodyne, and gradually affairs tend to return to their normal
level.

Through this period one very fine piece of church work was continued, the west front of Beverley Minster. It was probably begun about 1390 and took some thirty years to complete. It was thus finished ten years or more before either of the western towers of York was begun, though this is a fact that is very easily forgotten. The surpassing fame of York Minster tends to obscure its immense debt to the example set by Beverley, though nothing can hide the rather awkward junction between the Decorated front and the superimposed towers; at Beverley, where the architect was able to design the whole composition, there was no such difficulty, and the result is one of sublimity and grandeur: the tall slim towers of Beverley rush upwards like the bastions of some lofty cliff and avoid the appearance of instability by incorporating buttresses of great projection. From the ground to the topmost pinnacle the work mounts, gaining in spiritual impetus as it loses in weight. Seen from the front, it is the most over-whelmingly impressive of all English façades, but from other directions it is, alas, too big for the rest of the church. Another fault lies in the excess of panelling with which the walls and buttresses are encrusted—a concession to the decorative artist which weakens the first effect when one comes to a closer view (4, 7).

In spite of its defects, the Beverley front is one of the greatest of English designs, and one would like to discover the name of its architect. Unfortunately, the church records are at this period singularly unin-formative; it was decreed in 1391 that the office of master mason to the fabric should be abolished at the death of the then holder, but his name is not mentioned. It was of course reasonably certain by that time that the church would be completed under his supervision, or at least so far that there would be no excuse for further expenditure on retaining fees. There is one mason referred to among the town records of this period, William Rolston, who appears in 1407 as a resident in Walkergate, Beverley, while he and his wife Joan are mentioned in a later lawsuit concerning land in Holderness and premises in Beverley of which they were seized by knight-service. From the inquisitions taken it appears that Joan was the daughter of Thomas Snaith of Beverley, dyer, and his wife Cicely, sister of Thomas Lutton, citizen of York—evidently Rolston was well-connected through his wife, and the property was of some size. It descended to his daughter Isabella, who was born in or before 1403, and who married William Holme of Beverley. Thus far we are on safe ground, but it is disconcerting to find that at the same period there was a William Rolston or Rolleston of Beverley, prominent as a merchant and as one of the keepers of the town. Probably there were two different men of the same name, for while William Rolleston, merchant, occurs con-stantly from about 1390 to 1411 or later, the reference in 1407 to William Rolston as "mason" occurs in a list of seventy-one names, of which no other is provided with a trade description. It seems likely that the trade was added with a view to distinguishing the two men. In the same list occur two names as being of the fee of the Chapter, namely John Kervour and Nicholas Fenton, and in the "kervour" it is tempting to see the sculptor of the statues of the west front, of which one original still survives.

William Rolleston, or one of the men of that name, seems to have had an eventful career, for during the town riots of 1381–2, he was victimized by the discontented party, and in 1412 was excommunicated for a week for having procured the clandestine marriage of his daughter Joan to one William Ledes. Unpopularity with the mob of 1381 may not have indicated much amiss, and we are now accustomed to think of secret marriages in a most charitable way, but we can hardly condone the peculiar sense of humour which he displayed in 1408, when "one William Rolleston of Beverley and other evildoers of his company" caused translations into English of a royal pardon to the Provost of Beverley, Robert Manfeld, to be "placed on the doors of most of the inns of the town of Beverley". That Manfeld complained is not surprising, for his pardon was a general one covering "treasons, insurrections, rebellions, felonies, breaches of prisons and gaols, escapes of felons, receipts of felons, murders, rapes, larcenies, extortions, misprisions, oppressions, conspiracies, confederacies, maintenances and other trespasses and crimes committed by him". In spite of our complete ignorance of the antecedent facts, the bald relation of the Patent Rolls is sufficient to convey to us the full-blooded life of an English mediæval town.

Away in Oxfordshire another mason-architect was coming into prominence: Richard Winchcombe, who between 1408 and 1418 built the new chancel of Adderbury Church for the impropriators, New College, Oxford (102, 104). There and at other churches of the district he proved himself a designer of considerable skill, and reaped his reward in 1430, when the University appointed him director of the works of the new Divinity School, with a retaining fee of £2 a year, a gown worth 13s. 4d., and a salary of 4s. a week when he should be actually engaged upon the work. He retained the post for ten years, and then disappears from the scene, when his place was taken by Thomas Elkins, a mason of Barrington in Cotswold. Winchcombe and Elkins built the lower walls of the school, but the splendid pendant vault was the work of William Orchard in 1480, another proof, if proof were needed, of the melancholy state of the arts during the troubled middle of the century (106). Slowness is a chief symptom of the building works of this period, even when of small scale; for example, the Chantry of Henry V in Westminster Abbey was twenty years and more in course of construction, though under the constant supervision of John Thirsk, the Abbey master mason. It was a case, as Lydgate wrote in another connexion, of "for lack of money I might not speed".[1]

In spite of these difficulties, a few important churches were built in the provinces in the first quarter of the century; notable among them are Battlefield Church near Shrewsbury, a memorial to Henry IV's victory there in 1403; St. Nicholas Chapel at King's Lynn, between 1399 and 1419; and the chancel at Fotheringhay, Northants, where the influence of the London school is apparent in the nave of 1434, copied from the

---

[1] The refrain of *London Lyckpeny*, now commonly denied to Lydgate on grounds of style—a criticism stultified by the scribe's caption, stating that the surviving version had been "newly oversene and emended" in a later generation.

99   Norwich Cathedral, Retable. (Resurrection panel), *c.* 1380-1400

chancel, now long destroyed. This influence can almost certainly be traced back to Stephen Lote and Thomas Mapilton, who were concerned with the tomb of the Duke of York, founder of the college at Fotheringhay, who was killed at Agincourt in 1415. The reign of Henry IV was almost barren, but with the accession of his son recovery set in, though slowly on account of the reopening of the French war. But enough was done to show that the Perpendicular style was far from exhaustion, and that it was capable of wellnigh infinite adaptation to circumstances.

This tentative development of the style is well seen in the great screen at Canterbury and in the tomb of Henry IV, clearly from the same designer, probably Lote; the Erpingham Gate at Norwich, and the later work on the west front of the Cathedral, both probably due to James Woodrofe, a brilliant mason and carver; and the west front and south porch at Gloucester where, however, the less pleasant qualities of the West of England school reappear in the rather wiry mullions and pinnacles. In Suffolk the sturdy and finely proportioned flint tower of Walberswick Church was built by two local masons, Adam Powle of Blythburgh and Richard Russell of Dunwich, in 1426; the design was settled by the time-honoured method of using other buildings as models; the tower was to be like that at Tunstall, with windows like those of Halesworth (**101**). Of far greater aesthetic importance is the finely proportioned central tower of St. Augustine's, Hedon, in Yorkshire, one of the grandest compositions remaining to us (**18**). Here the architect was Robert Playser, who superintended the work from 1427 to its conclusion ten years later, dwelling rent free in rooms over the Grammar School and receiving a yearly fee of £1 in addition to his salary, and clothing worth 7s. annually. The tower of Hedon, more than any other building of its time, is evidence of the strength and vigour remaining in English art, even at this period of gloom

The structural carpenters had few opportunities in the early years of the century, but joinery and woodcarving continued to flourish. Hugh Herland had retired from the post of King's Chief Carpenter in extreme old age at the beginning of 1405, and his place was taken by William Toutmond, almost certainly identical with the inhabitant of Kingston-upon-Thames of that name who was dead by 1415. It is thus rather improbable that Toutmond was the designer of the excellent tester of Henry IV's tomb at Canterbury, a more likely candidate being John Wydmere, who was chief joiner from the beginning of 1394 until his death early in 1417. The tester, with its delicate pendent arcading and fine bratticing, is joiner's rather than carpenter's work, and instead of the imitation vaulting formerly customary, follows the newer fashion of the tombs of the Black Prince and of Richard II in holding a flat panel, painted on the under surface. There are more important paintings at the head and foot of the tomb, and though far below the level of design shown forty years earlier by the Black Prince's tester, are of great interest. One depicts the Coronation of the Virgin, who is supported by flying angels, while beneath are two kneeling figures of kings, probably representing Henry IV and Edward the Confessor.

To the painters of the period we shall shortly return: before leaving the carvers and imagers mention must be made of Nicholas Broker, coppersmith, who had cast the effigies of Richard II and Anne of Bohemia; his death did not take place until 1426, so that we may suppose him to have had considerable influence in carrying on the old traditions, while in 1414 William Godeyer, citizen and coppersmith of London, both devised and made an image in likeness of the mother of Henry V (Mary Bohun) to be placed on her tomb in the King's College at Leicester. In February 1415 Robert Broun, carver, made a swan and an antelope in wood for the King's great ship called the *Holigost*, and three years later carved other swans for the King's chamber in Shene Palace. To this period also belongs the early career of John Massingham, the great sculptor of the mid-century, who was probably the "John Massyngham, carpenter", imprisoned and later released in 1409, having left the service of John Dobson before the end of his term. This Dobson was a prominent London carpenter, and in 1402 had a grant of the office of the second of the King's Chief Carpenters on the death of Nicholas Walton; it is known that Massingham worked in wood as well as stone, and the comparative excellence of wood-carving during the fifteenth century suggests that a large proportion of sculptors would be recruited from the ranks of the carpenters.

Before turning to a consideration of the English painters of the period, it may be as well to look at the developments which were taking place across the Channel. There, less affected by trade depression than was England, and free from her political convulsions, the advance in technique which had characterized the late fourteenth century was maintained and carried still further. Under the patronage of the duc de Berri, there flourished the exquisite illuminator Paul of Limburg and his only less accomplished brothers Hans and Hermann, while Jan Maelweel lived until 1415. Independently of these masters, though doubtless linked with them by indirect channels, there was growing up the extraordinary art of the brothers Hubert and Jan van Eyck and of Robert Campin. The van Eycks did not of course invent the process of painting in oil, any more than John Dunstable invented counterpoint, but that they did introduce technical improvements can hardly be doubted. The growth of knowledge concerning their predecessors and contemporaries has destroyed some of their isolation, but nothing can take from them their proud position; we are nowadays by no means agreed as to the ultimate value of representational art and the capacity to reproduce, quasi-photographically, the features of persons and things, but that the van Eycks and Campin did initiate a new attitude to representation is certain. Brought up in the modern world of photography and exact perspective, one has to make mental adjustments when looking at earlier painting, but from van Eyck onwards it is a different matter; one is on known ground.

Within fifty years the methods of the advanced painters had so changed that in the work of the "Maître de Moulins" it is possible to feel something akin to shock at the extreme "naturalism" of faces and figures. But outside Flanders and Italy the transition was generally gradual, and in men such as Stephan Lochner of Cologne we recognize a half-way ground, meeting-place of the old and the new, of the "primitive" and the realistic. By the time Jan van Eyck died at the beginning of 1441, the art of north-western Europe had been profoundly modified, though it had not as a whole reached the threshold of the modern period. In England, however, the new influences had hardly penetrated at all; doubtless much allowance has to be made for the disturbed and depressed state of the country, but it is difficult on these grounds alone to explain why the close relations existing between England and the Netherlands, England and Burgundy, and England and North France, up to the 1440's, did not bring to our painting some reflection of the immense change which was taking place within a few miles of our coast. It seems that we must allow some weight to the innate conservatism of the English character when left to its own devices; under the pressure of a great connoisseur such as Richard II or Henry III, the English were able to put themselves in the forefront of the movement; take away the stimulus and they remained content to amble along at their old accustomed pace.

It is naturally difficult to assess the value of English art when it is certain that a very large proportion of the total output has been destroyed, but it seems unlikely that the losses of first-rank works, particularly works in the smaller and more portable kinds, would be proportional to the total destruction. The lack of really outstanding examples of English painting from the fifteenth century almost certainly implies that even when the country was filled to overflowing with wall- and panel-paintings, there was little that was first-rate, compared with the amazing progress just over the water. Of the little that is left to us, the "Four Scenes from the life of St. Etheldreda" belonging to the Society of Antiquaries, and formerly at Ely, is the most remarkable specimen; here the technique and general method of the Wilton Diptych, without its genius, survive, and the figures are competent and not lacking a certain naïve charm. Far higher in quality are the scene of Chaucer reading his poems to an audience of courtiers (in Corpus Christi College, Cambridge MS. 61), and the miniature of Hoccleve presenting his works to Prince Hal (in B.M. Arundel MS. 38). The latter certainly belongs to a date about 1412, but it is just possible that the Cambridge illumination was made before 1400. The manuscript was probably written for one of the family of John of Gaunt, and it seems significant that only the first miniature, a full-page scene, was completed, while the spaces for nearly a hundred more were left blank. One possible explanation of the facts would be to suppose the manuscript (Chaucer's *Troilus*) commissioned by Gaunt himself, and its illustration to have been interrupted by his death early in 1399, but it is possible that further examination of the extravagant costumes may deter-mine the date within definite and narrow limits. The background, of wellnigh Chinese fantasy, with its toy castles upon impossible crags, is quite unlike anything found elsewhere in English painting, and here again (and perhaps in the Hoccleve miniature) we seem to meet the influences

M

from the Low Countries and Rhineland typified in London by the work of Hermann Scheere and Herebrecht of Cologne.

There are remains of one or two Norwich paintings of around 1400, excellent of their kind, but betraying no awareness of the coming change; and there is the Coronation of the Virgin from Henry IV's tomb at Canterbury. This last undoubtedly belongs to the Royal School, of which the chief members at the time were Thomas Wright and Thomas Kent, who in 1413 were associated in the painting of banners with the arms of all the Kings of Christendom and other nobles of different kingdoms of the world, to stand round the hearse of Henry IV at Canterbury on the anniversary of his death. Wright had in 1400 been in touch with his predecessor Thomas Litlington, who thenceforth disappears from the scene, and Kent also first appears in 1400, and in 1403 was paid £5 for painting a chariot ordered for Philippa, the King's daughter. Wright and a number of other citizens were in 1422 declared creditors of William Lord Botreux for sums totalling over £300 and after Wright's death in 1424 his widow Alice gave receipts for the balance of the money, but there is no clue to the services which had been rendered by Wright to Lord Botreux. (See Appendix V, i.)

Another painter in the King's service was William Stone, also of London, who appears in 1406 and 1411, and in 1415 was painting the King's great ship with swans and antelopes and divers arms, and with the royal motto called "*une sanz pluis*", for which work he received £7 6s. 8d. In 1416 the Wardens of the London Painters' Company were Thomas Richer and John Northfolk (perhaps one of the leaders of the Norwich school); Richer was certainly one of the most influential London painters of the time, for when the Crown Inn at Rochester needed two signs in 1423–4, it was "Thomas Ryche" of London who painted them with angels and pictures for £8 6s. 8d. the pair, while the panels were made by Robert Cony, the King's Joiner. Richer continues to be mentioned from time to time as a London painter, and in 1429 he and Gilbert Melton, a London limner, were signally honoured by being ordered to go overseas in the retinue of the Duke of Bedford; there seems to be more than a possibility that they were the "ij peyntrys" who some eighteen months later were entertained to dinner by the Earl of Warwick at Rouen, on 22 April 1431, for later in that year Richer reappears in his old haunts, and in 1432 for some unexplained reason made a gift of all his goods and chattels to Henry Bourchier, Lord of Eu, Sir John Cornwall, Lord Fanhope, John Bekyngton, draper, and John Edward, tailor, after which surprising action he disappears from view.

In spite of the decline of art consequent upon the usurpation of 1399, there is much interesting information as to the patronage of the minor arts exercised by Henry IV, who was in his personal expenditure extremely lavish. During his first year his purchases included rich cloths and cushions worked with his arms and livery collar, a seal made by John Edmunds, citizen and goldsmith of London, for £13 10s., and £7 paid to John Norman, a London wheelwright, who had repaired divers chariots,

101 Walberswick Church: Tower, 1426–
Designers: Adam Powle and Richard Russell

100 Helmingham Church: Tower, 1487–1543.
Designer: Thomas Aldrych

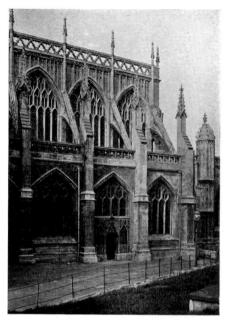

102 Adderbury Church:
Chancel interior

103 Bristol: St. Mary Redcliffe Church,
c. 1375–1400. Bristol school, perhaps by
Nicholas Waleys

104   Adderbury Church: Chancel, 1408–18. Designer: Richard Winchcombe

"whyrlys" and wheels for the use of Isabella, Richard II's Queen. He retained in his service Stephen Vyve, an embroiderer who had been sent to Richard II by the duc de Berri, and in 1401 paid £250 for eight collars purchased from Theodore the goldsmith of London and sent to the King's sister the Queen of Portugal, for the King's infant nephew. This would have been Prince Henry "the Navigator", or one of his brothers. In the following year Everard Gamenshede and Albright, goldsmiths of the city of London, received £79 for two tablets delivered to the King's sons John and Humphrey (afterwards Dukes of Bedford and Gloucester) to be presented by them to the Queen (their stepmother Joan of Navarre), and in 1406 Christopher Tildesley, the King's Goldsmith, executed the large order for jewelled collars already mentioned. In 1408 Drew Barentyn, another well-known London goldsmith, was paid no less than £550 for a collar of gold garnished with precious stones. Expenditure on jewellery was not so heavy under Henry V, but in February 1415 William Randolf was paid nearly £1,000 for 12 new dishes of pure gold, 4 dozen chargers of silver, and 8 dozen silver dishes for the King's use, and in 1418-19 another goldsmith, Conus Melver, received over £60 for making a silver image of the Blessed Virgin for St. George's Chapel at Windsor.

From the melancholy general picture of English art between 1400 and 1425, the remains of our music form a welcome relief. The musical

FIG. 105. *Go hert hurt with adversite*, song of the early fifteenth century.

harvest corresponding to the age of Chaucer came a generation late, and though its origins must have owed a great deal to Richard II, himself a composer, it is with Henry V and with his brother John, Duke of Bedford, that the English school of musicians is particularly identified. The best-known work is the stirring hymn for Henry's victory at Agincourt, but fine as this is, it has not the musical importance of a very considerable body of contemporary pieces, both religious and secular in character.

"Alas departynge" has already been referred to as an unforgettably lovely two-part song, and "Now wolde I fayne" and "Go Hert hurt with Adversite" are others which still have an instantaneous appeal; many more yield their delights only after the ear has become attuned to the feeling of the period. On the boundary of secular and religious music are the carols—and a very large proportion of old English carols, including the best of them, date from this period: "There is no rose of such virtue" might be described as the best of all, if there were not, among so many, the risk of an undeserved slight falling upon its equals—among the carols there should be something for all tastes.

Musically the most important works are preserved in two main sources: the first is now known as the Old Hall MS. and is definitely of English origin and history. The other great collection, in which English work occurs together with that of Continental composers, consists of the Trent Codices. Several other Continental collections contain English music, notably a manuscript at Modena, of which a transcription in score by W. B. Squire is in the British Museum. Both the English and foreign sources give, for the first time, the composers' names, and it is thus possible to trace the careers of some of these men, though their individual styles have as yet received comparatively little attention.

The Old Hall MS. is of unusual importance and not least in interest is the fact that it contains three compositions, a *Sanctus*, a *Benedictus*, and a *Gloria in Excelsis*, attributed to a "Roy Henry". The *Sanctus* is full of expression and grace, and its melancholy has been thought to confirm the usual identification of its author with Henry VI. In recent years Dr. Manfred Bukofzer has questioned this identification, mainly upon musical grounds, and would substitute Henry V. That Henry V, and not his son, was in fact the composer, seems to be all but certain on purely historical grounds. In the first place, the manuscript had some close connexion with at least two of the other composers whose works are included: "Damett" and "N. Sturgeon". Now on palaeographical grounds the manuscript itself (apart from its contents) belongs to the first rather than to the second half of the fifteenth century, and a period later than the reign of Henry VI (†1471) is absolutely excluded. This rules out one of the two candidates for identity with "Damett", viz. Thomas Danet (or Damet), a canon of Windsor who flourished in the reign of Edward IV and died on 18 September 1483. The other suggestion, generally accepted, puts forward the name of Thomas Damett (or Danett), who was "one of the chaplains of the king's chapel" when on 16 February 1431 he was presented to a prebend in St. George's Chapel in Windsor

Castle; on 5 August 1436, this prebend, and the prebend of Rugmere in St. Paul's Cathedral, London, which had been held by Damett, were granted to others, but no specific statement is made as to Damett's decease. His will was, however, proved in the following year (see Appendix V, ii), when Henry VI was a boy of sixteen; that a mere boy should have written the "Roy Henry" pieces is most improbable, and we are left with the alternatives: either the "Roy Henry" pieces are to be altogether dissociated from those of Damett, or their author was King Henry V. Thomas Damett's association with Henry V is moreover proven, for it was that king who presented him to the prebend of Rugmere in St. Paul's, where he was installed on 22 November 1418. He was also Rector of Stockton in Wiltshire from 1413 to 1435.

The "N. Sturgeon" of the manuscript has likewise been identified as Nicholas Sturgeon, who held various prebends, including one in St. George's, Windsor, from 1442, and died in 1454, but he too first appears in connexion with Henry V, who on 3 December 1419 granted him a pension: the grant specifies him as "one of the clerks of the Chapel Royal", which leaves no doubt as to his identity. Of the other names which occur several cannot be traced, but Cooke is as likely to be the "John Cook one of the clerks of the King's Chapel" who had preferment from Henry V in 1414 and again in 1417 (and who may have died in 1419), as his namesake who was a clerk of the Chapel from 1429 to 1455, and Forrest may well have been John Forrest, Dean of Wells from 1425 to his death in 1446, who had held various prebends at Lincoln from 1394 onwards, was Archdeacon of Surrey in 1414, and between 1415 and 1419 was holding prebends at Lichfield and York. The work of Forrest and a motet, inserted anonymously but known to be by Dunstable, were added to the manuscript after its substantial completion, and this also has been regarded as presumptive evidence that the original compilation took place before Dunstable was famous.

Forrest occurs again in the Modena manuscript, along with thirty pieces by Dunstable and a collection of other works by Englishmen, whose names include "Priamor" and "Polumier". There can be little doubt that we have here the attempts of a foreign scribe to cope with the names of John Pyamour and John Plummer, who were successively masters of the boys of the Chapel Royal. Pyamour, "one of the clerks of the Chapel Royal", first appears on 16 September 1419, when Henry V, who was with his army before Gisors, found time to grant him a corrody at the convent of Luffield, Northants, and next January Pyamour was commissioned to impress boys for the Chapel and take them across to the King in Normandy. In 1427 John Pyamour, clerk, went to France in the retinue of the Duke of Bedford, while on 31 July 1431 he is referred to as deceased in a new grant of the corrody which he had held at Luffield. John Plummer appears in 1440, was given commissions to impress boys for the Chapel in 1443 and 1444, and in 1445 was granted "the teaching, rule and governance" of the boys of the Chapel, with next year a grant of a yearly fee of forty marks for these "daily labours".

Apart from these men whose compositions are extant, there is abundant evidence of Henry V's interest in music in the pensions he granted to others of the chapel clerks, for example to Richard Blithe in 1419 and to William Gloucester in 1420, besides the numerous references, collected by Grattan Flood, to the King's special musical services. In October and November 1419, £5 for passage money was granted to Walter Wodehall, one of the organists of St. Paul's Cathedral ordered to proceed to Normandy to serve in the King's Chapel, and similar sums were allowed to a chaplain and four singing clerks. The Duke of Bedford continued this musical tradition, and in 1427 took to France not only John Pyamour, but also John Estcourt, Dean of the Royal Free Chapel of St. Martin's-le-Grand, and a certain "John Farley of Broghton, Lincoln, clerk, alias of Lyston, Devon, clerk, alias of St. Mary Ottery, Devon, clerk, alias of London, organ-player". Estcourt died before the end of the year, and Master Alan Kirketon became Dean of the Chapel maintained in Paris by the Duke as Regent of France. In 1428 Kirketon became a doctor of laws at Paris University and held several prebends in France, including a canonry at Rouen; he appears after Bedford's death as Rector of St. Peter, Oundle, Northants, and visited France in 1441 and 1442.

Except for a motet added to the Old Hall MS. without composer's name, the work of John Dunstable is practically unrepresented in English musical manuscripts. His career is most mysterious, for no specific facts of his life are known; he died on 24 December 1453 and was buried in St. Stephen's, Walbrook, in London, where his epitaph existed until the church was destroyed in the Great Fire of 1666. He is mentioned as setting an example followed by the Burgundian composers Guillaume Dufay and Gilles Binchois (who had lived in Paris under English rule), in the poem "Le Champion des Dames" written by Martin le Franc in 1443, and in one of two surviving manuscripts which once belonged to him is a Latin inscription "This book belonged to John Dunstable 'cn' musician of the Duke of Bedford". The contraction "cn" possibly represents "canonicus", a canon, and it is tempting to conjecture that his later years may have been spent as an Austin Canon of Dunstable Priory, known there perhaps under an alias which has up to the present concealed his identity from the prying eyes of historians. Another possibility is that he was a canon of some French or Burgundian church, but if so it is surprising that the fact should not be known, for there would be little likelihood of his appearing abroad except under the name by which he was famous.

If "cn" is correctly understood as implying canonical status, the composer and mathematician can hardly have been identical with the John Dunstable, who with his wife Margaret, had a grant of the manor of Bradfield in Cottered, Hertfordshire, in 1449, from Richard Whaplode, vicar of Sandon and Steeple Morden, and who, with his wife and another John Dunstable, gentleman,[1] obtained properties in the city of London in 1445; the John Dunstaple "armiger" who in 1441-2, was plaintiff in a suit

[1] Who, however, might possibly be the musician.

106 Oxford: Divinity Schools, 1430–55; vault 1480–83
Designer: Richard Winchcombe; of vault: William Orchard

107 Beverley: St. Mary's Church. West Front, c. 1380–1411. Nave and Tower, 1520–24

touching lands in Bassingbourne, Steeple Morden, and Litlington, Cambs.; the John Donstaple "armiger", nobleman, of the diocese of Lincoln, who had an indult of Plenary Indulgence in 1434; or the John Dunstable of "Kambregishere" who in the fifteenth century was assigned the arms: Sable a chevron ermine between three staples argent. Moreover, there is evidence that this layman did not die until 1459, six years later than the composer. Dunstable was almost certainly a cleric, but there seems to be a distinct possibility that his contemporary, the great composer and theoretician Lionel Power, was identical with the esquire of that name "of Canterbury" who in 1438 made a general release of all personal actions to one Thomas Ragoun, acknowledgment of the release being made in 1444. Canterbury was the nearest cathedral city to the Continent, and it was abroad that Power acquired his great reputation —coupled with the extremely rare combination of names there would seem to be in this a basis for further investigation.

To return to Dunstable: in the present meagre state of knowledge we can postulate a musical career lasting from the early years of the century to about 1435, the year of the Duke of Bedford's death, which was followed by the English withdrawal from Paris and the breaking of the alliance with Burgundy. These events could well account for Dunstable's retirement to England, where he apparently spent the remainder of his days in the study of astronomy and mathematics. Le Franc's remarks of 1443 show that his musical achievements had already won wide recognition more than ten years before his death, and the supposition that his music belongs to an earlier period than his scientific studies receives support from the fact of the survival of his music exclusively abroad, and of his astronomical treatises in England, where he died. When all has been said, less is known of Dunstable than of any first-rank genius in world history since the fifth century B.C., and it is an ironic commentary upon our attitude to genius that it is exclusively from foreign sources that we hear of Dunstable's far-reaching influence, and exclusively from other foreign sources that we derive his surviving musical output.

IV

INDIAN SUMMER

BETWEEN the premature frosts which closed the short summer of Plantagenet England in 1399, and the winter tempest of civil discord which swept the country from 1455 to 1471, came an Indian summer of the arts. This revival was due in the first place to Henry V, and after him to his two brothers and to his son, the pious and genuinely art-loving Henry VI. Henry of Monmouth had been a boy of eleven at the time of his father's banishment in 1398, and had been taken under Richard II's personal care. He seems to have been treated with kindness, and though taken to Ireland, a potential hostage, in the following year, Richard made no attempt to use this leverage against Bolingbroke. Henry V did not forget this generosity, to which he owed his life, and among his first acts as King was the reburial of Richard in the Abbey—in sentiment the younger Henry had more in common with Richard than with his own father. This bright promise was not fulfilled, for Henry V must needs renew the unfounded claims of his great-grandfather, and invade France; all the hopes founded upon Richard's entente with Charles VI were disappointed, and five centuries were to pass before the bitter breach was healed through the generous statesmanship of Edward VII.

In Europe, as a whole, there was a breath of hope; in 1414 the Council of Constance met to attempt a solution of the fantastic co-existence of rival Popes. Since the short-lived reunion of Eastern and Western churches, once again sundered in 1282, there had not been even a serious attempt to make common Christian cause against the Asiatic invasion of Europe. Deceptive as were the appearances favourable to unity, a brief period of brighter expectation broke the gloom of a moribund continent. A precursor of this new spirit was the visit of the Eastern Emperor Manuel II to the West in 1400, when he actually met Henry IV in England; his Western rival, Sigismund, spent two years from the opening of the Council of Constance in a vain effort to bring together the warring princes of France and England, and the Burgundian and Armagnac factions. Though he met with no success, the passage of his train through France and England must have brought about interesting personal encounters, particularly as among his entourage was the great German poet-composer, Oswald von Wolkenstein (c. 1377–1445), whose long sojourns in Italy had important results for the development of Northern music.

In 1414 Alexandre de Berneval, the principal master mason of Rouen, had visited England to buy alabaster; he sailed by long sea passage to Newcastle, and thence made his way overland to Chellaston, where he transacted his business with Thomas Prentis, the alabasterman whose

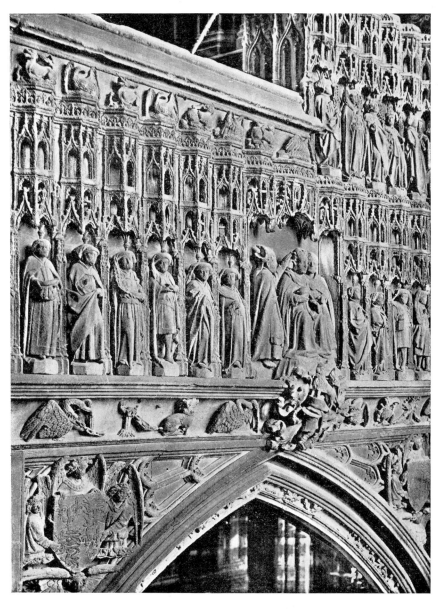

108   Westminster Abbey: Henry V's Chantry, *c.* 1422–50.
Designer: John Thirsk; sculptor: possibly John Massingham

109 Oxford, All Souls College: Gate Tower, 1438–43.
Designer: Richard Chevynton; sculptor: John Massingham

tomb of Ralph Greene still stands in Lowick Church, Northants (65). Berneval a few years later was one of Henry V's subjects, and in 1419 was appointed master mason of the King's works at Rouen, where the palace was about to be rebuilt. Henry V's artistic activities were naturally more in evidence in Normandy than in England; he was anxious to make a good showing in his regained Duchy, and at Caen for example, in 1418, he had the castle gardens laid out; but he did not altogether forget England, and besides providing funds for the resumption of work at Westminster Abbey, arranged for a supply of stone from Caen for the Abbey and for the Charterhouse, which he had founded by his palace of Shene in Surrey.

I have already mentioned the visit of the London painters Thomas Richer and Gilbert Melton to France in 1429, and it is at least possible that the John Stratford of London who went overseas in 1436 in the retinue of Sir Thomas Kyriel, the captain of Gournay, was identical with the John Stratford, citizen and painter of London, who was already a man of some standing in 1441, in 1447 was paid £10 by the hands of his wife for painting the King's barge with the arms of the King and Queen, and in 1461 was granted the office of King's Painter by Edward IV. Other comings and goings, besides the trading voyages of merchants, are marked by the issue of protections to English travellers, and of safe conducts to foreigners wishing to visit England. While Caen stone had been brought to England in Henry V's time, and continued to be a large import even after the loss of Normandy, stone and masons from Doncaster were ordered to be taken to the works of Calais in 1441, and in the previous year the Mayor of Norwich had been ordered to send to Calais certain men of Norwich skilled in carpentry.

In the other direction, Henry VI's marriage to Margaret of Anjou in 1445, and the Queen's subsequent solemn coronation, brought a swarm of overseas visitors, among them five minstrels of the King of Sicily (title of Margaret's father, the "good King René"), and two of the Duke of Milan. King René was the outstanding art patron of the age, and was himself a poet and musician; while a prisoner at Dijon in 1431 he learnt the art of glass-painting, and executed portraits on glass of Philip the Good, Duke of Burgundy, his captor, and of his predecessor, John the Fearless. René's importance as a painter has doubtless been exaggerated, but there can be no question of the immense significance of his Court, holding the balance between the arts of Italy, of France, and of the North.

From Constantinople came two Greeks, Andronicus and Alexius Effomato, workers in damascene gold, who were given a safe conduct for their stay in England at the beginning of 1445, probably in connexion with work for the marriage festivities, and at the end of 1446 Jacques Cordis, silversmith to the King of France, was permitted to sell goods to foreigners in London during the year 1447. Six years later the influx of artisans from Central Europe began with the permission granted to Michael Gosselyn and numerous other miners from Bohemia, Hungary, and Austria, who came to England to work in the King's mines. After

N

the disastrous interlude of the civil wars, we shall see that large numbers of Germans and Netherlanders, painters, sculptors, glaziers, and others, flocked to England to take advantage of the high standard of living and, no doubt, of the English shortage of first-rate artists. It was not that the wars actually destroyed the artists, but that they extinguished for a generation the demand for objects of the finest sorts.

The Wars of the Two Roses were still hidden in the future: in 1420 men could believe in a coming era of peace and plenty—even many Frenchmen, flattered by the emphasis laid on the "right line of St. Louis", and disgusted by the Dauphin's complicity in the murder of John the Fearless of Burgundy in 1419, were prepared to accept Henry V as Regent and his son as King. Seen in the light cast by later events, it is obvious to us that Edward III and Henry V were utterly in the wrong, and that the French resurgence brought about by Joan of Arc was, if a miracle, at any rate deservedly so. At the time, any honourable grounds for peace were acceptable to the great masses of both peoples, worn out by three generations of intermittent warfare. Lydgate went to Paris, where he made a verse translation of Laurence Callot's poem-pedigree of Henry VI, composed at the behest of the Duke of Bedford, Regent of France. Later on, Lydgate produced the official verses for Henry's coronation: the charming roundel:

> Reioice, ye reames of Englond & of Fraunce,
> A braunche that sprang oute of the floure-de-lys,
> Blode of Seint Edward and Seint Lowys,
> God hath this day sent in gouernaunce.
> God of nature hath yoven him suffisaunce,
> Likly to atteyne to grete honure and pris.
> O hevenly blossóme, o budde of all plesaunce,
> God graunt the grace for to ben als wise
> As was thï fader by circumspect advise,
> Stable in vertue, withoute variaunce.

and a series of verses for the three "subtelties" which concluded the three courses of the banquet—the manuscript fortunately preserves the menu of each course, as well as the verses (see Appendix IV).

Following the example set by Richard II, state banquets were the occasion for amazing displays of culinary art—no doubt the *Forme of Cury*, the cookery book "compiled of the chief masters cooks of king Richard the Second . . . the which was accounted the best and royallest viander of all christen Kings", still held the field, as *Mrs. Glass* did in the eighteenth and *Mrs. Beeton* in the nineteenth century. This great original in the science of household management was made with the assistance of "masters of physic and of philosophy that dwelt in his (Richard's) court", and one of its authors was probably John Goodrich, king's cook from 1363 to 1393, who died about 1398. Its receipts are not exclusively for the kitchens of royalty and nobility, for it begins with a large selection of "common pottages and common meats", though by the time Poached Eggs had been reached, one feels that the masters of philosophy rather than the cooks were responsible:

Take eggs, and break them in scalding hot water, and when they are boiled enough, take them up, and take yolks of eggs and raw milk and swing them together, and do thereto powder, ginger, saffron, and salt; set it over the fire, and let it not boil and take eggs boiled and cast the liquor "onoward", and serve it forth.

Henry's English coronation at Westminster took place on 6 November 1429, but he had to wait just over two years before his Paris coronation was arranged. A good part of the interval was spent by the King and Court in France, and the manuscript account book of the Earl of Warwick, Lieutenant of France and Normandy,[1] gives glimpses of the courtly life at Rouen in the year of the King's stay in France. On 6 April 1431 the Earl had to entertain the King with the two Dukes (presumably Bedford and York), two Barons, eight Knights, twenty-four Esquires and eighteen grooms who came "to drink" and then went away; they had not to be supplied with a meal. The King, with a slightly smaller retinue, came again two days later and seven times between 18 April and 12 August. After this the King moved to Paris, where preparations were at last being made for the coronation, and on 1 December the Countess of Warwick with her household started towards Paris by barge, occupying a week on the journey, which had to follow the indirect and winding course of the Seine. At Paris the Warwicks kept open house for the tailors and furriers of the city who were working on the King's robes, and for shipmen, bargees, burgesses, minstrels, merchants from Bruges and elsewhere, and many other representatives of the throng of visitors to Paris.

It is impossible here to detail all the stages of the Countess's return journey to Rouen, but soon after both Earl and Lady returned to England, and the records are particularly interesting as they give details of an early journey by wheeled vehicle, overland from Rouen to Calais, the stages being at Auffay, Dieppe, Eu, Abbeville, Rue, Montreuil, and Boulogne, leaving Rouen after breakfast on 12 January 1432 and reaching Calais in time for midday dinner on the 23rd, the journey time including days spent at Dieppe and Abbeville. The Earl's chariot and its repairs are often mentioned; it seems to have had four wheels and to have been drawn by five horses. Its general form may have been similar to that of the famous chariot depicted in the Luttrell Psalter of a century earlier, but probably there had been notable improvements in construction during that period, and there is reason to think that the Earl himself, and not merely his womenfolk, travelled by this means. On the journey to Paris, two chariots were taken by "schoute" up the river for the coronation and brought back again later, and a third was made at Rouen soon afterwards. These are all referred to as "the lord's chariots", while on the journey made by the Countess from London to Warwick by way of Reading, Burford, Tewkesbury, and Worcester, in the spring of 1432, her conveyance is termed "the lady's chariot" on more than one occasion. By 1395 there had been regular carriers from Oxford to London, Winchester, and

---

[1] It is surprising that this very important manuscript has not been published; Mr. E. G. Tibbits's projected edition deserves eager support.

Newcastle-on-Tyne, and although water transport was cheaper where it
was available, and riding was swifter, the great general increase in the
luxury of courts during the late fourteenth century is likely to have broken
down the prejudice against the use of the "ignoble" carriage by men.
It is known that the Emperor Frederick III employed a closed carriage
as early as 1474, and it would not be surprising if the old manners had
broken down some generations earlier.

It is of course necessary to guard against importing modern ideas into
the Middle Ages, but there is also a contrary danger: that of supposing
bygone ages to differ from our own in some essential way. It is particularly perilous to envisage the fourteenth and fifteenth centuries as lacking
sophistication; their civilization was not ours, but it was a rich and complicated one nevertheless. Lydgate, in his humorous *London Lickpenny*
drew a picture of mercenary dealings which is universal in its application,
from ancient Babylon, through the classic capital of which it was said
"Omnia venalia Romae", down to the present day. And on the credit
side he limned a busy world which was not so very different in kind from
the one we know:

> Famous marchauntys, that ferre cuntrees ryde,
>   With al ther greete rychesse and wynnynges,
> And artificerys, that at hom abyde,
>   So ferre castyng in many sundry thynges,
>   And been expert in wondirful konnynges,
> Of dyvers crafftys tavoyden al errour;
>   What may avaylle al your ymagynynges,
> Withoute proporciouns of weyghte and iust mesour?
>
> Rekne up phesyk with all ther letuaryes,
>   Grocerys, mercerys, with ther greet habundaunce,
> Expert surgeyns, prudent potecaryes,
>   And all ther weyghtes peysed in ballaunce,
>   Masouns, Carpenterys, of Yngelond and of Fraunce,
> Bakerys, browsterys, vyntenerys, with fresshe lycour,
>   All set at nought to rekne in substaunce,
> Yiff peys or weyghte doo lakke, or iust mesour.

Or, again, we find him reckoning up the sorts of "Cunning", that is
Knowledge, pure and applied:

> Whom folowyd Konnyng with hys genalogy—
> That ys to sey, Gramer, and Sophystry,
>   Philosophy Naturall, Logyk, & Rethoryk,
> Arsmetry, Geometry with Astronomy,
>   Canon & Cyuyle, melodyous Musyk,
>   Nobyll Theology, and Corporall Physyk,
>   Moralizacion of Holy Scripture,
>   Profounde Poetry and Drawyng of Picture——

Elsewhere he could run through the gamut of human experience in
search of proof that "Every thing draweth to his Semblable"—philosophers, gentlemen, merchants, musicians, painters, pie-bakers, prelates,
"plummers on stieplis and towris clymming aloft", broderers, beggars,
the turfman digging his turves and "the famous clerk" who "hathe ioye

of his librarye, as for tresore to him mooste acceptable"—all these and many more were pressed into the service of poetry by Lydgate's wellnigh endless patience. Or he would change his note, and in the bitterest pessimism declare the opposite: that things go by contraries, "the more I go, the further I am behynde", and concludes that:

> Thus al the world stant in variaunce:
> Late men dispute, whethir this be fortune?
> No man so loose, but he is tied with a luyne.

In this vein too is his haunting ballade, "That now is Hay some-tyme was Grase', in spite of its occasion: 'the commaundement of the Quene Kateryn as in here sportes she wallkyd by the medowes that were late mowen in the monthe of Iulij". When all of Lydgate's lines had been written, some 150,000 of them, he probably (for who has read them all?) never wrote one which more completely expressed the sadness of his century than one in this poem: "'Chekemate to beawtye,' seyth rymplyd age."

With the largest output in the language, Lydgate is by no means our greatest poet; but he is very far from being our worst, and he usually escaped being merely commonplace; there is an undercurrent of "sadness", in its old sense of solemnity, which gives strength and dignity, and he had Shakespeare's happy gift of using proverbs of hoary age with a fresh grace. Though it is anachronistic to describe Lydgate as England's Poet Laureate, he undoubtedly held a like position, provided verse for official occasions over a long period, and was certainly the chief Court poet from the death of Gower in 1408 until his own, at a date roughly coincident with the loss of the French provinces in the early 1450's. In spite of his monastic career, his knowledge of the Court and his stay in France afforded him wide opportunities for observation, and his mellowness and broad field of learning gave him a position in English letters almost comparable to that of Johnson in eighteenth-century London: through its prolonged distillation in the alembic of Lydgate's mind the transitional English of Chaucer became a modern language.

Holding a position in architecture somewhat analogous to Lydgate's in literature was Thomas Mapilton, King's Chief Mason from 1421 until his death in 1438. His family probably derived from the Derbyshire hamlet of Mappleton, close to Ashbourne and only five miles from Yeaveley, the almost certain source of Henry Yevele's family. John Mapilton is found as a marbler of London at the end of the fourteenth century, and died in 1407, and as is likely in the case of Yevele, he may have trained as a tomb-carver in the alabaster district near Tutbury. As early as the middle of the thirteenth century the family of "de Mapelton" occurs in the Ashbourne district, and several different branches of the family existed in 1300. We cannot therefore press very far the identity of surname between John and Thomas, but their common connexion with stone-working suggests a close relationship. Thomas first appears as the Master Mason of Durham Cathedral from 1408 to 1416, during the building of the cloisters, which had been begun by John Lewyn in 1390.

After spending eight years at Durham, Mapilton came to London, where he was described as "citizen and mason" in 1417; he had evidently entered the royal service and was closely associated with Stephen Lote, whose work on the tomb of the Duke of York he arranged to continue, in return for a rent-charge of 13*s.* 4*d.* for four years left him in Lote's will. Shortly before Lote's death in the winter of 1417–18, Mapilton was made co-executor of the will, and received a number of bequests: "my whole bed in my chamber at 'Schen' (Shene Palace) and all patterns that be there", a bed of "tapisserwerk" with a coverlet, and all of Lote's belongings from his kitchen and room in London. Mapilton was also to take over the unexpired term of John Studley, one of Lote's apprentices. The bequest of Lote's patterns shows that Mapilton inherited the "goodwill" and traditions of the practice established by Yevele and which had devolved upon Lote.

When Lote made a codicil to his will on 7 December 1417, in the "King's new lodge at Portsmouth", Mapilton was one of the witnesses, and soon after Lote's death, on 6 March 1418, Mapilton and Robert Rodyngton were commissioned to impress eight stone-cutters and to bring them beyond the seas to the King's presence with all possible speed. William Colchester was appointed King's Master Mason in Lote's place, but he was probably an old man, and such active work as going on campaign in Normandy would seem to have devolved on Mapilton. Now if Mapilton was retained by the King in Normandy until the peace of 1420, there is a possibility that he went very much farther. In 1417 the wardens of the works at Florence Cathedral agreed to the suggestion of Filippo Brunelleschi, that they should request the assistance of architects from France, Germany, England, and Spain, as well as from all parts of Italy, to determine the method to be adopted in vaulting the great central space of the Duomo. Directions were given to the Florentine merchants resident abroad, who were commissioned to spend any amount of money "to obtain the principal, most experienced and gifted men" of each country. After long delays, the body of architects met at Florence in 1420, and if the merchants followed out their instructions, Thomas Mapilton should have been of their number.[1]

Whether or no Mapilton actually travelled in Italy, he was promoted to the office of King's Master Mason on 6 June 1421, after Colchester's death, and about this time he was also called in by the authorities at Canterbury Cathedral, as architect for the works of the new south-west tower. Perhaps while travelling to Canterbury he arranged to advise the wardens of Rochester Bridge upon its repair in 1422, and in 1429 he undertook the rebuilding of St. Stephen's Church, Walbrook, in London, later superseded by Wren's masterpiece. The chief promoter of this church building project was Sir Robert Chichele, a wealthy London grocer and brother to the Archbishop, whose cathedral was in Mapilton's charge. Mapilton was one of the eight persons who laid memorial stones

[1] Guasti (*La Cupola di Santa Maria del Fiore*, 1857, p. 193), unable to discover corroborative documents, refers the whole story to "unfounded popular tradition".

in the foundations, and in the same year he was called as far as Bury St. Edmunds to survey the great western tower of the Abbey, approaching collapse. Throughout Mapilton's career he appears as a personage of distinction, and towards the end he joined the influential fraternity of Our Lady of the Assumption, maintained by the London Skinners, in 1436. Two years later he died, shortly before St. Stephen's, Walbrook, was completed, and Robert Westerley was appointed Chief Royal Mason in his stead.

The south-west tower of Canterbury, with its fine clustered pinnacles, is Mapilton's principal extant work, and it had a very marked influence upon the later towers of Kent and in the Home Counties generally. The summons to Bury suggests fame as a tower-builder, and he may have been personally responsible for other works now lost, and of which no record remains. Somewhat barren detail notwithstanding, Mapilton maintained the skill in composition which marks the Royal School and, though he died before the short cultural revival of Henry VI's maturity, he deserves credit for the fact that when the demand for their services came, there were artists and craftsmen trained and ready.

In assigning credit to Mapilton, I refer mainly to the London or Court School, for the fifteenth century saw the flowering of a number of distinctive local styles. The smaller churches and houses are distinctive of their regions, which quite often coincide roughly with boundaries of the ancient counties or sees. But these small buildings were for the most part designed and built by local men, sometimes under the supervision of a master from the nearest corporate town, or occasionally brought from a greater distance, presumably for personal reasons which now escape us. This vernacular architecture was endowed with remarkable vitality, and long survived the parent, more highly developed arts of the palace and great church or college, with which we are now more particularly concerned. What strikingly emerges from a large proportion of the country building contracts is that the local men undertook to copy, quite without apology or hesitation, admired works at a lesser or greater distance. For this reason, the real changes in architectural currency are marked in the first place by the greater works, carried out by skilled artists for wealthy patrons, determined to be in the forefront of fashion.

Of these greater men, many incidental records survive, and here it is only possible to deal with a few from each region. At this period, the important areas are five in number: London (with the Home Counties and Canterbury); East Anglia (with twin centres at Ely and Norwich); York and the North; Oxford and the West Midlands; Somerset and the West. This list is largely arbitrary, and could be indefinitely enlarged by addition and by the splitting apart of groups into their smaller component areas: thus Chester was the centre of a marked North-western style; Lincoln mediates between East Anglia and York; Bristol, Gloucester, Coventry and Oxford fought (metaphorically speaking) for supremacy in the Midlands and West, and so forth. The interdependence of all the regions except that of the North is noteworthy; hardly any striking innovations could be made by one school without a rapid spread taking place, and it will only be when the whole vast output of Perpendicular buildings has been examined in the light of positive (and not presumptive) dating, that the history of its progressive stages will be told. The major discovery of the age, that of fan-vaulting, did not penetrate to the North, but in Southern England it enjoyed an extended vogue, though very few works of large size were vaulted in this manner—but then there were not many large churches and chapels being built.

Among the London men not directly concerned with the King's works, John Croxton has already been mentioned, and another was Richard Beke, who worked at London Bridge from 1409 under John Clifford, whom he succeeded as Bridge Mason in 1417. When Mapilton (probably owing to an increasing amount of official work) gave up the post of consultant at Canterbury Cathedral, Beke succeeded him, and three years later, in 1435, left London to take up a permanent post in charge of the works of Christ Church, Canterbury. He was, however, recalled for consultation in 1438 by the London authorities, as the Bridge was in danger. For the remaining twenty years of his life (he died on 16 November 1458), Beke, so far as is known, fulfilled without interruption the regular demands of his post at Canterbury, where he was paid 4s. a week, and had also allowances of £1 a year for his house, 8s. for fuel, 10s. for clothes, and two pairs of hose, while he was insured even against ill-health by the provision in his agreement that if he should become unable "to be stere hym selft but for to lye stylle in hys bedde, or be privyd of hys bodyly sygzth and blynde" he should continue to receive all his allowances and half-pay.

John Thirsk, whose own name was originally Crowche, was a Yorkshireman, and most likely accompanied William Colchester on his return from York Minster to Westminster Abbey. Thirsk succeeded Colchester as Master Mason of the Abbey in 1420, and for many years continued the works of the nave and of Henry V's Chantry (108), while he also built the great reredos or screen behind the High Altar, completed in 1441. Though following the main outlines of the design as worked out by Yevele for the completion of the nave and west front, Thirsk shows markedly individual detail on the reredos, and though much restored, the canopied niches of the upper story of the west porch are probably his work. About 1448, on Henry VI choosing a position for his intended tomb in the Abbey, "oone callyd Thurske, that tyme beyng master-mason in the makyng of the Chapelle of King Henry the vth" came at the King's command "and in his presence with an instrument of iron whiche he browght with hym, markyd out the lengthe and brede of the saide sepulture there to be made. . . ." Another witness, deposing to this incident as evidence of Henry VI's intention of committing his saintly (and therefore valuable) bones to the Abbey, recollected that the instrument used was "an iron pykkes. Which done the said Kyng Henry seid to such as then there were present these wordes—'Forsoth and forsoth here is a good place for us'". Thirsk became Master Mason in Windsor Castle in June 1449, and died three years afterwards.

110 Sherborne Abbey from South-West, c. 1475–90. Designer: possibly William Smyth

112 Gloucester Cathedral: Lady Chapel, c. 1457–98

111 Sherborne Abbey: Presbytery, c. 1430–40

The Oxford and Cotswold school produced a number of men of distinction, successors to the Windsor, Winchester, and Wells traditions of William Wynford. Among them Richard Chevynton and Robert Janyns the elder are the most important: both were concerned with the building of All Souls College, Oxford, for Archbishop Chichele, Chevynton as master mason and Janyns as warden in constant supervision of the work, while Chevynton spent much of his time at the Burford quarries (**109**). The influence of Wynford's New College, both in planning and detail, is very evident, though the work shows an increased richness, reflecting to some extent the developments of the London tomb-masons and also the vivid detail of Somerset. Somerset influence may perhaps be accounted for if we accept the identity of the master carpenter at All Souls, John Branche, with the carpenter of the same name who took up the freedom of Wells in 1407, but the interval of over thirty years (All Souls was building from 1438 to 1443) renders the identity somewhat dubious. The fine roof of hammer-beam type, over the chapel, 70 feet long and 28 feet in span, is a worthy successor to the timber vaults of St. Stephen's Chapel and Winchester College, and the forerunner of the host of fine "angel" roofs of the rebuilt parish churches.

The London influences at All Souls are to be found in the plain window tracery and in the glass itself, by John Prudde, the King's glazier, and in the magnificent carved reredos and statuary by John Massingham, citizen and carver of London. The composition of the reredos shows a marked improvement upon that at New College, for the tiers of figures curve upwards to the middle instead of maintaining a level line. As has been previously mentioned, Massingham was probably trained as a carpenter by John Dobson, Hugh Herland's junior colleague, but his career as a carver is known only from three sets of references. In the first place he worked at All Souls, paid at the extremely high rate of 4s. 8d. a week, with board and lodging in addition; ten years later, in 1448-9, he was paid £10 for an image of the Blessed Virgin for Eton Parish Church—this image was made by him in London; lastly, in the years 1447-9 he received over £66 for work at the Beauchamp Chapel, Warwick, and in 1450 was to make the wooden pattern for the Earl of Warwick's effigy for the tomb within the chapel. This effigy was cast by William Austen, a London coppersmith, and Roger Webb, Warden of the Worshipful Company of Barber-Surgeons, was also engaged, apparently to tender expert advice on anatomical detail. The beautiful effigy, which still exists, is exceptionally lifelike in its details, and the veining of the hands is most delicately carried out (**2, 82**). From this work, and from the statue of Henry VI outside the main gateway of All Souls College (which Flaxman praised for its "purity of character and grace, and delicacy of workmanship") it is clear that Massingham was one of the great sculptors of his time, by no means an unworthy contemporary of Donatello.[1] A curious reference which probably alludes to a lost work of Massingham's was made by Isabel,

---

[1] One "Messyngham" was paid £7 13s. 4d. for painting the images of the new reredos of Winchester College Chapel in 1470-71. (Kirby: *Annals*, p. 52.)

o

widow of Richard Beauchamp, Earl of Warwick, in 1439, the year of her
husband's death. She desired that a statue should be made of herself
"all nakyd with her hair cast backward" according to the design and
model which Thomas Porchalion had for the purpose. It has been
suggested that Porchalion was the sculptor; this is extremely unlikely, as
Portaleyn or Porteheleyne, as he is variously called, was an esquire employed as a confidential and trusted agent by the Warwicks, and constantly busy on administrative business connected with the vast estates of
the family. Massingham is a much more likely candidate, in view of his
later association with the Earl's chantry chapel and memorial.

It seems not to have been suggested that Massingham may also have
been the sculptor of the groups and figures which adorn the Chantry of
Henry V in Westminster Abbey, but consideration of their style and
probable date, c. 1440–50, makes the attribution a likely one. It was
remarked by Lethaby that the work showed close observation of living
types, and it was precisely in this direction that Massingham's gifts lay.
The Chantry was, as we saw, a long time in building, though the curious
rather than beautiful iron screen was being finished by Roger Johnson,
of London, smith, in 1431. Thirsk, the master mason, was still engaged
on the work about 1448, and the preparation of the sculpture would
probably be one of the last jobs undertaken.

Robert Janyns, after the completion of All Souls, next appears at
Merton College in 1448, where he was in charge of the building of the
beautiful bell-tower, a genuine and original masterpiece (14). Early in
1449 he entered the King's service at Eton College, where he worked as
warden of the masons for fees of £10 a year. Undoubtedly a most gifted
man, he seems to have failed to reach any of the leading positions then
open to men of ability, but besides his existing work he is important as
the founder of a family of masons who carried on this branch of the
Oxford and royal traditions. Henry Janyns, probably his son, was the
first architect of Edward IV's new Chapel of St. George in Windsor
Castle, from 1475 to 1483, and a younger Robert, probably Henry's son,
was one of Henry VII's principal master masons.

Other Midland masons can only receive a brief mention: William
Horewode in 1434 undertook to build the nave and tower of Fotheringhay
Church, Northants, according to the design of the chancel already built,
with some specified variations. In certain clauses the "oversight of
master-masons of the countre" (i.e. district) suggests that Horewode was
himself a contractor pure and simple, and the design, which derives from
the London traditions, is probably to be attributed to one of the associates
of Lote and Mapilton. Perhaps of greater importance was the Hobbs
family of Gloucester: William Hobbys was in charge of repairs at
Gloucester Castle in 1441, and in 1455 John Hobbs, mason, was a tenant
of the Abbot of Gloucester in the parish of St. John; John contracted to
build a chantry chapel at the Black Friars of Worcester twenty years later.
It was at this period, the mid-fifteenth century, that Gloucester again
became the leading influence in the West Country, and we may possibly

114 Cambridge, King's College Chapel: West Front, 1446–
1515. Designer: Reginald Ely; of turrets and gable: John
Wastell

113 Windsor, St. George's Chapel: West Front, c. 1490–95.
Designer: probably Henry Janyns

115   Cambridge, King's College. Drawing, *c.* 1448, of projected tower.
Possibly by Reginald Ely

attribute to John Hobbs some part of the extensive works at Gloucester Abbey, including the tower, begun in 1450, and the Lady Chapel, which was carried on for some forty years from 1457 (**23, 112**). An alternative claimant as designer of the tower is the "John Gower" alleged by a traditional jingle as the builder not only of this but of Chipping Campden Church. The priory church at Great Malvern, whose tower closely follows that at Gloucester, was begun about 1450, and service was resumed in 1460, but completion was deferred by the civil wars.

The Western school provides several interesting names: Roger Growdon, who between 1449 and 1452 built the splendid tower at Totnes, Devon (**28**); and Richard Pope, freemason, who designed the sturdy central tower of Dunster Priory, erected by the local contractor, John Marys of Stogursey. But the true glory of the West is the anonymous presbytery of Sherborne Abbey, Dorset, with its magnificent vaulting, an individual blend of fan- and lierne-vault methods (**111**). The same principles were adopted later, with varied detail, for the nave vaults, and for vaults at Milton Abbey, Dorset, and in the tower of Wells Cathedral. The original design for the rebuilt choir must have been in existence by about 1430, but the rebuilding of the nave was not complete until 1490 —again an example of delay due to the disturbed state of the country. The Sherborne work is very distinctive, and must be the creation of a great master; it is quite possible that his name is known, but unconnected with any existing work through which the authorship of Sherborne could be traced.

At Norwich the outstanding figure is that of James Woderofe; with his brother John he was admitted to the freedom of Norwich in 1415, and both were working at the Cathedral five years later, when they received robes from the sacrist. James was master of the work of the great cloister in 1428, and brought the work to a conclusion in 1430. The keys of the cloister vault, with their fine carvings, are the work of Woderofe and his assistants John Horne and William Reppys, "gravour". In 1440 and later, Woderofe was working at the Cathedral, and to him can be attributed the partial transformation of the Norman west front, with its window closely following Yevele's great windows of Westminster Hall. Similarity of detail suggests the attribution to him of the rather earlier Erpingham Gate, built between 1411 and 1428. That Woderofe was a specialist of high standing is shown by the fact that in 1449 he was twice allowed generous sums for travelling from Norwich to the works of Eton College "with his gear", and in the following year had a reward of £7. Other East Anglian influences will be considered in connexion with Henry VI's great foundation at Cambridge.

Farther to the north, at Tattershall, Lincolnshire, Ralph Lord Cromwell, the Treasurer, was building an unusual palace-tower of brick; the bricks were made locally under the supervision of one Baldwin Docheman, who may have been a Fleming, but Dr. Douglas Simpson suggests, with perhaps greater plausibility, that he was a Hanseatic German, and points out the characteristic resemblances to work done in Prussia for the

Teutonic knights. Tattershall was in progress from 1433 to 1455, and is the prototype of much of the later brick architecture of Tudor times. At Louth, a great rebuilding of the church was going on, and with this John Porter may have had something to do; he was a prominent mason of Lincoln who was twice called to York Minster to give advice in 1450, took up the freedom of York in 1454, and was appointed Master Mason of the Minister there in 1456. He died in mid-winter of 1465–6, and in his will left legacies to churches at York and Lincoln and to the Gild of St. Mary at Louth.

The York school had declined since the advent of Perpendicular, for York itself had been especially hard hit by recurrent plagues, but we have already seen that splendid work had been done at Beverley, and later on at Hedon. At York Minster the chief works were the south-west tower, built 1432–42, and the central tower, whose construction was carried on over a period of many years after the initial work under William Colchester early in the century; the parapet was never finished (4). Thomas Pak, who took up the freedom of York in 1420, was the master during the building of the south-west tower, but the tower (or rather the pair, for the later northern twin is to the same design) though pleasantly proportioned, shows no improvement upon the towers of Beverley, which it closely follows. A fine vernacular work which still exists is the bridge at Catterick, built under the terms of a contract of 1421 by three masons, Thomas Ampilforde, John Garrett, and Robert Maunsell; here the precaution was taken of inserting the condition that the bridge was to be like that at Barnard Castle, deservedly famous for its strength and beauty. Before taking leave of York, mention must be made of the Guildhall, roofed in the ancient style with rows of timber posts instead of open trusses. The presence of certain corbels which have no function in the roof scheme adopted suggests that a trussed roof in one clear span of 43 feet was contemplated but abandoned. The mason was Robert Couper, admitted to the freedom in 1442; the work began early in 1448, and, as in so many other cases was delayed for many years before reaching completion about 1480. Couper died in 1459, by which time it seems probable that the roofing was in progress; the name of the carpenter is not certainly known, but at this period and until his death in 1466 the carpenter to the city was John Foulford. There is, however, evidence that the carvings (now destroyed) which formed the bosses of the roof, were the work of a number of hands.

Having made the circuit of the chief provincial schools, it is time to return to the great works which strike the keynote of the whole period: Henry VI's collegiate foundations at Eton and at Cambridge (114–15). In spite of the very extensive researches of Willis and Clark, of George Gilbert Scott, and more recently in the case of Eton, of Professor Douglas Knoop and Mr. G. P. Jones, the exact shares of different personalities in the design of these two colleges are somewhat obscure. It is certain that the King himself took a leading part in adapting the collegiate plan to his requirements, and in so far as there is a unity of conception behind Eton and King's College considered together, he deserves much of the credit. Next to the King, the principal architect was Robert Westerley, his master mason from 1439 to 1461, except for the two years 1449–51, when he was deprived of his office by the Act of Resumption. He had been in the royal service at least since the beginning of 1430, when he was commissioned to impress stone-cutters for the making of cannon-balls; there is no reason to doubt that he was the designer of the first scheme for Eton College, on which work began in 1441, but in 1448 John Smyth, previously warden of the Eton masons, is mentioned as master mason in the estimate for the enlarged new Chapel. This may, on the other hand, imply nothing more than that Smyth was resident master, while Westerley was moving over a wide area in connexion with the royal works elsewhere. John Wynwik also, warden of the masons of the King's Works, was associated with the Eton work in its early stages. On the whole, the probability is in favour of Westerley as the chief or even the sole designer (apart from the King himself) at Eton. The problem is less simple at King's College, Cambridge, where Reginald Ely seems to have been the only chief mason named in the documents from 1443 until the stoppage of work in 1461, at the overthrow of Henry VI. Ely himself lived on until 1471, when he may have been succeeded by John Wolrich, master of the second work which began in 1476 and lasted some ten years. It cannot as yet be considered as proven that Westerley had no control over the work at King's College, but stylistic considerations are in favour of the detail being by Ely; this is as far as it is advisable to go in the light of present knowledge (114–15).

It is at any rate safe to assume that both Westerley and Ely played leading parts in the design of these two buildings, and even after making due allowance for the King's own share in the work (a share which must have caused his architects many sleepless nights, as scheme was converted into scheme!) and for the miserably truncated and fragmentary remains of the original work, it must be admitted that these two men were among the great artists of history. For them, difficulties were made in order to be solved, and though other hands have added the crowning features to their work, we can but admire the beauty and finish of their designs and regret that their lot should have been cast in an age so gloomy and so uncongenial to artistic fruition. Of King Henry VI much has been written from divergent points of view; but there is perhaps room for a brief reconsideration of his character. In explaining his mental instability as an inheritance from his grandfather Charles VI, it tends to be overlooked that he may have inherited other qualities: the love of art and sensibility to aesthetic beauty which had characterized that earlier royal melancholic. From his father he inherited much of his religious sincerity, but without Henry V's bigotry; in spite of a prudish objection to the low-necked dresses of his court ladies and to the shameless manners of the hot spring at Bath, he maintained his gentleness under all provocations, and in the midst of a burden of wretchedness which fortunately falls to the lot of few kings or men. Let us forget for a time the niceties of usurpations and the administrative aspects of the regality, and be thankful for this King who was too saintly to achieve canonization.

Most of the interesting minor artists of the reign have already been dealt with; we have no great painter of the mid-century. When the Duke of Bedford died in 1435, his arms and others were painted on 350 shields by Thomas Daunte, painter of London, but we do not hear more of him, and soon afterwards John Stratford appears. Some of the odd fragments of paintings which are discovered from time to time may be attributed to Stratford's early career, as a portrait of Elizabeth Woodville of *c*. 1463 has already been ascribed to his later life. Another interesting person was Thomas Bee or Bye, senior warden of the Stainers' Company of London in 1441. In 1453 he was assigned by the Crown to assist John Lyalton, appellant, in a case of trial by battle, while Jenkyn of Stanlay "sergeant of the king's armures" was to make "sufficient armure and wepen" for Lyalton. Bee received a letter ordering him to "do and make for the said Lyalton such things concernyng the premisses as belongeth to yor craft", that is, the armorial shield, trappings and banners. In 1461 he appears as the new King's Glazier when Edward IV re-staffed the Civil Service; he died in 1472. It was probably Bee's successor William Neve who drew the painted glass portraits of Edward IV and his Queen which were given to Canterbury Cathedral in 1480; the details of the crowns and badges are so exquisitely painted that the artist must have had a wide experience of dealing with heraldic work of the finest order.

Sculpture in the mid-fifteenth century is on the whole of much greater importance than the painting; the bosses of the Norwich cloisters and Massingham's works have already been mentioned. The Beauchamp tomb at Warwick was made by John Essex, a London marbler of St. Paul's Churchyard, possibly successor to the shops which Stephen Lote had had there. The greater part of the actual working was let to John Borde, a Corfe marbler, but Essex was almost certainly the designer, for the work is of distinctively London style (116). This was in 1454, but the payments to Borde began some years earlier, and it is evident that several of the crucial documents are lost. Essex, however, was another of those concerned in the plans which Henry VI made for his tomb; many years later Thomas Fifelde who had been his apprentice deposed that in 1454 "Maysters Katermaynes and Marmayne . . . come to the howse of John Essex otherwyse callyd Herd marbelar with whom this deponent as he seithe than was apprentyse, which was in Powlys Chirchard of London where the crosse standyth, and desired the seide John to com to Kyng Henry the vj^{th} at that tyme being in his Palace of Westminster, to thentent to make a tombe for hym. Wherupon incontynently the seide John Essex sent for oone Thomas Stephyns copersmyth dwellyng in Guttyrlane of London, which seid John Essex and Thomas Stephyns went than forthe . . . to Westminster . . . furthermoore he saith that on the next day folowyng this deponent herde his saide maister John Essex and the forsayd Thomas Stephyns sittyng at soper in the howse of the said John Essex, say that they had bargayned with the seide Kyng Henry the vj^{th} for his tombe to

116 Warwick, St. Mary's: Beauchamp tomb, 1447–53.
Designer: John Essex; carver: John Borde; founder: William Austen

117 York Minster: Screen, 1475–1500. Designer: William Hyndeley

119 Yatton Church: West Front, *c.* 1400–40

118 Bath Abbey: West Front, 1501–39.
Designers: Robert and William Vertue

be made. . . . And how that they hadde receyved of the saide Kyng Henry for a rewarde or els in party of payment xl*s*. in grotes, of the which xl*s*. they than and there gave to this deponent a groote. . . . And he saithe there was no thyng done to the makyng of the seyd tombe as ferforth as he knewe be cause of the grete trowble that than dyd folowe."

Associated with Essex, Massingham, and Prudde the King's Glazier in the furnishing of the Beauchamp Chapel was Richard Bird, carpenter of London, who with John Haynes, contracted to make the desks with panelled backs, which still exist, and a screen about the organ in the Chapel, in 1450. Bird was an important London carpenter, a sworn viewer of carpenters' work for the city and warden of the Carpenters' Company in 1440, and busy on the Company's business for several years. He may possibly have been the designer of the great roof of the London Guildhall, burnt down in 1666, but whose hammer-beam outlines are preserved by a crude engraving, from which the restoration in Victorian times was "copied", only to be itself burnt down in the second "Great Fire" in 1940. These disasters lead to morose reflections upon the value of human activities, especially when they are seen in perspective with the thunderous tempest which was approaching the busy craftsmen and the gentle King of 1454; but in spite of what was still-born, and what was strangled at birth, King's College Chapel and much else that is worth the bitterness lived on through "the grete trowble".

V

PREGNANT WINTER

THE recovery of English art under Henry VI, though it witnessed to the power still left among the native craftsmen, was to some extent illusory. It was a revival of the surface, and went but skin deep. Beneath, the social and economic decay went on unchecked; Mr. L. F. Salzman quotes figures and facts which show clearly how impoverished many English towns had become.[1] In Winchester in 1430 there were 997 empty houses and 17 parish churches unserved, and in 1447 Lincoln was said to have scarcely 200 citizens remaining, through the withdrawal of merchants and continued pestilences; in 1439 Wallingford was greatly decayed, and in 1471 Yarmouth; about 1485 only 12 persons of substance were living in Grimsby. It may well be that this decline of the corporate town was partly due to the selfish policy of the guilds themselves, which drove trade out into the country and the unincorporated free towns—certainly the "little man" did comparatively well. On the other hand, a new and privileged commercial aristocracy was arising in the great East Anglian towns, and it is impossible from local conditions to make generalizations applicable to the whole country.

Probably the wool districts, notably Cotswold and Suffolk, suffered less than the average. But even in the production of parish churches there is a marked falling off for more than ten years from the start of the civil war in 1455. It used to be fashionable to divide English history into sections with the Black Death and the Wars of the Roses marking planes of cleavage, after which "nothing was ever the same again". More modern research has proved that this view does not account for the observed chronological order of changes, and that "the daily round, the common task" went on without showing any very marked symptoms of the crisis. It may be doubted whether the newer version tells us the whole truth. The Black Death was not responsible for many of the extraordinary developments in society once attributed to it; nor did the whole of the old English nobility die in the bloodthirsty conflict between York and Lancaster—but to nations as to individuals shock may be even more dangerous than actual injury, and just as the local fourteenth-century plagues in the city of York so depleted the ranks of its glass-painters that John Thornton had to be brought from Coventry to carry out the new east window of the Minster, so the aftermath of the Wars of the Roses saw an England practically deprived, not merely of first-class glaziers but of painters and

[1] This may have been partially compensated by a flow of persons to the little country towns in steep valleys where water-power fulling-mills were sited.

sculptors as well; poetry too was at a low ebb, its place being taken by a slowly growing stream of English prose.

Architecture, not being an art of the connoisseur, but one of sheer necessity, suffered less, but investigation of bequests to church building and similar enterprises shows how barren were the twenty years from 1450 to 1470 in comparison with the rich harvest of the 1440's and the great period of prosperous parish life inaugurated by Edward IV's restoration in 1471. It was not a question which depended on party divisions; it was a life-and-death problem in pounds, shillings, and pence. Henry VI, while he had the money, kept alive the Lancastrian tradition of building and art patronage; the reverses in France and trade decline had already turned off the tap before the revolution of 1461. Edward IV in the early years of his reign was even more circumspect, for he was balanced on a political razor-edge, which nearly destroyed him in 1470. Only after Edward's skilful blending of force and diplomacy had triumphed at Picquigny in 1475, wringing from Louis XI, the "universal spider", an annual subsidy in return for peace, did England regain its lost equilibrium (80).

The fall of Lancaster was the natural outcome of its accession to power; he who sups with the devil needs a long spoon, and he who lets out the forces of cupidity and insubordination will require superhuman strength and cunning to get them back into the bag. From the very first year of Henry IV, 1400, civil disturbance became epidemic, and the Regency period after the death of Henry V was disgraced by the perpetual wrangling between Gloucester and the Beauforts. In spite of this strife in high places, the older cultural order was maintained for a half-century on the shoulders of a few men who had been born in the English Golden Age. When these men died, an epoch closed for ever. The first of the irreparable losses was that of the Duke of Bedford in 1435—this early death doomed the English position in France. Humphrey, Duke of Gloucester, who shared his brother's love of art and science, but lacked his statesmanship, died in 1447; Hoccleve about 1450 and Lydgate some two years later. The fatal year 1453 saw the Turkish standard flying over Byzantium (29 May), the English finally driven from Guienne (19 October), and the death of John Dunstable (24 December).

On the Continent too there had been artistic losses: Jan van Eyck died in 1441, Robert Campin in 1444, Brunelleschi in 1446, Stephan Lochner in 1451, and Antonio Pisanello and Fra Angelico in 1455. On the other hand, the Continent did not lack for signs of a rebirth of cultural activity: 1440 or thereabouts saw the invention of printing from movable type, and the foundation of the Florentine Academy; from 1447 to 1453 the great equestrian monument to Gattamelata by Donatello was in progress; in 1450 Pope Nicholas V founded the Vatican Library. The loss of Constantinople and later of Athens (1456) and Trebizond (1461), though they sealed the fate of the Near East, brought crowds of scholars and artists flocking westwards, and several even reached England, where Emmanuel of Constantinople copied Greek manuscripts for George

Neville, brother of the "Kingmaker" Earl of Warwick, and Archbishop
of York from 1464 to his death in 1476.

The varying fortunes of the civil war must be studied in the political
histories, but the state of lawlessness engendered in the country affected
architecture in a positive as well as in a negative manner. While it made
it impossible for any large amount of money to be spent on churches and
buildings of luxury, the growth of mercenary private armies, the "livery
and maintenance" of bodies of retainers, led directly, as Dr. Douglas
Simpson has shown, to the introduction into England of a new form of
castle, typified by such a work as the great tower-house of Ashby-de-la-
Zouch, begun in 1474. Process of law was openly set at defiance, and the
Paston letters show how manor-houses could be seized by force and
garrisoned against their rightful owners in the 1450's. Money too was
losing its value: it is true that the silver standard itself remained un-
changed until Henry VIII debased the coinage in 1542, but the penny was
made of a decreasing quantity of silver. Originally weighing 22½ grains,
it fell slightly in the fourteenth century, then slumped to 15 grains by 1412
and was only 12 grains in 1464, little over half its original value. Although
food prices remained fairly stable, Sir William Beveridge and others have
shown that this did not hold true of other articles; the "little man" lived
in rude prosperity, but for his betters these were hard times indeed.

Apart from architecture, only two English works of first-class importance can be dated in this empty middle of the century, the dead-beat
between the back-stroke of the declining Middle Age and the forward
impulse of the New Learning. The first of these works is the forerunner
of modern English prose, the *Repressor of Over-much Blaming of the
Clergy*, by Reginald Pecock, Bishop of Chichester. Pecock, though
opposed to the Lollards and a lover of the time-honoured traditions of the
Church, opposed persecution and advocated reason and gentleness; he
furthermore put his trust in common sense, as where he pointed out with
sly humour to those who set up the Scriptures as a universal manual of
conduct: "In al holi scripture it is not expressid bi bidding, counseiling,
or witnessing, or by eni ensaumpling of persoon, that a lay man not preest
schulde were a breche, or that he schulde were a cloke, or that he schulde
were a gowne, or that he schulde die wollen clooth into other colour than
is the colour of scheep, or that men schulde bake eny fleisch or fisch in an
ovyn. . . ." It is not a thing to astonish us when we learn that this open-
mindedness was deemed so heretical that Pecock was deprived of his see
and of his privy councillor's seat, and banished to Thorney Abbey in 1459.

The other ray of light in the general gloom is provided by the drawings
in Thomas Chaundler's *Liber Apologeticus* and in his tract on William of
Wykeham, manuscripts which he almost certainly both wrote and illustrated with his own hand. The drawings, in a grizzale[1] method, include

[1] The englished spelling is intentional: can we not at least try to relearn the
art of digesting foreign words before putting them into general currency? Recent
events have replaced *détenu* by detainee, and I live in hopes of seeing (and eating)
crustoons rather than *croûtons*!

120   Ripon Minster: Nave, 1503–21.   Designer: Christopher Scune

121   Norwich Blackfriars' Church: Nave, *c.* 1450–60.

122 Norwich Cathedral: Nave vault, 1463–72. Designer: John Everard

elaborate groupings of figures, and architectural views of Winchester College and New College, Oxford. Both manuscripts date from close to 1460, when Chaundler was Chancellor of the University of Oxford; he was Warden of Winchester College in 1450 and of New College in the following year, and died as Dean of Hereford in 1490, a year earlier than John Rous the antiquary, whose illustrations in his Roll of the Earls of Warwick belong, however, to a later period, about 1480. There is no need to suppose that either Chaundler or Rous employed others to produce their drawings; in both cases the work is what might be expected of a talented amateur who had taken the trouble to learn what Lydgate had called the "cunning" of "Drawyng of Picture". Chaundler was by far the more accomplished artist of the two, and his work appeared just when it was most needed; but it seems significant that Pecock, Chaundler, and Rous were all clerics, and that they all belonged to an elder generation—Pecock was born *c*. 1395, Chaundler *c*. 1418, and Rous in 1411, so that his surviving drawings were made when he was nearly if not quite seventy.

The general historian closes the Middle Ages in 1453 because of the extinction of the Eastern Empire in that year; the simultaneous loss of Guienne marked a calamity just as noteworthy which befell England. Both tragedies were due in essence to an internal weakening of the power to resist the pressure of a changing world; both were followed by the replacement of a traditional culture by an alien one, imposed from without. At Constantinople the conqueror differed obviously in religion, in language, in traditions, from the men he displaced, though the early Ottoman Sultans were closely related in their culture, as they were in blood, to the late Byzantine Emperors whose throne they took. In England there was probably less of actual relationship between the ideals of the new world and those of the old, in spite of an apparent similarity, if not identity, of religion, language, and modes of life. Within a century, though the English language remained, England's religious outlook had been revolutionized, her arts destroyed: glass-painting and sculpture by natives simply disappeared; mural and panel painters were content to follow Holbein and Moro cautiously and at a great distance; the great principles of English manuscript book production and lettering were jettisoned, so that alone among Western nations England has no continuity of tradition leading from written to printed literature; even embroidery, the "English work", and heraldry weakened in face of foreign models and took their cue from pattern-books of international circulation.

There has been in recent years a great deal of hair-splitting on the subject of Puritans; Mr. Percy Scholes has written a long and scholarly work to prove that they were not guilty of the excesses against music which had been attributed to them. This is all perfectly true, and yet! Whether we use the label of "Puritan" or that of "Philistine" is relatively immaterial; we cannot disguise the obvious fact that England as a whole has been relatively indifferent to all forms of art during the past four centuries; relatively both to her own past, and to the standard of taste and appreciation common to other countries. We have, it may be said, made up for this by a much greater interest in science and hygiene, in which directions England (or Anglo-Saxondom as a whole) is alleged to lead the world. Whether this last defence is true or not I do not propose to argue: I am not discussing the whole of the activities of mankind, but primarily those cultural outpourings which can be termed art. The possession of a motor-bicycle cannot be accepted as a relevant defence to the charge of living contentedly in commonplace and unsuitable clothes in an ugly house.

England had helped to wound herself long before she was conquered by alien traditions and finally by the denial of tradition altogether. The supporters of "modern progress" point triumphantly to examples of mediæval jerry-building, mediæval guild exclusiveness, and mediæval filth, and loudly proclaim "*Nous avons changé tout cela*". The Middle Age had, as we have, its by-laws against jerry-building; it had in the King a really valuable check upon oppression and the exploitation of class by class; it made a determined effort to maintain reasonably sanitary conditions. We shall not reach any conclusion by mere polemics on this point and that: but we must not attempt to conceal the real changes that have taken place. England in the period before 1400 was able to produce art of all kinds in a quality and quantity sufficient to satisfy the exacting demands of her kings and other art-connoisseurs; and at the same time clothed and housed her people in an harmonious if frugal manner. Even the poorest of her churches, of which more than 10,000 ministered to the population, without counting monastic houses, contained something of positive beauty; although we may cavil at unsatisfactory design in Gothic work, it would be difficult to point to any mediæval church which could be called ugly when compared with modern examples of the unbeautiful.

When England acquiesced in Bolingbroke's usurpation of 1399, she sold her birthright for an illusion: the fallacy of popular control. When England suffered Oliver Cromwell to put trade in the saddle, she riveted chains upon her neck; and when she acclaimed that General Churchill who sold his King to the foreigner in 1688, she committed suicide. With the latter of these steps we are not concerned here; but they form a logical, almost a mathematic and predictable progression. My purpose in mentioning them is to bring out the ultimate gravity of the events of the fifteenth century: their effect was to reduce a flourishing country to the verge of spiritual bankruptcy. Only the advent of Tudor despotism saved what was left of England for a time, and in the process of weathering the storm had to jettison half the cargo that remained. What was saved included a growing vernacular literature, just budding into a new form: the drama; a stock of church music about to put forth buds and grow into the mighty tree which bore Fairfax, Tallis, Byrd, Morley, and Purcell before it was cut down; and an impoverished architecture which was nevertheless able on slight encouragement to take on new life, and which, even after it had been ruthlessly sacrificed by Henry VIII, continued to preside as a ghost over our buildings until mechanized cheap-jackery swept it away in the fervour of nineteenth-century progress.

The very real gap in English poetry is shown by the fact that while Hoccleve and Lydgate died in the early 1450's, Skelton was not even born until *c.* 1460, Dunbar until *c.* 1465, and Stephen Hawes until *c.* 1474. A whole generation was thus without leadership; in prose Sir Thomas Malory completed his glorious compilation *Morte D'Arthur* in 1470, and died in the following year; we may notice that the Sir Thomas Malory of Newbold Revell who is now accepted as the author was in early life in the retinue of Richard Beauchamp, the great Earl of Warwick, whose career also inspired John Rous and the author of the "Pageant" and whom we have already met at Rouen and Paris, and in effigy upon his tomb. *Morte D'Arthur* was not printed until 1485, so that its wide influence upon English really belongs to the final scene of the Middle Ages.

In the history of the English drama there is much that is obscure, and it is only in the Tudor period that we find sharply defined literary interludes by individual authors whose names are preserved. The earliest of these writers known to us is Henry Medwall, who was chaplain to Cardinal Morton, Archbishop of Canterbury from 1486 to 1500, and his surviving interlude, *Nature*, though probably written *c.* 1490, was not in print until forty years later. There had, however, been a very long development of dramatic action in England, largely connected with the presentation of scriptural and liturgical subjects. We have seen that there were already highly organized companies performing these plays and pageants in Richard II's time, and from the fifteenth century several important collections of local cycles of plays survive, and show that most of the corporate towns had their own texts, produced by the craft guilds. In addition to these mysteries or miracle-plays there were moralities, of which the earliest known, *The Pride of Life*, dates from the beginning of the century and was written in the neighbourhood of London. It cannot be said that either the mysteries or the moralities show very obvious resemblances to the plays of antiquity or of modern times, but that there were also forerunners of modern comedy and farce is proved by the survival of an English fragment of about 1300, the *Interlude of the Clerk and the Damsel*. In France there are the even earlier pastoral comedies to music (almost ballad operas) of Adam de la Halle of Arras, written between 1262 and 1289, and it is certainly easier to trace the development of the secular play in France than in England.[1]

As with English secular music, it is clear that much that once existed has been lost in the destruction caused at the dissolution of the monasteries, when the chief libraries of the country were scattered to the winds. Even as it is, the surviving bulk of English mediæval drama (mainly the cyclical mysteries) is probably greater than that of any other country; as for the much-canvassed problem of why dramatic presentation should have been

[1] See E. K. Chambers: *English Literature at the Close of the Middle Ages*, 1945, p. 65.

so largely in the hands of the craft guilds of the towns, it seems unnecessary to see in it more than a natural outcome of the close connexion between craft guilds and religious fraternities—a connexion which seems at times to have melted into practical identity, as in the case of the fraternity of the Resurrection maintained by the carpenters of York in 1487, and certainly earlier.

It is more difficult to account for the rise of the companies of players attached to various noblemen, but by analogy with other household departments, one would undoubtedly expect them to be founded upon royal precedent, and the ambiguous word "histrio" may be suspected to have implied rather more than a minstrel on some occasions, even though it were used on others as a precise equivalent. It is at any rate unquestionable that both King and noblemen employed regular companies of players by the last quarter of the fifteenth century, and that these troupes travelled from place to place giving entertainments and receiving rewards. Minstrels, jugglers, and "histriones" can be traced behaving in a similar manner as far back as the thirteenth century. We need not suppose that the form of their entertainments remained constant, but it is at least more probable that there was some form of continuity than that "his lordship's servants" should suddenly have sprung into being fully fledged. Against this may be advanced two main objections: first, the disappearance of the texts used by the companies of players; second, the instances where the word "histrio" is used in a sense indicating a minstrel. I cannot feel convinced that this latter argument has much weight when it is laid against the bulk of historical probability, which is in favour of a continuous development.

The other objection appears on the surface to be much stronger; but let us consider some analogous disappearances. We know, in the case of the drama itself, that by 1300 there existed a type of comedy capable of using the *Clerk and Damsel*; evidently this cannot have been the only piece of its kind, yet we do not seem to have any others. I think an equally cogent line of argument can be drawn from the disappearance of architectural drawings. We know from Continental sources that in the early thirteenth century, to go no further, working drawings were prepared for large churches such as that of Rheims, but the fragments we know owe their existence to their use as a palimpsest. In England we have at least one similar case, that of the Pepysian sketch-book at Magdalene College, Cambridge, some leaves of which contain in mutilated form both small-scale and detail drawings of window tracery and mouldings of the period 1350–1400. It is unthinkable that these drawings should have been the only technical drawings produced. The fact is that these have only survived by accident; the artist who needed a sketch-book, perhaps a monk or friar, collected up unwanted parchment from the mason's lodge or tracing-house, and by this chance preserved the drawings; so it must have been with the plays: the copies used by the craft guilds, which possessed corporate unity, in some cases survived. The casual bodies of strolling players had no archives, and with rare exceptions any written texts they possessed have been lost or destroyed.

123   Norwich Cathedral: Presbytery vault, *c*. 1472- .   Designer: John Everard

125 Eltham Palace: Great Hall, 1475–80.
Designer: Thomas Jurdan; of roof: Edmund Graveley

124 Hampton Court: Great Hall, 1531–36.
Designer: John Molton; of roof: James Needham

While writers were turning their attention to the drama and to experiments in prose composition, English merchants and seamen were beginning to undertake perilous ventures in the hope of discovering some substitute for the old markets they had lost. A hundred and fifty years earlier, Higden had described one of the most striking characteristics of the English: "They go to divers lands . . . they be y-spread so wide, and consider that every other land is their own heritage." Their wanderings had, however, received no special encouragement, and had not been directed towards specific objectives. In the meantime, the Portuguese had made great advances by process of working upon a definite plan, and by obtaining information and charts from Mediterranean pilots and natives of Africa, steadily pushed back the frontier of the unknown. The plan was that of Dom Enrique, "Prince Henry the Navigator", whose character seems to have been derived from his English Plantagenet mother: he had the stern absorption and scientific curiosity of that later prince, Rupert of the Rhine, without Rupert's swagger. Henry was an austere soul, but in his portraits as well as in Rupert's one can discern the fierceness of mind determined to thrust aside obstacles in the pursuit of truth.

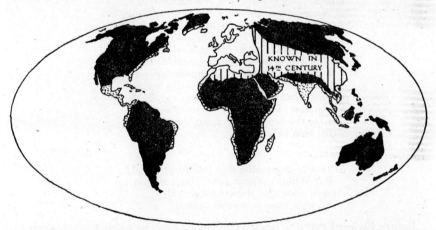

Fig. 126. The World contracts and expands—the dotted area had been opened up to Europe by *c.* 1530.

It seems that an abortive expedition was sent out into the North Atlantic by Christian I of Denmark in 1472, acting upon Portuguese advice, but this was twelve years after Prince Henry's death, and though the ships probably reached the American coast somewhere near that Vinland which had been discovered by Leif Eriksson in A.D. 1000, no direct results followed. It may be that rumours of this were the direct cause of the first British expedition to the West: the voyage of the *George* and *Trinity* of Bristol, laden in 1480 "not for the purpose of trading, but to seek and discover a certain island called the *Ile of Brasile*"; John Jay and Thomas Croft were the chief promoters, and the pilot was Lloyd, a Welshman, "the most scientific mariner of all England". The two ships set sail on 15 July, but after two months of vain search they were driven into port in Ireland, and the venture was not repeated until after the land-fall of Columbus had become public knowledge to the whole of Europe. For all that, the Bristol men had not sailed in vain; they were the pioneers of a vast expansion which was to make their language the most widely spoken upon the face of the earth.

It is time to return to the revival of culture within England itself; herald of the Tudor swan-song of Gothic art, the Court of Edward IV made a brave effort to rival the glories of the previous century. Edward IV, as rightful heir of the House of Plantagenet, had a great tradition to main-tain; like those of a later royal exile, Charles II, his luxurious tastes must have been reinforced by the contrasting poverty of his "travels". But in spite of his tastes, Edward IV knew how to be parsimonious when necessity was in the saddle, and not much is heard of his activity in building until after his restoration in 1471, when the "Kingmaker" had been overthrown, and Henry VI murdered. It was to the last ten years of his reign that his chief works belonged; Skelton catalogued them in his elegy on the King:

> I had enough, I held me not content,
> Without remembránce that I should die;
> And more ever to enroaché ready was I bent,
> I knew not how long I should it occupy:
> I made the Tower strong, I wist not why;
> I knew not to whom I purchased Tattershall;
> I amended Dover on the mountain high,
> And London I provoked to fortify the wall;
> I made Nottingham a place full royall,
> Windsor, Eltham, and many other mo:
> Yet, at the last, I went from them all,
> *Et, ecce, nunc in pulvere dormio!*

> .   .   .   .   .

> Where be my castles and buildíngs royall?
> But Windsór alone, now I have no mo,
> And of Eton the prayers perpetuall,
> *Et, ecce, nunc in pulvere dormio!*

Before Edward came to lie at Windsor he had, in a short space, seen his realm taking on a new guise; the spirit of the new richness and magni-ficence had reached England, though as yet without the Classic forms which manifested its appearance in Italy. During the years when Leonardo da Vinci was at work as a pupil in the studio of Verrochio, England saw the beginning of her last great era of native art—the last genuine outpouring of insular feeling. We cannot make a clear-cut separation between the Yorkist art revival of 1470–85 and the full flowering of its Tudor successor in 1500–30, but so much credit that is commonly given to the Tudors really belongs to Edward IV and Richard III, that it may be timely to insist upon their contributions to culture, especially to the promotion of architecture and music. Owing largely to the researches of Grattan Flood, a good deal is known of the English musicians of the time; most of those who achieved fame were at some period of their careers in the Chapel Royal, and they are consequently mentioned in many official documents. We saw that John Plummer, who in 1445 was given charge of the boys of the Chapel, is probably identical with the "Polumier" of the Modena manuscript; his successor, Henry Abingdon, was also a man of some standing, for in the same year, 1445, he was granted a yearly pension of £8 by Humphrey, Duke of Gloucester, whose private chapel he probably had in his charge. After Duke Humphrey's death, Abingdon entered the King's service, and in 1455 was granted the rule of the ten boys of the Chapel; he held the post until 1478, when it was granted to Gilbert Banaster. Abingdon was still alive in 1484, and his retirement was probably due to old age; his successor opened his career with a poem "The Miracle of St. Thomas", but is mainly remembered as the first of the Masters of the Chapel with a considerable surviving output of music.

For the coronation of Henry VII and Elizabeth of York, Banaster composed the anthem "O Maria et Elizabeth", and some motets and at least one song "My feerful dreme" from his hand are preserved. He did not long survive the coming of the Tudor dynasty, for he fell ill in the autumn of 1486 and died rather more than a year later, his work having devolved upon Laurence Squire, who was appointed to succeed to the Mastership. It was in 1486 that Henry VII recalled to England the great musical theorist John Hothby, who had been in Italy since his journey to Lucca in 1468. Hothby returned, only to die within a few months. Hothby's sojourn in Italy is proof of the esteem in which English music was held abroad, and English executants were also in demand: strange contrast to this century, when it is openly admitted that an English singer or ballet-dancer must assume a foreign name in order to succeed. Nicholas Sturgeon had been ordered in 1442 by the Privy Council to choose six singers to be approved by a messenger sent by the Emperor, to go overseas into the imperial service, and in 1471 the Duke of Milan sent Rayner, his Chapel Master, to seek English singers and musicians. At least one musical instrument, the "échiquier d'Angleterre", was considered typically English, and this is of great interest, for the "exchequer" or "chequer", as we might term it, was the earliest form of the spinet and harpsichord, and thus the ancestor of the pianoforte. Perhaps the first mention of it occurs in 1360, when Edward III gave as a parting present to his captive, King John of France, "j. instrument appelle l'eschequier", but Reese considers it possible that the Robertsbridge Priory manuscript of instrumental music may be intended for the chequer rather than for the organ—this manuscript dates from some time previous to the Black Death.

A goodly number of English musicians of the Yorkist and early Tudor period are represented by extant works, notably Sir William Hawte, a layman of Canterbury (c. 1436–c. 1499); William Newark (c. 1450–1509); William Pasche (c. 1450–1525); Richard Hygons (or Hugo), who studied under Abingdon and was master of the choristers of Wells Cathedral in 1474 and died in 1509; and most notable of all, Robert Fayrfax. Pasche was a gentleman of the private chapel maintained by Anne, Duchess of

Q

Exeter; he was a married layman, but his greatest work is a mass "Christus resurgens", and his fame found him a place in Morley's list of English practitioners of music. Newark was a gentleman of the Chapel Royal in 1477, and succeeded Squire as Master in 1493; he composed many songs and devised musical entertainments for the Court. Among his songs is a two-part setting of Lydgate's "Tied with a line", an early example of the setting by a famous composer of words by a famous poet.

Fayrfax was born about 1465, the fourth son of Sir Thomas Fayrfax of Walton, Yorkshire. Robert graduated as a Bachelor of Music at Cambridge in 1500, but was a gentleman of the Chapel by 1496, and soon afterwards was organist of St. Albans Abbey. He was Doctor of Music at Cambridge in 1504, his "exercise" being the 5-part Mass "O quam glorifica", and in 1511 he was also granted the Oxford doctorate; the first known instance of an Oxford grant of the degree of Doctor of Music. He was pensioned as one of the poor knights of Windsor in 1514, was frequently paid for composing music for Henry VIII, led the King's singing men at the Field of the Cloth of Gold, and died at St. Albans in 1521. Of his work, and of that of his close associates William Cornish (*c.* 1468–1523) and John Taverner (*c.* 1495–*c.* 1548), Mr. Gerald Hayes has written: "there is a soberness combined with a sense of clear beauty of line in their work that has no parallel until the middle period of Palestrina, and it is doubtful if even his work has more genuinely musical content. It is a form . . . (which) rises to its highest development in the work of Fairfax: one *Gloria* by Fairfax can give more feeling of inspired spiritual exaltation than a dozen Masses by Josquin, Clemens, Willaert, and Goudimel."

Further discussion of the new music will have to await the Tudor period, when indeed Fayrfax himself and the others just mentioned, as well as a galaxy of younger men, enjoyed their great period of composition. Let us return for the present to the architecture of Edward IV, which as Skelton has told us, was extensive. The work at the Tower of London comprised an outer wall of defence on the west side, the famous brick Bulwark, but this disappeared in the seventeenth century. Tattershall was not of course built by Edward, but became forfeit to him on the death of Humphrey Bourchier, Lord Cromwell, at the battle of Barnet in 1471. The work at Dover is represented in 1481 by a payment of £33 6s. 8d. to William Elys, brickmaker, in part payment of a greater sum due to him for the making of "twenty hundred thousand" bricks for the repairs of Dover Castle; of the parapet walk added to the Roman (and mediæval) walls of London some scanty fragments remain just north of Tower Hill, and can be seen in old engravings to have consisted of diapered brickwork: this was the doing of Sir Ralph Joceline, Mayor in 1477. At Nottingham, little is left, and to see Edward's work of real aesthetic importance we have to visit the great hall of Eltham Palace or St. George's Chapel at Windsor.

The work at Eltham was doubtless carried out to the designs of the King's chief craftsmen at Westminster, Thomas Jurdan, the master mason (elsewhere referred to as "the devizer of buildings") and Edmund

127   Kirby Muxloe Castle, 1480–84. Designer: John Cowper

128   Raglan Castle: Great Gatehouse, c. 1460–1530

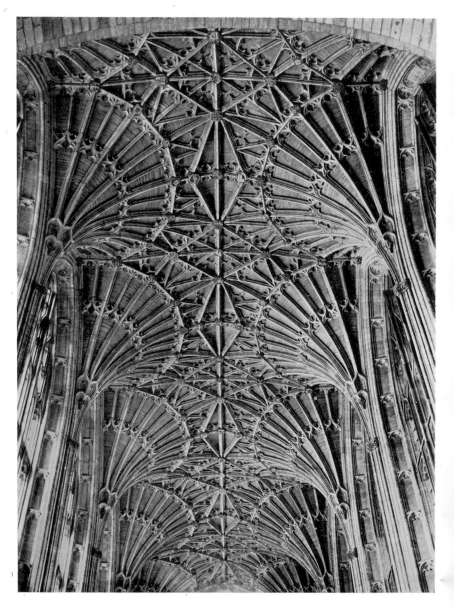

129   Sherborne Abbey: Nave vault, *c.* 1475–90.
Designer: possibly William Smyth

Graveley, the carpenter. Jurdan or Jordan may have been the hard-hewer of that name who had worked at Eton College for two years from 1444; he was certainly the chief mason of London Bridge from the beginning of 1461, and on 27 July of that year became Serjeant of the King's Masonry; he continued to hold both of these posts until his death in the spring of 1482; his official post brought him in the usual fees of £18 5s. a year, with robes and perquisites, and the post at London Bridge another 3s. 4d. a week. Though not such an architectural pluralist as Yevele had been, Jurdan was evidently a well-to-do and influential man.

So, too, was his colleague Edmund Graveley, the King's Carpenter, who first appears as a member of the London Carpenters Company in 1444, and was still living forty years later, when he had a re-grant of the office of King's Chief Carpenter from Richard III. In 1461, when he first had it from Edward IV, he was given only a miserable pittance of 4d. a day, instead of the usual 12d., in proof, were any needed, of the poverty and retrenchment with which the reign of York opened. Eltham Hall is a notable building, and ranks with Hampton Court and Westminster as one of the three surviving royal halls of first-class size. Although a simple adaptation of an old Decorated pattern was used for the window tracery, Jurdan showed a pleasant fantasy in his detail of the cusping, and the vaulting of the oriel is strong and excellent work. Graveley's roof is of less excellence; it has the appearance of being an adaptation of the Westminster design to a four-centred arch, but is in reality of quite different and much weaker construction. Besides this, it lacks the lightness of Herland's great conception, and its heavy lines of horizontal mouldings and deep pendants make a poor substitute for the flying angels which float effortlessly, bearing up the coat-armour of Richard II. Eltham, designed about 1475, only eighty years after Westminster, shows a distinct falling off, but it contains nevertheless the embryo of something new (125).

The fifteenth century was ruled by the London craftsmen; almost a regular dynasty of masons from London Bridge succeeded to the office of King's Master Mason, and the King's Carpenters were prominent members of the Carpenters' Company. After Jurdan came Thomas Danyell, who had been his apprentice at the Bridge from 1461 to 1465; Danyell probably died in 1487, but even his five years of office were not uninterrupted, for in 1483 the office was granted over his head to Robert Stowell, though given back a few months later. In consequence it is impossible to say, until the details of style have been worked out, who was the responsible architect for the works of Richard III's brief reign; for example, the alterations at Sudeley Castle in Gloucestershire, where there are signs of impending change. Stowell had a long and interesting career, for he succeeded Thirsk as Master Mason at Windsor in 1452, and after losing this post ten years later (apparently as a Lancastrian) he migrated to Westminster and eventually became the Abbey master in 1471. He held this post until his death in 1505, his work including the vaulting of three bays of the nave in 1489, and also the design of the new parish church of St. Margaret's beside the Abbey, where extensive work was in progress from 1488, the nave being complete in 1504, a year before Stowell's death. In 1476 he had contracted to alter the south aisle of Broxbourne Church in Hertfordshire, and we catch later glimpses of him as a "gentilman" of the town of Westminster, and as Warden of the Guild of St. Mary there in 1502.

Robert Stowell may perhaps have been related to John Stowell of Wells in Somerset, a freemason who was working on the Cathedral there in 1457–8, when he took up the freedom, and who in 1470 contracted to make the carved Jesse reredos for the church of St. Cuthbert; the reredos which though greatly mutilated still stands in the south transept. Other Wells masons were John Turpyn, who was paving the cloisters by contract in 1457–8, and who may have been responsible for the other great works of Bishop Bekynton; and William Smyth, master mason of the Cathedral at his death in 1490, when he was succeeded by William Atwodde, who took up the freedom in 1498—Smyth was probably the designer of the fan-vaulted cloister Lady Chapel at Wells, of which only a few fragments remain, in tantalizing resemblance to the contemporary Sherborne nave.

I have allowed myself to wander away for a space from the supreme work of Edward IV: the new chapel of St. George in Windsor Castle (113, 130). Work began at the end of 1474, and was carried on during the last nine years of the King's reign under the supervision of Henry Janyns, who received £12 a year and an annual robe worth 10s., as well as rewards, generally amounting to £3 or more in the year. Henry, as we have seen, was probably the son of Robert Janyns, the builder of the Merton College bell-tower; Henry also was at Eton College, where he was apprentice to John Clerk, the warden of the masons, in 1453, and left the works with Clerk in the following year. At Windsor the architectural position is complicated by the fact that Robert Leget (or Legate) was chief mason of the Castle from 1462 to 1484 or later, and in 1479 was making the great bay window of the Queen's Chamber. It seems probable that while Leget was responsible for normal upkeep and works belonging to the castle proper, the new Chapel was considered from the start as a separate undertaking (as indeed it has always remained). Henry Janyns should probably be considered as architect of the Chapel, apart from its west front and the vaults, all of which were later additions, though the choir must have had its timber roof by 1481, when the stalls were being set up, and "vowtyngstone" for the aisles and ironwork for the windows are mentioned. The magnificent iron screen of Edward IV's tomb was the work of John Tresilian, smith, who had a Cornish name, at any rate (133). The chief carpenter was John Squyer and the glazier James Skynke, who was very likely a foreigner. Foreign carvers were employed on the stalls and imagery, but the chief carver appears as William Berkeley, or William Baker, from 1480 to 1483. One wonders whether this can be the same William Baker who was painting remarkable grizzale frescoes upon the walls of Eton College Chapel close by in precisely the same years. It seems very likely, and if Baker and Berkeley are versions of the same name, it would hardly seem that he could have been an alien.

The problem of the influx of foreign workers into England at this period becomes extremely involved, for while some retained names marking their origin, others were very chameleons and failing external evidence pass as natives in englished guise. I am inclined to think that a very large proportion of the sculpture and carving of first-rate jobs from about 1470 onwards was done by immigrants, mainly Flemings. Not all of these men betrayed their origin in a very obvious, much less blatant, manner. But quite apart from indications of Renaissance detail, which only appeared at a later date, there is a strangeness of feeling about much of the work of the last generation of the fifteenth century. This apparent difference is exceedingly difficult to describe, and may be due to a subjective reaction, but to some extent it can be supported by the evidence for the presence of foreign workers.

Scotland, less able to be artistically self-supporting than England, had gone to France and to Flanders even earlier. In 1441 Melrose Abbey engaged Cornelius de Aeltre, master carpenter and citizen of Bruges, to provide new stalls for their choir; we find a master Cornelisse van Aeltre very busy at Bruges from a rather earlier period, directing the works of carpentry on the civic fortifications and making toll-booms for the port, from about 1383 to 1414 and perhaps later; the Melrose contractor is more likely to have been a son of the same name. In England, at York Minster, there were two carvers of the name of Dam; James, who took up the freedom of York in 1456-7 as a carver, and who appears at the Minster between 1469 and 1479 working indifferently on wooden bosses and on stonework and crockets. David Carver of 1471 is David Dam, carver, in 1485, and there can be little doubt that these two men with an almost unknown surname (in England) and with unusual Christian names (for England at that time) were from overseas. The town of Dam or Damme lies not far from Bruges, and there was an extensive Bruges family surnamed "de Dam" or "van den Damme". In fact, in 1494 there is one Jacop van den Damme, one of the principal men of the craft of paternoster-makers of Bruges, who might well be a close relation of the York men. It has to be remembered that the wool trade put York into direct communication with Bruges, then the commercial centre of Northern Europe.

In architecture, England still held her own; until the real influx of classical pattern-books and designers in the reign of Henry VIII, English building was itself wholly a native product. Besides the masters of the Royal School, each region of England was producing talented men, some of them of very great importance. Beginning with East Anglia, I will pass by Cambridge, where John Wolrich was in charge of the start of the second work of King's College Chapel in 1476. Of broader significance was John Cowper, who was to Waynflete, Bishop of Winchester, very nearly what Wynford had been to Wykeham a century earlier. Cowper first appears as an apprentice at Eton College between 1453 and 1459; in 1460 he returned to the College to work as a full-blown freemason for a fortnight, and then for a time disappears, the battle of Northampton and the political revolution practically stopping work. Waynflete was one of the trustees of the College, and may have given Cowper employment; at any rate, Cowper is next found as a mason of Winchester in 1477 and in 1478, contracting with Waynflete and with the latter's Oxford foundation, Magdalen College, to repair the bridge of Bramber in Sussex. Soon after this Cowper moved to Tattershall in Lincolnshire, where Waynflete was completing the fine collegiate church (25, 75). While living at Tattershall, Cowper obtained further employment as master mason to William Lord Hastings for the new brick-built castle of Kirby Muxloe in Leicestershire (127). Between October 1480 and Lord Hastings' execution in June 1483, much work was done, and Cowper spent his time between Kirby and Tattershall; the advanced, apparently "Tudor" character of the design of Kirby is very marked, and Cowper undoubtedly profited by his knowledge of the earlier brick tower of Tattershall Castle.

About the same time a brick tower was built for Waynflete at Esher Palace in Surrey, and a brick schoolhouse of his foundation at his birthplace, Wainfleet, in Lincolnshire. At both these works Henry Alsbroke, carpenter, Cowper's colleague at Tattershall Church, seems to have been concerned, and one can hardly doubt that these buildings also are to Cowper's design; the tower at Buckden Palace in Huntingdonshire, built for the Bishop of Lincoln at the same period, is another of the early works in brick in the style which Cowper may be said to have initiated. Though by no means the first to use brick on a large scale in England, Cowper is the first architect to adapt the material to a distinctive national style, and as such he deserves a very high place among our architectural inventors.

Norwich continued to be a great centre of activity; from about 1450 the chief mason at the Cathedral was John Everard, who also appears with the alias of Abbot. He had been admitted to the freedom of the city in 1429–30, and had charge of various routine works of paving, whitewashing the church and so forth, but in 1463 the great work of vaulting the Norman nave was undertaken, and in 1472 this was followed by the similar vaulting of the presbytery (122-3). There are few more completely satisfying works than these vaults, and they belong to that class of supremely successful masterpieces which gives the lie to the accusation of decadence so often levelled against Perpendicular: it would be difficult to discover anything more articulate and alive than the star patterns of the nave vault, contrasting as they do, and to such advantage, with the heavy and solemn Norman arcades below.

Everard's contemporary at Norwich Cathedral was William Howlett, carpenter, who no doubt was responsible for the timber roofs and for the great centrings needed; is it possible that in the famous misericord of an owl being attacked by small birds, we have an intentional play upon his name? The fable of the owl and the birds is of course much earlier, and the date of these misericords has been put at about 1420, too early for Howlett. But on another misericord, one of the same pattern as that of the owl, two wrestlers are shown, with other figures in the background, and the costumes, and especially a tall hat, seem to me to be more typical

131 Sherborne Abbey: Nave, c. 1475–90.
Designer: possibly William Smyth

130 Windsor, St. George's Chapel: Nave, 1474–1503.
Designer: Henry Janyns; of vaults: William Vertue

132 Westminster Abbey: Tomb of Henry VII. Bronze screen, *c.* 1510.
Designer: perhaps Lawrence Emler; founder: Nicholas Ewen

133 Windsor, St. George's Chapel: iron screen, *c.* 1482–83.
Smith: John Tresilian

of 1460 than of 1420. The suggestion is at best a minor point, and I will leave it to the experts to reach a valid conclusion.

Outside Norwich itself were masons with provincial practices, such as the Thomas Aldrych of North Lopham who in 1487 contracted to build a bell-tower of knapped flint for Helmingham Church in Suffolk (100), to be like the tower at Framsden, and who twenty years later inserted a new great east window at Thetford Cluniac Priory. Of greater importance was William Hyndeley of Norwich, who entered the freedom in 1466 and left six years later to take up the post of Master Mason to York Minster. He remained at York until his death in 1505, when he left not only mason's tools, but also tools pertaining to "les gravyng in plaite", which may indicate that he produced monumental brasses or that he was experimenting in the new art of engraving designs, practised in Germany by Martin Schongauer at an earlier date, and by Dürer at about this time. The statues of kings on the York rood-screen, with their sharply undercut hair and somewhat wiry vividness of expression, could well be the work of a man accustomed to engraving, and it is certain that Hyndeley was the designer of the screen as a whole (117).

The West of England produced another great anonymous at Sherborne Abbey, where the nave and its vaulting were designed to harmonize with the choir but were far from mere imitations of it (110, 129, 131). Further comparison may show that this mason was the William Smyth whom we saw at Wells before 1490; another work with similar feeling is the ruined cloister of Muchelney Abbey. In the north-west of Somerset, at Yatton, William Stonhowse was working on the steeple in 1446 (119); in the same church a new rood-loft was erected in the years 1446–54 by John Crosse, a local carpenter. In Cornwall, a very noteworthy contribution to the local style had been made between 1469 and 1472 in the building of Bodmin Church by local contractors, the principal mason being Richard Richowe, and the chief carpenter John Sam. The seating, pulpit, and screen, were added in 1491–5 by Mathy More, carpenter and joiner, for the sum of £95. Remains of this work show that it was executed in a wonderfully rich style, peculiar to Cornwall, and quite unlike the typically English work of the period.

More conventional are the choir-stalls of St. Asaph Cathedral, made between 1471 and 1495; these look like Chester work, and may possibly exhibit the style of William Frankelyn alias Temple, who was Master Carpenter of Chester Castle from 1461, and of the counties of Chester and Flint from 1463 to 1503. At Lichfield was another centre of wood-carving, for in 1459 Thomas Karver of that city undertook to supply forty choir stalls for the conventual church of Nuneaton, Warwickshire. Returning to the London area, we find Walter Nicholl of Southwark contracting with Bishop Waynflete to carve the roodloft for Eton College Chapel between 1475 and 1477, the west side being modelled upon that of Winchester College Chapel, and the east side like that in the Hospital of St. Thomas of Acre in London. Walter the carver twice visited Waynflete at Winchester with the college authorities in 1476, once in company with the chief mason and carpenter. Of nearly the same date are the immense reredoses of Winchester and St. Albans; both are unquestionably from the same shop, and equally without doubt are London work. They have something of the masterly grouping which marked Massingham's masterpiece at All Souls of forty years earlier, but have become more separated from the architecture, more clearly individual structures with a life of their own. In this they are inferior to Massingham's work, but they are immensely impressive, drop-scenes upon the eternal pageant of the Redemption. We may owe these to Walter Nicholl, for he seems to have been the principal carver of the period in the capital, and was in touch with Winchester at least at the right time.

It has already been admitted that English painting (of real importance, that is) came near to extinction in the fifteenth century; such painters as there were seem to have concentrated upon portraiture and the quasi-portraiture of saintly figures to fill up the panels of church-screens. Of the screen-paintings still extant, the finest of this period are at Ranworth and Sparham in Norfolk, and Southwold in Suffolk. The screen at Southwold, though it has been a good deal restored, shows to the best advantage the tradition of English church decoration; gold and sombre browns and reds are set off with cream mouldings, and the saints have the grandeur of the best heraldic figures. These are decoration, albeit of the finest order, but the remains of a set of imaginary portraits of Saxon kings painted for the Coronation Chapel at Kingston-upon-Thames and now in the possession of the Society of Antiquaries are, in their own way, great art. They do not compete with the productions of the great Flemings, nor even with the work of Germany at this period, in the main stream of artistic experience, but they glow with all the mysticism of earlier English painting and portraiture. These, and a number of portraits of reigning kings—Edward IV, Richard III, and Henry VII—represent the final phase of the native Court School, though most if not all of the portraits of kings that we now have are only copies after lost originals. Finest of all these portraits is that of the Lady Margaret, mother of Henry VII, now in the National Portrait Gallery. Here, or in the kings of the Society of Antiquaries, we probably have the work of John Serle and his school. Serle succeeded John Stratford as King's Painter in 1473, and continued to hold the office in the first years of Henry VII, in 1486 for example being paid for painting divers figures, beasts, and armed men upon the King's landing stairs at Westminster. But with the coming of the Tudors, English painting died down, and it was not until after Holbein had showed us a new way of looking at life that the Hilliards were able to rediscover an English art of painting in a later generation. The yarn which had provided a strong thread from the days of Matthew Paris and the Chichester Roundel, through the painters of Westminster and St. Albans to Master Hugh and Gilbert Prynce, had been spun out thinner and thinner—like the House of Plantagenet which in a sense gave it birth: it gave out, came to a direct stop.

VI

FROZEN SPRING

THERE is a definite relation between the various phases of each cultural cycle; this was well brought out by Mr. Sacheverell Sitwell in discussing the relation of Mozart to Bach—when the Rococo is reached, something of the strength of the Baroque has been sacrificed. It so happens that in the art cycle of the Renaissance this is particularly noticeable, for all aesthetic values changed with the coming of the Revolutionary period, and one sees the whole Renaissance neatly trimmed and bordered, pinned on a board for inspection, and as far as England is concerned we mentally label the beginning "1500" and the end "1800", and leave it at that. If we wish, we can subdivide the picture into four: first a time of experiment; then a "classic" culmination in the work of Inigo Jones for Charles I; a second triumphant resorting of the pattern in the Baroque of Wren and Vanbrugh; and, after the stately pudding-time of the Kents and Woods (civic virtue taking breath on a landing), the fragile Rococo of the brothers Adam. My use of the words "classic", Baroque, and Rococo, is not intended to have an exact connotation; they are simply convenient symbols to express universally relative values.

If we look at Gothic art, we shall find that something very similar happened, though owing to the greater natural vitality of Gothic form and construction, it cannot be put in a jar for inspection. Here the four phases will be found in the Early English, Decorated, Perpendicular, and Tudor styles, Commonwealth austerity corresponds closely to the hard economical work of the Black Death, and the interlude of civic pride occurs in the fifteenth century. We could find further parallels to support the thesis that history repeats itself; the murders of Edward II and of Charles I, and the revolutions of 1399 and 1688 show points of resemblance, and something more striking occurs in the final phases of each cycle. At the very last gasp, as it were, we can discern signs of a rebirth: just before he died, Mozart had begun to compose in a new manner— that of the Requiem, of the F minor Fantasia for a mechanical organ, of the finale of the Jupiter symphony—a manner which not only grew out of his own style but equally from that of Bach. Similarly Blake, who had mastered the polite methods of the eighteenth-century engraver from Basire, somehow acquired from his mediæval studies an older power filled with dynamic energy.

It is the world's loss that neither Mozart's nor Blake's new styles were fulfilled: the forces of a changing human focus swept them away. Now whether we believe or no in historical parallels, similar events took place in the Europe of three centuries before. A glimpse was vouchsafed of an art too advanced, too sublime for mankind's state of development—instead of going on, a great backward plunge was taken. Taken wholly in painting and sculpture, almost wholly in architecture, partially in writing, but slightly in music. It is only in music that unbroken progress can be traced in a steady line from the Dark Ages to the death of Purcell in England, and to the death of Mozart in continental Europe. If we take the most universal output of each composer (a qualification particularly necessary in the case of Purcell, much of whose work was in a popular foreign idiom), a direct genealogy can be traced backwards, step by step—from Purcell back to Matthew Locke, William Lawes, Orlando Gibbons; from Gibbons to Bull and Morley; from them to Byrd; from Byrd to Tallis and Tye, from them to Taverner and Fayrfax, and so into the heart of the school of Dunstable.

This wonderful succession in musical history depends upon the long life of Byrd; had he died at the age of Mozart, it is more than doubtful if any of the rest would have been possible. In similar fashion, such continuity in English roof construction as was maintained through the sixteenth century was due to the long career of John Russell, the King's Chief Carpenter, who, brought up under his father Richard Russell and under Humphrey Coke, lived into the reign of Elizabeth and at the end of his life was advising Trinity College, Cambridge. Thus it is that the roofs of the halls of the Middle Temple and Gray's Inn, and even that of Lambeth Palace, rebuilt by Wren, show their descent from Hampton Court, Christ Church, Eltham, and Westminster Hall.

In literature both the accidental and the universal aspects of the age can be seen; Skelton, the one great poet of the time in England (for Wyatt and Surrey only began to write in 1535 and later, in a new atmosphere), appears full of frivolity on the surface; his jerky "modern" rhythms seem type of the Rococo only—yet when he wished he could sound a deeper organ-note than Milton, plead God's cause with man in accents more pathetic, more moving than those of Herbert or Crashaw. If we would approach to an understanding of that terrible cult of the dying Jesus which lay at the heart of the latest Middle Ages, Skelton's "Woefully Arrayed" will be perhaps a surer guide than even Grünewald's ghastly imaging of the Crucifixion. Of Grünewald's masterpiece, Friedländer writes that the reason why all pleasurable contemplation is not swept away by a torrent of horror is "because the master communicates to us his vision and, thereby, his religious fervour in such purity and so decisively, that our imagination . . . experiences the distant, sublime myth; and the fearsomeness becomes deeply affecting drama. In the picture Christ dies not once, not here: on the contrary, everywhere and always; hence never and nowhere." The same may be said of Skelton's poem.

"Woefully Arrayed" was set by Skelton's almost exact contemporary, William Cornish, who likewise set "Mannerly Margery Milk and Ale", a piece in Skelton's quite other manner. In his satires many of the extravagances of modern verse were anticipated, and some modern poets have consciously borrowed from Skelton. But it is dubious whether any of them have achieved a subtler obscurity than:

> Esebon, Marylebone, Whetstone next Barnet;
> A trim tram for an horse-mill it were a nice thing;
> Dainties for damoiselles, chaffer far fet:
> Bo-ho doth bark well, but Hough-ho he ruleth the ring;
> From Scarpary to Tartary renown therein doth spring,
> With "He said", and "we said", ich wot now what ich wot—
> *Quod magnus est dominus Judas Scariot.*

Nor is it common to find in work of the present day anything so brilliant (in this kind) as an earlier verse of "Speak, Parrot":

> With my beaké bent, my little wanton eye,
> My feathers fresh as is the emerald green,
> About my neck a circulet like the rich rubý,
> My little legs, my feet both feat and clean,
> I am minion to wait upon a queen:
> "My proper Parrot, my little pretty fool!"
> With ladies I learn, and go with them to school.

The antipathy to Wolsey which runs through so much of Skelton's verse, though it does less than justice to the ability of the great Cardinal, gives rise to some interesting descriptions of the new frivolity of architecture and decoration, such as this from "Colin Clout":

> Building royally
> Their mansions curiously,
> With turrets and with towers,
> With hallés and with bowers,
> Stretching to the stars,
> With glass windows and bars;
> Hanging about the wallés
> Cloths of gold and pallés,
> Arras of rich array,
> Fresh as flowers in May . . .

and allusions to lesser personalities have their value, as for example the reference to the rich woolman, Thomas Spring of Lavenham, in "Why come ye not to Court?"

> Good Spring of Lavenham
> Must count what became
> Of his cloth-making:
> He is at such taking,
> Though his purse wax dull
> He must tax for his wool
> By nature of a new writ.

Spring was one of the principal benefactors of Lavenham Church; his bequest of £200 in 1523 enabled the tower to be carried up to its present height, though it was never fully completed.

In this changing environment, the Englishman himself was changing; the loss of Guienne in 1453 had altered the whole basis of English polity. No longer a compact group of realms astride the narrow seas, England had to turn her back upon the whole European system and look outwards. The new attitude had very far-reaching results in the next four centuries for the world at large, and the "Pax Britannica" in the days of our grand-fathers seemed to foreshadow the millennium. We are now disillusioned, and possibly there is a tendency to undervalue the reality of the benefits conferred by the expansion of Britain. On the other hand, quite apart from the effects upon other peoples, it would be dishonest to pretend that the change did not have some very adverse results so far as the English character is concerned.

The English of the fourteenth century, as we see them through the eyes of Chaucer and Langland, were a markedly natural people: natural in their vices as in their virtues. They lacked artifice, had a broad and fairly good sense of humour, had acquired from the Celts a mystical sense of priceless value, and in spite of their position on the circumference of the known world were mellowed by constant contacts with lands lying nearer the centre. The need for adventurous spirits who would brave the unknown and learn how to deal with savage peoples in regions devoid of civilization produced a new mental attitude; one which emphasized all the boisterous self-assurance already present in our character, and rein-forced it with a growing sense of superiority which is particularly trying to those foreigners who do not belong to barbarous and savage tribes, and possibly also to some of those who do.

It is unnecessary to seek in any one circumstance a key to this gradual alteration of attitude, but it is not altogether fanciful to suppose that a major factor was the loss of our supplies of really excellent wine. The Emperor Julian had noticed the ale-drinking habits of the North, where grapes lacked, and refused to recognize the true Bacchus in this liquor smelling "of goat". Centuries later, the Norman Conquest brought the grape itself to England, but the climate did not allow of good wine being made. Under the Plantagenets the connexion with the best wine districts of France was exploited to the full, and our imports rose steadily from an annual 10,000 tons in the early years of Edward I's reign to some 15,000 by 1400. Through the mid-century and after the loss of Guienne, the amount dropped to rise again in the early Tudor period, and then finally to drop, as imported and home-made beer took its place. The warm geniality of the wine-drinker, so well exemplified in Chaucer, the vintner's son (and which marks so strong a contrast between the modern Germans of the wine districts and those farther north and east), deserted the great generality of Englishmen. The much less flexible good-fellowship of the northern ale-drinker itself gave ground before the inferior brew, beer, which has the dubious advantage of keeping longer, owing to its content of hops. Later still even ale and beer were supplanted by tea and slops, as Ludovici and others have pungently complained.

All this was still hidden in the distant future when Henry Tudor "picked the Crown of England out of a thorn-bush" in 1485: for the time being the new dynasty brought with it increasing prosperity, and if the country did not excel an earlier age in putting on the land "a white

134   Christchurch Priory: Salisbury Chapel, *c.* 1530.   Designer: probably
Thomas Bartewe

135   Westminster Abbey, Henry VII's Chapel: vault over the Lady Margaret's
tomb, 1503–19.   Designer: probably Robert Vertue

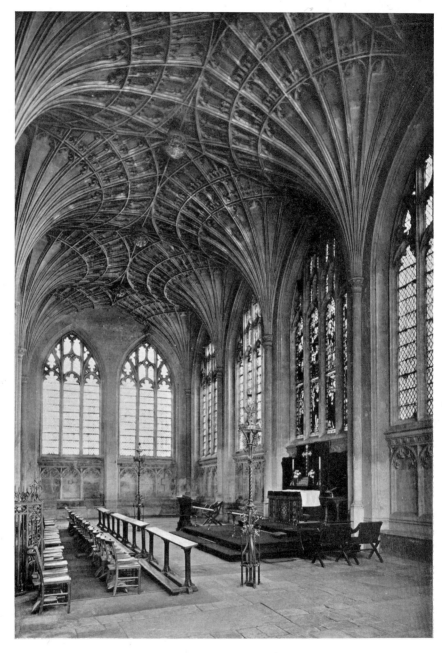

136   Peterborough Cathedral: Eastern Chapels, *c.* 1496–1508.
Designer: probably John Wastell

137   Cambridge, King's College Chapel: interior looking east, 1446–1515
Designer: Reginald Ely; of vaulting, John Wastell

138   Oxford, Christ Church: Hall Oriel, 1525–29.
Designers: John Lebons and Henry Redman

robe of churches", it did at least rebuild a great many, and added towers or chapels to many others. This volume of work was made possible by the great advances in the organization of masons and other building craftsmen. The greater towns all had their guilds of building operatives, and there were also building by-laws and the equivalent of the modern district surveyor to see them carried out and to settle disputes. These surveyors, known as viewers or searchers of their respective crafts, are found in London in the thirteenth century, and later appear at other cities such as York and Norwich. The system of training by apprenticeship was also fully developed, and even in the smaller country towns master masons and master carpenters could be found who were capable of building normal houses and chantry chapels to their own design. Here and there in the quarry districts or in the great cities were firms of mason-contractors specializing in the production of details and ornaments ready cut (143-4). The first large firm of this type for which there is any strong evidence was that of William Orchard of Headington Quarry near Oxford, who was both architect and contractor, and took a leading part in Oxford building during the thirty years preceding his death in 1504. His great works are Magdalen College and the vault of the Divinity Schools, which had remained unfinished for a whole generation (15, 106, 140). William Botoner, better known as William of Worcester, mentions the new vault as being built in the year 1480, and gives the dimensions of the building, including the library above, built for the collection bequeathed by Humphrey, Duke of Gloucester (see Appendix I).

Apart from development in organization, improvement in technical methods has to be considered. We have already seen that great advances were made during the fourteenth century, and the sequence of events showed that to a great extent the demand produced the supply; in other words, the necessity of fulfilling the wishes of royal and noble patrons for larger halls and chapels and for windows and decoration of greater refinement, provoked the invention of the artists concerned. In the fifteenth century the stimulus was removed, and in most directions there was retrogression: Battlefield Church, near Shrewsbury, built for Henry IV about 1408, could still be provided with glass of the most exquisite beauty, yet towards the end of the century there were no first-class English glass-painters left (66). Eltham shows structural and aesthetic decadence when compared with Westminster Hall roof. On the other hand, there had been partial advances in certain directions.

At Cambridge, under the master hand of Reginald Ely, the turreted gatehouse was being improved towards its final, successful form; John Branche at All Souls and other carpenters in East Anglia and Somerset were perfecting the "angel roof"; diligent local masons were improving the standard of church towers by selective imitation of the steeples of the greater churches. If indeed it may be attributed to the fifteenth rather than to the late fourteenth century, we have the adaptation of fan-vaulting as a structural expedient for works of large span. The late F. E. Howard dealt almost exhaustively with the fan-vaults that now exist, but had to confess that unless transitional examples have been lost, there is no link between the small fan-vaults of the Gloucester cloister and the high vaults of Sherborne, the first fan-work on a large scale, designed about 1430–40 (111).

As a decorative toy, the fan-vault appears in stone at Tewkesbury in the third quarter of the fourteenth century, and before the end of the century the Gloucester cloisters were being covered with a structural vault of this form. It was not, however, in masonry that the first high vault

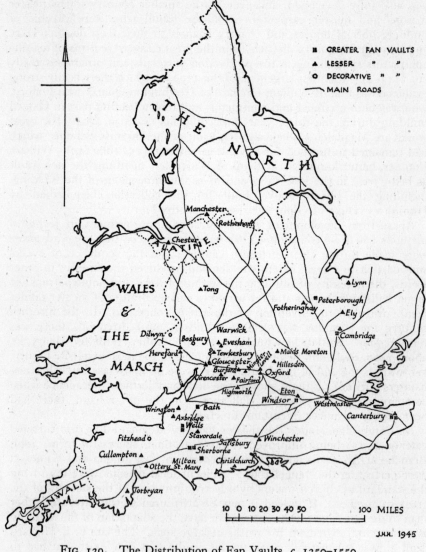

FIG. 139. The Distribution of Fan Vaults, c. 1350–1550.

of fan type appeared, but in timber: Hugh Herland's wooden vaulting of
c. 1390 for Winchester College Chapel has the effect, though not the
geometrical definition, and covers the considerable area of 96 feet by
30 feet. It may be that important early examples of the new type of work
are lost, but it is at least equally possible that the masters who had been
brought up in the tradition of lierne stellar vaulting were loath to give it
up—the fan's principal advantages lie in cheapness and reduction of
thrust, but except possibly at Sherborne, no fan-vault attains the exquisitely modulated effects of the nave vaults of Canterbury, Winchester,
and Norwich.

The fan-vault was cheap because it was standardized in its parts; all
the ribs were of the same curvature; it was easy to build because rib-and-
panel design was only apparent, and in most cases the whole work was cut
from the solid block; it was consequently less "alive" than other vaults
and needed less buttressing. Aesthetically, the device was not so satisfactory, and many of the finest late vaults are either not fans at all (Divinity
Schools and Cathedral choir, Oxford, and Christchurch Priory, Hants)
or only partially of fan form (Henry VII's Chapel). In spite of the many
ways in which the fans could be arranged (Howard classified them), there
was a grave danger of the monotony which afflicts all shop- and mass-
produced work. It must be admitted that there are a few supreme examples
of admirable fan-vaults, but these were the work of great masters, men
such as John Wastell and the brothers Vertue, of whom we shall hear
more later.

So numerous were the important architects of the period that only a
selection can be mentioned here. As had been the case for some two
hundred years, the Royal School in London was able to control the fashion,
forming a fusion between the inventions of East and West: the work of
the Canterbury masons and of those from Oxford and Cotswold. Among
the latter group, William Orchard has been mentioned, but though he
worked for Bishop Waynflete and visited London, he does not seem to
have been employed by the Crown. Orchard's work is good late Perpendicular, but shows little sign of the approaching florid treatment of detail.
Something of the new "Rococo" work is visible in Bishop Alcock's Chapel
at Ely, begun in 1488, and it is clearly present in the decorative tracery
on the central tower of Canterbury Cathedral—detail from the hand of
John Wastell, Archbishop Morton's master mason, who very possibly
found the grand composition of the tower already sketched by his predecessors. Certainly Bell Harry in its outlines belongs to the great school
founded by Yevele rather than to the newer and slighter feeling of the
time of its erection—roughly 1490–7 (**3, 22**).

Wastell's later career is entirely associated with East Anglia; he appears
at Bury St. Edmunds in 1498, and was master mason at the completion
and vaulting of King's College Chapel between 1508 and 1515 (**114, 137**).
From its extremely close resemblance to this Cambridge work, Wastell
must also be presumed the architect of the new work of Peterborough
(**136**)—when it is remembered that Morton came to Canterbury from Ely,

and that he had inaugurated the great drain from Peterborough to Wisbech still known as Morton's Leam, there seems some reason for supposing that Wastell's own origins were in the eastern counties; there had been Wastells near Bury and across mid-Suffolk by the early fourteenth century. Canterbury had her own masons, and is the probable source of the family which provided the two greatest masters of the time, the brothers Robert and William Vertue.

The family of Vertue is found in Essex in the mid-fifteenth century, but its known members were prominent woolmen who migrated from Bocking and Witham to Colchester, for which town John Vertue the younger was a member of Parliament in 1484 and in 1485–6. He was dead by 1499, in which year died a Robert Vertu, of Rochester. Robert may have been a scion of the Essex family who crossed the Thames estuary, or he may of course have been of entirely independent origin. The masons first appear as joint architects of the new abbey church at Bath in 1501, and simultaneously as King's masons in charge of works at the Tower of London, Greenwich Palace, and Windsor Castle (113, 130, 142). Robert Vertue, Robert Janyns, and John Lebons were the three master masons of Henry VII in 1506, when they submitted an estimate for his tomb at Westminster.

Robert Vertue was probably the chief designer of Henry VII's Chapel, but he died in the autumn of 1506, and during the last ten years of its building his brother William, as official King's Master Mason, would have been in charge. The detailed history of this period has yet to be written, and it would be rash to attempt a critical discrimination between the styles of the several men who were leaders of the Royal School; their work resembled, as do peas in a pod, and while the "office of works" manner can easily be recognized (for example, from that of Wastell), the individual contributions of Robert and of William Vertue, of Robert Janyns the younger, of John Lebons or Lubbyns, and of Henry Redman, still need the most careful sorting out. William Vertue had a fondness for breaking up his lines of cusping and tracery by the introduction of straight lines and diamond shapes among the simple and ogee curves; Robert was more interested in the diverging lines of fan-ribs or the sweep of the vertical up-rush of his mullions.

Until exhaustive analysis of all the surviving detail has been made, solutions must necessarily be tentative, and based upon subjective reactions to the work. I would suggest, using the known facts of the case as a foundation, that we see Robert Vertue's style at Bath Abbey and in the aisle vaults of Henry VII's Chapel; Robert Janyns's contribution in the window of star-polygonal plan, as in Henry VII's Tower at Windsor, and in the Chapel—perhaps the west front of St. George's Chapel is also largely influenced by his touch; William Vertue would then be regarded as a specialist in vaulting: he certainly carried out most of the vaults of St. George's Chapel, and almost certainly the dizzy canopy at Westminster, the crowning glory of what Norden called "this mirror of art and architect" (1, 135, 147–8).

140 Oxford, Magdalen College: Chapel doorway, 1475–80
Designer: William Orchard

142 Windsor Castle: Henry VII's Tower, 1498–1500.
Designer: Robert Janyns, junior. A detail of Mackenzie's
engraving

141 Thornbury Castle: Oriel windows, 1511–22.
Designer: possibly Robert Janyns, junior

Lebons just possibly came from Somerset, and in the oriel of Christ Church hall at Oxford (138) his hand is seen—it has a West-Country richness which would well accord with a Somerset origin. His colleague Henry Redman, however, is chiefly important for the attention he gave to the new uses of brick; Hampton Court Palace perfects into a living style the usage which John Cowper had begun but never finished at Kirby Muxloe. Redman for many years was also the official colleague of William Vertue, and it is difficult, perhaps impossible, to determine their shares in royal work. Vertue was the architect of Corpus Christi College, Oxford, according to the accounts, yet here we have a strict and sober building, admirably fulfilling its purpose, yet in appearance more closely related to Redman's Hampton Court than to the richly detailed work Vertue himself had in hand at Westminster.

William Vertue and William East, the chief contractor at the building of Corpus, as well as Humphrey Coke the carpenter, their colleague, were the victims of assault by two men who had been suborned by Fellows of Brasen Nose Hall, in 1512. East was seriously injured, and the ruffians were imprisoned until his recovery, when they were fined, and East and Vertue agreed not to prosecute the matter further in the King's Courts. East came from Abingdon, and Vertue and Coke from London, and there may possibly have been ill-feeling against them as "foreigners", but it seems likely that some more subtle university feud was in progress.

When Robert Vertue died in 1506, he left instructions that he should, if possible, be buried in the Abbey Church of St. Augustine at Canterbury, and his widow Eleanor subsequently lived at Canterbury. William, on the other hand, bought property at Kingston-upon-Thames, as Hugh Herland had done a century before, and maintained his "country house" —well-to-do craftsmen had been acquiring houses or lands in the suburban villages or farther out in the Home Counties since Henry III's time at least, so that the advent of the dormitory-town is by no means modern. From 1501 until his death in 1527, William Vertue was responsible for a very large amount of work, either by himself or in collaboration. Apart from the important buildings already mentioned, he was concerned with the design of the Chapel of St. Peter in the Tower of London after the destruction of the old chapel by fire in 1512; with work at Woking Palace; designed, in collaboration with Redman, the west side of the court and Lupton's Tower at Eton (150), and doubtless also Lupton's Chantry Chapel there. In his later years he had charge of important preparations for the Field of the Cloth of Gold in 1520, and the two-storied cloister of St. Stephen in the Palace of Westminster, completed under Redman after his death (159-169).

The work of the brothers Vertue typifies the architecture of their age; it is as brilliant, and possibly more attractive than the Rococo extravaganzas of a Balthasar Neumann, and if its construction lacks something of sincerity, it is still efficient and devised by a skill approaching that of a magician. At Bath the result is marred by some unfortunate second thoughts and by the interruption of work at the Dissolution, but the

s

asymmetry of the tower is handled with supreme genius, and the west front, baldly proclaiming the aisles and exhibiting the angelic ladders of Bishop King's dream, deserves more praise than it has yet received (27, 118). Henry VII's Chapel is, in its own way, one of the wonders of the world, and in spite of fire and restoration and members' hat-racks and tape-machines, St. Stephen's cloister is still one of the gems of Westminster.

The early exuberance of the Tudor building was a phenomenon of the Court School (like the "aureate diction" of the Court poetry), and where it reached out into the country it was carried by courtiers acquainted with the royal architects and their work, or was produced by local men imitating the latest fashions. Hence it was that fan-vaulting and bay-windows of many facets are not found in the North. Where rich work does appear in the counties north of Trent it may be accepted as a sign of the employment of a southern mason: the splendid tower of All Saints Derby (now the Cathedral) was built between 1510 and 1532 under the direction of John Otes, who had been a mason-setter at King's College, Cambridge, under John Wastell in 1508 (19). At Cambridge, Otes was paid 3s. 8d. a week, the pay received by the wardens, and 4d. more than that received by the normal skilled masons, while at Derby he received only the standard rate of 3s. 4d. but was described as a freemason, and doubtless had a yearly retainer and a gown in addition.

An earlier work of unusual character is the church of Steeple Ashton in Wiltshire, where the nave was rebuilt and chapels added to the chancel between 1480 and 1500 at the charges of two families of wealthy clothmen of the place, the work being carried out by Thomas Lovell, freemason. Stone high vaults were intended, but only built in wood (145). This was before the great eruption of court works, but the manner in which style could be rapidly disseminated is exemplified by the case of one Cheney, a mason working under Redman on Wolsey's Hampton Court, who in 1521 was allowed time off to go to Reading and design new arcades and a font for St. Lawrence's Church. Similarly, William Burden of Ely, evidently a prominent freemason, worked at Cambridge (he was concerned with the building of Great St. Mary's Church in 1512–14, and perhaps earlier) and was employed between 1505 and 1511 on the provision of the details for Little Saxham Hall in Suffolk. At Croscombe in Somerset, when a chapel and vestries were added to the church between 1506 and 1512, the churchwardens obtained the services of John Carter, an Exeter freemason, though this entailed a journey of sixty-five miles in each direction.

Many churches were engaged in completing works begun before the civil wars; Boston "Stump" in Lincolnshire, the famous beacon tower of the parish church, had been started as early as 1309, but the two lower stages of the present tower date from the second quarter of the fifteenth century; later it was decided to raise the tower instead of adding a spire, and the bell-chamber was built—finally, in the first quarter of the sixteenth century, came the graceful lantern with its flying buttresses (158). Masons' marks prove the lantern to be of quite a distinct period, apart from the

143   Bromham Church: Tocotes Chapel, *c.* 1490–92.   144   Devizes, St. John's Church: South Chapel, *c.* 1490

Mass production in the fifteenth century

146 Oxford Cathedral: Presbytery vaulting, *c.* 1480–1500. Designer: possibly William Orchard

145 Steeple Ashton Church: South Nave Aisle, *c.* 1480–1500. Designer: Thomas Lovell

obvious change of style. In northern Lincolnshire, another great steeple was in progress, that at Louth. Here also a great part of the church and the lower stages of the tower had been in process of rebuilding during the middle of the fifteenth century. Then came a pause, and only in 1501 was the spire begun (157).

The first master mason at the building of Louth spire was John Cole, who remained in charge of the work for four years; from the spring of 1505 his place was taken by Master Christopher Scune, a north-country-man who was in charge of the rebuilding of the nave of Ripon Minster, begun in 1503. A possible explanation of the employment of Scune lies in the position of Louth Park Abbey as a daughter house of Fountains, close to Ripon. At Fountains, Abbot Marmaduke Huby built a particu-larly fine tower in the early days of the century, and this tower has marked resemblances of style to Scune's work at Ripon (155). It is at least a tenable hypothesis that Scune designed Huby's tower; that the Louth churchwardens consulted the sacrist of Louth Park, and that their request for the name of an experienced steeple builder was thus forwarded to Fountains. Scune was undoubtedly a man of considerable reputation, for between 1508 and 1515 he obtained the post of master mason to Durham Cathedral (156), and was still at work there in 1519, while he appears at Ripon in 1521 supervising the masons at work on the fabric, Robert Squyer being the resident master or warden. By this time Ripon nave was nearing completion (120); Louth spire had been finished in 1515, and the weathercock made in York from a great basin captured from the King of Scots at Flodden. Thus after two hundred years Bannockburn was avenged—James IV was dead, and Skelton could boast:

> Your Seven Sisters, that gun so gay,
> All have ye lost and cast away.
> Thus Fortune hath turned you, I dare well say,
> Now from a king to a clot of clay . . .

By common consent Louth steeple is the most perfect completed tower and spire of parochial scale in England; as in so many other instances, several brains had a part in its design, and more than one pair of hands set out its details. We do not know who first prepared the masterly scheme of its composition, but it may well have been John Porter, a prominent master mason of Lincoln, called into consultation by the authorities at York Minster in 1450 and who six years later obtained the office of master mason there. He had taken up the freedom of York in 1454, and when he died in 1466 left, among other legacies, one to the Guild of St. Mary of Louth. This implies some connexion with the town, and his journeys to York, a distance of seventy-five miles from Lincoln, prove him to have had a widespread reputation.

Christopher Scune, though he merely supervised the erection of Louth spire, was undoubtedly an architect of real genius; the nave of Ripon is a strong and finely balanced work, and contrasts with the inserted arches which were underpinning the falling central tower. The new casing of the tower piers consists on plan of a continuous deep roll moulding, uninterrupted by any fillets; these giant piers thus have the natural sweep of a tree and it is difficult to resist the suggestion of physical growth (120). From the piers spring stilted arches, acutely pointed, whose unusual curve approaches the parabolic catenary curve of forces employed in building by the ancient Hittites and by the Sassanids of Persia, and again by twentieth-century engineers using reinforced concrete. The Ripon arches were never completed, and the lop-sided result bears witness to the calamity which so soon overtook English architecture. The tower at Fountains Abbey, which is either by Scune or by an architect with closely related style, shows the same mastery over the physics of stone-and-mortar, with which a parallel command of psychical effects goes hand in hand. The modern tourist approaches Fountains from Ripon through the most skilfully designed vistas of the landscapist, and repeated pilgrimages only increase the sense of surprised wonder with which the Abbey ruins at last strike upon the eye. Now in ruin, as once in splendour, the tower is the keynote. From the harsh tenets of St. Bernard, the Cistercians had trodden a weary road, yet who will grudge them their sublime disobedience, which raised at Fountains a witness to man's divine ancestry, more convincing than fifty sermons?

The top stage of the Fountains tower is lit by square-headed windows with uncusped lights; here is another sign of the revulsion from the Southern tendencies towards artificiality and encrusted decoration. There was no decadence in an age which, in spite of every temptation, could produce such towers as those of Fountains and Louth; such domestic work as Kirby Muxloe and Hampton Court. In music, if the bass is properly constructed, the work will last; in like manner, sincere and true structure is the ground-bass of architecture. A lovely melody, coloured passages of notes; rich decoration, paintings, and imagery—all these have their place and can enhance the effect upon ear and eye; without a solid background they are as sounding brass and a tinkling cymbal. Amid the frippery antics of the budding Renaissance, men like Scune and Henry Redman could appreciate these truths and put them into practice. Classic details were arriving as a mere surface veneer; because they were new they had an advantage over the Gothic details which sprang out of the inherited traditions of four centuries; these architects with a sublime courage began to throw off their adventitious aids in the face of the enemy, and appear clad only in their native worth.

It was Wolsey whose luxurious tastes had aroused such passionate indignation among the Conservatives: men like Skelton who foresaw the catastrophe which Skelton, for one, did not live to see. Yet from the point of view of their art, there is a curious reversal of positions; Skelton the political conservative wrote poetry of the most subtle modernism; Wolsey hung with rich tapestries a palace of enormous size, but built of brick in a restrained and dignified style. From the straightforward composition of Hampton Court, relieved by its calculated asymmetries, springs the whole, or almost the whole, of later English vernacular building. The charm of the English house, the harmonious repose of our villages and country towns, owes its being very largely to the fact that the work begun by Cowper at Kirby Muxloe was completed by Henry Redman—if the brick Tudor style had not become an integral part of the traditions of the Court School, the later history of the English house might have been as unfortunately mannered as that of the French.

Speaking of German Baroque, Dr. Pevsner remarks that "one can see from the devotion to-day of the peasants in these . . . churches that their style is not the style of a privileged set of virtuosi, but the style of the people. And yet it is by no means a simple style. Much of it seems naïve, but the more one tries to penetrate, the more is one overwhelmed by its complexity and depth." The words might be echoed, and with even greater truth, of the second phase of English Tudor. The first phase, which produced Bath Abbey and Henry VII's Chapel, had some of the characteristics of the virtuoso's architecture; it appeals to a highly cultured and artificial taste, though it escapes banality and the purely meretricious by its superb sense of structural values. Now, to the same sense of construction was added this intriguing quality—deceptive naïvety. In his supreme moments Wren could play in this manner, as he did at St. Stephen Walbrook; but such exceptions simply prove that great genius can triumph even over the deepest erudition and virtuosity.

At Hampton Court we may sigh our relief that Wren's attempt to modernize the Palace (surely one of his least inspired and most blighting works) stopped short of the original courts built for Wolsey (149). Here, after disentangling the accretions of Henry VIII, we can appreciate in all its freshness and clarity Redman's great conception—of all the works that we have left, this is the noblest offspring of a single brain. Westminster Hall alone gives a deeper pang to the emotions, but it is the product of three men—William Rufus's master mason who gave it its plan and proportions, and Henry Yevele and Hugh Herland, who devised its present form. Hardly one of our Gothic cathedrals or castles was born singly, of one mind; so we get at best (at Westminster and Canterbury for example) a quilt made up of patches—samples from the workshops of genius mountaged together.

There is a great deal of information about Henry Redman's career: his father Thomas Redman was master mason at Westminster Abbey for ten years after Robert Stowell's death in 1505, so that Henry, who succeeded him in this post, no doubt had excellent chances of imbibing the very best of both practice and precept. From Henry's will, it appears that the family came from Hepmangrove in the parish of Bury beside Ramsey, and it may well be that the immediate forebears of Thomas had been master masons to Ramsey Abbey. Farther back the family took its name from a different and unusual occupation: the Redman or Reedman of the fifteenth and sixteenth century was a corruption of the Abbot's *Rideman*, or riding bailiff, whose office seems to have been hereditary. At any rate, as far back as the middle of the twelfth century, an extent shows "Robertus Rideman" holding four acres at "*Hecmundegrave*" by the service of two bowls of honey, and the family continues in the same place all through the thirteenth and fourteenth centuries. It must have been in the knowledge of this amazingly long tradition that Henry Redman was careful to leave the reversion of "my dwellyng howse with the lands not bequest" to "the next heyre male of my blood beyring the name of Reedmans in Huntingdonshire, besyde our Lady of Reedbone", a chapel at Hepmangrove which has long since disappeared.

The list of Redman's works is a long one, but many are lost or altered; with John Lebons he designed Cardinal College at Oxford, whose remains surround Tom Quad at Christ Church (138, 153-4). At Greenwich Palace he built in 1519 the two startling Tilt Yard Towers which dominate the old drawings and views, and between 1515 and 1522 the tower of St. Margaret's Westminster, now much changed by rebuilding. The great hall of Wolsey's York Place' and other works there were roughly contemporary, and like the work at Christ Church, were still in progress when Redman died on 10 July 1528; on the following day a letter to Wolsey mentioned that Henry VIII "is sorry for the death of Mr. Redman, his mason". He was buried in his parish church at Brentford, ancient capital of Middlesex, where a brass asks us: "Pray for the Soule of Henry Redman sumtyme chefe Mr. Mason of ye Kyngs works and Johane his wyf speciall benefactors of this churche . . . which Henry deceased July 10, 1528. On whose soulle Jhesu have Mercy."

The masons were not the only Englishmen of genius in the royal service; through the whole of the reigns of Henry VIII, Edward VI, and Mary, and for part of that of Elizabeth, the Crown had in its employ a dynasty of great carpenters. The greatest of these was Humphrey Coke, who first appears upon the Scottish Border in 1496, as a member of a commission to impress craftsmen and labourers for defensive works; three years later he was appointed chief carpenter of Berwick-on-Tweed, and is described as of London. Soon he was in the South, having a hand in the designs of the new work at Eton College in 1510, and a few years later designed the timberwork for Corpus Christi College, Oxford. In 1519 he became King's Chief Carpenter, and next year was busy preparing for the Field of the Cloth of Gold, with William Vertue (159). Apart from this official work he also acted as chief carpenter for Wolsey after the death of Richard Russell in 1517, and had heavy responsibility as chief carpenter for the building of the Savoy Hospital. He managed to find time to serve as warden of the Carpenters Company from 1506 to 1510, and again in 1519, and several items in the books of the company suggest that he had a private practice in London as well. After acting as chief carpenter for Cardinal College between 1525 and the stop of the work in 1529, he died in March 1531 and was buried in the Chapel of the Savoy. (See Appendix V, v.)

Of Coke's existing works, by far the greatest in importance is the hall roof at Christ Church, where the mistakes of Eltham have been corrected, and the whole composition improved almost out of recognition (154). In

147   Westminster Abbey: Henry VII's Chapel, 1503–19.
Designer: probably Robert Vertue; of vault: William Vertue

148 Westminster Abbey: Henry VII's Chapel, 1503–19.
Designer: probably Robert Vertue

the case of roofs of such a wide span as 40 feet, there is no very great latitude for variation in structure, for some form of hammer-beam truss is almost inevitable. It is wonderful how, in spite of this handicap, each of the masters of English roof construction was able to impress his own individuality upon the materials at his command. Coke's roof appears strong in spite of its low pitch, yet is graceful rather than heavy, and its parts are all admirably proportioned. His earlier and simpler work at Corpus Christi College also shows a happy mastery of scale—it provides exactly the covering needed by a small hall of comparatively homely size. The suites of horizontal mouldings betray Coke's knowledge of Eltham, but here they are happily restrained, and proportioned to the whole.

Coke's successor, James Nedeham, seems to have been endowed with persistent pushfulness—the son of Christopher Nedeham or Nedam, a London carpenter, he became free of the Carpenters Company in 1514, and in the following year paid for licence to "present" an apprentice bound to him for seven years. In 1522 he went abroad on foreign service, and was a master carpenter in the war with France which lasted until 1525; on his return he was pensioned by grant of an office as gunner in the Tower of London, and became one of Wolsey's servants in connexion with the works at York Place, Westminster. After Wolsey's fall, Nedeham was retained by the King, and continued to work at York Place during its conversion into the new royal palace of Westminster. By 1530 he was being referred to as "one of the King's master carpenters" and succeeded to the office of chief carpenter immediately on Coke's death in the following March.

Nedeham had evidently attracted the notice of Thomas Cromwell when working under him for Wolsey, for at Cromwell's rise to eminence in 1532 the then clerk and surveyor of the works, Thomas Flower, was called upon to resign, and the vacant post given to Nedeham—a revolutionary appointment, for though literate (specimens of "Jamys Nedam's" well-formed signature exist in plenty) Nedeham was no clerk in the old sense. Soon after this appointment Nedeham was engaged on "Cromwell's work", and this was almost certainly the "large and spacious" house in Throgmorton Street, of whose erection Stow tells a curious story. "This house being finished, and having some reasonable plot of ground left for a garden, he (Cromwell) caused the pales of the gardens adjoining to the north part thereof on a sudden to be taken down; twenty-two feet to be measured forth right into the north of every man's ground; a line there to be drawn, a trench to be cast, a foundation laid, and a high brick wall to be built. My father had a garden there, and a house standing close to his south pale; this house they loosed from the ground, and bare upon rollers into my father's garden twenty-two feet, ere my father heard thereof; no warning was given him, nor other answer, when he spake to the surveyors of that work, but that their master Sir Thomas commanded them so to do; no man durst go to argue the matter, but each man lost his land, and my father paid his whole rent, which was 6s. 6d. the year, for that half which was left. Thus much of mine own knowledge have I thought good to note, that the sudden rising of some men causeth them to forget themselves."

The advent of Nedeham brought in a new era in the royal building construction; for the first time it became usual to have large amounts of overtime worked at night and in the men's meal-times and the time of their afternoon siesta. Everything must be done post-haste, and ill fare the slacker. These methods made for Nedeham bitter enemies among the older clerics of the civil service, and he was several times accused of taking commission on materials he ordered, and of drawing double pay, because "he makes his own book and pays without comptrolment". However it was achieved, work in immense quantity was carried out during Nedeham's term of office; extensions or rebuilding were taking place at Hampton Court, Greenwich, Whitehall (York Place), the Tower of London, and at several of the lesser royal manors; the fantastic and shoddy extravagance of Nonsuch was rushed up, and the more solidly built coastal forts planned by the German engineer Stephen von Hashenperg. Of Nedeham's personal share in all this work it is difficult to speak, but fortunately we know that he made the drawings and prepared the moulds for the great roof of Hampton Court hall in 1532–3: this added a new form to those already employed for roofs of large span, for its slopes are double. This double-slope roof is commonly called "Mansard" from its supposed seventeenth-century French inventor, but it appears quite early in the eastern counties as a local form (the so-called kerb-roof), though so far as extant examples are concerned, not in works of the main stream until Hampton Court (124).

When Nedeham was promoted to the office of clerk and surveyor, John Russell became chief carpenter. Son of Richard Russell, a prominent Westminster carpenter who had worked for Wolsey until his death in 1517, John had married Christine, the daughter of Humphrey Coke, and became heir to the extensive Coke properties in the Strand. Living on until 1566, it is to John Russell more than to any other figure that we must attribute the continuity of the English tradition of timber construction. The onset of Renaissance detail was not able to smother the sturdy vigour of the English hammer-beam roof, and the line of descent passes on from Christ Church, Oxford, through Hampton Court, to Gray's Inn, the Middle Temple, and Trinity College, Cambridge. Finally, after the disastrous interlude of the Civil War, the old methods asserted themselves in the new roof of the hall of Lambeth Palace, which, in spite of its somewhat incongruous pendants and cornices, retains a goodly portion of the gracious nobility of Westminster Hall.

If John Russell was the last of the mediæval carpenters, John Molton held a similar place among the master masons; he was probably in the king's service before 1526, when he was one of the witnesses to William Vertue's will, in the following year became master mason of Bath Abbey, and in 1528 succeeded to the offices of master mason to the King and to Westminster Abbey at the death of Henry Redman. Molton seems to have been a careful but perhaps rather spiritless imitator of Redman,

149　Hampton Court: Great West Gatehouse, 1515–25.
Designer: Henry Redman

150　Eton College: Lupton's Tower, 1516–20.
Designers: William Vertue and Henry Redman

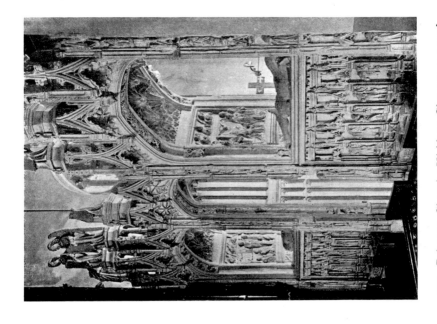

The Monument intended for King Henry the fixde.

151   Paignton Church: Kirkham Chantry, *c.* 1500?

152   Design for tomb of Henry VI, *c.* 1500.
Probably by Robert Vertue

though his great gatehouse at St. James's Palace is a worthy work with which to bring the story of English architecture to a close. Here, within the palace, as at Hampton Court and Nonsuch, Molton was powerless to prevent the invasion by foreigners of the whole domain of decoration, furniture, and fittings. In the architectural details of the new coastal forts, notably in the beautiful little castle of St. Mawes, Molton was writing the epitaph of Gothic art, and when he died, five days before his royal master in the January of 1547, the tale was told.

Other royal masons there were, and a few in the provincial centres, who prevented the total extinction of the lamp. Thomas Pettyt, who was in charge of the repairs at Wark Castle in Northumberland in 1543, and who two years later produced the exquisite "Platt of the Lowe Countrye att Calleys" now among the Cotton manuscripts, was one of the men who carried on the old manner in works of stern necessity. Pettyt, in all probability, was the architect of the bold blockhouse at Lindisfarne which frowns at the North Sea like an Arthurian hold. At York Minster, bridging the period of transition, was John Forman, whose term of office began in 1523 and lasted until his death in 1558. Between 1525 and 1536 he entirely rebuilt the church of St. Michael-le-Belfry, beside the Minster, a sturdy example of Northern Tudor, devoid of the frivolities of the South (**167**). He seems also to have carried out building for Wolsey at some of his northern manors, Southwell, Scrooby, or Cawood, before the Cardinal's downfall, as he was one of the many servants to whom large sums of money (in Forman's case £58) were due.

Finally, something must be said of the remarkable figure of Thomas Bartewe or Bertie, master mason of Winchester Cathedral in 1532, and father of the Richard Bertie who married the Duchess of Suffolk and founded the Bertie line in the peerage of England. When J. H. Round pointed out the true paternity of Richard Bertie, he was so delighted to be able to "debunk" fanciful and snobbish theories that he erred gravely in the opposite direction. He even goes so far as to imply villein origins by speaking of the family property at Bersted near Maidstone as a typical yardland or virgate, forgetting the "enclosed" character of Kent, and that in any case masons were of free blood, and generally speaking of good yeoman standing. As a matter of fact, the Berty, Barty, or Bertyn family had been settled in or close to Bersted for over a century when Robert Berty died in 1501, leaving his substantial properties there and in Maidstone to his sons Thomas and William. He left them also the significant bequest of "my working Toles such as be for macyns crafte". In 1509 his widow Margaret or Marion received a general pardon, which tells us that after leaving Bersted she had been living at Godstone, and at the time of receiving the pardon was dwelling in Colchester.

Her son Thomas was in Winchester by 1520, and by 1532 was not only master mason at Winchester Cathedral, where the vaulting of the presbytery aisles was in progress, but deputy Treasurer of Wolvesey as well. This was of course an office of importance under the Bishop, then Stephen Gardiner. To Bartewe may be attributed the general remodelling

T

of the presbytery begun by Bishop Fox in the 1520's; the work has marked resemblances to the current practice of the Royal School, as exemplified by William Vertue, but lacks Vertue's genius (163). Bartewe was, however, an accomplished architect, and after the Dissolution transformed Titchfield Priory into that Tudor Place House which is now in ruins (134, 164). A letter written to Wriothesley, the client, by John Crayford, in April 1538, concludes with a postscript to the effect that Bartyew had told him "that smoke shall not be avoyded by the chymneys of your chieffe lodgings if the steple stand"—so the Priory tower had to come down. Immediately after this he was in the King's employ, being charged with the building of Calshot Castle on the Solent in 1539, and then with that of Hurst Castle from 1541 to 1544, when on the completion of the works he was appointed first captain of the castle. In 1550 he received a grant of arms, and when he died five years later he left goods to the value of over £40 at Hurst and at Winchester, where he had a house. If the fame of Thomas Bartewe has been somewhat overshadowed by the academic prowess of his son Richard, who went up to Oxford in 1533 at the age of sixteen, and by the distinction of the noble lines descended from them, he still deserves to be remembered not the least among English worthies, a man who won his family a place in history by the confident exercise of his art.

Of the arts other than architecture little remains to be said: between 1486 and 1502, Robert Fyll succeeded to John Serle as King's Painter, and at Henry VII's funeral in 1509 John Broun, William Whytyng, and John Wolfe, appeared as the three King's painters. At the beginning of 1512 Brown was appointed Serjeant Painter, and held the office until he was discharged as "impotent and feeble" twelve years later. As Alderman Sir John Browne he is honoured by the Painter-Stainers Company as the donor of premises for their common hall in 1532, the year of his death. Vincent Volpe succeeded to Brown, but from Holbein's first visit to England in 1526 the whole course of our art was changed, and it is needless to follow further the careers of the last of the English court painters of the Middle Age. On the other hand, the King's Players were growing in importance, and as early as 1494 "the players of the King's interludes" are named as receiving five marks yearly per person: the four players named were John English, Edward Maye, Richard Gibson, and John Hamond, while nine years afterwards their number had increased to five by the addition of William Rutter and John Scott, Maye having fallen out. Through the reign of Henry VIII the King's players, and sometimes also the Queen's players, are found receiving rewards at places as far apart as Durham, Thetford, Oxford, and Shrewsbury—for a considerable proportion of their time they must have been on tour, as were the court minstrels and the bear-leaders—royal bears passed through Louth, for example, in 1537, 1541, and 1543, the "beerward" on each occasion receiving 20*d.* from the churchwardens.

Some of the musicians of the Tudor age have already been mentioned: the great Fayrfax, Newark, and Cornish the associate of Skelton. Grattan

153   Oxford, Christ Church: Great Gate, 1525–29.
Designers: John Lebons and Henry Redman

154   Oxford, Christ Church: Hall, 1525–29.   Designers: John Lebons and Henry
Redman; of roof: Humfrey Coke

Flood recovered the careers of a much greater number, and showed the links by which the English school maintained continuity with the past of Dunstable and Power. As with all the arts, the conflict of the Roses had for a time damped down the fires of invention, but Láng goes too far when he claims that "the horrors of the war between 1455 and 1485 put an end to the flourishing musical culture of England". That the leadership of European music passed to the Netherlands masters cannot be denied, but England followed her own course in steady fashion, and her Church music at least never required to be brought back from the Continent, while the keyboard remained almost an English monopoly until the seventeenth century. While a real gap occurred in the series of English poets in the middle of the fifteenth century, no such calamity befell our music.

Henry Abyngdon succeeded Plummer as Master of the Chapel Royal in 1455 and held the post for twenty-three years, while a new generation grew up around him. Also the Master of St. Katherine's Hospital at Bristol, he was "the grand old man" of musical circles; a doggerel epitaph, said to be a joke perpetrated by Sir Thomas More, refers to

> . . . old Henry, no freend to mischievous envy,
> Surnam'd Abyngdon, to all men most hartily welcom

and mentions that he had been a clerk at Wells. There he was the master of Richard Hygons, who passed on the Wells tradition to Richard Bramston and he in turn to William Parsons, who lived into the reign of Elizabeth.

Through the tradition of the Chapel Royal, Abyngdon was connected with the flourishing generation of composers who followed his successor Gilbert Banaster, some of whom, Cornish, Fayrfax, and Newark, we have already met. Outside the immediate circle of the Court the Countess of Richmond, Henry VII's mother, proved herself an important patroness of music, having in her service the song-writer Thomas Farthing and the more notable Hugh Ashton, composer of masses and of a number of highly developed pieces in variation form for the exchequer or virginals. No work comparable to this of Ashton's is known in Europe, and it must have been the outcome of a native school sprung up to give expression to the English keyboard instrument.

If Ashton was pre-eminent in music for the virginals, the great master of the organ was John Redford, born about the time of Bosworth Field, and successively choir-boy, Vicar-Choral, and Organist and Master of the Choristers at St. Paul's Cathedral. He held these last posts from 1525 to 1540, and during this period had among the boys under his charge Thomas Tusser, who in his *Hundreth Good Pointes of Husbandrie* (1557) tells of his schooling and his good fortune in coming under Redford's guidance:

> But mark the chance, myself to vance
> By friendship's lot to Paul's I got,
> So found I grace a certain space
> Still to remain
> With Redford there, the like no where,
> For cunning such and virtue much
> By whom some part of music's art,
> So did I gain.

Besides his musical and educational work, Redford wrote a dramatic interlude "Wit and Science", parts of which are set to music.

The grand manner of English music was carried on through the stormy mid-century by the "three T's", John Taverner, Christopher Tye, and Thomas Tallis. Taverner became a chorister at Tattershall College in Lincolnshire soon after 1500, and Master of the Choristers there in 1524. Two years later he received a like appointment at Wolsey's newly founded Oxford College, where the services under his direction were reported by Cromwell to Wolsey in 1528 to be "solemn and full of harmony". Taverner became infected with heretical opinions and resigned his post in 1530, to take an active part in the suppression of the monasteries, under Cromwell. He married Rose Parrowe of Spalding (perhaps the "good marriage" he had been so loath to lose by leaving Tattershall in 1526), and died and was buried at Boston in 1548.

Whereas Taverner's change of faith proved disastrous to his musical talents, Tye and Tallis were both able to accommodate themselves to the needs of the reformed service. Tye began his career as a chorister at King's College, Cambridge, about 1510, and was organist of Ely Cathedral from 1541 to 1561, when he took orders and spent the last twelve years of his life as rector of several country parishes. His works include settings for both the Roman and English services. So also do those of Tallis, who was a London choir-boy, perhaps at St. Paul's Cathedral, soon after 1520, and became organist to Waltham Abbey. After the abbey's dissolution, he entered the Chapel Royal, and so extensive was the work of his forty years' career thereafter that he has been termed "father of English cathedral music". Through him the great tradition passed to his pupil and colleague William Byrd, and thus beyond the limits of our period.

Last of all, a few words must be added as to the fate of English sculpture. That the leading freemasons were still at times sculptors is shown by the contract of employment entered into in 1488 between the Prior and Chapter of Durham and John Bell, who was to serve the convent for life in "all their works of masonry with imagery and other". So far as wood-carving is concerned, there was a remarkable school at Ripon under the leadership of William Brownfleet or Bromflet. His shop produced an amazing series of works of the highest order, characterized by marked individuality of design and by exquisite workmanship. The chief works of this shop, so far as is known, comprised the choir-stalls at Ripon, made in 1489–94, those at Manchester of 1505–9, a set for Bridlington Priory completed about 1518, and those of Beverley Minster, made about 1520. Brownfleet also contracted to make a loft in Ripon Minster in 1518, was paid a reward of 6s. 8d. for his supervision of the carpenters at work on the fabric there in 1520–21, and in 1522 travelled to York, Weighton, and Hull, to purchase boards for the Minster fittings. In this same year he was engaged on carvings behind the High Altar of Ripon, now lost. He was undoubtedly an artist of great originality and distinction, and also held high civic office as wakeman or mayor of Ripon in 1511. In the exquisite Ripon misericords telling the story of Jonah and the whale we

156 Durham Cathedral: Central Tower, 1465–90.
Designer: probably Thomas Barton

155 Fountains Abbey: Tower, c. 1510–25.
Designer: possibly Christopher Scune

157　Louth Church: Steeple.　Tower, *c.* 1460–90; Spire, 1501–15.
Designer: perhaps John Porter; of spire, John Cole

158 Boston Church: Tower, *c.* 1425–50. Lantern, *c.* 1510–20, perhaps by
John Tempas

LE CHAMP DE DRAP D'OR

THE INTERVIEW OF HENRY THE KING OF ENGLAND AND THE FRENCH KING FRANCIS I BETWEEN GUISNES AND ARDRES IN THE MONTH OF JUNE 1520

FROM THE ORIGINAL PICTURE TWELVE FEET SIX INCH IN LENGTH AND SIX FEET PRESERVED IN THE ROYAL APARTMENTS AT WINDSOR CASTLE

159   The Field of Cloth of Gold, 1520.   William Vertue and Humfrey Coke.
From the engraving published by the Society of Antiquaries

probably possess works from Brownfleet's own hand, while other carvings done by his assistants reflect his mastery with varying degrees of success (78).

The other important northern firm of carvers was that of Drawswerd, of York. Thomas Drawswerd took up the freedom in 1495, and was working for the Minster in 1498; he was Chamberlain of York in 1501 and Sheriff in 1505–6, when he submitted an estimate for image-work in Henry VII's Chapel at Westminster. In 1508 he was elected an alderman, and at about this time is believed to have produced the existing rood-screen of Newark-on-Trent. His public career was crowned in 1512 by his election as Member of Parliament for York, and in 1515 and again in 1523 he was Lord Mayor. At his death in 1529 he left extensive house property in York to his wife Maud and to his children, George and Maud.

Drawswerd was probably the last of the great English sculptors; his rival for the Westminster work in 1506 was one Lawrence Ymbar, who was to make wooden patterns for bronze to be cast by Nicholas Ewen. It may be that the existing bronze screen is to Ymbar's design. It is, however, very doubtful if Ymbar was English. He does not appear elsewhere under this name, but it seems extremely likely that he was identical with the Laurence Emler who was paid 40s. in 1492 by the London Bridge authorities for making a new statue of St. Thomas "wrought in stone, standing upon the wall on the west side of the said bridge". Now this raises a further presumption: that the sculptor of St. Thomas and competitor for the tomb-work was no other than the Laurence Emler, native of Swabia in Almain, who, with the heirs of his body lawfully begotten in England, was granted a patent of denization on 8 January 1506. Several parts of Germany were producing great sculptors during the latter part of the fifteenth century: for example, Veit Stoss, of Nuremberg, born about 1447, who after a long sojourn in Poland from 1477 to 1496, returned to his native city and died there in 1533; Tilman Riemenschneider of Würzburg, who was born c. 1460 at a small hamlet in the Harz, became a master woodcarver in 1485 and died in 1531; and Hans Leinberger of Landshut in Bavaria, who worked largely in wood, from 1513 until after 1530.

A number of the statues in Henry VII's Chapel are of unusual interest, and are undoubtedly foreign work, though tinged with English influences; other statues may be by Englishmen, such as John Hudd or Robert Belamy who were working on the royal buildings at Westminster and at the Tower in 1500. The Bellamy family seem to have been settled at Canterbury for two or three generations. There is, however, nothing to connect these men with statues in the round such as that of St. Thomas, carved by Emler, and it would be hazardous to put forward any known English name as that of the author of the grand head of the Almighty now in the Winchester Cathedral Library (160). This enigmatic work is of tremendous power, and translates into stone Skelton's thought:

> O Maker of mankind, that forméd day and night,
> Whose power imperial comprehendeth every place!

Its date has been placed by Mr. T. D. Atkinson at the end of the fifteenth century, or in the opening years of the sixteenth, and this agrees well with all the relevant material, though there is literally nothing with which it can fairly be compared, except perhaps the wooden figure of Jesse at Abergavenny Priory.[1] It has certainly traces of a relationship with the earlier English iconography of God the Father, as in the woodcarving at St. Mary's Hall, Coventry, where something of the same repose and calm are seen. Winchester, which had possessed classic statues in the twelfth century, produced the College Madonnas about 1390, and the delicious fragmentary Madonna (now in the Cathedral choir) rather later, is, above all English cities, the one where such a work by a native would be conceivable. Against this is the general decline of the period, and the fact that foreigners were being extensively employed in London, where a good proportion of the carvers' shops must have been still in English hands. For the present, the great Head of Winchester must remain a mystery, but it is not too late for some document to be found which may attribute it positively to Emler, or to some local artist whose fame has been quenched by the bitter rage of the iconoclast. Meanwhile, in sombre majesty, the sightless eyes of the Universal Father gaze down upon a closed chapter of human existence.

---

[1] But Mr. L. E. Tanner has recently drawn my attention to a splendid head now preserved in the Upper Library at Westminster Abbey; it is probably a portrait of John Islip, Abbot 1500–32.

160   Winchester Cathedral: Head now in Library, *c.* 1500

161   Abergavenny Priory: Figure of Jesse (wood), *c.* 1500

162   Chester Bridge, 1347. Designer: Henry Snelleston

VII

SURVIVAL AND RETROSPECT

THE triumph of classic detail over the traditional methods of Northern Europe was due to a change of fashion; a change imposed by a few royal and distinguished patrons fascinated by novelty, or led to believe that by furnishing their regality in the trappings of antiquity, they would themselves become Roman Emperors. Taste is fickle, and it would be as fruitless to compare the aesthetic sense of Henry VIII or Francis I with that of Richard II or Charles VI, as it is to conduct any prolonged discussion upon matters which in the last resort can be decided only by opinion. The lover of the classic will doubtless proclaim the kings of the Renaissance as possessed of a higher degree of discrimination than their predecessors, while all that I need do in rebuttal of their judgment is to appeal to that of those mighty monarchs under whose sway Europe was thickly encrusted with the gems of Gothic art.

Under Henry VIII and Wolsey, although many Flemish and German artists were retained, there was a widespread invocation of Italian methods and personnel. Castiglione's *Courtier*, written in 1514 just after Machiavelli had composed his *Prince*, was published at Venice in 1528; both of these works rapidly became text-books of a new world. Everywhere the older styles were ignored in the courtly scramble after the new, and in England the centuries-old knowledge of the master masons was driven into exile by the superficial studies of dilettanti provided with foreign pattern-books. As a natural result, even where Gothic building was still done, the detail began to go wrong; the craftsmen lost their grip and took to copying at second- and third-hand the capitals and cornices they saw around them, and by the end of the sixteenth century the old style had disappeared from general use. It must be stressed, however, that wholehearted foreign planning and composition were rare; the bony skeleton of the English house fortunately remained much what it had been, and developed naturally along the lines laid down by changing social habits.

We may picture contracting firms of old standing in the provinces, and apprentices and journeymen of the Gothic masters such as Orchard, Lebons, and Vertue, continuing to carry out work with stock details, very little altered. One great centre of this Gothic survival was at Oxford, and another seems to have been in Warwick. Generally speaking, the Midlands were the last part of England to succumb to the pattern-books and the amateur-professional architects. Gothic was recognized as typical of church work and of university colleges, and the last great building erected in almost wholly traditional style was Wadham College, built by Somerset-shire craftsmen between 1610 and 1613. So successful was this that Inigo Jones, in spite of his travels in Italy and his official position as Surveyor of the King's Works, designed the Chapel of Lincoln's Inn in 1618 in a closely similar style.[1] The window tracery is of the same type as that at Wadham, and shows undoubted West Country influences.

At Oxford, Wadham College was not alone in adhering to the older principles of design: at Jesus College in 1621, at Exeter College in 1624, in the rebuilding of Oriel College from 1619 to 1642, and at St. Mary Hall in 1639-40, Gothic masonry and timberwork of a high standard are still found. In 1640 the great staircase of Christ Church was covered with a fan-vault of noble design but jejune detail; F. E. Howard's suspicion that it may have been worked out from the original sketches of 1525 is very possibly justified. During the period of the Laudian revival in the Church of England, a good deal of quasi-Gothic detail was employed in repairs to country churches, and in 1631-4 a complete church, St. John's at Leeds, was built in Gothic style, though its internal woodwork is of very rich Jacobean character. On the other hand, traditional timber construction for houses was employed by the great master carpenter John Abel, who built fine market halls and houses along the Welsh Border in the reign of Charles I, though he too employed Jacobean detail for church screens. The fall of Oxford to the Parliamentary troops on 24 June 1646 marks the end of the Gothic period.

After the Restoration came another stage in the break-up of the style, a period which might be called the post-Gothic. Before the Civil War there had been in certain districts a living body of tradition, capable not merely of continuing to put up small houses in the vernacular manner but of building an Oxford college or a complete parish church. In the post-Gothic phase these survivals were practically extinguished, and such Gothic designs as were made were self-conscious imitations: witness Wren's experiments, of which by far the most successful is the steeple of St. Dunstan-in-the-East, London. There was at the same time the emergence of a curious blend, a kind of Gothic Baroque, of which a fine specimen is to be found in the nave and tower of St. Mary's, Warwick, rebuilt to the designs of Sir William Wilson of Sutton Coldfield after the fire of 1694. Wilson had himself been a stonemason, and was concerned with the repairs of Lichfield Cathedral after the devastation of the siege. His views on detail can hardly be praised, but the grasp of space shown in the Warwick nave, and the composition of the dominating tower put him into an altogether higher category than the mere imitators of past forms.

Among the craftsmen who worked on the tower of St. Mary's was Samuel Dunkley, minister of the Baptist Chapel on Castle Hill, who on weekdays earned a scanty livelihood as a "Poor Mason of Warwick". In 1704 Dunkley "designed, built, carved, and finished" the portal of approach from the south transept to the Beauchamp Chapel; doubtless

---

[1] Even if Jones was not the designer, he certainly gave his approval to the design. John Clarke, freemason, made the drawings and carried out the work.

this was based on what he could recollect of the old work before the fire, but there is a spontaneity and a warm enthusiasm for Gothic form which come as a surprise at this date, and all the more springing from a non-conformist's love for his old parish church. The history of Gothic architecture in Warwick goes even further: the tower and spire of St. Nicholas' Church were pulled down in 1748, and a new steeple of simple Gothic design erected. Thirty years later the rest of the church was rebuilt to match, the interior possessing a naïve charm of its own. Baroque concepts of space here triumph even more completely than in the nave of St. Mary's, and the detail and mouldings are derived from the latest Perpendicular. Though a small provincial work, this church contains in embryo all the elements needed for the growth of a new style based upon the past. It is a tragedy that no real master should have adopted the "Gothick" movement and transmuted its pinchbeck fantasies into the gold of great art.

We do not even know who was responsible for St. Nicholas, Warwick —certain local accounts ascribe it to "one Johnson,[1] a Warwick architect", while others give the credit for the nave to "Joe Collins". Others again would attribute the building to Francis Hiorne, F.S.A. (1744–89), who built Gothic churches at Stony Stratford, Bucks., in 1776, and at Tetbury, Glos., in 1781. A wooden model of the church, the property of Professor A. E. Richardson (one of a collection of models of Warwick buildings of the mid-eighteenth century) shows the church exactly as it is but with an alternative and richer spire. Clearly Francis Hiorne could not have designed the tower in 1748, but it may have been the work of his father, William Hiorne, of Warwick (1715–76), joint designer (with his brother David) of the Shire Hall. Let us not belittle the taste of the Hiornes or of Joe Collins (whoever it was); in this strange and pathetic little work lies more of real formative energy than in all the insipid trivialities of the classic taste of 1780. Nowadays we sigh for the balance and leisure of the silver age of the brothers Adam, for it has the facile charm of a passing breeze; but the extreme niceties of taste pander only to the moment. Seeking to be sure of the refined shadow of a shade, the very substance is lost.

Not by bread alone does man live, but not by subtle essences either, and that which does not contain in itself the strength and cohesion to bind together past and future will not survive. Hence, we may say, the French Revolution, the fall of Constantinople, the Reformation. Taste pushed onwards towards a logical conclusion is steadily climbing a branch from the trunk out: with every step taken the bough becomes thinner and the moment of forces greater. Finally, the crack, the snap, the plunge. Sometimes the falling body saves itself upon another branch, leading in a different direction. For a moment there was such a recovery, when Joe Collins or another was working at Warwick St. Nicholas in 1779 and 1780; only for a moment, for the promised bough proved a twig.

[1] Probably Thomas Johnson, who died at Sidbury, Worcestershire, in 1786. (M. Whiffen in *Burlington Magazine*, LXXXVIII (March 1946), 76.)

U

Quite another form of survival from the Gothic era occurs at King's Lynn, where the nave of St. Margaret's Church was destroyed by the fall of the south-west spire in 1741. The new nave, strikingly akin in its detail and tall pier-bases to St. Nicholas, Warwick, is as striking a contrast in its method of treatment. Here is a strong, even slightly clumsy, Tudor building, inheritor of the qualities of such a church as John Forman's St. Michael-le-Belfry in York. So close is the resemblance that the gap of over two centuries seems hardly to be believed (168). Yet we have its exact dates: begun after the collapse of 1741, it was completed by 1750, the year when Horace Walpole first contemplated the building of Strawberry Hill—at least, the year in which he first referred to his Gothic ideas. It seems hardly likely that we are here concerned with two sets of entirely unrelated circumstances, for the Walpole family estates were in the neighbourhood of Lynn, the centre of their great political influence. Horace Walpole himself represented Castle Rising in Parliament from 1754 to 1757, and Lynn from 1757 to 1768. The disaster to the great church and its gradual rebuilding must have impressed themselves upon his receptive mind, and it may well be that it was this accident that determined the course of a budding fantasy, and thus stage by stage to the Gothic Revival itself.

It is not a part of my purpose to follow the course taken by the Revival, and I have given only a minimum of information concerning the period of survival from 1550 to 1750. It is time to glance back over the whole Gothic scene, to consider in what it differed from succeeding centuries, and to seek the benefits to be derived from such a study. We have in the first place to visualize our period as a panorama seen from a distance, or with eyes half shut, so that the great mountains and valleys, but not the lesser waves and undulations of the scenery, appear with full value—still better, slightly exaggerated for emphasis.

English art, and especially English architecture, suffer from the fact that their literature can be divided into two distinct categories which fail to cohere. On the one side are the works on the philosophy of art, written by aestheticians and academic theorists. They are usually so generalized that not only are facts wanting in the exposition: one is sometimes tempted to feel as one reads that the learned authors have entirely disregarded the minutiae of time and place, and are soaring in the free air of their unfettered imagination. Opposite are the painstaking studies of local schools, of individual buildings, individual technical problems, occasionally of individual men. These detailed studies are the separate bones, nerves, and sinews which go to make up a living organism, but so often they remain sterile and unlinked—one cannot visualize from them a social whole any more than one can see the resultant picture in the loose pieces of a jig-saw emptied on the table.

Some places, some arts, have been more fortunate than others. Westminster Abbey was the fortunate peg on which Lethaby could hang his brilliant realization (in the French sense) of the facts of mediæval life and art in London. More recently there has been a concentration of interest

163 Winchester Cathedral: Presbytery, *c.* 1520–32. Designer: Thomas Bartewe

164   Titchfield Place, 1537–40.   Designer: Thomas Bartewe

on the subject of stained and painted glass. Mr. Knowles produced a series of essays which strike deep into vital problems under the guise of an historical approach to the York glaziers; on a wider canvas Dr. Herbert Read treated the whole of English coloured glass as a means of re-stating the central facts of art history as a whole. These are notable steps in the right direction; modern life has become a thing of such infinitely numerous parts that the specialists drift steadily apart by the day and hour. We await with impatience, or else with complete indifference, the coming of a super-scientist, a man of the stamp of Aristotle, Roger Bacon, Leonardo, or Goethe raised to a yet higher power, who will effect a universal synthesis.

Meanwhile there lies before us the much slighter task of looking back upon a past era, a space of time, a social system already completed—in the hope of finding in it some promising analogy to our own case. How to begin to classify the manifestations of this period? The chronological method is the only natural one, and in following out the detail of some parts of the picture it is the method I have already used. In dealing with the special case of glass, Dr. Read has seen the English art in a threefold division, whose three parts together cover the time from the first vestiges of the craft in our country up to the present day. He calls these three parts the Age of Reason (1150–1350), the Age of Sentiment (1350–1500), and the Age of Fancy (1500–1900). It will be realized from earlier chapters that I do not altogether accept this division as applicable to our culture viewed as a whole.

In the first place, I do not think that the Middle Ages and the Renaissance can be regarded as forming a single cycle of existence, except possibly in the case of music. This apparent exception may be due to the fact that music is the most highly abstracted of the arts, the least connected with physical necessities. It thus develops more slowly and matures when all else is in the grave or the museum. If this view can be accepted it means that while the progress of polyphonic music started level with the other arts in the Dark Ages, it had only reached in 1800 a position parallel to that of culture generally some three centuries earlier.[1] For me, then, the whole cycle is represented by the space covered in Dr. Read's two first periods—roughly 1150 to 1550. Again, Dr. Read considers that the period after 1350 is the beginning of the wave of Humanistic

---

[1] Mr. Paul H. Láng in his recent book, *Music in Western Civilization*, warmly denies even this exception to the rule, and holds that music was hardly, if at all, behind the other arts. In a sense, this may well be true—contemporary arts necessarily reflect one another to some extent; but European music is the only major art which can show a direct and unbroken development through the period of the sixteenth-century Renaissance. In any event I find it difficult to accept Dr. Read's thesis: it seems closer to the facts to regard the "humanism" of the fourteenth century as the fruition of that of the twelfth, whose ripening had been delayed by the scholastic revival of dialectic. It is very doubtful whether sweeping generalizations can give much assistance to us; but for what they are worth I venture to suggest the terms Integrative and Disintegrative Art, as applying to the Gothic Age from 1100 to 1550, and overlapping it, the "Modern" Age from 1450 down to our times. It is at least apparent that we now stand upon the threshold of a new age of integration.

Art, and that it sprang up through the dying growth of Gothic Art, which received its death-blow in the plague of 1349. Now a lot depends on what is meant by humanism—at an earlier stage I tried to show that it contains a deceptive paradox. In relation to art, it surely means (to take an obvious example) the philosophy behind such a phenomenon as the realistic painting of the van Eycks. As I have tried to bring out, the quasi-photographic viewpoint of the van Eycks was only the outcome of a very long process, which was already far advanced in the early thirteenth century, when Villard de Honnecourt and Matthew Paris drew lions or elephants from the life, and carvers so far forgot scholastic precepts as to attempt to copy nature.

It is quite needless to take a further step with Ruskin, and say that the art of living forms is "good" and that of the abstract "decadent". All that is here in question is the objective fact that the craftsman, the artist, in this particular period *was trying* to improve his capacity for the portrayal of natural forms. It does not concern us whether his intention was morally or aesthetically a good one; historically, the one vital fact is that his intention existed. And so for me, the cycle of "Stylized Portrayal of Nature" includes part of what Dr. Read terms Gothic, and part of what he calls Humanism. To me, the lively and brilliant art of the late fourteenth century appears as the goal towards which England (among other countries) had been struggling for two hundred years; for five hundred, if we prefer to include the three centuries from the Danish invasions to the introduction of Gothic elements.

The tale told by the human artefacts is a very different one from that which reaches the student of scholastic philosophy. The links between the cloistered man of learning and his brother in the shop or at the banker were undoubtedly very close: Miss M. D. Anderson has pointed out that many of the beasts carved in the Middle Ages show a pronounced "literary bias", and the amount of detail derived from goldsmiths' work and illumination. But long before 1350 the correspondences were becoming looser, the links were drawing apart. The crude, uproarious, sometimes almost bestial humour of the balance of the carvings should tell us of the increasing emphasis on a counter-current, sweeping art out of the hands of the pious and the literary—from the prison of second-hand information into the open air. The pious, in line with the iconoclastic movements of earlier and later ages, looked with grave suspicion upon *all* forms of art. The *Physiologus* informs us that Sirens charm men to sleep and tear them to pieces, this being the end reserved for "those who delight themselves in theatrical pleasures, which are tragedies and comedies and music". One of the troubadours, after a distinguished career, had to obtain absolution "from the sin of poetry". The polemics of St. Bernard prove how rigidly antipathetic to art as such were the official pillars of the Church.

Bearing these things in mind, and also the activities in the Civil War of William Dowsing in East Anglia and Richard Culmer in Kent, among a host of other violent iconoclasts, we get a picture of the Gothic spirit emerging from the warder's grasp in the middle of the twelfth century, standing in free equilibrium in the age of Chaucer, and being hustled off in chains by the new (and presumably unconscious) imitators of St. Bernard. The piety of a Henry VI, though it included reprobation of low-necked dress for ladies and of the free-and-easy nudism of the hot spring at Bath, was not directed against art by any means, as the records of architecture, music, poetry, and the drama at his court abundantly testify. True piety, renunciation of the flesh, is content in itself; puritanism is fired by a lust to destroy.

The puritan frenzy of destruction was still present in our blood when interest in the form and spirit of Gothic reawakened in the mid-eighteenth century. Hence it is that instead of adapting the constructive principles of Gothic to new uses, only the surface detail was investigated, and became a good excuse for pulling down what was built in other fashions, to put up a "Gothic" sham in its place. A number of the earliest of the Gothic revival works did not even serve any purpose, but were artificial ruins. Here again is the taste which has become so over-refined that it destroys itself. What then was the secret of the true Gothic taste of the Middle Ages?

Since the "Revival of Learning", which is largely identical with the revival of Plato, European man has progressively passed through the stage of taking himself as the measure of the universe to the point where he is prepared to accept the physical atoms of which the universe consists as the measure of himself. In both cases, the final decision is made in the human brain, and if a deity is invoked, it is a *deus ex machina*, manufactured in the ideal image of the man of the moment. Thus we have seen God the Astronomer, God the Chemist, God the Mathemat, and God the Electrician. Whatever the choice, the Deity is made to preside over a perfectly classified and inflexible system.

The men of the Middle Ages were for the most part uninterested in system for its own sake. The scholastic theologians developed one, it is true, but their system centred on God as a revealed matter of Faith and, far from being built up on observed facts, was in flat contradiction to the facts in all directions but one: the theologians at least knew a good deal about human nature. If we concern ourselves with ethics at all, we still find that the theological virtues and vices, and the seven deadly sins with their contrary virtues, are capable of covering all situations. It would be a great mistake to suppose that the Church's system was a fully perfected and unchanging one: in spite of failure to cope adequately with the exercise of real "free will", the system to-day is still in process of mutation, and bit by bit swallows facts which three or four centuries ago were enough to burn the men who proclaimed them.

The system of the Middle Ages, compared to the many systems of modern times, differed in that it took its rise in a Faith transcending the facts observable through the senses, and in its flexibility. In these qualities the mediæval system was in series with those of the great ethnic religions which had gone before, or which still bear fruit in the Far East. In so far as the mind of a normal man reflects the official system in which his generation has been brought up, that of the mediæval European above all things betrayed this readiness to adjust itself to circumstances. Let us examine a few of the practical outcomes of this attitude so different from that of the present day.

To us, the first questions to be asked are What?, Where?, and When? We expect the answers to be exact, and lending themselves readily to classification and quantitative analysis. A name must be accurately spelt in order that it may be found in the dictionary or encyclopedia without difficulty or delay. We accept spellings which represent neither etymology nor phonetics, provided only they are recognized. Very few persons in the Gothic age were troubled by these scruples; variation of spelling was the rule, and it is reasonably certain that there was parallel variation in pronunciation. Thus mediæval English was able to play with infinitely variable rhymes and assonances which we have lost by standardization.

The matter went beyond questions of sound and orthography: I well remember the surprise with which I met for the first time a fifteenth-century index. It set forth all the names of tenants contained in a manorial survey of 1464, but the alphabetical order was of Christian names! Mr. Herbert Chitty tells me of an amusing instance where this method of indexing caused confusion to the modern investigator: early students of the lists of Winchester scholars actually referred in print to the boy at the head of the first list as Captain of the School in 1394—only later was it observed that each list was set in the order of the boys' Christian names.

From What? we proceed to Where? It is only in the age of the internal combustion engine that places have been provided with prominent name-plates for the avoidance of human intercourse on the road; only in the age of the stage-coach that mile-posts and direction boards became usual. The mediæval traveller was content either to follow the road known to him or to his fellows, or else hired a guide as the Countess of Warwick did at Windsor in 1432. For official use, lists of computed mileages were made out, and from them and from a modicum of rough-and-ready observation the "Gough" Map, or rather its original, was compiled about the time of Edward I. Though grossly inaccurate by modern standards, the Gough Map is perfectly adequate for its purpose, but again it demonstrates the outlook of its time by being orientated to East instead of to North. Other mediæval maps were differently orientated, yet their users must have been quite at ease. To-day, if we were faced with a series of outlines of countries, including our own, purposely changed in orientation, how many of us would name them without hesitation?[1]

An extension of the problem of position is that of space: neither the antique world nor the Middle Ages was tied down to the fixed viewpoint in art. This development, which seems so logical to us, was not essential

[1] Just after writing this I was pleased to see an admirable map of "Our Neighbours in Europe" oriented to the South-East, heading an exhibit in the Guildford Central School's Geographical Exhibition, due to the enterprise of Miss L. M. Budden.

165 Rochford Church: Tower, *c.* 1490–1510

166 Ashwell Church, *c.* 1340–81. London school

168 King's Lynn, St. Margaret's Church: Nave, 1742–50.
Designer: Bartholomew Brettingham of Norwich

167 York: St. Michael-le-Belfry Church, 1525–36.
Designer: John Forman

to the mental comfort of the mediæval art-patron. The chariot in the Luttrell Psalter, which appears in combined elevation of side and both ends, and the diverse vanishing-points of chequered pavements in the paintings, point to a vision which was prepared to move around a fixed object and to receive several impressions, yet at the same time. This, an impossibility in real life, was not unwelcome in the artistic counterfeit.

The question When? was sometimes left unanswered. Many documents were not dated at all, even when they were of legal importance. Others were fixed in time by the citation of the King's regnal year, or by the year of office of a mayor or such-like official—these methods had been normal in Mesopotamia four thousand years earlier. The era of the Incarnation, which might have been thought all-important to the Age of Faith, was in fact less and less used the earlier we seek for it. Its common use is a mark of the coming collapse, and it was reserved for the age of agnosticism to adopt it as a convenient standard for astronomical calculation. The minor divisions of time were regulated by seasonal considerations, and "daylight saving" was accomplished by the simple method of rising at dawn and going to bed when it was dark. The resulting long day in summer and short day in winter, as well as the gradual change from one to the other, were graphically shown by the "scratch-dial" whose canonical hours varied appropriately with the position of the sun. Mechanical clocks were introduced late in the fourteenth century, but were a rarity until 1500.

Before leaving this series of contrasts between the fixed and the flexible, I must refer to currency and to musical notation. English money was based on the silver penny, and these pennies were normal currency; the pound, nominally of 240 pence, was never coined until 1489, and its twentieth part, the shilling, not until 1504. Accounts were none the less kept in pounds, shillings, and pence, though items were often stated in "marks", of which three were equivalent to two pounds, though no such coin as the mark was ever issued. It might be thought that so complicated a system would lead to insolvency, but mistakes in mediæval book-keeping are seldom serious, and often due to the cumbersome Roman numerals.

In music the staff notation came into being at the end of the Dark Ages in time to aid the course of the polyphonic development, and was afterwards rendered more flexible by the use of different key signatures. Whereas in our day many competent singers have to be coaxed into learning by systems such as tonic sol-fa, and only a few are really at home in sight-reading, the mediæval singer was prepared to read from a page in which the position of the clef was constantly changing, in order to keep the high and low notes within the compass of the stave. Here is perhaps the most remarkable mental flexibility of all, even if we suppose a majority of the choristers to have learnt by rote. In every case it is of course not the average, but the highest level of achievement that really counts—the best performances of 1400 and of 1900 may not have differed much from one another, but they sprang from two quite different habits of mind.

The attitude of looking at things from a number of points of view simultaneously instead of from one fixed viewpoint is possibly shown also in the cookery of the Middle Ages. We are astonished when we read of the vast number of different meats which were served as part of the same course at a banquet; but to the man of the time (at least to the man of culture) cooking was one of the arts, and its practitioners were rewarded as fine artists. Master Thomas Beauchef (did he get his name from the Derbyshire Abbey, or from his skill?), who had cooked for the Black Prince and became one of Richard II's cooks, was in 1383 "an old man and not able to labour as he used to do", and he was in consequence granted for life his fee in the kitchen, his wages in the household, and his yearly robe as he had been accustomed to take them, "with licence to go away for recreation and return when he pleases". The *Forme of Cury*, which Beauchef and John Goodrich may have compiled in their pensioned retirement, shows us the great variety of eatables in use, in spite of the lack of many of those imported foods on which we pride ourselves. Not that imported foods were not well in evidence: the shopping lists of monasteries and noblemen show how much was already familiar. One of the Earl of Warwick's purchases of spicery in London in 1432 included pepper, ginger, sugar, saffron, dates, figs, raisins, almonds, cloves—and in the previous year there was an item at Rouen which showed that in some respects taste has not changed materially in five hundred years: for cherries, "Strauberyes et Creyme"—7s. 6d.

The same feeling pervades the whole of the social life of the age: at a time when a salad had fourteen ingredients apart from its dressing, how many forms of decoration might be found in a chapel? There was the decorative panelling of the stone walls themselves, and the intricacies of the vaulting; the encaustic tiles of the floor and the patterned glass of the windows; wooden screens, stalls, and perhaps organ-loft; carved reredos with alabaster figures, richly painted and gilded; panel paintings in the screens or arranged as a retable, themselves provided with gilt embossed gesso backgrounds akin to sculpture; private pews hung with pictured tapestry, and an altar-cloth and vestments of the most costly broderer's work; wrought iron grilles and gates, and sacred vessels from the gold-smith. Even the bookbindings might be encrusted with engraved clasps set with jewels, and the service-books themselves were certain to be exquisite examples of penmanship still further beautified by the brush of the miniaturist. Over the tombs would hang helms from the armourer (often outworn or old-fashioned ones, since the new were too valuable), and heraldic shields and banners, these last the stainer's contribution. The mere number of craftsmen of manifold misteries in a London of less than 50,000 inhabitants would prove the extent to which art was inter-woven with social life (11, 12, 43, 44, 63-7, 95, 161, 175, 176).

It was architecture, "the mistress art", which held all these parts together and which alone was capable of achieving out of their diversity an over-ruling unity of composition. Architecture was, and is, able to do this only when it rests upon a sound structural system, and every age has to confront its own problems of construction with its own solutions. This keeps the architects as a group busy and alive, responsive to changing conditions. We have seen that owing to such changes in conditions and in requirements, the architecture of 1400 differed greatly from that of a century earlier. The change was not, as used often to be said, one from perfection to decadence: the real situation has been brilliantly summarized by Mr. Greening Lamborn, who tells us: "It is only the raw amateur, ignorant of constructive technique, who supposes that because Perpendicular detail has not the naïvety, naturalness, and variety of earlier work it must be a decadent stage of Gothic. For Gothic construction was progressive to the last, and was never more alive and vigorous than when it was suddenly interrupted by the Reformation." Writing two generations earlier, Paley perceived something of this, for he wrote: "there is such a mass of really high art in the work of this (the Perpendicular) period, that the student must be careful not to slur it over, in indulging any predilection he may have formed for earlier work."

Sound construction was arrived at by methods which we regard as empiric; but an ounce of practice is worth a ton of theory, and the constructional disasters of modern times show that the knowledge obtained from test-samples and the application of formulae is not infallible, any more than were the old master builders, who preferred to waste material and be on the safe side. Trial-and-error is dangerous when the experiment takes place over the heads of large congregations or of the King and his justices sitting on the Bench, even though the penalty were not that prescribed by Hammurabi's Code early in the second millennium B.C.— "If a builder has built a house for a man and his work is not strong, and if the house he has built falls in and kills the householder, that builder shall be slain."

Fortunately, the Gothic architects could profit from the mistakes of their Romanesque predecessors, and most of the great collapses were those of Norman towers supported on piers of rubble masonry. In addition to this, models were in use, and must have been employed to test structural methods as well as for the display of the design to noble clients. There was of course a background of traditional usage, and much of this was set down in such manuscript text-books as the surviving album of Honnecourt, and the later German treatises of which that of Matthäus Roriczer on Pinnacles was printed in 1486. Hahnloser mentions another tractate, the *Unterweisung* of Lorenz Lacher, printed in 1516, and a manuscript pattern-book of the late fifteenth century discovered at Vienna; this last contains cut-out profiles of mouldings on parchment, evidently for use as master-templates.

The use of such pattern-books and text-books implied a certain standard of literacy among the master craftsmen, and from time to time positive evidence can be discovered; in the thirteenth century and later craftsmen were sometimes appointed as keepers and controllers of building works, and were responsible for keeping accounts as well as for correspondence with such tradesmen as lead and marble merchants living at a distance. At the end of the period signatures are quite frequent, and in 1517 Henry

x

Smyth, master mason of the Savoy Hospital, made a bequest of "all my Bokis of purtiturys", undoubtedly "portraitures" or patterns and designs. It is now generally admitted by historians that literate laymen were numerous from the thirteenth century onwards, but it may not be out of place to stress this in view of the tendency in certain quarters to equate the master craftsmen with the building foreman of the present day, and then to take away from him even elementary education. Mr. J. W. Adamson brings forward an instance of 1373, where out of 28 witnesses examined in a suit 14 were laymen, and of these 14, 11 were set down as literate; and another similar case of 1466 where out of 20 witnesses only 2 were clerks, while of the remaining 18, at least 7 were literate, including 2 merchants, 2 husbandmen engaged in agriculture (out of 7), one of a pair of tailors and one of a pair of shipmen. We have already seen that in 1408 William Rolleston caused English translations of letters patent to be fixed to the inn-doors of Beverley, and Mr. Adamson gives a slightly later case of 1424, where one Walter Aslak was stated to have posted "Englische billes rymed in partye" on the city gates of Norwich on the Norfolk shire-day.

As far back as the reign of Edward I we have the unimpeachable evidence of Henry de Bray, a Northamptonshire squire, whose estate book gives proof not only of his literacy but of his wide interests, and speaking of the fifteenth century Mr. Hilary Jenkinson concludes from his exhaustive studies of English handwriting that "there was an extensive and widely recognized system of elementary business education". It is also a significant fact, in keeping with the evidence from other sources, that he finds "the latter part of the reign of Henry VI . . . a period of bad taste in penmanship and slovenly writing". This time, 1450–60, marks one of the lowest ebbs of English cultural activity of all kinds, and we must think, not that constant progress was being made from the thirteenth through the fourteenth and fifteenth to the sixteenth century, but that if we have good evidence of wide literacy in the middle of the fifteenth century (as we have from the Paston and Stonor letters, for example), then there was probably literacy even wider in the brilliant epoch at the close of the fourteenth, when the spread of the Scriptures in English so greatly alarmed the dignitaries of the Church.

The King and many of the nobility and gentry were of course literate during our period, and the King especially had an important role to play in encouraging book production. During Edward I's passage through Sicily on crusade in 1270 he had lent to Guido delle Colonne a manuscript on which the latter based his Troy Book; Richard II's library in 1384, while he was still a youth, contained thirteen French romances and a two-volume Bible; in 1425 there occurs mention of John Burnham as having been librarian to Henry V, and handing over the books to a successor, John Depeden; while in 1480 Piers Bauduyn "stacioner" was paid for binding some of Edward IV's books: "Titus Livius, the Holy Trinite, Frossard, the Bible, Le Gouvernement of Kinges and Princes, thre smalle bookes of Franche, La Forteresse de Foy, Book of Josephus,

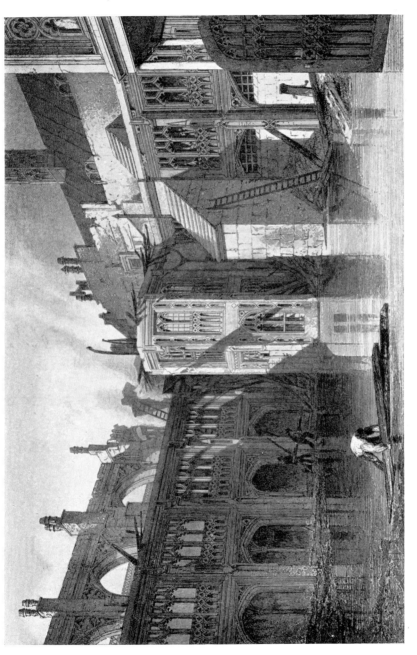

169   Westminster Palace: St. Stephen's Cloister, 1526–28.   Designers: William Vertue and Henry Redman.
From Brayley and Britton's *Houses of Parliament*

171 Walsoken Church: Font, 1544

170 Northleach Church: Font, *c.* 1400?

the Bible Historial." The whole extent of this library was doubtless much greater.

Not only literacy, but many other aspects of the social life of the Middle Ages have been persistently underestimated: communications, for instance, and health and sanitation. It is no longer believed that even in the seventeenth century the road system was as bad as it used to be customary to represent it—when travellers were benighted or their carriages bogged in a mire, the facts were recorded in such reminiscences as Pepys's *Diary*; but when we consider the vast travels of William Worcester about 1480, and John Leland between 1536 and 1542, it is evident that even "tourist travel" was quite possible, and a similar impression is derived from the earlier narratives of pilgrims such as Simon Simeon and Hugh the Illuminator in 1323, or Margery Kempe in the early fifteenth century, to say nothing of Chaucer's cavalcade. In summing up the evidence for English road travel Professor F. M. Stenton concludes "that for the ordinary mediæval traveller, the waterways of England were never more than an occasional supplement to a road-system which on the whole was sufficient to his needs", and shows evidence that the normal rate of fast travel was about thirty miles per day, while on exceptional occasions even forty miles a day might be reached, though the general average of all traffic was probably nearer twenty (see Appendix III).

Something has already been said of the development of the carriage and of the service of public carriers; to this may be added that in 1397 the sum of £400 was paid in respect of making the Queen's chariot, after Richard II's second marriage, while in 1400 John Norman, wheeler of London, was paid £7 due to him for repairs effected to divers chariots, "whyrlys" and wheels for the use of Isabella the late Queen. In 1480 the King had some kind of state coach, for the wardrobe accounts include payments for the "Reparacion off the Kinges Carre"; items which may be compared with those for the Earl of Warwick's chariot of 1431. As to accommodation for travellers, the incident of William Rolleston already referred to shows that there were in 1408 a fair number of inns in Beverley, and the innholders of London were of sufficient importance to become incorporated in 1515, though there must have been extensive accommodation for the stranger long before this.

Sanitation has been elevated into a principal fetish; the disposal of sewage and by-laws of a sanitary character have come to be regarded as of greater importance than the layout of gardens or the general convenience and appearance of houses. Evidence of the strenuous efforts made by mediæval authorities to secure public health has been quoted as though it were proof of the ignorance and dirty incompetence of the Middle Ages as a whole. Recently there has been a most timely change of front, and the body of evidence brought forward by scholars such as Mr. Lynn Thorndike and Mr. Ernest Sabine is convincing as to the precautions taken both in English and Continental cities to avoid disease and to maintain a good standard of public cleanliness. Mr. Sabine's studies of the records concerning butchering, public sanitation, and civic cleaning in mediæval London are of absorbing interest, and it comes as a surprise to learn that the square mile of the ancient city contained at least thirteen public conveniences—I cannot do better in this connexion than to quote Mr. Sabine's conclusion: "If citizens are to be judged by the time and money expended in their efforts to make their latrines comfortable, clean, and sanitary, then many citizens of mediæval London must have deserved wholehearted praise and respect." As a delightful instance of the punishment being fitted to the crime I must also quote from the Calendar of French Rolls, which includes an order of 18 October 1441 to the authorities of Calais commanding them "to have all offensive matter cast by soldiers and others into the streets of the town to the detriment of health, at once removed by the offenders themselves to a spot selected upon outside the walls".

In fact, while in many purely cultural matters the Middle Ages were ahead of modern times, they were also not so far behind in the conduct of material affairs. I cannot here enter upon the much greater field of social life, but a few words may be said upon the position of women in mediæval times. In this age, when widespread education has brought at least modernized versions of Chaucer's *Prologue* and of sections of *Piers Plowman* within the compass of everyman's general reading, it can hardly be needful to demonstrate the extent to which women of different classes moved freely in society and travelled about on pilgrimage or pleasure bent, or upon both at once. But as an aftermath of the nineteenth-century books written with a legalistic bias, it is still customary to emphasize that the mediæval wife was her husband's chattel, that she could not make a will without her husband's consent, and so forth. This was indeed the state of the law, but we should do well to consider carefully our present legal system before we criticize that of the past. Seldom do laws reflect current life; they are usually anything from a generation to a century out-of-date by the time they are passed, and when they do give evidence of exact circumstances, these are more commonly exceptional than universal.

It used to be impressed upon us, as a sure proof of our own progress from bondage to freedom, that the mediæval villein (the majority of the population), not only had to seek his lord's licence before he could marry, but that he had to pay for the privilege. In view of the modern prevalence of divorce, such a system does not now seem so cruel as perhaps it did to our grandparents; but the late Miss Levett showed from her studies of long series of manorial rolls that the "merchet" fee was, at any rate by the fourteenth century, mainly of economic significance, and that though the lawyers might correctly deem it to be a sure mark of servile blood, it was thought less a badge of shame than a possibly burdensome registration fee. Girls frequently went to school, and Leach drew attention to Mary Mareflete who in 1404 appears on the Corpus Christi Guild Roll of Boston as "mistress of the schools". It is even probable that reading (though not necessarily writing) was more widely spread among mediæval women than among men. Education was available, as we have seen, even to the poor; Richard II would not hear of the exclusion of villeins' children from school, and Miss Levett found that in one small manor of St. Albans Abbey in 1331-3, no less than nine boys paid for licences to attend school —these boys were of course all of villein blood, and there would also have been scholars from the free families.

Something has already been said on the subject of royal relief of the poor—it was to the King rather than to the monastic houses that the poor looked for alms; the records of the monasteries, where they survive, do not suggest that any very large proportion of their income went to the poor—not even what they were supposed to distribute by their rule. It has to be remembered, on the other hand, that the great monastic estates did give normal employment to a great mass of people, and even a scholar as little sympathetic to the monks as Dr. Coulton holds that life on church lands was slightly preferable to that on manors in lay hands. But the most enviable lot of all was certainly that of the residents upon the "ancient demesne" of the Crown. It was to the King's lands, and to lands which had once been the King's, that men looked for a symbol of relative freedom and prosperity; it was to the King on progress that the poor looked for food; it was to the King's person that every free man looked for redress of grievances past bearing—and every bond man also, if he could but find means to evade manorial custom and get a hearing. There was a sentiment of loyalty towards the King as a human individual which found expression in ballads of royal escapades incognito, like those of Haroun al Rashid, and the same motive is seriously expressed in polite verse by Hoccleve; referring to Edward III:

> O worthi king! benyngne Edward the laste!
> Thow haddist ofte in herte a drede impressid,
> Which that thyn humble goost ful sore a-gaste;
> And to know if thou cursed were or blessid,
> A-mong the peple ofte hastow the dressed
> In-to contre, in simple array allone,
> To herë what men seide of thi persone.

England lived on the personality of her kings: the existence of English art springs very largely from Henry III; Edward I made possible a true nationhood and national culture. It was to the weakness of Edward II and to the bad example of Henry IV that we owed the two worst outbreaks of piracy around our shores: Mr. L. F. Salzman has remarked "the beginning of the reign of the incompetent Edward II was one of the periods when the sea was most unsafe; . . . just a hundred years later, under Henry IV, there was another tremendous outbreak of lawlessness". The land as well as the sea was unsafe in the days of Edward II; in February of 1322, Master William of Eyton, mason of Lichfield Cathedral, and his seven assistants, as well as their four labourers under one Walter, took an oath to help the Chapter in the defence of the close, and to warn them of any impending danger or "sinistrum" (in France the noun *sinistre* still covers the dangers of fire, riot, and the like). Some years later, during the ascendancy of Mortimer after the murder of the King, a certain Robert Malvoysin (no fortunate name in the circumstances!)

asked the Chapter to allow him to live in the close with his wife and family "because of the peril which threatens in these days".

Some disasters our kings were powerless to prevent: the great famine of 1315, the last in western Europe, was widespread, and seems to have been caused by heavy rain in 1314 followed by torrential floods in the following summer. It was not until the end of 1316 that Europe, including England, began to recover from the blow. Likewise the Black Death could not be stayed upon its terrible march across Asia to the Crimea and thence on merchant vessels to every part of the West. In modern times

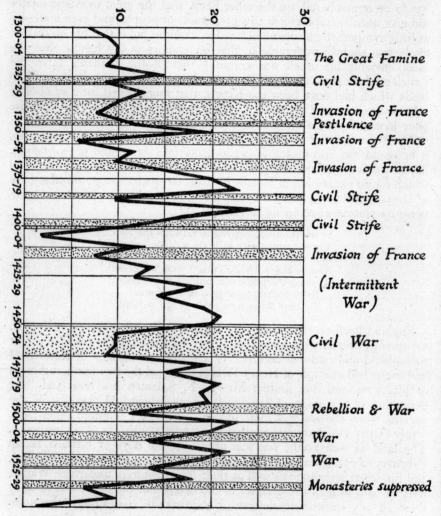

FIG. 172. Graph to show number of important building works under-taken in England in each period of five years, from 1300 to 1550, compared with disturbing factors.

173 Cambridge: Christ's College, 1505–11.
Designer: William Swayn; carver, possibly Ralph Bolmone

174 Tiverton Church: carving of ship, 1517

175   Ramsey Abbey: Silver-gilt Censer

176   Ramsey Abbey: Silver-gilt Incense-boat. Silverware, probably late
fourteenth century, now in the Victoria and Albert Museum

Europe has known nothing comparable in horror except perhaps the epidemic of influenza which swept the world soon after the war of 1914–18. Famine and pestilence, though their effects may be softened, are not altogether within human control. There remains the third disaster, war. Here is a problem which should be capable of human solution, unless we believe it to be irrevocably determined by the positions of the heavenly bodies or by the incidence of spots upon the surface of the Sun.

If war is to be avoided, it must be by the rulers of the peoples; the whole course of history cannot show an example of the working of machinery whereby a democracy has averted war. Once the ferment has begun, the suggestibility of the human mass to propaganda is immensely increased—it should lie within the hands of sovereignty to guide the peoples in peace. Here lies the greatest indictment of the Middle Ages as a whole; they brought down their own towering structure in ruins by continued and fruitless war, and for this many kings must be held responsible. Many, but not all. Edward I, Edward III, the Black Prince, all were warriors, all fell short of success in so far as they relied upon war as an instrument of policy. Yet in Richard II we have the spiritual ancestor of Edward VII, and Richard, who has no title, might well bear that of the Peacemaker. Under him English civilization, English culture, English art, reached their highest peak; under his sceptre the clouds of war were being rolled away from England, from France, and from western Europe; in his person the beneficent doctrine of divine right regained a great portion of its lost power. Drayton asked concerning the victor of Agincourt, who once more plunged France and England into blood and misery, when England should again see such a King Harry? After several centuries of bitter and repeated lessons from which we fail to learn, is it not more pertinent to ask: Where can we find again such a King Richard?

Appendix I

SOME LITERARY REFERENCES TO BUILDING

(i) Geoffrey of Vinsauf: *Poetria Nova*, c. 1210, lines 43–8, 55–6.

> Si quis habet fundare domum, non currit ad actum
> Impetuosa manus: intrinseca linea cordis
> Praemetitur opus, seriemque sub ordine certo
> Interior praescribit homo, totamque figurat
> Ante manus cordis quam corporis; et status ejus
> Est prius archetypus quam sensilis . . .
>
> . . . .
>
> Circinus interior mentis praecircinet omne
> Materiae spatium. . . .

[If a man has to lay the foundations of a house, he does not set rash hand to the work; the inward line of the heart measures forth the work in advance and the inner man prescribes a definite order of action; the hand of imagination designs the whole before that of the body does so; the pattern is first the prototype, then the tangible. . . . The inner compasses of the mind must encircle the whole quantity of material beforehand.]

Text from E. Faral: *Les Arts Poétiques du XIIe et du XIIIe Siècle*, 1924, p. 198.

(ii) Pilgrimage of Simon Simeon and Hugh the Illuminator from Ireland to Palestine, 1323. The Palace of Westminster.

Almost immediately joined to the same monastery (Westminster Abbey) is that most famous palace of the kings of the English; in it is that well-known chamber on whose walls are all the histories of the Wars of the whole Bible painted beyond description, with most thorough and perfect inscriptions in French, to the no small wonder of beholders and with the greatest royal magnificence.

Text in *Itinerarium Symonis Symeonis*, ed. J. Nasmith, 1778, pp. 5–6.

(iii) John Gower: *Confessio Amantis*, 1390, book vii, lines 2412–31. The Emperor and his Masons.

> Lo nou, hou thilke time it ferde
> Toward so hih a worthi lord:
> For this I finde ek of record,
> Which the Cronique hath auctorized.
> What Emperour was entronized,
> The ferste day of his corone,
> Wher he was in his real Throne
> And hield his feste in the paleis

Sittende upon his hihe deis
With al the lust that mai be gete,
Whan he was gladdest at his mete,
And every menstral hadde pleid,
And every Disour hadde seid
What most was plesant to his Ere,
Than ate laste comen there
Hise Macons, for thei scholden crave
Wher that he wolde be begrave,
And of what Ston his sepulture
Thei scholden make, and what sculpture
He wolde ordeine therupon.

Text in *The English Works of John Gower*, ed. G. C. Macaulay, vol. II, 1901, p. 299.

(iv) John Lydgate: Troy Book, 1412–20, book ii, line 479 onward. King Priam rebuilds Troy. (A few letters modernized.)

The sorwe aswaged, & the syghes olde,
By longe processe, liche as I yow tolde,
This worthi kyng, callyd Priamus,
Is in his herte nowe so desyrous,
Up-on the pleyn, that was so waste & wylde,
So strong a toun of newe for to bilde,
At his devyse a cite edefye,
That schal thassautys outterly defye
Of alle enmyes, and his mortal foon,
With riche tourys & wallys of hard stoon.
And al aboute the contres enviroun,
He made seke in every regioun
For swiche werkemen as were corious,
Of wyt inventyf, of castyng merveilous;
Or swyche as coude crafte of gemetrye,
Or wer sotyle in her fantasye;
And for everyche that was good devysour,[1]
Mason, hewer, or crafty quareour;
For every wright and passyng carpenter,
That may be founde, owther fer or nere;
For swyche as koude grave, grope, or kerve,
Or swiche as werne able for to serve
With lym or stoon, for to reise a wal,
With bataillyng and crestis marcial;
Or swiche as had konyng in her hed,
Alabastre, owther white or redde,
Or marbil graye for to pulsche[2] it pleyn,
To make it smothe of veynes & of greyn.
He sent also for every ymagour,
Bothe in entaille, & every purtreyour
That coude drawe, or with colour peynt
With hewes fresche, that the werke nat feynt;

[1] architect.   [2] polish.

Y

And swiche as coude with countenaunces glade
Make an ymage that wil nevere fade:
To counterfet in metal, tre, or stoon
The sotil werke of Pigmaleoun,
Or of Appollo,[1] the whiche as bokis telle,
In ymagerye alle other dide excelle;
For by his crafty werkyng corious,
The towmbe he made of kyng Daryus,
Whiche Alysaundre dide on heyghte reise,
Only for men schuld his fame preise,
In his conquest by Perce whan he went.
And thus Priam for every maister sent,
For eche kerver & passynge Joignour,
To make knottis with many corious flour,
To sette on crestis with-Inne and with-oute
Upon the wal the cite rounde aboute;
Or who that wer excellyng in practik
Of any art callyd mekanyk,
Or hadde a name flouryng or famus,
Was after sent to come to Priamus.
For he purposeth, this noble worthi kyng,
To make a cite most royal in byldyng,
Brod, large, & wyde, & lest it were assailled,
For werre proudly abouten enbatailled.
And first the grounde he made to be sought,
Ful depe and lowe, that it faille nought
To make sure the fundacioun;
In the place where the olde toun
Was first ybilt, he the wallis sette;
And he of lond many myle out mette,
Aboute in compas, for to make it large,
As the maysters that toke on hem the charge
Devysed han the settyng and the syyt,
For holsom eyr to be more of delyt.
And whan the soille, defouled with ruyne
Of walles old, was made pleyn as lyne,
The werkmen gan this cite for to founde,
Ful myghtely with stonys square & rounde,
That in this world was to it noon lyche[2]
Of werkmanschip, nor of bildyng riche,
Nor of crafte of coryous masounry.
I can no termys to speke of gemetrye,
Wherfore as now I muste hem sette a-syde;
For douteles I radde never Euclide,
That the maister and the foundour was
Of alle that werkyn by squyre or compas,
Or kepe her mesour by level or by lyne;
I am to rude clerly to diffyne
Or to discrive this werk in every parte,
For lak of termys longyng to that arte.
But I dar wel of trouthe affermyn here,

---

[1] Apelles.   [2] like.

In al this world ne was ther never pere
Un-to this cite, and write it for a sothe,
As in his boke my mayster Guydo[1] doth.
And tha tit myght in prosperite,
In hyghe honour and felicite,
From al assaut perpetuelly contune,
It reysed was in worschip of Neptune,
And namyd Troye, as it was to-forn,
Lyche the firste that was thorugh Grekis lorn.
The lenthe was, schortly to conclude,
Thre dayes Journe, lyche the latitude,
That never I herd make mencioun
Of swiche another of fundacioun,
So huge in compas nor of swiche larges,
Nor to counte so passyng of fayrnes,
So edyfied or lusty to the syght.
And, as I rede, the walles wern on highte
Two hundrid cubites, al of marbil gray,
Maskowed[2] with-oute for sautis and assay;
And it to make more plesaunt of delyt,
A-mong the marbil was alabaster white
Meynt in the walles, rounde the toun aboute,
To make it schewe with-Inne and with-oute
So fresche, so riche, and so delitable,
That it alone was incomparable
Of alle cites that any mortal man
Sawe ever yit, sithe the world began.
And at the corner of every wal was set
A crowne of golde with riche stonys fret,
That schone ful bright ageyn the sonne schene;
And every tour bretexed[3] was so clene
Of chose stoon, that wer nat fer a-sondre,
That to beholde it was a verray wonder.
Ther-to this cite compassed enviroun,
Hadde sexe gatis to entre in-to the toun:
The first of al & strengest eke with al,
Largest also and most principal,
Of myghty bildynge allone peereles,
Was by the kyng callyd Dardanydes;
And in story, lyche as it is fownde,
Tymbria was named the secounde;
And the thridde callyd Helyas;
The fourte gate hight also Cethas;
The fyfte Troiana; the syxte Anthonydes,
Strong and myghty bothe in werre & pes,
With square toures set on every syde.
At whos corners, of verray pompe & pride,
The werkmen han, with sterne & fel visages,
Of riche entaille, set up gret ymages,[4]
Wrot out of ston, that never ar like to fayle,

---

[1] Guido delle Colonne.   [2] machicolated.   [3] battlemented.
[4] compare the stone figures at Carnarvon and at Alnwick Castles.

Ful coriously enarmed for batayle.
And thorugh the wal, her fomen for to lette,
At every tour wer grete gunnys sette,
For assaut and sodeyn aventurys;
And on tourettis wer reysed up figurys
Of wylde bestis, as beris and lyouns,
Of tigers, bores, of serpentis and dragouns
And hertis[1] eke, with her brode hornes,
Olyfauntes and large Unicornes,
Buglis, bolys, and many grete grifoun,[2]
Forged of brasse, of copur and latoun,
That cruelly by sygnes of her facys
Up-on her foon made fel manacys.
Barbykans and bolewerkys huge,
A-fore the toun made for highe refuge,
Yiffe nede were, erly and eke late;
And portecolys stronge at every gate,
That hem thar nat noon assailyng charge;
And the lowkis[3] thikke, brode, and large,
Of the gatys al of yoten[4] bras.
And with-Inne the myghty schittyng[5] was
Of strong yrne barres square and rounde,
And grete barrerys picched in the grounde,
With huge cheynes forged for diffence,
Whiche nolde breke for no violence,
That hard it was thorugh hem for to wynne.
And every hous, that was bilt with-Inne,
Every paleys & every mancioun,
Of marbil werne thorugh-out al the toun,
Of crafty bildyng & werkyng most roial.
And the heght was of every wal
Sixty cubites from the grounde acountid;
And ther was non that other hath surmountid
In the cite, but of on heght alyche,
In verray sothe, bothe of pore and riche,
That it was harde of highe estat or lowe
Hous or palys asounder for to knowe,
So egaly of tymbre and of stoon
Her housis wern reysed everychon.
And if I schulde rehersen by and by
The korve knottes by crafte of masoúnry,
The fresche enbowyng,[6] with vergis right as linys,
And the vowsyng ful of babewynes,[7]
The riche koynyng, the lusty tablementis,[8]
Vynnettis rennynge in the casementis[9]——
Though the termys in englisch wolde ryme,
To rekne hem alle I have as now no tyme,
Ne no langage pyked for the nonys,
The sotil Joynyng to tellen of the stonys,
Nor how thei putten in stede of morter,

---

[1] harts. [2] wild oxen, bulls. [3] locks. [4] cast. [5] shutting. [6] arching.
[7] vaulting, grotesques.   [8] quoins, cornices.   [9] leaf ornamentation.

In the Joynturys copur gilt ful clere,
To make hem Joyne by level & by lyne,
Among the marbil freschely for to schyne
Agein the sonne, whan his schene lyght
Smote in the gold, that was bornyd[1] bright,
To make the werke gletere on every syde.
And of this toun the stretis large & wyde
Wer by crafte so prudently provided,
And by werkemen sette so and devided.
That holsom eyr amyddis myght enspire
Erly on morwe to hem that it desyre;
And Zephirus, that is so comfortable
For to norysche thinges vegetable,
In tyme of yere, thorugh-oute every strete,
With sugred flavour, so lusty & so swete,
Most plesantly in the eyr gan smyte,
The Cytezeyns only to delyte;
And with his brethe hem to recomfort,
Whan thei list walke hem silven to disport.
And thorugh the toun, by crafty purviance,
By gret avys and discret ordynaunce,
By compas cast, & squared out by squires,
Of pulsched marbil up-on strong pilleris,
Devised wern, longe, large, and wyde,
In the frountel of every stretis syde,
Fresche alures[2] with lusty highe pynacles,
And moustryng[3] outward riche tabernacles,
Vowted a-bove like reclinatories[4]
That called werne deambulatories,
Men to walke to-gydre tweine & tweyne,
To kepe hem drie whan it dide reyne,
Or hem to save from tempest, wynde, or thonder,
Yif that hem list schrowde hem silve ther-under.
And every hous cured was with led;
And many gargoyl & many hidous hed
With spoutis thorugh, & pipes as thei ought,
From the ston-werke to the canel raught,
Voyding filthes low in-to the grounde,
Thorugh gratis percid of yren percid rounde;
The stretis paved bothe in lengthe & brede,
In cheker wyse with stonys white & rede.
And every craft, that any maner man
In any lond devise or rekene can,
Kyng Priamus, of highe discrecioun,
Ordeyned hath to dwellyn in the toun,
And in stretis, severyd her and yonder,
Everyche from other to be sette a-sonder,
That thei myght, for more comodite,
Eche be hym silfe werke at liberte:
Gold-smythes first, & riche Jowellers,
And by hem silf crafty browdereris,

[1] burnished.   [2] cloisters.   [3] showing.   [4] canopied couch

Wevers also of wolne & of lyne,
Of cloth of gold, damaske, and satyn,
Of welwet, cendel, & double samyt eke,
And every clothe that men list to seke;
Smythes also, that koude forge wele
Swerdis, pollex,[1] and speris scharp of stele,
Dartis, daggeris, for to mayme & wounde,
And quarel hedis scharp and square y-grounde.
Ther wer also crafty armoureris,
Bowyers, and faste by fleccheris,
And swyche as koude make schaftes pleyn,
And other eke that dide her besy peyn
For the werre to make also trappuris,
Bete[2] baners and royal cote armuris,
And by devise, stondardis & penowns,
And for the felde fresche & gay gytouns.[3]
And every crafte that may rekned be,
To telle schortly, was in this cite.
And thorugh this toun, so riche & excellent,
In the myddes a large river went,
Causyng to hem ful gret commodite;
The whiche on tweyne hath partid the cite,
Of cours ful swyft, with fresche stremys clere,
And highte Xanctus, as Guydo doth us lere.
And as I rede, that up-on this flood,
One eche-asyde many mylle stood,
Whan nede was her grayn & corn to grinde,
Hem to sustene, in story as I fynde.
This river eke, of fysche ful plenteuous,
Devided was by werkmen corious
So craftely, thorugh castyng sovereyne,
That in his course the stremys myght atteyn
For to areche, as Guido doth conjecte,
By archis strong his cours for to reflecte
Thorugh condut pipis, large & wyde with-al,
By certeyn meatis artificial,
That it made a ful purgacioun
Of al ordure & fylthes in the toun,
Waschyng the stretys as thei stod a rowe,
And the goteris in the erthe lowe,
That in the cite was no filthe sene;
For the canel skoured was so clene,
And devoyded in so secre wyse,
That no man myght espien nor devyse
By what engyn the filthes, fer nor ner,
Wern born a-wey by cours of the ryver—
So covertly every thing was cured.
Wher-by the toun was outterly assured
From engenderyng of al corrupcioun,
From wikked eyr & from infeccioun,[4]

---

[1] pole-axe.   [2] paint.   [3] small standards.
[4] Note theory of hygiene, and Lydgate's knowledge of sanitary arrangements such as those of the Abbey of Bury.

That causyn ofte by her violence
Mortalite and gret pestilence.

(Lines 765–926 are omitted, as they do not concern building.)

But I wil furthe of this story wryte,
And on my maner boistusly endyte,
How Priamus was passyng dilligent,
Right desyrous, and inwardly fervent,
Yif he myght, among his werkes alle,
To bilde a paleys and a riche halle,
Whiche schulde ben his chose chef dongon,
His royal se and sovereyn mansioun.
And whan he gan to this werke aproche,
He made it bilde highe up-on a roche,
It for tassure in his fundacioun,
And callyd it the noble Ylyoun.
The sight of whiche, iustly circuler,
By compas cast, rounde as any spere[1]—
And who that wold the content of the grounde
Trewly acounten of this place rounde,
In the theatre first he moste entre,
Takyng the lyne that kerveth thorugh the centre,
By gemetrie, as longeth to that art,
And treblid it, with the seventhe part,
He fynde myght, by experience,
The mesour hool of the circumference,
What lond also, pleynly eke with al,
Contened was with-Inne the stronge wal—
The creste of whiche, wher it lowest was,
Hadde in hight ful sixe hundred pas,
Bilt of marbil, ful royal & ful strong,
And many other riche stoon a-mong;
Whos touris wern reysed up so highe,
That thei raght[2] almost to the skye;
The werk of whiche no man myght amende.
And who that list by grecis[3] up ascende,
He myghte seen in his inspeccioun
To the boundis of many regioun
And provincys that stoode rounde aboute.
And the wallys, with-Inne and with-oute,
Endelong with knottis grave[4] clene,
Depeynt with azour, gold, zinopre, & grene,
That verraily, whan the sonne schon,
Up-on the gold meynt[5] among the stoon,
Thei gaf a light, with-outen any were,[6]
As Phebus doth in his mydday spere—
The werke of wyndowe, and eche fenestral,
Wrought of berel and of clere cristal.
And amyddys of this Ylyoun,
So fresche, so riche of fundacioun,
Whiche clerkys yit in her bokis preyse,

---

[1] sphere. [2] reached. [3] steps. [4] bosses carved. [5] mingled. [6] doubt.

Kyng Pryam made an halle for to reyse,
Excellyng alle in bewte & in strenthe
The latitude acordyng with the lengthe.
And of marbil outeward was the wal;
And the tymbre, most nobil in special,
Was halfe of cedre, as I reherse can,
And the remenant of the riche eban,
Whiche most is able, as I dar specefye,
With stoon to Joyne by craft of carpentrie;
For thei of tymbre have the sovereynte.
And for to telle of this Eban tre,
Liche in bokys sothly as I fynde,
It cometh out of Ethiope and Ynde,
Blak as is get[1]; and it will wexe anoon,
Whan it is korve, harde as any stoon,
And evermore lasten and endure,
And nat corrupte with water nor moysture.
And of this halle ferther to diffyne,
With stonys square by level and by lyne
It pavid was, with gret diligence
Of masownry and passyng excellence.
And al above, reysed was a se,
Ful coriously of stonys and perre,[2]
That callid was, as chefe and principal,
Of the regne the sete moste royal.
To fore whiche was set by gret delyt
A borde of Eban and of yvor whyt,
So egaly Joyned and so clene,
That in the werk ther was no rifte sene;
And sessions wer made on every syde,
Only the statis by ordre to devyde.
Eke in the halle, as it was covenable,
On eche party was a dormant table
Of evor eke, and this eban tre;
And even ageyn the kynges royal see,
In the party that was ther-to contrarie,
I-reised was by many crafty stayre,
Highe in the halle, in the tother syyt,
Right as lyne in the opposyt,
Of pured metal and of stonys clere
In brede & lengthe, a ful rich auter.[3]
On whiche ther stood, of figure & visage
Of masse gold, a wonderful ymage,
To ben honoured in that highe sete,
Only in honour of Jubiter the grete.
And the statue, for al his huge weyghte,
Fiftene cubites complet was of heighte,
A crowne of gold highe up-on his hed,
With hevenly saphirs & many rube red
Fret enviroun, with other stonys of Ynde;
And among wer medled, as I fynde,

---

[1] jet.   [2] precious stones.   [3] altar.

Whyte perlis massyf, large, & rounde;
And for most chefe al dirkenes to confounde,
Was a charbocle, kyng of stonys alle,
To recounfort & gladyn al the halle,
And it tenlumyn in the blake nyght
With the freschenes of his rody light.
-The valu was ther-of in-estimable,
And the riches pleynly incomperable;
For this ymage, by divisioun,
Was of schap and proporcioun
From hed to foot so maisterly entayled,
That, in a point, the werkeman hath nat failed
It to parforme by crafty excellence. . . .

Text in *Lydgate's Troy Book*, ed. H. Bergen, vol. I (E.E.T.S., E.S., XCVII),
1906, pp. 158–174.

(v) *The Court of Sapience*, *c.* 1465, stanzas 211–13, lines 1471–91,
Description of the Castle and Mansion of Wisdom.

Whan I had seene that souverayn solempne syght,
Dame Sapience led me a lyte besyde
Unto a comly Castell shynyng bryght,
Full of all solace, delyte, lust and pryde,
In whos circuite wyth vawtes large and wyde
Of parfyte blys yset were towrys sevene,
The heyghte of whyche astyeth up to hevene.

The dyke of hit, yformyd wyth delyte,
Fulfyllyd was wyth watyr of Quiete;
The marble stoone, the alabaustre whyte
By geometry so frendly gan meete,
That such a wall in hede, body, and feete,
With precyous stones illumyned at devyse,
Was never seen; hit passeth paradyse.

Uppon a Rooche hit was groundyd and set,
And every Botras full of ymagery,
Yche pynnacle, corner, towre and toret
Wyth golde and perle and stonys curyously
Depeyntyd was and powdryd lustyly;
And on the yate, illumynyd wyth all blys,
Wyth goldyn lettres thys wrytyn was ywys: . . .

Text in *The Court of Sapience*, ed. R. Spindler (Beiträge zur Englischen Philo-
logie, Sechstes Heft), 1927, p. 182 ff.

(vi) **William Botoner alias Worcestre measures the new Divinity Schools
at Oxford, 1480. (Translation.)**

The new school of divinity with the library above . . . contains in length
30 yards, each yard of 3 feet, and in breadth 32 feet, and in height from the
bottom up to the upper "walplate" of "frestone" 80 feet, and in height to
the new vault or arch now worked in the year of Christ 1480, from the ground
or floor level 32 feet.

Text in *Itinerarium Willelmi Botoner dict. de Worcestre*, ed. J. Nasmith, 1778, p. 281.

Note: I have omitted references from Chaucer and Langland, and the well-known description of a Friary Church in *Pierce the Ploughman's Creed*, of which the original may be found in Skeat's *Specimens of English Literature*, and a good modernization in Clapham and Godfrey: *Some Famous Buildings and their Story*, pp. 256–7. Further important collections of relevant documents and extracts will be found in Dr. Coulton's *Social Life in Britain*, and *Life in the Middle Ages*, vol. II.

Appendix II

DISTURBED STATE OF THE COUNTRY UNDER EDWARD II AND MORTIMER

(i) The Lichfield masons take an oath to defend the Close, 1321/2.

Upon the Ides (5th) of February (1321/2) Master William of Eiton, mason, with his seven masons swore to help the Chapter (of Lichfield Cathedral) in the defence of the Close and to forewarn the Chapter if they should hear of any impending harm or danger. Also the four servants under Walter swore the same.

Lichfield Chapter Acts, Bodleian MS. Ashmole 794, f.2d. (translation).

(ii) Robert Malvoysin and his family seek protection, 1328.

30th December, 1328. Robert Malvoysin asked the Chapter that by their licence he might live within the Close with his wife and family on account of the danger which was threatening (*ymminebat*) in these days. (Permission was granted provided that accommodation could be found.)

Lichfield Chapter Acts, as above, f.20d. (translation).

Appendix III

A NOBLE HOUSEHOLD
IN THE FIFTEENTH CENTURY

Extracts from the Household Accounts of Richard Beauchamp, Earl of Warwick, 1431-2 (Translation).

f.I. *14th March, 1430/31.* (Cost of the account book.)
And for this paper bought by Duffeld at Roon (Rouen) of Peris parchemyn maker together with binding. 15s. tournois.

f.IV. *Tuesday 20th March.*
. . . cords bought for the lord's chariot (*chariet*). 7s. 6d.

f.IXd. *Saturday 31st March, 1431.*
. . . for 3 loads of rushes (*summis Cirpium*) bought of Halshide for the chamber of the lord and lady. 23s.

f.XXXII. *Sunday 13th May.*
And for 1 "gelycloth" bought of John Gratam. 3s. 9d.

f.LIII. *Saturday 23rd June.*
Also the King came with 2 dukes, 6 knights, 18 esquires, 20 yeomen to drink and went away.
. . . "besommes" bought for the kitchen.

f.LXXVI. *Monday 6th August.*
The lord went away with 11 esquires, 13 yeomen, 12 grooms, 8 pages and 26 horses after breakfast. Also there came Madame Tolbot with 1 damsel, 1 esquire, a nun of Cane (Caen), Haux Cordwaner, Norrys, Richard Beauchamp, Master John Upton to dinner and supper and went away. Also there came (left blank).

f.XCV. *Friday 14th September.*
Also paid for the making and mending of 2 "gardevyands" of . . . (illegible) with iron in the Cellar. 28s. 4d.

f.CXXd. *Monday 5th November.*
And for 4 new wheels bought and made for the lord's chariot with ironwork and nails and with the mending of the body of the said chariot together with the oversight and . . . (illegible) by John Ball with 4 traces (*treys*) bought for the same work. £9 6s. 8d. tournois.

f.CXXVIId. *Monday 19th November.*
Of the marriage of James Dryland and Alice Lyghtfot—
There came Madame Talbot with 2 damsels and 4 squires to dinner and supper and the night. Also came the Earl of Stafford, Lord de Audeley, Sir William Peyto and 10 esquires and 13 yeomen, also Jamys Dryland with 8 grooms, Madame Blont, Madame Peyto, Madame Godard with 8 damsels, 6 wives of burgesses of the city, Hampton's wife, Borow's wife with 2 damsels, 8 burgesses

of the city, Master John Upton, 4 of the King's yeomen of the Crown to dinner and went away. Also (left blank).

f.CXXXIV. *Saturday 1st December.*

And in expenses of the lady Countess of Warwick going by water from Roon to Paris beginning on Saturday the first of December going by water and staying for 7 days and so to Friday on which day at night she entered Paris—with Madame Talbot, 2 damsels, 3 esquires, 1 groom, Madame Godard with 1 damsel, 1 esquire, the wife of Mr. John Somerset with 1 damsel, 2 yeomen, 1 page, 4 officers of the King, 1 esquire of the Cardinal with 1 yeoman, 2 "armerers" with 54 persons guests for the same time.

f.CXXXIVd.

And for 1 "schoute" hired at Roon carrying the lord's gear and provisions viz. wheat, oats, and fish, with firewood (*focali*) and other things to Paris against the King's coronation for the expenses of the hospice of the lord and lady. £tournois 82. 3s. 4d.

And to 1 "fousett" hired to go with the lady, carrying her household with the lady's gear from Roon to Paris before the King's coronation, with all accounted for £t 45.

And to 15 bargees (*Nauigancioribz*) hired for the barge of the lord duke of Bedford carrying the lady Countess of Warwick with lady Talbot and the damsels of the lady with other damsels and with divers officers of the King from Roen to Paris against the King's coronation with 10s. tournois paid for bridge customs. £t 60. 10s.

And given by the hands of the lord and lady to the master of the barge . . . in Reward for his labour going from Roon to Paris. £t 8. 5s.

And in expenses of Richard White with 2 grooms going with the gear of the lord and lady and about the provisions from Roen to Paris and returning to Roen and with carrying gear . . . from the quay (?) of Paris to the lord's hospice with all accounted for 20s. 10d. sterling. £t 8. 14s. 6d.

f.CXXXVII. *Thursday 13th December.*

. . . 32 officers of the King with tailors and skinners of the city (Paris) working on the King's robes; the laundryman (*lavynder*) and 1 woman, the keeper of the hospice, Hugford with 1 page and 4 "plastrer", Weysford, "pursevaunt", 2 merchants of the city to dinner and went away. Also came 6 "schipmen" to dinner and went away. Also came (left blank).

(Note: "one woman, keeper of the hospice" (1 *femina cust' hospic'*) may refer to the same individual; in which case, the concierge).

f.CXXXVIIId. *Sunday 16th December.*

The lord and lady with Madame Talbot went away by reason of the King's Coronation. Also came "le lavynder", 1 woman, the keeper of the hospice— to dinner and supper and went away. Also came Nanfan with 2 yeomen, Forsted with 1 yeoman, Rafe Mountford, Baudewyn Mountford with 1 page, Hugford with 1 page, Raulyn of the pantry (*de pant'*), Robert de Chapell, Blyth with 1 page, Thomas Say, 1 burgess of the city—to supper and went away.

f.CXLd. *Thursday 20th December.*

. . . 3 burgesses of the city, 4 "mynstrell", Bolvyll with 1 page, 4 "vynters"— to dinner and went away.

f.CXLIII. *Tuesday 25th December, Christmas Day.*
. . . 13 burgesses of the city, 6 "marchaunts de Roon", 4 chaplains of that city, 11 "souder", 3 "marchauntys de Brugis" . . .

f.CXLIIId. *Wednesday 26th December.*
. . . 14 "bargemen" of the lord and lady to dinner and went away.

f.CXLIV. Sendenys (St. Denis). For Supper.
And for expenses of the lord Earl and lady Countess with their household and 44 horses staying at "Seynt denys" on Wednesday 26th December and Thursday 27th of the same month for a day and a night. . . .
(Expenses of the return journey follow; the stages given are Mantes, Vernon, Château Gaillard, Pont-de-l'Arche. Rouen was reached in time for supper on Sunday 30th December.)

f.CXLVI. . . . And for a ship called 1 "schoute" hired at Paris to carry the lord's gear viz. 2 chariots, 1 "carre", 10 "punchonns", 2 pipes of wine and (? ale) of the gear of the lord and lady in part payment. £t 11.
. . . (a total, giving rate of exchange) £t 67. 10s.—£8 3s. 9d. stg.

(f.CXLIX). *Friday 4th January* (1432).
And for the making of 1 chariot of the lord overseen by John Ball. 27s. 6d.

f.CLIII. *Saturday 12th January.*
At Roon for breakfast and went away.
(The stages of the journey to Calais were Auffay, Dieppe, Eu, Abbeville, Rue, Montreuil, Boulogne).

f.CLVII. Caleys (Calais) for dinner.
Wednesday 23rd January.

f.CLXVI. Caleys for breakfast early and went away.
Saturday 9th February.
   Dovere.
And for expenses of the lord and lady there viz. on Saturday for dinner and the lady with Madame Talbot . . . damsels and part of the household went to Canterbury on pilgrimage. . . .
(The stages of the Countess's journey to London were "Rewell", Canterbury, Faversham, Gravesend.)

f.CLXIX. London. *Wednesday, 13th February.*
The Lady Countess, Madame Talbot, 7 damsels, 2 chaplains, 8 esquires, 1 trumpet, 11 yeomen, 16 grooms, 18 pages and 27 horses to supper and stayed. And there came the wife of Mr. John Somerset with 1 damsel, 1 esquire, the Rector of Stanford with 1 page, Busch, Shirley with 1 page, Thomas Poyntz with 3 yeomen, 14 bargemen, Henry, Robert, John, Bay—for the same time, altogether 94 persons. Also came Monsieur de Ewe with 3 esquires, John Laurens with 3 yeomen to drink and went away.

f.CLXXd. *Saturday 16th February.*
And for the carriage of the lord's gear from ship viz. 11 carts hired from Senkatrens (St. Katharine's) to the lord's hospice in London 4s. 8d. Also for 3 men hired to carry the gear into the lord's hospice 16d. Total 6s.

f.CLXXIV. *Saturday 23rd February.*
. . . 4 of the lord's tenants of Waltamstow, 1 tenant of the lord from "devyn schire" to dinner and went away.
(a certain John Ferrur of Walthamstow is several times mentioned).

f.CLXXIVd. *Sunday 24th February.*
. . . 4 of the lord's tenants of Waltamstowe to supper and went away.

f.CLXXV. *Monday 25th February.*
There came the surveyor with 1 esquire, 4 yeomen, Robert Andrewz with 2 yeomen, Boyvyle with 3 yeomen, Hugford with 1 yeoman, Vampage with 1 page, Thomas Poyntz with 1 yeoman, 1 page, Schirley with 1 page, Randull Mullyngs with 1 page, the Rector of Stanford, Busch, Rokenet, John Aylewey with 1 page, John Phelip, William Coke with 1 page, Henry Robert(s), Thomas Ferrur, 9 "bargemen", "le lavynder", Borton, 4 falconers, John Denby, Gateley, John Ray, Bongay with 1 yeoman—to dinner and supper and went away.

f.CLXXVI. Wages of servants. (*Tuesday 26th February.*)
And for the wages of Thomas Stugh the lord's yeoman staying at Waltamstow to give hay and feed to the horses of the lord and servants for 6 days per day 3*d.*—18*d.* Also for 4 grooms of the "carr" and chariot for the same time—3*s.* Also for 3 grooms of the lord keeping the horses and hackneys for the same time—3*s.* Also in wages of 4 pages of the lord's household for the same time per day 1½*d.*—3*s.* Total 11*s.* 6*d.* (hire of a stable "at Hugh Colene".)

f.CLXXVIIId. (*Wednesday 27th February.*)
And for the expenses of the lady Countess with Madame Talbot, 7 damsels, 3 chaplains, 6 esquires, 8 yeomen, 12 grooms, 7 pages, 14 bargemen with 1 barge and 19 horses viz. 1 "palfrey", 1 "somer", 5 mares for the chariot, 12 "haks"—at Braynford (Brentford) going by water from London to Caversham and so to Warwick.

f.CLXXIX. Staines. *Thursday 28th February.*
. . . for 1 "kynderkyn" of ale bought for the lady's barge containing 15 gallons of ale price per gallon 1½*d.*—22½*d.* Also for 4 (*sic*) hired from Stanis for carrying the servants of the lady with 1 "botell hors" and 1 guide (*gyd*) to Wynsore. 3*s.* 4*d.*

f.CLXXIXd. Windsor. *Saturday 1st March.*
. . . given to 1 "gyd" for going through "Wiltschr" for the lady's chariot. 8*d.*

f.CLXXX. Marlow. *Sunday 2nd March.*
. . . given to 3 small boats hired by Colier and 4 men from Wynsore to Marlowe appointed to carry the lady with her servants 6*s.* 8*d.* Also for 5 horses hired at Marlow for carrying the lady's servants to Caversham. 3*s.* 4*d.*

f.CLXXXd. Henley. *Monday 3rd March.*
. . . Given to William Hurre and Edward "bargeman" with their 6 fellows one day at London and afterwards for 13 men for 7 days going by water . . . from London to Stanis each man per day 4*d.* 32*s.* 8*d.* Also given to the same Hurre for 1 "towynglyn" for the lady's barge 3*s.* 4*d.* Also for expenses of the same Hurre with 13 fellows by the way for bread and firewood etc. 6*s.* Also paid to the same Hurre for 1 cable . . . for the lady's barge 3*s.* 4*d.* Also paid to the

same Hurre for 8 men at London going with the lady to "seynt katryne" 3s. Also given to William Hurre and Edward with their said 12 fellows in Reward for their labours by the lady's hands 13s. 4d.

f.CLXXXI. Caversham. *Tuesday 4th March etc.*
. . . paid to William de Backhowse going with 1 cart and 7 horses to Warwick. 2s. . . .

f.CLXXXId. Walyngford et Abynton (Abingdon). *Monday 10th March.*
. . . for "veryyngs" at Dorchester and Moreton 3s. 8d. Also for 4 horses' hire and 3 men to help the lady's chariot by the way 14d. . . . Also for 5 new collars with 4 pairs of traces and 6 hames (*hamis*) bought by John Carter for the lady's chariot 11s. 4d. Also paid for 1 cart hired with 2 men and 7 horses for carrying the lady's gear from Caversham to Warwick 26s. 8d.

f.CLXXXIId. Tewkysbery et Worsester. *Wednesday 12th March etc.*
. . . Also paid to 2 men with 5 horses hired from Whetyngton (? Whittington near Cheltenham) to Warwick for helping the lady's chariot 6s. 4d. Also paid to John Nele going with the lady's chariot with the said horses from Tewkysbery to Warwick, by the lady's hands 6s. 5d.

f.CLXXXIII. Bordisley (Bordesley, Worcs.) *Friday (14th) March.*
. . . paid for 14 horses hired at Redyng (Reading) to carry the lady's servants from Caversham to Warwick viz. for 8 days, each horse per day 4d., 37s. 4d. Also for 2 "hakeneymen" hired for taking the said horses back from Warwick to Reading 8s. 8d.

(*Note :* From London to Staines, and from Abingdon to Warwick, road transport was used. Caversham Manor (on the north bank of the Thames opposite Reading) belonged to the Earl of Warwick; at Bordesley near Redditch was a Cistercian Abbey. The stages and times are set out in the following table:

Date	Place	Mile-age	Journey Time	Stay	Speed
26/27 Feb.	London				(Road)
27 Feb.	Brentford	9	Morning	Night and morning	(Below)
28/29 Feb.	Staines	10	Afternoon	Two nights	
1 March	Windsor	8½	Day	Night	
2 „	Marlow	13¼	Day	Night and morning	
3 „	Henley	8¾	Afternoon	Night	(River)
4/9 „	Caversham	9¾	Day	Six nights	
10 „	Wallingford	16	Morning		
	Abingdon	13	Afternoon	Night	15½ m.p.d.
11 March	Burford	23	Day	Night	
12 „	Tewkesbury	31	? Day	Night	
13 „ (?)	Worcester	15	Morning	Night	(Road)
14 „ (?)	Bordesley	21	? Day	? Night	
15 „ (?)	Warwick	16	? Morning		25 m.p.d.
18 days on route		194¼	9½ days		20½ m.p.d.

f.CLXXXVIId. (London).
Also for 8 quarters 3 bushels of oats bought from John Ferrur of Walthamstow price the quarter 2s.—17s. . . . bought of Jankyn Ferrur there. . . . And by gift and present (*exhennio*) of the lord's tenants of Walthamstow 10 quarters of oats whence 9 quarters issued to Denysh at London for the lord's horses there.

f.CLXXXVIII/IX. (French and English measures.)
. . . (illegible) "myn" of oats makes 5 bushels of measure of England . . . the "myne" of wheat contains 4 bushels of measure of France at Rouen which make 3 bushels of measure of England lacking the third part of one "peck" of that measure. . . . "mew" contains 24 "mynes".
(Note: for French old measures see *H.MSS.Comm.*, Rep. IX, p. 76).

f.CCII. Hire of ships.
And for 2 ships hired at Rouen by Duffeld for carrying the lord's and lady's gear with wines to Honfleur and divers gear of the servants of the same lord and lady 55s. for 1 "lodsman" hired—£t 35. 15s. Also for 1 great ship hired there for carrying the said gear to London with £t 8. 5s. given to a "lodesman"—£t 58. 15s. Also for the expenses of Roger Savage, White, Robert "capell", Bartholomew, Thomas Say, 3 yeomen with 8 grooms of the lord going by sea and guarding the said provisions for 5 weeks 3 days with their carriage and costs £t 33. 15s.—£t 128. 5s.—£15.10.11 sterling. . . . 1 "geldyng" bought for the lord's chariot 26s. 8d. sterling.

f.CXCIX. Spices bought at London.
½ lb. pepper bought . . . Feb. 8d. Also for ¾ of Ginger bought 22½d. Also for 1 quarter of sugar 8d. Also 3 oz. "Saffren" 2s. 10d. Also for 3 lbs. dates bought 12d. Also for 4 lbs. Figs and Raisons 7d. Also for 4 lbs. Almonds 7d. Also for 1 quarter of Cloves 11d. Also 2 lbs. Ginger bought 4s. 8d. Also for 2 lbs. Pepper 2s. 8d. Also for 2 lbs. Sugar bought 4s. 8d. Also 1 "queyer papir" bought 4d. Total 21s. 5½d. Sterling.

(*Note:* Food bought at Rouen included: Red and white wine, beer (*bere*); Beef, mutton, veal, bacon, kid, sucking pig, calves' feet; geese, pullets, pigeons, egrets; salt fish, plaice, soles, flounders, porpoise, bream, "bremettz", perch, carp, roach, trout, salmon, mullet, "Rogetts", "Whits", "barbell", "codlyngs", "cheven", "Thornba", eels, conger, mussels, crawfish; milk, cream, butter, eggs; peas, beans, onions; cherries, strawberries, pears, plums, nuts; vinegar, verjuice, mustard, herbs.)

MS. Account Book of Richard Beauchamp Earl of Warwick, 14th March 1430/1 —13th March 1431/2. Warwick Corporation Records.

Appendix IV

MEALS COMMON AND UNCOMMON

(i) *The Forme of Cury, c.* 1400.

First . . . commune pottages and commune meetis . . .
    4. Caboches in potage.
Take caboches and quarter hem, and seeth hem in gode broth, with oynonns
y mynced, and the whyte of lekes y slyt, and corve smale, and do thereto
safronn and salt and force it with powdor douce. (? all-spice.)
    8. Gourdes in potage.
Take young gowrdes, pare hem, and kerve hem on pecys. Cast hem in gode
broth, and do thereto a good partye of oynonns mynced. Tak pork soden
(boiled); grynd it, and alye it therewith, and with yolkes of ayren (eggs).
Do thereto safroun and salt, and messe it forth with powdor-douce.
    18. Connates (Marmalade of Quinces).
Take connes (quinces) and pare hem; pyke out the best and do hem in a pot
of erthe (earthenware). Do thereto whyte grece (lard), that he stewe thereinne,
and lye (mix) hem up with hony clarified, and with rawe yolkes, and with a
lytell almaund mylke, and do thereinne powder-fort (strong spices) and
safronn; and loke that it be yleeshed (cut into slices).
    76. Salat.
Take parsel, sawge, garlec, chibollas (young onions), oynons, leek, borage,
myntes, porrectes (leaves of onion or leek?), fenel, and ton tressis (cresses),
rew, rosemarye, purslarye (purslane); lave, and waishe hem clene; pike hem,
pluk hem small with thyn honde, and myng hem wel with rawe oile. Lay on
vynegar and salt, and serve it forth.

Text in *Antiquitates Culinariae*, ed. R. Warner, 1791, pp. 1–35.

(ii) Lydgate's Subtleties at the Banquet of Henry VI, 1432.

The Soteltes at the Coronation Banquet.

This was the first cours at his coronacion, that is to say, first:

ffurmentie, with venyson. Viande Royal plantid with losenges of golde.
Borehedes in castelles of earmed with golde. Beef. Moton. Signet. Capon
stued. Heron. Grete pike. A redde lech with lions corven theryn of white.
Custadc Rooial with a leparde of golde sittyng theryn. Fritour like a sonne
with a flour de lice therynne. A sotelte, Seint Edward and Seint Lowes
armed in cote armours bryngyng yn bitwene hem the Kyng in his cote
armour with this scripture suyng:

> Loo here twoo kynges righte perfit and right good,
>   Holy Seint Edwarde and Seint Lowes:
> And see the braunch borne of here blessid blode;
>   Live, among Cristen moost sovereigne of price,
>   Enheretour of the floure de lice!

God graunte he may thurgh help of Crist Jhesu
This sixt Henry to reigne and be as wise
And hem resemble in knyghthod & vertue.

Here foloweth the second course; that is to wite:

Viande blank, barrid of golde. Gely partid writen and notid Te Deum
Laudamus. Pigge endored. Crane. Bitore (bittern). Conyes. Chikyns
endored. Partrich. Pecok enhakyll. Greate breame. Leches white with an
antelop of redde corven theryn, a crowne about his neck with a cheyne of
golde. Flampayne poudred with lepardis and floure de lices of golde. Fritour,
a lepardis hedde with 2 ostrich fethers. A sotelte, themperour and the kyng
that ded is, armed, and here mantelles of the garters; and the kyng that nowe
is, knelyng bifore hem with this resoun:

Ageinst miscreauntes themperour Sigismound
    Hath shewid his myght which is imperial;
Sithen Henry the Vth so noble a knyght was founde
    For Cristes cause in actis martial;
    Cherisshyng the Chirch Lollardes had a falle,
To give exaumple to kynges that succede
    And to his braunche in especiall
While he dothe regne to love God & drede.

The 3d course sueth; that is to say:

Blaunde Surrey poudrid with quatrefoulis gilt. Venyson rostid. Egrettes.
Curlewe. Cokkes. Plover. Quailis. Snytes (snipe). Grete birdes. Larkes.
Carpe. Crabbe. Lech of 3 colours. A colde bakemete like a shelde quarterly
redde and white, set with losenges & gilt, and floures of borage. Fritour
crispes. A sotelte of Our Lady sittyng and hir Childe in hir lappe, and she
holdyng in hir hand a crowne and Seint George knelyng on that oo side and
Seint Denyse on that other side, presentyng the Kyng, knelyng, to Our Lady,
with this reason folowyng:

O blessid Lady, Cristes moder dere,
    And thou Seint George, that callid art hir knight;
Holy Seint Denyse, O martir moost entier,
    The sixt Henry here present in your sight,
    Shewith of grace on hym your hevenly light,
His tendre yougth with vertue doth avaunce,
    Bore by discent and by title of right
Justly to reigne in England and in Fraunce.

Appendix V

WILLS OF CERTAIN PERSONS MENTIONED

(i) Thomas Wryght, painter, 1424. (Translation.)

In the name of God Amen. the 26th day of February in the year of our lord 1423 (142¾) and the year of King Henry the Sixth after the Conquest of England the second I Thomas Wryght citizen and "Peyntor" of London of whole mind and being in my good remembrance do set make and ordain first my testament of my last will in this manner. First I bequeath and commend my soul to God my almighty creator and to the Blessed Virgin Mary His Mother and to all the Saints and my body to be buried in the churchyard of the church of St. Giles without "Crepilgate" in the suburb of London next to the tomb of Agnes late my wife. And I will first and before all after that my body is buried that all my debts in which I am lawfully bound shall be paid then I will that my funeral expenses shall be decently and reasonably made according to the good discretion and ordinance of my executors. Also I bequeath to the high altar of the aforesaid church of St. Giles for my tithes and oblations forgotten and withheld 6s. 8d. Also I bequeath to the fabric of the nave of the same church 13s. 4d. Also I bequeath to each chaplain and clerk of the same parish taking part in my burial 8d. Also I bequeath to the fraternity of St. Giles aforesaid 6s. 8d. Also I bequeath to the fraternity of St. Luke[1] in the same church 6s. 8d. Also I bequeath to each of the five orders of friars of London to pray for my soul 2s. 6d. Also I bequeath to Nicholas Benton 40s. Also I bequeath to John my apprentice 20s. The residue of all my movable goods not bequeathed wherever they may be after my debts first paid and all my bequests (set forth) below fulfilled I bequeath to be divided into two parts of which the first part of the same residue I bequeath to be distributed for the soul and souls [sic] abovesaid by my executors for pious uses as shall seem best to them to please God and to profit the salvation of my soul and as they should wish to answer before the celestial Judge on peril of their souls and the other part or moiety I give and bequeath to the aforesaid [sic] Alice my wife to do and dispose therewith at her free will for ever. Of this my beforemade testament I make and ordain my faithful executors namely the aforesaid Alice my wife the principal executor William Dogge my father-in-law and for his labour about the premises one hundred shillings sterling. In witness whereof &c.

Proved &c the last day of February in the year of our lord above written ... administration was granted to John the executor [sic] ...

Prerogative Court of Canterbury, Register Luffenam, fo. 2.

(ii) Thomas Damett, Canon of St. Paul's, 1436. (Translation.)

In the Name of God Amen. the fifteenth day of July in the year of our lord 1436 I Thomas Damett Canon and Residenciary of the Cathedral Church of St. Paul London of whole mind and perfect memory in the hospice of my

---

[1] This fraternity was specially supported by the London painters.

dwelling at London first do set make and ordain my testament in this manner. That is to say first I bequeath my soul to almighty God the Blessed Mary and all the Saints and my body in ecclesiastical burial to be buried in "le Pardon-cherchawe" London. Also I bequeath to my mother £40 of good and lawful money of England 1 silver cup "chaced" and covered with writing and "benedictus qui venit in nomine domini". Also I bequeath to the same 1 dozen of silver spoons and a silver salt with gilt edges. Also I bequeath to the same 4 yards of violet "duguyd". Also I bequeath to the same the remainder of pewter vessels and of "countrefeett" not new with a dozen of "pewtervessell countrefeett" with 2 "chargeors". Also I bequeath to the same certain utensils of my hospice to the value of £10 according to the discretion of my executors. Also I bequeath to my mother's maid called Katherine 5 marks. Also I bequeath to Katherine the daughter of my sister 40s. Also I bequeath to William Sherman the son of my sister 100s. and a chest well bound with iron and painted with all and singular my books of small price according to the discretion of my executors. Also I bequeath to the parish church of "Stokton" my vestment bordered (?) with damask with white fringes (crinis) together with 60s. to be distributed among the men and women of the same parish suffering the greatest need. Also I bequeath to the parish church of "Somercotes" towards buying things needful for the choir 40s. Also I bequeath to the parish church of "Ouynton" in the diocese of Wynton 13s. 4d. Also I bequeath to the hospital of St. Thomas in "South-werk" 3 pairs of sheets according to the discretion of my executors. Also I bequeath to the convent of St. Mary "de Overey in Southwerk" 1 "bordecloth de work" with 2 towels according to the discretion of my executors. Also I bequeath to the celebrants of divine service within the Castle of "Wyndesor" 40s. Also I will that there should be distributed for the soul of John Selby 20s. And for the soul of Thomas Gentill 26s. 8d. Also I bequeath to each person in priest's orders (in ordine sacerdotali) within the Church of St. Paul wearing the habit 12d. Also I bequeath to each vicar of the same church 12d. Also I bequeath to each verger of the same church 8d. Also I bequeath to the choristers of the same church 5 marks. Also I bequeath to the bell ringer of the same church 12d. Also I bequeath to William Wheler my servant 20s. Also I bequeath to John Bacheler my servant 20s. Also I bequeath to John Botiller my servant 10s. Also I bequeath to John Shelford my servant 10s. Also I bequeath to my godson called Wayte at "Wyndesor" 13s. 4d. Also I bequeath to my godson at "Stokton" called Mascall Junior 13s. 4d. Also I bequeath to the common library at "le presteshouse" next the church of St. Paul aforesaid my book called "Speculum curatorum". Also I bequeath to each of my executors 26s. 8d. Also I bequeath to sir William Bothe overseer of this testament with my mother 1 "Bordcloth de damascworch". Also I bequeath to my mother 1 "Shipcofr" well bound with ironwork. Also I will that 40s. should be distributed among the parishioners of "Somercotes" suffering need. Also I bequeath to the parish church of "Stokton" a missal, on the second leaf "dignetur per dominum nostrum &c". Also I bequeath to the Charterhouse of London my book called "Speculum humane salua-cionis". Also I bequeath to sir John Browne a yellow robe lined with blue (blodio) "Bokerham" together with a hood of the same. Also I bequeath to Katherine my and my mother's kinswoman 1 "myddelpot de Brasse" 1 ladle and a half-dozen of "pewtervessell garnesshed". Also I bequeath to the same 1 pair of "blanketts" 1 pair of sheets of the middle sort and 1 red coverlet with 1 "canevas". Also I bequeath to Katherine Damett 1 "bordcloth de pariswerk" 1 "towell" 1 pair of "shets" 1 pair of "Blanketts" 1 "canevasse" and a half-dozen of "pewtrevessell countrefete" with 1 brass pot and ladle. Also I bequeath to Katherine Damett apprentice of London daughter of my brother when she shall come to marriageable years 100s. Also I bequeath to Margaret Sherman daughter of my sister 1 mazer with 1 silver and gilt band (*bend*/). Also I bequeath to Seuer Acres Grocer of London 1 pair of silver salts covered. Also I bequeath to his wife 1 silver and gilt "goblett" with 1 blue boss (*blodio knopp*) "enamayled". Also I bequeath to Master Reginald Kentwode a "bordcloth de damascwork". Also I bequeath to sir John Bernyngham 1 penner with its appurtenances of Paris work. Also I will that immediately after that my soul shall have left my body 400 masses shall be celebrated for my soul and the souls of all the faithful departed. Also I will that these things above bequeathed which tend to works of charity or piety for me and for my soul shall also accrue to the merits and benefit of others to whom I am in any way rightfully bound and that they should share with me in all things which may be done for me and my soul as if they were personally expressed. Also I will that four priests shall say each day two psalters for six days before and after my obit for my soul and that they shall receive for each psalter 16*d*. Also I will that a priest of virtuous repute shall celebrate before the Crucifix called "le Roode at the Northdore" for my soul for three years if my goods bequeathed shall be sufficient for this. Also I will that one of the brothers of the Charterhouse shall celebrate each day for three years a Requiem mass for my soul after my death. And I will that the same brother shall receive for each mass 2*d*. The residue of all my goods and chattels wheresoever they may be both in goods and in other things only after my debts fully paid I give and bequeath to sir William Woborne sir John Fuller Seyar Acrez and Thomas Pebley my executors that they having God before their eyes may ordain and dispose as is afore said in place of alms as they shall best know and shall wish to answer before the celestial Judge in the stern examination of judgment. In witness whereof I have set my seal with these present [No witnesses named]. Given at London the day month and year of the lord abovesaid

Proved the 14th of April 1437 . . . administration granted to sir William Woborne, sir John Fuller chaplains & Thomas Pebley the executors. . . .

Prerogative Court of Canterbury, Register Luffenam, fo. 21.

(iii) Robert Vertue, freemason, 1506. (Contractions expanded, Arabic numerals substituted for Roman, and modernized use of capitals, i and j, and u and v.)

In the Name of God Amen. The 10th day of May the yere of our lord God 1500 and sixe and the 21th yere of the Reigne of kyng Henry the VIIth I Robert Vertue Citezein and Fremason of London beyng in my hole & stedfast mynde ordeyne and make this my testament in maner and forme folowing. First I geve and bequeth my soule to almighty God my maker and saviour and to our blessed Lady Seynt Mary His Moder and to all the holy company of heven and my body to be buried within the church and monastery of Seynt Augustyne without the walls of Caunterbury in the Countie of Kent Orells in suche place where it shall please God of His mercy for me to dye /. Also I bequeth unto the high aulter of the parisshe church of Seynt Paule without Caunterbury aforsaid for my tithes and offeryngs forgoten or negligently withholden in dischargyng of my soule / 3*s*. 4*d*. Also I bequeth to the sustentacion of the work of the same church 6*s*. 8*d*. Also I Renownce and utterly Revoke all maner testaments and wills by me made before the date herof and this my present testament and last will to stand and take effect / Also I will that myn executors underwritten anon after my decesse doo fynde an honest preest of goode name and fame to syng and pray for my soule the soules of my fader and moder and all cristen soules in the parisshe church of Seynt Paule aforsaid by the space of an hole yere next after my decesse / he having for his salary and wages for the same yere 10 marks sterling/. Also I bequeth to my lord of Seynt Augustyns to have my soule in his blissed remembrance 6*s*. 8*d*. To Master prior 5*s*. To the supprior 4*s*. To the Chaunter / 3*s*. 4*d*. And to every preest in the same house folowing 20*d*. And to every Novice there 12*d*. Item I bequeth to dan Symeon Vertue a gobelett with a cover parcell gilte and half a dosen spones of silver. And also I bequeth unto William Vertue my son ayenst he cometh oute of his apprentishode £20 / a pece of silver gilte covered and all myn apparell for my body Except my beste gowne my best dowblett and my best Jackett and my best ryng with a dyamond which I bequeth unto my brother William Vertue /. Also I bequeth unto my son Robert Vertue £20 in money and a flatt pece of silver with a cover parcell gilte and half a dosen sponys of silver /. The which money plate and stuff to theym so bequethed I will that anon Immediatly aftir my decesse be delivered into the Custody and keping of my said brother William he to see the dispocion therof according to this my bequest. So that the said money plate and stuff be layd in sure and sauf keping for the performance and fulfilling of this my present testament as he wold I shuld doo for him in like case /. And if any of the said William & Robert my sonnes decesse before their bequests comyng to their hands than I woll that the part of hym so being dede remayn unto that other overlyving and if both the said William and Robert my sonnes decesse bifore their said bequests come to their hands than I will that all their parts be distributed amongs the childern of my said broder William by his discrecion evenly with oute any colour. Also I bequeth for a trentall of masses to be said for my soule the day of my decesse / 10*s*/. Also I bequeth to the Gray freers Observants in Caunterbury to pray for my soul amongs all christen soules/.[*sic*] The Residue of all my goods moevable and unmoevable in this my present testament no graunted not bequethed my detts paide and myn obite kept I freely geve and bequeth unto Elinore my Wif whom I ordeyne and make my principall executrice and William Vertue my brother hir coexecutor they to doo for the helth of my soule as they can seme best by their discrecions to please God and moost mede for my soule / And for the accomplisshement and fulfillyng of this my present testament and last Will wele & truely to be done / I ordeyne and make William Kynder of the Citie of Caunterbury to be overseer / And I bequeth to either of my said executor and overseer 20*s*. for their true and diligent labour in this behalf. Sealed with my seale the day & yere abovesaide /.

This is the last Will of me the said Robert Vertue[1] made the day and yere abovesaid as to the disposicion of all my lands and tenements that is to say / First I will that anon aftir my decesse Elianore my Wiff have hold and peasibly enjoye my newe tenemente at Grenewich aforsaid unto the tyme that William my son come oute of his apprenticehode / She keping the reparacions

---

[1] The testament disposed of personalty ; the will of real estate.

during the same tyme And then the said William to enjoye the same Newe tenement to hym and to the heirs of his body laufully begoten / And over that I will that the said Elianore have and enjoye all my lands and tenements in the parisshe of Hayron [Herne] in the Countie of Kent unto the tyme that the said Robert have the same lands and tenements to hym and to the heirs of his body laufully begoten / Saving onely I will that the said Elianor my Wif kepe the reparacion of the said house and tenements during hir tyme / And over this I will that thesaid Elianore my Wif have hold and peasibly enjoye all myn other houses and gardyns sett and lying in Caunterbury & withoute. To have and to hold unto thesaid Elianore for terme of the liff of the same Elianore / I will that the said houses and gardeyns with their appurtenances remayn to thesaid William my son / To have and to hold to hym to his heirs and assignes for ever of the chieff lorde of that fee by service therof due and of right accustomed. And if it happen that thesaid William or Robert to decesse oon of theym bifore that other without heirs of the bodies of theym laufully begoten as God defend that then the lenger lyver of theym to be others heyre /. To have and to hold to hym to his heirs and assignes of the chief lord of that fee by service therof due and accustomed. And if it happen that the said William and Robert my sonnes without heirs of their bodies laufully begoten to decesse Than I will that if thesaid Elianore be than on lyve that she shalhave all my said howses or tenements and gardeyns aswell in the townes of Grenewiche and Hayron as in Caunterbury or withoute / To have and to holde unto the same Elianore for terme of hir lif She keping sufficient reparacion during all the same tyme /. And aftir the decesse of thesaid Elianore I will that all thesaid houses or tenements and gardeyns aswell in Grenewiche and Hayron as in Caunterbury or withoute to remayne to my broder William Vertue / To have and to hold to hym and to the heirs of his body laufully begoten. This present testament and last Will was sealed by the said Robert Vertue with his owne propre seale in the presence of Robert Janyn John Lobyns the Kyngs maister masons and John Mance notary publique /. By me Robert Vertue /

Proved . . . 12th December 1506 by oath of Elianore and William Vertue the executors. . . .

Prerogative Court of Canterbury, Register Adeane, fo. 13.

(iv) William Vertewe, esquire, Master Mason to the King, 1527

In the Name of God Amen. the 11th day of March the yere of our Lord a Thousande fyve hundred twenty and six (1526/7) The 18 yere of the Reigne of king Henry the eight / I William Vertewe Squier maister mason unto the kings grace abovesaid / being of hole and parfite mynde and memory lawde be unto almighty God / ordeyn and make this my last will and testament / in maner and fourme folowing that is to say First I bequeth my soule to almighty God my saviour and Redemer to our blissed Lady Saint Mary His Mother / and to all the celestiall company of heven to pray for me / and my body to be buried in the parishe Church of Kingeston Where as my wife lieth buried / Item I bequeth to the high awter of Saint Margaret of Westmynster for my tithes necligently forgotten 12*d*./ Item I bequeth to the said Church of Saint Margaret / 40*s*. / towards the makyng and performyng of a Tabernacle of Saint Kateryn within the said Church / Item I geve and bequeth to my doughter Margery the wife of Thomas George twenty pounds /

to be delivered to hir and hir Childern by the hands of John Agmondesham my sonne in lawe / after his discrecion and as he shall thinke necessary to be delivered by parte porcion or all at all tymes / Item I geve and bequeth to the said John Agmondesham and to my doughter his wife to their heires of their bodies laufully begotten and assigns / all that my londes and tenements the Inne called the Thre Cranys in the town of Kyngeston aforsaid / Soo that the said John Agmondesham his wife heires or assignes shall fynde or cause to be founde a prest to syng masses for my soule my Wifs soule my father and mother soule and all christen soules / during the space of fyve yeres Immediatly after my decesse / paying or cause to be paid to the said prest for his salary by yere £6 13s. 4d. of good and laufull money of Inglond quarterly by egall porcions / Also all other my londes and goodes within the Realme of Inglond I geve and bequeth to the said John Agmondesham and his wife their heires and assignes. Item I geve and bequeth to John Carsse my servant £6 13s. 4d. The residue of my goodes both moveable and unmoveable to me belonging by juste title specialties or otherwise except oonly my forsaid legacis and bequests to other persones / my funerall expenses and detts weale and truely discharged I interly and freely geve to the said John Agmondesham to dispoase for my soule helth as he shall thinke best. Which John Agmondesham I ordeyn and make sool executor of this my last Will and testament. Written the day and yere abovenamed with these witnesses Master William Mote Curat of the Church of Saint Margaret aforesaid George Lord John Mayborne Thomas Sylvester Richard Trice Richard Sadsford "Tonsor" John Carsse Robert Joys John Molton with many others.

Proved 22nd March 1526(/27) on oath of John Agmondesham.

Prerogative Court of Canterbury, Register Porch, fo. 17.

(v) Humfrey Cooke, Carpenter, 1531.

In the Name of God Amen. The 14th day of Marche in the yere of our lord God 1500 and thirty (1530/31) and the 22th yere of the reigne of King Henry the eight I Humfrey Cooke Citizen and Carpynter of London being hole of mynde and in good memorye Laude and praysing be unto allmighty God make ordeyne and dispoase this my present testament conteyning therin my Last Will in maner and fourme folowing / that ys to wytte / First I bequeth my soule to allmighty God my creatour saviour and maker / to the most blissid Virgyn His Mother / our Lady Sainte Marye and to all tholy and blissid company of saintes in hevyn and my body to be buryed in the churche of thospitall of Henry late King of England the VIIth called the Savoye / before the ymage of Sainte George in the same churche. Item I woll that all suche debts and duetyes as I owe to anny manner parsonne or persons of right or of conscience shalbe weale and truely contentid and paid and after that my debts be paid / and my funerall charges doon I woll that all my goodes cattalls and debts shall after the laudable use and custome of the Cytie of London be devided into three egall parts whereof I give and bequethe to Alice my wife / one equall parte for and in the name of her full porcion and parte of all my said goodes cattalls and debts to her aftre thuse and custome of London belonging / and the second egall parte of all my said goodes cattalls and debts I give and bequethe to Roger Cooke Christeane Russell my childern now being of full age and to Humfrey Cooke Margarete Cooke and Elisabethe Cooke my childerne now being of noneage egally

amongest them to be devided and to be deliverd to the said Humfreye or
Margarete and Elisabethe / and to every of them at their full ages of 21 yeres
or ells at suche tyme as it shall fortune them to be maryed and if it shall
fortune anny of the said Humfrey Margarete and Elisabeth my said childerne
to decease before that it shalhappin them to come to their said full age of
21 yeres / or ells fortune to be maryed Than I will that the porcion and parte
of hym her or them so deceasing before full age / and not maryed shall
remayne to the other of my said childe or childerne now of noneage surviving
egally betwne them to be devided and to be delivered as is aforesaid and if yt
shalhappin all my said thre childern before their said full ages or mariages to
decease Than I woll that all the said porcion and parte of goodes to my said
3 childerne bequethed shall remayne to Roger Cooke my sonne and to
Cristeane my doughter egally betwene them to be devided if they shalbe then
lyving and if they shall not then be lyving then I will that the childerne of
the said Roger and Christeane shalhave all the said porcions egally amongest
them to be devided and the thirde egall parte of all my said goodes cattalls
and debts I reserve unto my selfe and to myne executours underwritton to
and for the perfourmannce of my legacyes and bequestes herafter ensueyng
that is to wytte / First I bequethe to the highe aulter of the parrishe church
of Saincte Martyne in the Feelde next Charing Crosse where I am a
paryshener for my tythes and oblacions by me necligently forgotton or
withholdin in discharge of my soule and conscience 13s. 4d. sterling Item
I will that my bodye be honestly buryed as apperteynithe to my degree / And
my ultimum vale doon at my said parrishe churche after the discrecion of
myne executours Item I woll that the 4 poore men that shall bere torches
aboute my bodye at my buryall shalhave 4 blacke gownes of the value eche
of them of 6s. 8d. a peace Item I will that my crafte and occupacion of
carpynters and all other brotherhoodes as I am of shalbe at my burying and
every of them to be honestly rewardid for their labours after the discrescions
of myn said executours Item I bequethe to Alice my wife my best cuppe.
Item I bequethe to Cristeane my doughter hir mothers best gowne / and I
bequethe to Margarete hur suster her said mothers second gowne And I
bequethe to Elisabethe my daughter hir said mothers thirde gowne Item
I will that the foresaid Alice my wife shalhave and enjoye all my landes and
tenements with the appurtenances sett and being in the parryshes of Sainte
Margarete at Westmynster and Saint Martens in the Feelde whiche I have
for termes of yeres aswell of the lease and graunte of Thomas late lord
Cardynall of Ingland and late Busshopp of Durham as of the graunte and
lease of the parsonne and churchewardeynes of Sainte Botulphes without
Aldersgate of London during as many yeres of the termes that be yett for to
come by the said twoo severall leases or graunts as she shall fortune to leave /
she during her same life keping all suche covenants and payments as I stand
bounden and am charged to doo by vertue of the said severall leases and over
and besides that I will and gyve to the said Alyce my wyfe for terme of her
life oon annuytie or annuall rent of 53s. 4d. sterling goyng out of my three
tenements sett to gethirs besides the Christofer in the said parryshe of Sainte
Martyn in oon of the whiche tenements oon Henry Barbour now dwellithe
in another of them Robert Pynner now dwellyth and in the thirde tenement
one Wyllyam Wharlete now dwellyth in Item I will that the Vicar and
churchewardeyns of the foresaid churche of Sainte Martens for the tyme
being shall yerely during 20 yeres / next after my decease take perceyve and
have out of my tenement callid the Christofer one annuall rent of 26s. 8d.

AA

sterlinges for and towardes the supportacion and maynteynyng of the morowe
masse kepte in the said churche / And I wolle that aswell my feoffes as myn
executours shall peasably permytte and suffre aswell the said Alice and her
assignes as the said Vicar and churchwardens and their successours Vicar and
churche wardens of the said churche for the tyme being to have and to
perceyve the said severall annuall rents quarterly to be paid and I wolle that
as often as the said severall annuall rents or either of them shalhappin to be
behinde unpaid during the life of the said Alice or any tyme during the said
20 yeres That then and so often that shalbe leafull aswell to the same Alice
or to her assignes in the said 3 tenements to enter and distrayne and the
distres so takin for the said rente so being behinde to retayne and kepe tyll
the same rent so being behinde be fully paid as to the said Vicar and churche-
wardens and to their successours in the said tenement callid the Christofer
to entre and for the said annuall rent of 26s. 8d. so being behinde to distrayne /
and the distresses so takyn to retayne and kepe till the same annuall rent of
26s. 8d. so being behinde be fully paid / and aftre the decease of the said
Alice my Wife I will that every of Cristeane and Margarete if they shalbe
then lyving shalhave eche of them twoo of my six tennements sette gythers
in the said parrishe of Sainte Margarete / that is to say those 4 tenements of
20s. a peace of yerely rente during all the yeres that I have yet for to comme
to of and in the same And I wil that the foresaid Elisabethe my doughter
shal after the deceas of my said Wife have one other of the foresaide 6 tenements of twenty shillinges by yere / and the other of the same tenements of
lesser rent with the forge and gardeyne during as many yeres as thanne shalbe
for to comme / and if anny of my said 3 daughters shall fortune to decease
before my said wife / Than I will that the survivour or survivours of them
after her decease shall have egally to be devided betwne them the porcion or
porcions of the said tenements forge and gardeyne to her or them so deceasing
above bequethid during all the termes of yeres That than shalbe for to
comme / Item I wil that after the decease of the said Alice my wife that John
Russell my sonne in lawe and the foresaid Christeane my doughter his wife
shalhave all the interest and termes of yeres that I have for to come of and in
the house with thappurtenances that I now dwell in Item I woll that all
thissues rents and revenues that shall come and growe of my tenement callid
the Christofer with thappurtenances and of all other my landes and tenements
being free holde sett and being in the foresaid parrishe of Sainte Martyn
besides the reparacions therof kept and the foresaid yerely annuytie of 53s. 4d.
during the life of my said Wife and the foresaid 26s. 8d. appointid for the
foresaid morowe masse shalbe takin and yerely leavid by thands of myn
executours by the permission and suffraunce of my feofes during the noneage
of Humfrye Cooke my sonne / and unto suche tyme as the same Humfreye
shall comme and accomplishe his full age of 21 yeres / to and for the finding
and noryshing up of the said Humfrey my sonne / and of the said Margarete
and Elisabethe my doughters now being within age during the tyme of their
noneage egally to be devyded aftre the discrescion of my Executours &
supervisours. And after that yt shall fortune my said sonne Humfrey to
comme to his full age of 21 yeres Than I wolle gyve & bequethe to the same
Humfrey all the said tenement callid the Christofer and all other my landes
and tenements being freholde above expressid except the foresaid annuall
rent of 53s. 4d. appointid to my said wife during her life And also the foresaid
26s. 8d. appointed for the foresaid morowe masse during the said terme of
20 yeres To have and to holde to the said Humfrey my sonne and to theires

of his body laufully begotton forever / And for defaulte of suche yssue / the remaynder thereof to the foresaid Christeane / Margarete / and Elisabethe my doughters and to theires of their bodies laufully begotten forever And for lacke of suche issue the remaynder therof to Roger Cooke my sonne and to theires of his body laufully begotton forever And for lacke of suche yssue I will that the foresaid tenement callid the Christofer and other my landes and tenements being free hold above expressid shalbe solde by myn executours or thexecutours of my executours to the moste profyte that they canne / by thassent and agreement of my feoffes and the mony comyng of the same sale to be distributid and disposaed in deades and warkes of mercye / petye / and charytie for the welthe of my soule and all christen soules after the wise discrescions of myn executours or theire executours by thadvise of my super-visours and feoffes that then shall fortune or happin to be on lyve./ The Residewe of all my foresaid goodes cattalls and debts above nat bequethed after that my debts be paid my funerall charges doon and thise my legacyes and bequests expressid in this my testament and last will perfourmed and fulfillid I wolle shalbe distributed and disposaed in deades and werks of mercye / petye / and charytie for the welthe of my soule after the wise discrescion of myn executours and of thexecution of this my testament and last will I make and ordeyne Alice my wife and John Aylmere citizin and free mason of London myn executours And I bequethe to the same John Aylmer for his labour in that behalf 20s. And of thoversight of thexecution of this my testament and last will I make and ordeyne Barthilmewe by goddes sufferaunce priour of saint Mary Overey and Maister William Holgill clerke maister of the Savoye overseers These wyttnesses John Wylford Scryvener Barth.. priour of Saint Mary Overey maister William Holgill clerke with others.

In the Name of God Amen This is the laste will and Codycell of me Humfrey Cooke which I will to be adjoynid and annexid to my testament Item I bequethe to the maynteyning of Ihus masse to be song with note everye Fryday within the parishe church of Sainte Martyn at Charinge Crosse during the terme of 20 yeres every yere 26s. 8d. to be takin of the profytts of my house where in Wylliam Wharleton dwellithe within the said parrishe Item that every of my childerne shalhave one silver spone callid the Appostles Item that Antonye my prentise shalhave all suche toolis as he dothe occupye and a grote Item that Margarete Lyde shalhave a halydaye gowne furrid all this to be fulfillid by myne executours gevyn the 18th day of Marche about 5 or 6 aclocke before noone of the same day These being present Wyllyam Skynner Vicar of Sainte Martens foresaid James Gaver Nicholas Hatfeeld Robert Tomson Edwarde Nicolson & John ap Richard.

Proved 10th July 1531 by oath of the religious man sir Bartholomew prior of St. Mary Overey Masters William Holgill and William Skynner clerks John Wilford and Cristine Russell being examined . . . administration granted to Alice the relict and John Aylmer executors. . . .

Prerogative Court of Canterbury, Register Thower, fo. 5.

A SELECT CLASSIFIED BIBLIOGRAPHY

As explained in the preface, no references are given for details of the careers of mediæval master masons and carpenters. For this reason, in the general bibliography which follows, the heading *Architecture (Personalities)* includes a large body of articles from periodicals. Elsewhere few entries other than books are given, but many references to periodicals will be found in the list of Abbreviations following this Bibliography. Some works will be found in more than one section, but remarks are not repeated.

I. GENERAL WORKS

Brockhaus' *Konversations Lexicon.*
Cambridge Ancient History, 12 vols., 1923–39.
Cambridge Medieval History, 8 vols., 1924–36.
Camden Society—Publications (in progress).
Diccionario enciclopedico Hispano-Americano de litteratura, ciencias y artes.
Dictionary of National Biography.
Enciclopedia Italiana.
Encyclopaedia Britannica, 11–13th ed.; 14th ed.
English Place-Name Society—Publications (in progress).
Groves' *Dictionary of Music and Musicians*, 4th ed., 6 vols., 1938–40.
London Survey Committee and London County Council—*Survey of London* (in progress).
New English Dictionary.
Philips' *Historical Atlas, Mediæval and Modern.*
Philips' *International Atlas.*
Royal Commission on Ancient Monuments (Wales)—Inventories (in progress).
Royal Commission on Historical Monuments (England)—Inventories (in progress).
Scholes's *Oxford Companion to Music.*
Victoria County Histories.
Walpole Society—Publications (in progress).

II. PERIODICALS

The number of periodicals relevant to the subject is so large that only a brief selection is attempted here; most of those listed have been used extensively, even if not consistently nor exhaustively.

Antiquaries Journal (Society of Antiquaries of London).
Archaeologia (Society of Antiquaries of London).
Archaeological Journal (Royal Archaeological Institute).
Ars Quatuor Coronatorum (Lodge Quatuor Coronati No. 2076).
Associated Architectural Societies—*Reports.*
British Academy—*Proceedings.*
British Archaeological Association—*Journal.*
Burlington Magazine.
Economic History Review (Economic History Society).

English Historical Review.
Genealogists' Magazine (Society of Genealogists).
Geographical Journal (Royal Geographical Society).
Geography (The Geographical Association).
History (The Historical Association).
History Teacher's Miscellany, The.
Institute of Historical Research—*Bulletin.*
Library, The (Bibliographical Society).
Musical Association—*Proceedings.*
Notes and Queries.
Royal Historical Society—*Transactions.*
Royal Institute of British Architects—*Journal.*
St. Paul's Ecclesiological Society—*Transactions.*
Speculum (Mediæval Academy of America, Cambridge, Mass.).

III. HISTORY

BENNETT, H. S.: *Life on the English Manor*, 1937.
CALTHROP, D. C.: *English Costume*, 1066–1830, 1936.
CLARKE, M. V.: *Fourteenth Century Studies*, 1937.
    Important essays on specialized subjects by an expert.
COULTON, G. G.: *Life in the Middle Ages*, 4 vols., 1928–30.
    Social Life in Britain from the Conquest to the Reformation, 1938.
    Two invaluable source-books of the widest scope.
    The Medieval Village, 1931.
    Medieval Panorama, 1940.
    Immense impact of garnered fact; somewhat inclined to see the "bad old times" from superior (?) platform of to-day. But grandly readable in a manner nowadays rare.
CRUMP, G. C., JACOB, E. F., Etc.: *The Legacy of the Middle Ages*, 1926.
    Valuable essays by experts.
DARBY, H. C., Etc.: *An Historical Geography of England before* 1800, 1936.
    Standard.
DAVIS, H. W. C.: *Medieval England*, 1924.
    Barnard's *Companion* brought up-to-date; valuable.
EKWALL, E.: *Concise Oxford Dictionary of English Place-Names*, 1940.
    Standard; indispensable.
GROSS, C.: *Bibliography of British Municipal History*, 1897.
    The Sources and Literature of English History, from the Earliest Times to about 1485, 1915.
    Indispensable standard bibliographies.
HOMANS, G. C.: *English Villagers of the Thirteenth Century*, Cambridge, Mass., 1942.
    Valuable, documented picture of mediæval country life.
HUMPHREYS, A. L.: *A Handbook to County Bibliography*, 1917.
JENKS, E.: *Edward Plantagenet*, 1923.
    The most detailed modern study of Edward I.
JUSSERAND, J. J.: *English Wayfaring Life in the Middle Ages.*
    One of the very few modern classics on the Middle Ages.
KELLY, F. M., and SCHWABE, R.: *A Short History of Costume and Armour, chiefly in England, I,* 1066–1485, 1931.
    Accurate, well written, and well illustrated.

KINGSFORD, C. L.: *English Historical Literature in the Fifteenth Century*, 1913.
    Henry V, the Typical Mediæval Hero, 1923.
LEACH, A. F.: *The Schools of Mediæval England*, 1915. Standard.
OMAN, C.: *The Great Revolt of* 1381.
ORWIN, C. S. and C. S.: *The Open Fields*, 1938.
    The best general study of the open field system.
POWER, E. E.: *Medieval People*, 1924, etc.
    Perhaps the layman's best introduction to the period, but delightfully
    written by an expert, with full references.
ROGERS, J. E. T.: *History of Agriculture and Prices in England*, 1259–1793,
    6 vols., 1866–92.
    Invaluable collection of facts; theories unreliable.
SALZMAN, L. F.: *English Industries of the Middle Ages*, 1923.
    English Life in the Middle Ages, 1926.
    English Trade in the Middle Ages, 1931.
    England in Tudor Times, 1926.
    All four crammed with valuable and often amusing facts.
STEEL, A.: *Richard II*, 1941.
    A political history, with brief glimpses of cultural matters.
TOUT, T. F.: *Edward the First*, 1920. Standard short life.
    Chapters in the Administrative History of Mediæval England, 6 vols.,
    1920–33.
    Indispensable for details of mediæval ways and means.
UNWIN, G.: *Finance and Trade under Edward III*, 1918.
WALLON, H.: *Richard II*, 2 vols., Paris, 1864.
    In French; no longer up-to-date, but a sympathetic view.
WEISS, R.: *Humanism in England during the Fifteenth Century*, 1941.

IV. ART

ADLER, G.: *Handbuch der Musikgeschichte*, 2nd ed., 2 vols., 1930.
Architectural Publication Society's *Dictionary*, 7 vols., 1849–92.
    Of far greater value than nowadays seems to be realized.
BAUCHAL, C.: *Nouveau Dictionnaire biographique et critique des Architectes
    français*, Abbeville, 1885.
EITNER, R.: *Biographisch-bibliographisches Quellen-Lexikon der Musiker und
    Musikgelehrten*, 10 vols., 1900–4.
FLETCHER, B. F.: *A History of Architecture*, 1896 and frequent editions.
    The standard general history.
LETHABY, W. R.: *Mediæval Art*, 1904.
    Important, like all the author's work.
    Architecture.
    A brilliant little book.
MICHEL, A.: *Histoire de l'Art*, 18 vols., Paris, 1905–29.
    Standard.
MORTET, V., and DESCHAMPS, P.: *Recueil de textes relatifs à l'histoire de l'archi-
    tecture . . . en France* (–1300), 2 vols., Paris, 1911–29.
    Fundamental.
RIEMANN, H.: *Handbuch der Musikgeschichte*, 2nd ed., 5 vols., 1920–3.
RUSKIN, J.: *The Seven Lamps of Architecture*, 1849, etc.
    Wrong-headed, but still one of the most vital as well as readable books
    on art.

SAUNDERS, O. E.: *A History of English Art in the Middle Ages*, 1932.
Important; excludes architecture.
STREET, G. E.: *Gothic Architecture in Spain*, 1865.
Now chiefly important for Street's demonstration that the architects of
mediæval Spain were the master-craftsmen.
THIEME, U., and BECKER, F.: *Allgemeines Lexikon der bildenden Künstler*,
Leipzig, 1907–.
Standard, though unfinished. International in scope, but very weak in
mediæval English artists.
VASARI, G.: *Le vite de' piu eccellenti pittori, scultori, ed architette*, Florence, 1550,
etc.
Still a standard classic, though proved wrong in some details.

V. ENGLISH ARCHITECTURE

I. GOTHIC ARCHITECTURE IN GENERAL

ATKINSON, T. D.: *A Glossary of Terms used in English Architecture*, 6th ed., 1946.
English Architecture, 12th ed., 1946.
Both standard; of (large) pocket size.
BLOXAM, M. H.: *Gothic Ecclesiastical Architecture*, 11th ed., 3 vols., 1882.
BOND, F.: *Gothic Architecture in England*, 1906.
An Introduction to English Church Architecture, 2 vols., 1913.
Both standard, and complementary; on the analytical method.
BRIGGS, M. S.: *A Short History of the Building Crafts*, 1925.
The Architect in History, 1927.
Both excellent; complementary, condensed, and international.
CLAPHAM, A. W., and GODFREY, W. H.: *Some Famous Buildings and their
Story*, 1912.
Valuable essays and illustrations.
CLARK, K.: *The Gothic Revival*, 1928.
GODFREY, W. H.: *The Story of Architecture in England*, 1931.
A History of Architecture in London, 1911.
Both admirable.
INNOCENT, C. F.: *The Development of English Building Construction*, 1916.
Standard.
JACKSON, T. G.: *Gothic Architecture in France, England, and Italy*, 2 vols., 1915.
NICHOLSON, C. A.: "Construction and Design" in *R.I.B.A. Journal*, 1912,
3 S., vol. XIX, p. 621 ff.
PALEY, E. G.: *Gothic Mouldings*, 1891.
PARKER, J. H.: *An Introduction to the Study of Gothic Architecture*, 12th ed., 1898.
A B C of Gothic Architecture, 3rd ed., 1882.
A Glossary of Terms used in Gothic Architecture, 3 vols., 1850.
All three standard.
POWER, C. E.: *English Mediæval Architecture*, 2nd ed., 3 vols., 1923.
PRENTICE, S.: *The Heritage of the Cathedral*, 1937.
A "popular" book, written with fine enthusiasm.
PRIOR, E. S.: *A History of Gothic Art in England*, 1900.
The Cathedral Builders in England, 1905.
Brilliant but lop-sided; obsessed by the thirteenth century and by the
West of England "school" of masons.

RICKMAN, T., and PARKER, J. H.: *Gothic Architecture*, 7th ed., 1881.
Standard.

SCOTT (SIR), G. G.: *Lectures on Mediæval Architecture*, 2 vols., 1879.

SCOTT, G. G.: *An Essay on the History of English Church Architecture*, 1881.
Valuable.

WILLIS, R.: "Vaults of the Middle Ages", in *R.I.B.A. Transactions*, I, 1842.
Indispensable.

II. WORKS WITH ENGRAVED PLATES OF GOTHIC DETAIL

BILLINGS, R. W.: *Carlisle Cathedral*, 1840.
Durham Cathedral, 1843.

BOWMAN, H.: *Ecclesiastical Architecture of Great Britain*, 1846.

BOWMAN, H., and CROWTHER, J. S.: *Churches of the Middle Ages*, 2 vols., 1857.

BRANDON, R. and J. A.: *Analysis of Gothic Architecture*, 1847, etc.
The Open Timber Roofs of the Middle Ages, 1849.
Parish Churches, 2 vols., 1858.

BRITTON, J.: *Architectural Antiquities*, 5 vols., 1807–26.
Cathedral Antiquities (13 parts), 5 vols., 1814–35.
Both series largely unsuperseded; for vanished details indispensable.

CARTER, J.: *Ancient Architecture of England*, 1795, etc.
A pioneer work.

COLLING, J. K.: *Details of Gothic Architecture*, 2 vols., 1852–6.

DOLLMAN, F. T.: *Analysis of Ancient Domestic Architecture*, 1863, etc.

FERREY, B.: *Christ Church, Hampshire*, 1834.

FREEMAN, E. A.: *Window Tracery in England*, 1857.

MACKENZIE, F.: *The Architectural Antiquities of the Chapel of St. Stephen, Westminster*, 1844.
Exquisite drawings, to be used with caution. Part of what is shown is imaginary, and careful reference to text needed.

PARKER, J. H.: *A Glossary of Terms used in . . . Gothic Architecture*, 3 vols., 1850.

PUGIN, A.: *Specimens of Gothic Architecture*, 2 vols., 1821.

PUGIN, A. and A. W.: *Examples of Gothic Architecture*, 3 vols., 1838.

RICKMAN, T., and PARKER, J. H.: *Gothic Architecture*, 7th ed., 1881.

SCOTT (SIR), G. G.: *Gleanings from Westminster Abbey*, 2nd ed., 1863.

SHARPE, E.: *Architectural Parallels*, 1848.
The Mouldings of the Six periods of British Architecture, 3 parts, 1871–4.
Standard, but incomplete.
The First (Lincoln) Excursion of the Architectural Association, 1871.
A Treatise on the Rise and Progress of Decorated Window Tracery in England, 2 vols., 1849.

SHARPE, E., JOHNSON, J., and KERSEY, A. H.: *The Churches of the Nene Valley*, 1880.

STEWART, D. J.: *On the Architectural History of Ely Cathedral*, 1868.

TURNER, T. H., and PARKER, J. H.: *Domestic Architecture in England during the Middle Ages*, 3 vols. in 4, 1851–9.
Standard; still by far the most important work on the subject, and a rich source of documented material for manners, meals, gardens, and everything related to the home.

WEALE'S *Papers on Architecture*, 4 vols., 1844.
Whichcord's measured drawings of Maidstone Church in vol. IV are a shining exemplar.

WILLIS, R.: *The Architectural History of Canterbury Cathedral*, 1845.
"The Architectural History of Winchester Cathedral", in *Proceedings of the Archaeological Institute at Winchester*, 1845-6.
Both indispensable.

III. CHURCH ARCHITECTURE

ALLEN, F. J.: *The Great Church Towers of England*, 1932.
Standard, but inadequate except for the south-western counties.
ATKINSON, T. D.: *English and Welsh Cathedrals*, 1912.
BATSFORD, H., and FRY, C.: *The Cathedrals of England*, 1936.
The Greater English Church, 1940.
BOND, F.: *Gothic Architecture in England*, 1906.
An Introduction to English Church Architecture, 2 vols., 1913.
The Chancel in English Churches, 1916.
BUILDER, THE: *Cathedrals of England and Wales*, 1894.
Contains large-scale plans.
BUMPUS, T. F.: *The Cathedrals of England and Wales*, 1926.
COX, J. C.: *The English Parish Church*, 1914.
Standard.
COX, J. C., and FORD, C. B.: *The Parish Churches of England*, 1935.
A good introduction, but reference should also be made to Cox's original work (above).
CROSSLEY, F. H.: *The English Abbey*, 1935.
English Church Monuments, 1150–1550, 1924.
English Church Craftsmanship, 1941.
English Church Design, 1945.
All admirable studies, well illustrated.
HOWARD, F. E.: *The Mediæval Styles of the English Parish Church*, 1936.
HOWARD, F. E., and CROSSLEY, F. H.: *English Church Woodwork*, 1250–1550, 1933.
Both standard, and of first-class importance.
LAMBORN, E. A. G.: *The Parish Church—its Architecture and Antiquities*, 1929.
A little book in the great tradition.
MARTIN, A. R.: *Franciscan Architecture in England*, 1937.
Standard.
PALMER, R. L.: *English Monasteries in the Middle Ages*, 1930
POWYS, A. R.: *The English Parish Church*, 1930.
PRENTICE, S.: *The Heritage of the Cathedral*, 1937.
PRIOR, E. S.: *The Cathedral Builders in England*, 1905.
STRZYGOWSKI, J.: *Early Church Art in Northern Europe*, 1928.
Origin of Christian Church Art, 1923.
Involved and subjectively written, but contain unusually valuable material and thought.
THOMPSON, A. H.: *The Ground Plan of the English Parish Church*, 1911.
The Historical Growth of the English Parish Church, 1913.
Both standard manuals.
The Cathedral Churches of England, 1925.
Especially valuable for the subject of the craftsman.
English Monasteries, 1923.

IV. MILITARY, DOMESTIC, AND CIVIC ARCHITECTURE

ADDY, S. O.: *The Evolution of the English House*, 1933. Standard.

BATTEN, M. I.: *English Windmills in Kent, Surrey, and Sussex*, 1930.

CLARK, G. T.: *Mediæval Military Architecture in England*, 2 vols., 1884.
Standard, but theories unreliable.

CLAY, R. M.: *The Mediæval Hospitals of England*, 1909.

DOLLMAN, F. T.: *Analysis of Ancient Domestic Architecture*, 1863.

GARNER, T., and STRATTON, A.: *The Domestic Architecture of England during the
Tudor Period*, 2nd ed., 1929.
Standard.

GOTCH, J. A.: *The Growth of the English House*, 1909 and 1929 editions.

HARVEY, A.: *The Castles and Walled Towns of England*, 1911.

HENDERSON, C. J., and COATES, H.: *Old Cornish Bridges*, 1928.

HENDERSON, C. J., and JERVOISE, E.: *Old Devon Bridges*, 1938.

HEWINS, G. S.: *Notes on Ancient Tithe Barns*, 1938.
Valuable listing.

JERVOISE, E.: *The Ancient Bridges of the South of England*, 1930.
The Ancient Bridges of the North of England, 1931.
The Ancient Bridges of Mid and Eastern England, 1932.
The Ancient Bridges of Wales and Western England, 1936.

LLOYD, N.: *A History of English Brickwork*, 1925. Standard.
A History of the English House, 1931.
Covers all periods; richly illustrated.

SMITH, D.: *English Windmills in Bucks, Essex, Herts, Middlesex, and London*,
1932.

THOMPSON, A. H.: *Military Architecture in England during the Middle Ages*,
1912.

TIPPING, H. A.: *English Homes* (Periods I and II), 3 vols., 1921, 1924, 1937.
Reprinted from *Country Life* with revisions; of varying value, but
superbly illustrated.

TOY, S.: *Castles*, 1939.
Covers all periods up to sixteenth century A.D.

TURNER, T. H., and PARKER, J. H.: *Domestic Architecture in England during the
Middle Ages*, 3 vols. in 4, 1851–9.

VALLANCE, A.: *The Old Colleges of Oxford*, 1912.

WILLIS, R., and CLARK, J. W.: *The Architectural History of the University of
Cambridge*, 4 vols., 1886.
Standard. Perhaps the finest detailed architectural study ever published
—strong both in documents and structure.

V. ARCHITECTURAL DETAILS

ALLEN, F. J.: *The Great Church Towers of England*, 1932.

ANDERSON, M. D.: *The Medieval Carver*, 1935.

BAGGALLAY, F. T.: "The Use of Flint in Building", in *R.I.B.A. Transactions*,
N.S., I, 1885.

BOND, F.: *Woodcarvings in English Churches. I—Misericords*, 1910. *II—Stalls
and Tabernacle Work, Bishops' Thrones, and Chancel Chairs*, 1910.
Fonts and Font-Covers, 1908.
All standard.
Screens and Galleries in English Churches, 1908.
The Chancel in English Churches, 1916.

BOND, F. B., and CAMM, B.: *English Church Screens and Rood Lofts*, 2 vols., 1909.
BURY, T. T.: *Remains of Ecclesiastical Woodwork*, 1847.
CESCINSKY, H., and GRIBBLE, E. R.: *Early English Furniture and Woodwork*, 2 vols., 1922.
  Valuable.
COOK, G. H.: *Mediæval Chantries and Chantry Chapels*, 1947.
COX, J. C.: *Pulpits, Lecterns, and Organs*, 1915.
  Bench-Ends in English Churches, 1916.
CROSSLEY, F. H.: *English Church Monuments*, 1150–1550, 1921 and 1933.
  Standard.
GARDNER, A.: *Alabaster Tombs of the Pre-Reformation Period in England*, 1940.
  Standard.
HOWARD, F. E.: "Fan Vaults" in *Archaeological Journal*, LXVIII, 1911.
  "On the Construction of Medieval Roofs", in *Archaeological Journal*, LXXI, 1914.
HOWARD, F. E., and CROSSLEY, F. H.: *English Church Woodwork*, 1250–1550, 2nd ed., 1927.
MACKLIN, H. W.: *The Brasses of England*, 1907.
  Standard.
PEVSNER, N.: *The Leaves of Southwell*, 1945.
SIMPSON, F., junior: *Ancient Baptismal Fonts*, 1828.
VALLANCE, A.: *English Church Screens*, 1936.
  Old Crosses and Lychgates, 1920 and 1933.
  Both standard.
WILDRIDGE, T. T.: *The Grotesque in Church Art*, 1899.

VI. ARCHITECTURAL PERSONALITIES

ANDREWS, F. B.: *The Mediæval Builder*, 1925.
  "Further Notes on the Mediæval Builder", in *Birmingham Archaeol. Soc. Trans.*, LV, 1931 (1933).
Architectural Publication Society: *Dictionary*, 1849–92.
BAUCHAL, C.: *Nouveau Dictionnaire biographique et critique des Architectes français*, Abbeville, 1885.
BAYLEY, J.: *History of the Tower of London*, 1821.
BECKER, M. J.: *Rochester Bridge*, 1387–1856, 1930.
BISHOP, H. E., and PRIDEAUX, E. K.: *The Building of Exeter Cathedral*, 1922.
BIVER, P.: "Tombs of the School of London at the Beginning of the Fourteenth Century" in *Archaeol. Jnl.*, LXVII, 1910.
BOYLE, J. R.: *History of Hedon*, 1895.
BRAYLEY, E. W., and BRITTON, J.: *History of the Ancient Palace . . . at Westminster*, 1836.
BRITTON, J.: *Architectural Antiquities*, V, 1826 (Appendix).
BROWNE, J.: *Fabric Rolls and Documents of York Minster: or A Defence . . . ,* new ed., 1863.
BUSHELL, W. D.: *Elias de Dereham* (Harrow Octocentenary Tracts, XII), 1906.
CHAPMAN, F. R.: *Sacrist Rolls of Ely*, 1291–1360, 2 vols., 1907.
CHATWIN, P. B.: "The Decoration of the Beauchamp Chapel, Warwick", in *Archaeologia*, LXXVII, 1928.
CLARK, G. T.: *Mediæval Military Architecture in England*, 2 vols., 1884.
COULTON, G. G.: *Art and the Reformation*, 1928.

CUNNINGHAM, W.: "The Organization of the Masons' Craft in England", in *Proc. Brit. Academy*, VI, 1911–12.

DALLAWAY, J.: *Discourses upon Architecture in England*, 1833.

DAVIS, R. H. C.: "Masons' Marks in Oxfordshire and the Cotswolds", in *Oxfordshire Archaeol. Soc.*, 84th Rep., 1938–9.

DAYNES, G. W.: "A Masonic Contract of A.D. 1432", in *Ars Quatuor Coronatorum*, XXXV, 1922.

DUDDING, R. C.: *The First Churchwardens' Book of Louth*, 1941.

FERREY, B.: "Early Mediæval Superintendents", in *R.I.B.A. Trans.*, 1860–1.

FLETCHER, J. M. J.: "Elias de Dereham", in *Wiltshire Archaeol. and Nat. Hist. Mag.*, XLVIII, 1939.

FOWLER, J. T.: *Extracts from the Account Rolls of the Abbey of Durham* (Surtees Soc., XCIX, C, CIII), 1898–1900.

FOWLER, T.: *Corpus Christi College* (Oxford Hist. Soc., XXV), 1893.

FRANKL, P.: "The Secret of the Mediæval Masons", in *Art Bulletin*, XXVII, 1945.

FROTHINGHAM, A. L.: "The Architect in History, during the Dark Ages", in *The Architectural Record*, XXVI, New York, 1909.

GARROD, H. W.: *Ancient Painted Glass in Merton College, Oxford*, 1931.

GOODMAN, A. W.: "The Choir Stalls, Winchester Cathedral", in *Archaeol. Journal*, LXXXIV (1927), 1930.

HAHNLOSER, H. R.: *Villard de Honnecourt—Kritische Gesamtausgabe des Bauhüttenbuches ms. fr. 19093 der Pariser Nationalbibliotek*, Vienna, 1935.

HARVEY, J. H.: "The Mediæval Carpenter and his Work as an Architect", in *R.I.B.A. Journal*, 3 S., XLV, 1938.

"The Last Years of Thetford Cluniac Priory", in *Norfolk Archaeology*, XXVII, 1939.

"The Medieval Office of Works", in *B.A.A. Journal*, 3 S., VI, 1941.

"The Western Entrance of the Tower of London", in *London and Mddx. Archaeol. Soc. Trans.*, N.S. IX, pt. 1, 1944.

"Henry Yevele, Architect, and his Works in Kent", in *Archaeologia Cantiana*, LVI, 1944.

Henry Yevele, 1944; and 2nd ed., 1946.

"The Education of the Mediæval Architect", in *R.I.B.A. Journal*, 3 S., LII, 1945.

"Some Notes from the York Guildhall", in *The Builder*, CLXIX, 1945, 165 ff.

"The Building Works and Architects of Cardinal Wolsey", in *B.A.A. Journal*, 3 S., VIII, 1943.

"Cardinal College, Oxford, and its Architects", in *Oxoniensia*, VIII–IX 1945, 145 ff.

"Mediæval Buildings", in J. Lees-Milne, etc.: *The National Trust*, 1945.

"Side-Lights on Kenilworth Castle", in *Archaeological Journal*, CI, 1946.

"The Later Architects of Winchester Cathedral", in *Winchester Cathedral Record*, No. 15, 1946.

"St. Stephen's Chapel and the Origin of the Perpendicular Style", in *Burlington Magazine*, LXXXVIII, Aug. 1946.

In W. P. Blore, etc.: "Recent Discoveries in the Archives of Canterbury Cathedral", in *Archaeologia Cantiana*, LVIII, 1946.

"Some Details and Mouldings used by Yevele", in *Antiquaries Journal*, XXVII, 1947, 51 ff.

HARVEY, W. and J. H.: "Master Hugh Herland, Chief Carpenter to King Richard II", in *Connoisseur*, June 1936.

HOBBS, J. W.: "The Travelling Masons and Cathedral Builders", in *A.Q.C.*, XL, 1928.

HOBSON, T. F.: *Adderbury Rectoria* (Oxfordshire Record Soc., VIII), 1926.

HONEYMAN, H. L., and RUSSELL, J. C.: "Master Elias Dereham and his Connexion with Durham", in *Trans. of Archit. and Archaeol. Soc. of Durham and Northumberland*, 1938.

HOPE, W. ST. J.: "The Funeral, Monument, and Chantry Chapel of King Henry the Fifth", in *Archaeologia*, LXV, 1914.
Windsor Castle, 2 vols., 1913.
"The Heraldry and Sculptures of the Vault of the Divinity School at Oxford", in *Archaeological Journal*, LXXI, 1914.

HOWLETT, R.: "A Fabric Roll of Norwich Guildhall", in *Norfolk Archaeology*, XV, 1904.

JACOB, E. F.: "The Building of All Souls College, 1438-43", in *Historical Essays in Honour of James Tait*, 1933.

JUPP, E. B., and POCOCK, W. W.: *Historical Account of the Worshipful Company of Carpenters*, 1887.

KNOOP, D., and JONES, G. P.: "The First Three Years of the Building of Vale Royal Abbey, 1278-80", in *A.Q.C.*, XLIV, 1931.
"Castle Building at Beaumaris and Caernarvon in the Early Fourteenth Century", in *A.Q.C.*, XLV, 1932.
"Masons and Apprenticeship in Mediæval England", in *Economic History Review*, April 1932.
"The Evolution of Masonic Organization", in *A.Q.C.*, XLV, 1932.
"Masons' Wages in Mediæval England", in *Economic History* (Supplement to *Econ. Journal*), January 1933.
The Mediæval Mason, 1933.
"The Building of Eton College, 1442-60", in *A.Q.C.*, XLVI, 1933.
"London Bridge and its Builders", in *A.Q.C.*, XLVII, 1934.
"Some Notes on Three Early Documents relating to Masons", in *A.Q.C.*, XLIV, 1931.
"Henry Yevele and his Associates", in *R.I.B.A. Journal*, 3 S., XLII, 1935.
"The Repair of Beaumaris Town Wall, 1536-8", in *Trans. Anglesey Antiquarian Soc.*, 1935.
"The Rise of the Mason-Contractor", in *R.I.B.A. Journal*, 3 S., XLIII, 1936.
An Introduction to Freemasonry, 1937.
    Contains valuable collection of biographies of mediæval masons.
"The Impressment of Masons for Windsor Castle, 1360-3", in *Economic History*, February 1937.
"The Sixteenth Century Mason", in *A.Q.C.*, L, 1937.
"Latlaying the Groundwork", in *Miscellanea Latomorum*, September 1937.
"Notes on Three Mediæval Master Masons", in *Miscellanea Latomorum*, November 1937.
"The Decline of the Mason-Architect in England", in *R.I.B.A. Journal*, 3 S., XLIV, 1937.
"The Impressment of Masons in the Middle Ages", in *Economic History Review*, November 1937.
"Overtime in the Age of Henry VIII", in *Economic History*, February 1938.
"The English Mediæval Quarry", in *Economic History Review*, November 1938.
"The London Masons' Company", in *Economic History*, February 1939.

"Master Walter of Hereford, Cementarius", in *Miscellanea Latomorum*, December 1939.

KNOOP, D., JONES, G. P., and HAMER, D.: *The Two Earliest Masonic MSS.*, *B.M. Bibl. Reg.* 17 *A*.1; *B.M. Add. MS.* 23198, 1938.

KNOOP, D., JONES, G. P., and LEWIS, N. B.: "Some Building Activities of John, Lord Cobham", in *A.Q.C.*, XLV, 1932.

"Some new documents concerning the building of Cowling Castle and Cobham College", in *Archaeologia Cantiana*, XLVI, 1934.

LAW, E.: *History of Hampton Court Palace*, 3 vols., 1885–91.

LEACH, A. F.: "William of Wykeham", in *Encyclopaedia Britannica*, 11–13th ed., 1910, etc.

LETHABY, W. R.: *Westminster Abbey and the King's Craftsmen*, 1906.
Westminster Abbey Re-examined, 1925.
Both standard, and of far wider scope than the titles suggest.
"Old St. Paul's", in *The Builder*, CXXXIX, 1930.

LLOYD, N.: *A History of the English House*, 1931.

MARSH, B.: *Records of the Worshipful Company of Carpenters*, 6 vols., 1913–39.

MYLNE, R. S.: *Master Masons to the Crown of Scotland*, 1893.

NICHOLS, J. G.: "Henry de Yeveley, one of the Architects of Westminster Hall" in *London and Mddx. Archaeol. Soc. Trans.*, II, reprinted in *Gentleman's Magazine*, N.S., XIX, 1865.

OLIVER, G.: *Lives of the Bishops of Exeter*, 1887.

OSWALD, A.: "Canterbury Cathedral: the Nave and its Designer", in *Burlington Magazine*, LXXV, 1939.

PANTIN, W. A.: "Tackley's Inn", in *Oriel Record*, June 1941; reprinted in *Oxoniensia*, VII, 1942.

PAPWORTH, W.: "Notes on the Superintendents of English Buildings in the Middle Ages", in *R.I.B.A. Trans.*, N.S., III, 1887.

PEVSNER, N.: "Terms of Architectural Planning in the Middle Ages", in *Warburg Inst. Journal*, V, 1942.
"The Term 'Architect' in the Middle Ages", in *Speculum*, XVII, 1942.

PURVIS, J. S.: "The Ripon Carvers", in *Yorkshire Archaeol. Soc. Journal*, XXIX, 1929.
"The Use of Continental Woodcuts and Prints by the Ripon School of Woodcarvers", in *Archaeologia*, LXXXV, 1935.

RACKHAM, R. B.: "The Nave of Westminster Abbey", in *Proc. Brit. Academy*, IV, 1909–10.
"Building at Westminster Abbey, 1298–1348", in *Archaeological Journal*, LXVII, 1910.

RAINE, J.: *Catterick Church*, 1834.
Fabric Rolls of York Minster (Surtees Soc., XXXV), 1858.
See also Browne, J., for further details.

Ripon, Memorials of (Surtees Soc., LXXIV, LXXVIII, LXXXI, CXV), vols. III, IV, 1888, 1908.

ROGERS, J. E. T.: *Oxford City Documents* (Oxford Hist. Soc., XVIII), 1891.

ROSENAU, H.: *Design and Medieval Architecture*, 1934.

RUSSELL, J. C.: "The Many-sided Career of Master Elias of Dereham", in *Speculum*, V, 1930.

RUTTON, W. L.: "Sandgate Castle, A.D. 1539–40", in *Archaeologia Cantiana*, XX, 1893.

SALZMAN, L. F.: MS. Documentary History of Building in England to A.D. 1549. Soc. of Antiquaries MS. 670.

SAUNDERS, H. W.: *An Introduction to the Rolls of Norwich Cathedral Priory*, 1930.
SCOTT, G. G.: *Gleanings from Westminster Abbey*, 2nd ed., 1863.
SIMPSON, W. D.: "James de Sancto Georgio", in *Trans. Anglesey Antiquarian Soc.*, 1928; reprinted in *Scottish Archaeological Studies*, 2nd Series, 1936.
"The Warkworth Donjon and its Architect", in *Archaeologia Aeliana*, 4 S., XIX, 1941.
"Herstmonceux Castle", in *Archaeological Jnl.*, XCIX, 1943.
SMITH, J. T.: *The Antiquities of Westminster*, 1807.
STANLEY, A. P.: *Historical Memorials of Westminster Abbey*, 1–3rd edns., 1868, etc.
STEIN, H.: *Les Architectes des Cathédrales gothiques*, Paris, 1909.
"Comment on désignait les architectes au moyen âge", in *Mémoires de la Soc. nat. des Antiquaires de France*, 1918.
STEWART, D. J.: *The Architectural History of Ely Cathedral*, 1868.
"Notes on Norwich Cathedral", in *Archaeological Journal*, XXXII, 1875, pp. 16, 155, 471 ff.
STREET, G. E.: *Gothic Architecture in Spain*, (Chapter XXI), 1865.
SWARTWOUT, R. E.: *The Monastic Craftsman*, 1932.
  Standard; an important book.
THOMPSON, A. H.: "The Building Accounts of Kirby Muxloe Castle, 1480–4", in *Trans. Leicester Archaeological Soc.*, XI, 1915–16.
The Cathedral Churches of England, 1925.
"Cathedral Builders of the Middle Ages", in *History*, N.S., X, 1925–6.
"Mediæval Building Documents and what we learn from them", in *Trans. Somerset Archaeological Soc.*, XLVI, 1920; reprinted in *Miscellanea Latomorum*, N.S., XII, 1927–8.
"Master Elias of Dereham and the King's Works", in *Archaeological Journal*, XCVIII, 1941.
TOPHAM, J.: *An Account of the Collegiate Chapel of St. Stephen at Westminster*, 1834.
TURNER, T. H.: *Some Account of Domestic Architecture in England from the Conquest to the end of the Thirteenth Century*, 1851.
VIBERT, L.: "Chaucer and Henry Yevele", in *A.Q.C.*, XLIV, 1931.
WELCH, C.: *History of the Tower Bridge and of other Bridges over the Thames*, 1894.
WILLIAMS, W. J.: "Archbishop Becket and the Masons' Company of London", in *A.Q.C.*, XLI, 1928.
"A Masonic Pilgrimage through London", in *A.Q.C.*, XLII, 1929–31.
"The King's Master Masons", in *A.Q.C.*, XLIII, 1930.
"Masons and the City of London", in *A.Q.C.*, XLV, 1932.
WILLIS, R., and CLARK, J. W.: *The Architectural History of the University of Cambridge*, 4 vols., 1886.
WONNACOTT, W.: "Henry Yvele, the King's Master Mason", in *A.Q.C.*, XXI, 1908.
WOODRUFF, C. E.: "The Rebuilding of the South-West Tower of Canterbury Cathedral", in *Archaeologia Cantiana*, XLV, 1933.
WOODRUFF, C. E., and DANKS, W.: *Memorials of Canterbury Cathedral*, 1912.

VI. ENGLISH SCULPTURE

ANDERSON, M. D.: *The Medieval Carver*, 1935.
ATKINSON, T. D.: "Medieval Figure Sculpture in Winchester Cathedral", in *Archaeologia*, LXXV, 1935.

BOND, F.: *Woodcarvings in English Churches, I—Misericords,* 1910. *II—Stalls, etc.,* 1910.
  Fonts and Font-Covers, 1908.
CHATWIN, P. B.: "The Decoration of the Beauchamp Chapel, Warwick", in *Archaeologia,* LXXVII, 1928.
CROSSLEY, F. H.: *English Church Monuments,* 1150–1550, 1921 and 1933.
FRYER, A. C.: *Wooden Monumental Effigies,* 2nd ed., 1924.
GARDNER, A.: *A Handbook of English Medieval Sculpture,* 1935.
  · Standard; see also Prior and Gardner below.
  Alabaster Tombs of the Pre-Reformation Period in England, 1940.
GARDNER, S.: *English Gothic Foliage Sculpture,* 1927.
HOPE, W. H. ST. J.: "The Funeral, Monument, and Chantry Chapel of King Henry the Fifth", in *Archaeologia,* LXV, 1914.
HOWARD, F. E., and CROSSLEY, F. H.: *English Church Woodwork,* 1250–1550, 1927.
LETHABY, W. R.: *Westminster Abbey and the King's Craftsmen,* 1906.
  Westminster Abbey Re-examined, 1925.
MASKELL, A.: *Wood Sculpture,* 1911.
PRIOR, E. S.: "A Sketch of English Mediæval Figure Sculpture", in *Walpole Society,* I, 1912.
PRIOR, E. S., and GARDNER, A.: *Mediæval Figure Sculpture in England,* 1912.
  Standard; see also Gardner, above.
UNDERWOOD, E. G.: *A Short History of English Sculpture,* 1933.
VALLANCE, A.: *English Church Screens,* 1936.
  Old Crosses and Lychgates, 1920 and 1933.

VII. ENGLISH PAINTING

BORENIUS, T.: "English Primitives", in *Proc. Brit. Academy,* XI, 1924.
  "An English Painted Ceiling of the late Fourteenth Century", in *Burlington Magazine,* LXVIII, 1936.
BORENIUS, T., and TRISTRAM, E. W.: *English Medieval Painting,* 1927.
  Standard.
CONSTABLE, W. G.: *Exhibition of British Primitive Paintings,* 1924.
ENGLEFIELD, W. A. D.: *History of the Painter-Stainers Company of London,* 2nd ed., 1936.
JAMES, M. R., and TRISTRAM, E. W.: "The Wall-Paintings in Eton College Chapel and in the Lady Chapel of Winchester Cathedral", in *Walpole Society,* XVII, 1929.
JONES, E. A.: "English Mediæval Painters", in *Burlington Magazine,* LXXXII, 1943.
  Useful listing from deeds in rolls of the Court of Husting.
KENDON, F.: *Mural Paintings in English Churches during the Middle Ages,* 1923.
KUHN, C. L.: "Herman Scheerre", in *Art Bulletin,* XXII, 1940.
LETHABY, W. R.: "London and Westminster Painters of the Middle Ages", in *Walpole Society,* I, 1911–12.
  "Mediæval Paintings at Westminster", in *Proc. Brit. Academy,* XIII, 1927.
  "The Westminster Portrait of Richard II", in *Burlington Magazine,* LXV, 1934.
PAGE, W.: "The St. Albans School of Painting", in *Archaeologia,* LVIII, 1902.
RICKERT, M.: "Herman the Illuminator", in *Burlington Magazine,* LXVI, 1935.

SHAW, W. A.: "The Early English School of Portraiture", in *Burlington Magazine*, LXV, 1934.
THOMPSON, D. V.: *The Materials of Medieval Painting*, 1936.
Standard.
TRISTRAM, E. W.: *English Medieval Wall Painting—the Twelfth Century*, 1945.
The first of an intended series of standard monographs on the period.
UNDERWOOD, E. G.: *A Short History of English Painting*, 1933.

VIII. ENGLISH GLASS-PAINTING

ASHDOWN, C. H.: *History of the Worshipful Company of Glaziers of the City of London*, 1919.
DRAKE, M.: *A History of English Glass-Painting*, 1912.
Finely illustrated.
EDEN, F. S.: *Ancient Stained and Painted Glass*, 1913.
KNOWLES, J. A.: "Disputes between English and Foreign Glass-Painters in the Sixteenth Century", in *Antiquaries Journal*, V, 1925.
"Additional Notes on the History of the Worshipful Company of Glaziers", in *Antiquaries Journal*, VII, 1927.
Essays in the History of the York School of Glass-Painting, 1936.
Important; of much wider scope than the title suggests.
LE COUTEUR, J. D.: *Ancient Glass in Winchester*, 1920.
English Mediæval Painted Glass, 1926 and 1932.
Both admirable.
NELSON, P.: *Ancient Painted Glass in England*, 1170–1500, 1913.
POWELL, H. J.: "The Picture-Windows in New College Ante-Chapel", in *Burlington Magazine*, VIII, 1906.
READ, H.: *English Stained Glass*, 1926.
Standard; finely illustrated.
SALZMAN, L. F.: "The Glazing of St. Stephen's Chapel, Westminster, in 1351–2", in *Journal of Brit. Soc. of Master Glass-Painters*, I.
"Mediæval Glazing Accounts", in *Jnl. of B.S. Master Glass-Painters*, II.
WOODFORDE, C.: "Glass-Painters in England before the Reformation", in *Jnl. B.S. Master Glass-Painters*, VI.
"English Stained Glass and Glass-Painters in the Fourteenth Century" in *Proc. Brit. Academy*, XXV, 1939.

IX. ENGLISH ILLUMINATION

HARRISON, F.: *English Manuscripts of the Fourteenth Century*, 1937.
HERBERT, J. A.: *Illuminated Manuscripts*, 1911.
The Sherborne Missal (Roxburghe Club), 1920.
JAMES, M. R., and MILLAR, E. G.: *The Bohun Manuscripts* (Roxburghe Club), 1936.
KUHN, C. L.: "Herman Scheerre", in *Art Bulletin*, XXII (September 1940), 138 ff.
MILLAR, E. G.: *English Manuscript Illumination from the Tenth to the Thirteenth Century*, 1926.
English Illuminated Manuscripts of the Fourteenth and Fifteenth Centuries, Paris and Brussels, 1928.
The Luttrell Psalter, 1932.
"The Egerton Genesis and the M. R. James Memorial M.S.", in *Archaeologia*, LXXXVII, 1938.

Pächt, O.: "A Giottesque Episode in English Medieval Art", in *Warburg Inst. Journal*, VI, 1943.
Rickert, M.: "Herman the Illuminator", in *Burlington Magazine*, LXVI, 1935. "The Reconstruction of an English Carmelite Missal", in *Speculum*, XVI, 1941.
Saunders, O. E.: *English Illumination*, 2 vols., 1928.
Thompson, E. M.: *English Illuminated Manuscripts*, 1895.
Wormald, F.: "The Fitzwarin Psalter and its Allies", in *Warburg Inst. Journal*, VI, 1943.

X. ENGLISH MUSIC

Adler, G., Koller, O., Orel, A., Ficker, R., and others: *Sechs, Sieben, Trienter Codices*, 7 vols. (Denkmäler der Tonkunst in Österreich, VII, Bd. 14, 15; XI, Bd. 22; XIX, Bd. 38; XXVII, Bd. 53; XXXI, Bd. 61; XL, Bd. 76), 1900–33.
Contains most of Dunstable's works, and those of other English composers of the fifteenth century.
Carnegie-Oxford Edition: *Tudor Church Music*, vols. I, III, 1923–4; vol. X, 1929.
These vols. contain works by Taverner, Hugh Ashton, and others.
Davey, H.: *History of English Music*, 2nd ed., 1921.
Flood, W. H. G.: *Early Tudor Composers*, 1925.
Important; documented biographies of thirty-two composers.
Fuller-Maitland, J. A.: *English Carols of the Fifteenth Century*, 1891.
Contains the Agincourt song, "There is no Rose", etc.
Galpin, F. W.: *Old English Instruments of Music*, new ed., 1932.
Standard; charmingly written.
Gibbon, J. M.: *Melody and the Lyric from Chaucer to the Cavaliers*, 1930.
Glyn, M.: *Early English Organ Music* (Plainsong and Mediæval Music Soc.), 1939.
Transcriptions from keyboard works of Dunstable, Redford, Tallis, Taverner, Tye, etc.
Láng, P. H.: *Music in Western Civilization*, 1941.
Covers an immense field; valuable sidelights.
Oxford History of Music, 2nd ed., 8 vols., 1929–34.
Good, but outdated by Reese; see below.
Prunières, H.: *A New History of Music* (transl. E. Lockspeiser), 1943.
Documented general history; good chapters on Middle Ages.
Pulver, G.: *A Biographical Dictionary of Old English Music*, 1927.
Ramsbotham, A., Collins, H. B., and Hughes, A.: *The Old Hall Manuscript* (Plainsong and Mediæval Music Soc.), 3 vols., 1933–8.
Transcriptions of all but fragments of the most important English musical MS., with introductory matter.
Reese, G.: *Music in the Middle Ages*, 1940, 1942.
Standard; the only comprehensive documented history, but stops at 1450.
Stainer, J.: *Early Bodleian Music*, 3 vols., 1901–13.
Facsimiles and transcriptions; valuable.
West, J. E.: *Cathedral Organists*, 1921.
Wooldridge, H. E., and Hughes, H. V.: *Early English Harmony*, 2 vols., 1897–1913.
Facsimiles and transcriptions; valuable.

XI. OTHER ARTS

AMHERST, A. M. T.: *A History of Gardening in England*, 1896, etc.
"A Fifteenth Century Treatise on Gardening", in *Archaeologia*, LIV, 1895.

BLOOM, J. H.: *English Seals*, 1907.

British Museum: *A Guide to the Mediæval Antiquities*, 1924.

CHAFFERS, W.: *Gilda Aurifabrorum*, 1883.

CHAMOT, M.: *English Mediæval Enamels*, 1930.

CHRISTIE, A. G. I.: *English Mediæval Embroidery*, 1938.
Standard.

GARDNER, J. S., and WATTS, W. W.: *Ironwork to the End of the Mediæval Period* (Victoria and Albert Museum), 4th ed., 1927.

HARTLEY, D.: *Mediæval Costume and Life*, 1931.
Full of practical points, often overlooked.

HILDBURGH, W. L.: "Varieties of Circumstantial Evidence in the Study of Mediæval Enamelling", in *Speculum*, XVII, 1942.

HOWGRAVE-GRAHAM, R. P.: "Some Clocks and Jacks, with Notes on the History of Horology", in *Archaeologia*, LXXVII, 1928.
Everything earlier on the subject is rendered out of date.

JACKSON, C. J.: *English Goldsmiths and their Marks*, 2nd ed., 1921.
An Illustrated History of English Plate, 2 vols., 1911.

KELLY, F. M., and SCHWABE, R.: *A Short History of Costume and Armour (chiefly in England, 1066–1800)*, 1931.
Historic Costume, 1490–1790, 2nd ed., 1929.

KENDRICK, A. F.: *English Embroidery*, rev. ed., 1913.
Burlington Fine Art Club Exhibition of English Embroidery, 1905.

KINGSFORD, H. S.: "English Mediæval Seal-Engravers", in *Archaeological Journal*, XCVII, 1940.

LETHABY, W. R.: "The Broderers of London and *Opus Anglicanum*", in *Burlington Magazine*, XXIX, 1916.

London Museum: *Medieval Catalogue*, 1940.

LONGHURST, M. H.: *English Ivories*, 1926.

MACKLIN, H. W.: *The Brasses of England*, 1907.

RAVEN, J. J.: *The Bells of England*, 1906.

SYMONDS, M., and PREESE, L.: *Needlework through the Ages*, 1928.
Valuable; well illustrated.

THOMSON, W. G.: *A History of Tapestry*, rev. ed., 1930.
Standard.

WALTERS, H. B.: *Church Bells of England*, 1912.

WARNER, R.: *Antiquitates Culinariae*, 1791.
Contains "The Forme of Cury" and other mediæval cookery.

WOODFORDE, C.: "Some Mediæval Leaden Ventilating Panels", in *Journal of the Brit. Soc. of Master Glass-Painters*, IX, 1944.

ABBREVIATIONS USED IN THE NOTES

With the exception of certain periodicals, and a few special cases, the abbreviations follow a definite principle: the first letter is always the initial of author or editor; in the case of two joint authors or editors, the first two letters represent the initials of both names. The last letter or letters are the initials of significant elements of the title. Volume numbers in series are always indicated by Roman Capitals, except in the case of the Early English Text Society, Original Series (O.S.). The three abbreviations N.S., O.S., and S., indicate New Series, Original Series, and (preceded by a numeral) Series, respectively. S, not preceded by a numeral nor followed by the period, always refers to the periodical *Speculum.*

A   *Archaeologia* (Society of Antiquaries of London).

AAC   T. D. Atkinson: "Local Character in the Ancient Architecture of Cambridgeshire", in CAS Proc., XL, 1945, 24 ff.

AB   *Art Bulletin* (College Art Association, Providence, R.I.).

ACC   A. H. Allcroft: *The Circle and the Cross*, 2 vols., 1927–30.

ACR   Académie des Inscriptions et Belles Lettres, Paris, *Comptes Rendus.*

AEC   J. W. H. Atkins: *English Literary Criticism—The Medieval Phase*, 1943.

AEH   S. O. Addy: *The Evolution of the English House*, rev. ed., 1933.

AFS   T. D. Atkinson: "Medieval Figure Sculpture in Winchester Cathedral", in A, LXXV, 1935, 159 ff.

AHA   T. D. Atkinson: "The Sources of Hampshire Architecture in Past Times", in HFC, XV, pt. 2, 1942, 146 ff.

AJ   *Archaeological Journal* (Royal Archaeological Institute).

AKM   C. Aldenhoven: *Geschichte der kölner Malerschule*, Lübeck, 1902.

ALE   J. W. Adamson: "The Extent of Literacy in England in the Fifteenth and Sixteenth Centuries", in L, 4 S., X, 1930, 163 ff.

ALS   *Atti Liguri* (Società Ligure di Storia Patria, Genoa).

AM   *Acta Musicologica* (International Society for Musical Research).

AMC   M. D. Anderson: *The Medieval Carver*, 1935.

ANJ   *Antiquaries Journal* (Society of Antiquaries of London).

ARA   W. O. Ault: *Court Rolls of Ramsey Abbey*, 1928.

ARR   H. E. Allen, ed.: *The English Writings of Richard Rolle*, 1931.

ASP   M. Arnold: *The Study of Poetry*, 1880.

B   *The Builder.*

BAA   British Archaeological Association *Journal.*

BAC   A. Burroughs: *Art Criticism from a Laboratory*, New York, 1939.

BAH   M. S. Briggs: *The Architect in History*, 1927.

BCA   F. Bond: *An Introduction to English Church Architecture*, 2 vols., 1913.

BCR   F. B. Bond and B. Camm: *English Church Screens and Roodlofts*, 2 vols., 1909.

BDA   C Bauchal: *Nouveau Dictionnaire biographique et critique des Architectes français* Abbeville, 1885.

BDG   C. R. Beazley: *The Dawn of Modern Geography*, 3 vols., 1897–1906.

BEB   *The Estate Book of Henry de Bray* (c. 1289–1340), ed. D. Willis (CS, 3 S., XXVII), 1916.

BFG   V. Belaiev: "The Folk-Music of Georgia", in MQ, XIX, 1933, 417 ff.

BFY J. Browne: *Fabric Rolls and Documents of York Minster, or A Defence . . .* rev. ed., 1863.

BGA F. Bond: *Gothic Architecture in England,* 1906.

BGS A. Burkhard: "Two Late-Gothic German Sculptors", in S, VIII, 1933, 165 ff.

BJD M. Bukofzer: "John Dunstable and the Music of his Time", in PMA, LXV, 1938, 19 ff.

BLD M. Bukofzer: "Über Leben und Werke von Dunstable", in AM, VIII 1936, 102 ff.

BLH G. Bertie: *Five Generations of a Loyal House,* 1845.

BLP C. Babington and J. R. Lumby: *Polychronicon Ranulphi Higden* (RS), 9 vols., 1865–86.

BLW E. Buckle: "On the Lady Chapel by the Cloister of Wells Cathedral" in SPA, XL, 1894, pt. ii, 32 ff.

BM *The Burlington Magazine.*

BMA M. Bloch: "When did Simone Martini go to Avignon?", in S, II, 1927, 471 ff.

BMC F. Bond: *Wood Carvings in English Churches—I. Misericords,* 1910.

BOC W. G. Benham: *The Oath Book or Red Parchment Book of Colchester* 1907.

BPP A. Bright: *New Light on Piers Plowman,* 1928.

BPR *The Black Prince's Register,* 4 vols., 1930–3.

BRB M. J. Becker: *Rochester Bridge,* 1387–1856, 1930.

BRC W. G. Benham: *The Red Paper Book of Colchester,* 1902.

BSM M. S. Bunim: *Space in Mediæval Painting and the Forerunners of Perspective,* New York, 1940.

BTL E. K. Broadus: *The Laureateship,* 1921.

BTP T. Borenius and E. W. Tristram: *English Medieval Painting,* Paris, 1927.

BVS A. Burkhard: "Veit Stoss", in S, X, 1935, 31 ff.

BWB W. H. B. Bird: *The Black Book of Winchester,* 1925.

BWY M. K. Bennett: "British Wheat Yield for Seven Centuries", in EHJ, III, 1934, 12 ff.

BYC W. Beveridge: "The Yield and Price of Corn in the Middle Ages", in EHJ, I, 1927, 155 ff.

CAH *Cambridge Ancient History,* 12 vols., 1923–39.

CAR G. G. Coulton: *Art and the Reformation,* 1928.

CAS Cambridge Antiquarian Society.

CCH *Calendar of Charter Rolls.*

CCM P. B. Chatwin: *The Collegiate Church of St. Mary, Warwick* (Guide).

CCR *Calendar of Close Rolls.*

CEE A. G. I. Christie: *English Medieval Embroidery,* 1938.

CFP A. Clutton-Brock: *An Introduction to French Painting,* 1932.

CFR *Calendar of Fine Rolls.*

CFS M. V. Clarke: *Fourteenth Century Studies,* 1937.

CGE H. Cescinsky and E. R. Gribble: *Early English Furniture and Woodwork,* 2 vols., 1922.

CGF A. W. Clapham and W. H. Godfrey: *Some Famous Buildings and their Story,* 1912.

CGW J. D. Le Couteur: *Ancient Glass in Winchester,* 1920.

CJB S. B. Chrimes: "John, first Duke of Bedford, 1389–1435", in IHR, VII, 1929–30, 110 ff.

CKN　F. Collins: "The Kinges Note", in S, VIII, 1933, 195 ff.

CMG　G. G. Coulton: "Medieval Graffiti, especially in the Eastern Counties", in CAS, 8vo Publ., XIX, reprinted as *Medieval Studies, No.* 12, 1915.

CMH　*Cambridge Medieval History*, 8 vols., 1924–36.

CMP　G. G. Coulton: *Medieval Panorama*, 1940.

CMS　E. K. Chambers: *The Mediæval Stage*, 2 vols., 1903.

CPC　R. W. Chambers: "Poets and their Critics: Langland and Milton", in PBA, XXVII, 1941, 109 ff.

CPL　*Calendar of Papal Letters.*

CPP　W. G. Constable: *Catalogue of the Exhibition of British Primitive Paintings*, 1923. 1924.

CPR　*Calendar of Patent Rolls.*

CPW　H. Chitty and S. Pitcher: *Medieval Sculptures at Winchester College*, 1932.

CRB　A. W. Clapham: *English Romanesque Architecture before the Conquest*, 1930.

CS　Camden Society.

CSB　P. B. Chatwin: "The Decoration of the Beauchamp Chapel, Warwick", in A, LXXVII, 1928.

CSD　T. W. Cole: *Scratch Dials*, 1938.

CSE　F. R. Chapman: *Sacrist Rolls of Ely*, 2 vols., 1907.

CSP　O. Cargill and M. Schlauch: "The Pearl and its Jeweller", in PMLA, XLIII, 1928, 105 ff.

CST　Cymmrodorion Society *Transactions.*

CUS　T. W. Cole: *Origin and Use of Church Scratch Dials*, N.D.

CWD　M. V. Clarke: "The Wilton Diptych", in BM, LVIII, June 1931, and reprinted in CFS.

DAH　A. Dolmetsch: *Translations from the Penllyn MS. of Ancient Harp Music*, 1937.

DBE　A. Dorner: "Ein Schuler des Meisters Bertram in England", in PKJ, LVIII, 1937, 40 ff.

DCP　H. Denifle and A. Chatelain: *Chartularium Universitatis Parisiensis*, 4 vols., 1894–7.

DDF　O. Delepierre: "A Document from the records of West Flanders", in A, XXI, 1846, 346 ff.

DEG　M. Drake: *A History of English Glass-Painting*, 1912.

DHG　H. C. Darby, etc.: *An Historical Geography of England*, 1936.

DHP　H. A. L. Dillon and W. H. St. J. Hope, edd.: *A Pageant of . . . Richard Beauchamp, Earl of Warwick*, 1914.

DHT　P. Durrieu: *Les Heures de Turin*, Paris, 1902.

DIE　F. Devon: *Issues of the Exchequer, Henry III–Henry VI*, 1837.

DKR　*Reports* of the Deputy Keeper of the Public Records.

DLB　M. Deanesly: *The Lollard Bible*, 1920.

DME　H. W. C. Davis, ed.: *Medieval England*, 1924.

DMM　R. H. C. Davis: "Masons' Marks in Oxfordshire and the Cotswolds", in OAS, 84th Rep., 1938–9.

DPC　H. S. Davies: *The Poets and their Critics—Chaucer to Collins*, 1943.

DRC　L. L. Duncan: *Index of Wills in the Rochester Consistory Court*, 1440–1561, 1924.

DRH　P. Durrieu: *Chantilly, Les Tres Riches Heures du Duc de Berry*, Paris, 1904.

DSC   W. Dodsworth: *Salisbury Cathedral*, 1814.
DSM   E. Duncan: *The Story of Minstrelsy*, 1907.
DTO   *Denkmäler der Tonkunst in Osterreich.*

EAS   Essex Archaeological Society *Transactions.*
EB   *Encyclopaedia Britannica.*
ECR   *Economic History Review* (Economic History Society).
EEH   H. E. Wooldridge and H. V. Hughes: *Early English Harmony*, 2 vols., 1897–1913.
EEL   C. Edwards: *The World's Earliest Laws*, 1934.
EETS Early English Text Society.
EHJ   *Economic History* (Supplement to *Economic Journal* of Royal Economic Society).
EHR   *English Historical Review.*
EPL   W. A. D. Englefield: *History of the Painter-Stainers Company of London*, 2nd issue, 1936.
ERN   J. L'Estrange and W. Rye: *Calendar of the Freemen of Norwich*, 1317–1603, 1888.

FAC   M. J. Friedländer: *On Art and Connoisseurship*, 1942.
FAP   E. Faral: *Les Arts Poétiques du XIIe et du XIIIe Siècle* (Bibliothèque de l'École des Hautes Études, Fasc. 238), 1924.
FBB   F. J. Furnivall: *The Babees Book, etc.* (EETS, O.S. 32), 1868.
FBH   H. Fierens-Gevaert: *Les Tres Belles Heures du . . . Duc de Berry*, 1924.
FCC   *Chronicle* of Friends of Canterbury Cathedral.
FCR   W. H. G. Flood: "The English Chapel-Royal under Henry V and VI", in SIM, X, 1908–9, 563 ff.
FEW   F. J. Furnivall: *The Fifty Earliest English Wills in the Court of Probate, London* (EETS, O.S. 78), 1882.
FHB   T. Faulkner: *History and Antiquities of Brentford, Ealing and Chiswick*, 1845.
FLF   E. B. Fitzmaurice and A. G. Little: *Materials for the History of the Franciscan Province of Ireland, A.D. 1230–1450* (Brit. Soc. of Franciscan Studies, IX), 1920.
FME   F. J. Furnivall, ed.: *The Story of England by Robert Mannyng of Brunne* (RS), 2 vols., 1887.
FPD   D. Flower: *The Poetical Works of E. C. Dowson*, 1934.
FPF   H. Fierens-Gevaert: *Histoire de la Peinture Flamande*, 3 vols., 1927–9.
FPR   W. H. G. Flood: "Entries relating to Music in the English Patent Rolls of the Fifteenth Century", in MA, IV, 1912–13, 224 ff.
FRB   F. J. Furnivall, ed.: *Robert of Brunne's Handlyng Synne* (EETS, O.S. 119, 123), 1901–3.
FRL   A. Finn: *Records of Lydd*, 1911.
FSC   W. E. St. L. Finny: "The Church of the Saxon Coronations at Kingston", in SAC, XLVIII, 1943, 6 ff.
FSE   J. H. Fabre: *Souvenirs Entomologiques*, 10 vols., 1879–1907, definitive reissue 1914–25.
FTC   W. H. G. Flood: *Early Tudor Composers*, 1925.
FWE   (J. H. Fabre), *The Works of*, transl. into English by J. A. Teixeira de Mattos and B. Miall, 1912–.
FWL   C. T. Flower: *Public Works in Mediæval Law* (Selden Soc., XXXII, XL), 1915–23.

GAB L. Gilliodts van Severen: *Inventaire des archives de la ville de Bruges*, 9 vols., 1871–85.
GAL R. W. Goulding: *Annals of Louth*, 1918.
GAS *Gesta Abbatum Monasterii S. Albani,* ed. H. T. Riley (RS), 3 vols., 1867–9.
GCH Gervase of Canterbury: *Historical Works*, ed. W. Stubbs (RS), 2 vols., 1879–80.
GEB L. Gilliodts van Severen: *Cartulaire de l'ancien Estaple de Bruges*, 6 vols., 1908–9.
GEH J. A. Gotch: *The Growth of the English House*, 1909–27.
GER J. A. Gotch: *Early Renaissance Architecture in England*, 1914.
GES A. Gardner: *A Handbook of English Medieval Sculpture*, 1935.
GGM H. W. Garrod: *Ancient Painted Glass in Merton College, Oxford*, 1931.
GJ *Geographical Journal* (Royal Geographical Society).
GLK V. H. Galbraith: "The Literacy of the Medieval English Kings", in PBA, XXI, 1935, 201 ff.
GLR V. H. Galbraith: "A New Life of Richard II", in H, N.S., XXVI, 1941–2, 223 ff.
GPA C. Glaser: *Les Peintres Primitifs Allemands . . .*, Paris, 1931.
GRE J. A. Gotch: *Architecture of the Renaissance in England*, 2 vols., 1891–4.
GSD A. R. Green: *Sundials*, 1926.
GST T. Garner and A. Stratton: *The Domestic Architecture of England during the Tudor Period*, 2 vols., 2nd ed., 1929.
GYC J. Goodchild: "The Architect of Yeovil Church", in SPA, LXXXIX, 1943, pt. ii, 87.

H *History* (Historical Association).
HCC J. Hornell: "The Fishing and Coastal Craft of Ceylon", in MM, XXIX, 1943, 40 ff.
HCJ R. P. Howgrave-Graham: "Some Clocks and Jacks, with Notes on the History of Horology", in A, LXXVII, 1928, 257 ff.
HDS A. Holländer: "The Doom-Painting of St. Thomas of Canterbury, Salisbury", in WAM, L, 1944, 351 ff.
HET *Historical Essays in Honour of James Tait*, 1933.
HEV W. E. C. Harrison: "An Early Voyage of Discovery", in MM, XVI, 1930, 198 ff.
HFC Hampshire Field Club *Proceedings*.
HFV F. E. Howard: "Fan Vaults", in AJ, LXVIII, 1910–11, 1 ff.
HHY J. H. Harvey: *Henry Yevele*, 1944; 2nd ed., 1946.
HIV J. B. Hurry: *Imhotep the Vizier and Physician of King Zoser*, 2nd ed., 1928.
HK A. M. Hocart: *Kingship*, 1927.
HKM G. Hayes: *King's Music*, 1937.
HLC T. Hearne: *Peter Langtoft's Chronicle as . . . improved by Robert of Brunne*, 2 vols., 1725.
HLM E. Holmes: *Life of Mozart* (Everyman Edition).
HLR W. H. Hart and P. A. Lyons: *Cartularium Monasterii de Rameseia* (RS), 3 vols., 1884–94.
HMB T. D. Hardy: *Catalogue of Materials for British History*, 3 vols., 1862–71.
HMC Royal Commission on Historical Manuscripts.
HMW R. C. Hoare: *Modern Wiltshire (Heytesbury Hundred)*, 1824.

HNR G. Hennessy: *Novum Repertorium Ecclesiasticum Parochiale Londinense*, 1898.

HOW J. H. Harvey: "The Medieval Office of Works", in BAA, 3 S., VI (1941), 1943.

HPM A. M. Hocart: *The Progress of Man*, 1933.

HRP *Hoccleve's The Regement of Princes*, ed. F. J. Furnivall (EETS, E.S. LXXII), 1897.

HRR S. H. D. Holton: "Richard the Redeless", in RHS, N.S., X, 1896, 120 ff.

HS Harleian Society.

HSD E. Horne: *Scratch Dials*, 1929.

HSM J. A. Herbert: *The Sherborne Missal* (Roxburghe Club), 1920.

HSP J. H. Harvey: "St. Stephen's Chapel and the Origin of the Perpendicular Style", in BM, LXXXVIII, 1946, 192 ff.

HVH H. R. Hahnloser: *Villard de Honnecourt—Kritische Gesamtausgabe des Bauhüttenbuches ms. fr. 19093 der Pariser Nationalbibliotek*, Vienna, 1935.

HVT G. C. Homans: *English Villagers of the Thirteenth Century*, Cambridge, Mass., 1942.

HWC W. H. St. J. Hope: *Windsor Castle*, 2 vols., 1913.

IBC C. F. Innocent: *The Development of English Building Construction*, 1916.

IHR *Bulletin* of the Institute of Historical Research.

ILN *Illustrated London News*.

JAS E. F. Jacob: "The Building of All Souls College, 1438–43", in HET.

JCC M. R. James: *Catalogue of MSS. in Corpus Christi College, Cambridge*, 1912.

JES M. R. James: "An English Medieval Sketchbook, No. 1916 in the Pepysian Library, Magdalene College, Cambridge", in WS, XIII, 1924–5.

JGR *John of Gaunt's Register*, 1372–6; 1379–83 (CS, 3 S.), 4 vols., 1911–37.

JHE H. Jenkinson: "The Teaching and Practice of Handwriting in England", in H, N.S., XI, 1926–7, 130, 211 ff.

JMG *Journal* of the British Society of Master Glass-Painters.

JMP E. A. Jones: "English Medieval Painters", in BM, LXXXII, 1943, 77.

JPR H. Johnstone: "Poor-Relief in the Royal Households of Thirteenth-Century England", in S, IV, 1929, 149 ff.

JWW *The Works of the Emperor Julian*, with transl. by W. C. Wright (Loeb Classical Library), 3 vols., 1913–23.

KAD O. Kurz: "An Architectural Design for Henry VIII", in BM, LXXXII, 1943, 81 ff.

KAS T. D. Kendrick: *Anglo-Saxon Art*, 1938.

KEG S. Kramer: *The English Craft Guilds*, 1927.

KFD T. F. Kirby: "On some Fifteenth-Century Drawings of Winchester College, New College, Oxford, etc.", in A, LIII, 1893.

KHS C. L. Kuhn: "Herman Scheerre", in AB, XXII, 1940, 138 ff.

KJM D. Knoop and G. P. Jones: *The Mediæval Mason*, 1933.

KMP F. Kendon: *Mural Paintings in English Churches during the Middle Ages*, 1923.

KPF J. A. Knowles: "The Periodic Plagues of the Fourteenth Century", in AJ, LXXIX, 1922.

KSA L. W. King: *History of Sumer and Akkad*, 1916.

KSE H. S. Kingsford: "English Medieval Seal-Engravers", in AJ, XCVII, 1940, 154 ff.

KWS T. F. Kirby: *Winchester Scholars*, 1888.

KYG J. A. Knowles: *Essays in the History of the York School of Glass-Painting*, 1936.

L *The Library* (Bibliographical Society).

LAA A. Ludovici: *A Defence of Aristocracy*, 2nd ed., 1933.

LAG *Lydgate's The Assembly of Gods*, ed. O. L. Triggs (EETS, E.S., LXIX), 1896.

LBD A. E. Levett: *The Black Death on the Estates of the See of Winchester*, 1916.

LBL W. R. Lethaby: "The Broderers of London and *Opus Anglicanum*", in BM, XXIX, 1916, 74 ff.

LCP D. H. Lawrence: (Collected) *Poems*, 3 vols., 1939.

LDA C. E. Lugard: *Calendar of Derbyshire Eyre and Assize Rolls*, 1938.

LEF H. S. Lucas: "The Great European Famine of 1315, 1316, and 1317", in S, V, 1930, 343 ff.

LEH N. Lloyd: *A History of the English House*, 1931.

LGM R. Lloyd: *The Golden Middle Age*, 1939.

LGP P. A. Lemoisne: *Gothic Painting in France, Fourteenth and Fifteenth Centuries*, 1931.

LHM G. Hulin de Loo: *Les Heures de Milan*, Brussels, 1911.

LHP E. A. G. Lamborn: "Heraldry and the 'History of Parliament'", in NQ, CLXXXIX, 1945, 125 ff.

LKC W. R. Lethaby: *Westminster Abbey and the King's Craftsmen*, 1906.

LLP D. H. Lawrence: *Last Poems*.

LMC P. H. Láng: *Music in Western Civilization*, 1941.

LMH A. E. Levett: *Studies in Manorial History*, 1938.

LMP *The Minor Poems of John Lydgate*, ed. H. N. MacCracken and M. Sherwood (EETS, E.S. CVII and O.S. 192), 1910–34.

LPC E. A. G. Lamborn: *The Parish Church—its Architecture and Antiquities*, 1929.

LPH *Letters and Papers of Henry VIII*, 21 vols. in 36, 1864–1929.

LSP W. R. Lethaby: "Old St. Paul's", in B, CXXXIX, 1930.

LTD C. E. Lugard: *Trailbaston Rolls of Derbyshire*, 3 vols., 1933.

LWP W. R. Lethaby: "The Westminster Portrait of Richard II", in BM, LXV, 1934, 220 ff.

LWR W. R. Lethaby: *Westminster Abbey Re-examined*, 1925.

MA *The Musical Antiquary*, 4 vols., 1909–13.

MEC J. A. F. Maitland: *English Carols of the Fifteenth Century*, 1891.

MEI E. G. Millar: *English Illuminated Manuscripts of the Fourteenth and Fifteenth Centuries*, Paris and Brussels, 1928.

MGE G. C. Macaulay: *The English Works of John Gower* (EETS, E.S., LXXXI–II), 1900–1.

MGW G. C. Macaulay: *The Works of John Gower*, 4 vols., 1899–1902.

MHA A. Michel: *Histoire de l'Art*, 18 vols., Paris, 1905–29.

MLM H. Mersmann: *Letters of Mozart* (transl. by M. M. Bozman), 1938.

MLP E. G. Millar: *The Luttrell Psalter*, 1932.

MM *The Mariner's Mirror* (Society for Nautical Research).

MMC F. W. Maitland: *Select Pleas in Manorial Courts* (Selden Soc. II), 1888.

MPH J. Hall, ed.: *The Poems of Laurence Minot*, 3rd ed., 1914.

MQ *The Musical Quarterly* (New York).

MSL B. Miall: *Social Life in the Insect World* (transl. from J. H. Fabre), 1911.

NA *Norfolk Archaeology* (Norfolk and Norwich Archaeological Society).
NFA J. LeNeve: *Fasti Ecclesiae Anglicanae*, ed. T. D. Hardy, 3 vols., 1854.
NMG A. Nutt: *The Mabinogion* (trans. from the Welsh by Lady C. Guest), 1902.
NPC N. H. Nicolas: *Proceedings and Ordinances of the Privy Council*, 7 vols., 1834–7.
NPP N. H. Nicolas: *Privy Purse Expenses of Elizabeth of York, etc.*, 1830.
NQ *Notes and Queries.*
NSS J. Nasmith: *Itinerarium Symonis Simeonis*, 1778.
NTM A. P. Newton, etc.: *Travel and Travellers of the Middle Ages*, 1926, reissue 1930.
NWA J. G. Noppen: "The Westminster Apocalypse and its Source", BM, LXI, Oct. 1932, 146 ff.
NWP J. G. Noppen: "Early Westminster and London Painting", in BM, LIV, Apr. 1929, 200 ff.
NWW J. Nasmith: *Itinerarium Willelmi Botoner dict. de Worcestre*, 1778.

OAS Oxfordshire Archaeological Society.
OEP *The English Poems of Charles of Orleans*, ed. R. Steele (EETS, O.S. 215), 1941.
OHM *The Old Hall Manuscript*, transcribed by A. Ramsbotham, H. B. Collins, and A. Hughes. (Plainsong and Mediæval Music Society), 3 vols., 1933–38.
OSH B. H. St. J. O'Neil: "Stefan von Haschenperg, an Engineer to King Henry VIII, and his Work", in A, XCI, 1945.

PBA *Proceedings* of the British Academy.
PBD E. E. Power: "The Effects of the Black Death on Rural Organization in England", in H, III, 1918–19, 109 ff.
PCB E. S. Prior: *The Cathedral Builders in England*, 1905.
PCC C. R. Peers: "Carnarvon Castle", in CST, 1915–16.
PCR J. S. Purvis: "The Ripon Carvers", in YAJ, XXIX, 1929, 157 ff.
PEA N. Pevsner: *An Outline of European Architecture*, 1942.
PEG J. H. Parker: "On the English Origin of Gothic Architecture", in A, XLIII, 1871.
PFC M. M. Postan: "The Fifteenth Century", in ECR, IX, 1938–9, 160 ff.
PFP H. Peake and H. J. Fleure: *The Corridors of Time—III. Peasants and Potters*, 1927.
PGA E. S. Prior: *A History of Gothic Art in England*, 1900.
PGM R. A. Pelham: "The Gough Map", in GJ, LXXXI, 1933, 34 ff.
PHM H. Prunières: *A New History of Music*, transl. by E. Lockspeiser, 1943.
PKJ *Jahrbuch der Preuszischen Kunstsammlungen* (Berlin).
PMA *Proceedings* of the Musical Association.
PMC A. Pirro: *La musique à Paris sous le règne de Charles VI, 1380–1422*, Strasbourg, 1930.
PMLA *Publications* of the Modern Language Association of America.
PMM F. A. Paley: *A Manual of Gothic Mouldings*, 4th ed., 1877.
PPT E. E. Power and M. M. Postan: *Studies in English Trade in the Fifteenth Century*, 1933.
PRB R. Pecock: *The Repressor of Overmuch Blaming of the Clergy*, ed. C. Babington, 2 vols., 1860.
PRC E. E. Power: "The Opening of the Land Routes to Cathay", in NTM.

PRS　J. S. Purvis: "The Use of Continental Woodcuts and Prints by the Ripon School of Woodcarvers in the early Sixteenth Century", in A, LXXXV, 1935.

PSP　W. Page: "The St. Albans School of Painting", in A, LVIII, 1902, 286 ff.

PSR　E. Prestage: "The Search for the Sea Route to India", in NTM.

PWT　E. E. Power: *The Wool Trade in English Medieval History*, 1941.

QEE　D. B. Quinn: "Edward IV and Exploration", in MM, XXI, 1935, 275 ff.

RA　*Revue Archéologique*, Paris.

RCM　M. Rickert: "The Reconstruction of an English Carmelite Missal", in S, XVI, 1941, 92 ff.

RDM　H. Rosenau: *Design and Medieval Architecture*, 1934.

RFY　J. Raine: *Fabric Rolls of York Minster* (SS, XXXV), 1858.

RHF　B. J. H. Rowe: "King Henry VI's Claim to France in Picture and Poem", in L, 4 S., XIII, 1932–3, 77 ff.

RHI　M. Rickert: "Herman the Illuminator", in BM, LXVI, 1935, 39 ff.

RHP　J. E. T. Rogers: *History of Agriculture and Prices in England*, 1259–1793, 6 vols., 1866–92.

RHS　*Transactions* of the Royal Historical Society.

RIT　Royal Institute of British Architects: *Transactions*.

RKB　E. Rickert: "King Richard II's Books", in L, 4 S., XIII, 1932–3, 144 ff.

RKM　H. Reiners: *Die Kölner Malerschule*, 1925.

RMM　G. Reese: *Music in the Middle Ages*, 1940; reissue 1942.

ROL　W. L. Renwick and H. Orton: *The Beginnings of English Literature to Skelton*. (Introductions to English Literature, I), 1939.

RP　*Rotuli Parliamentorum*, 7 vols. and index, 1771–1832.

RPP　J. H. Round: *Peerage and Pedigree*, 2 vols., 1910.

RRK　J. Ramsay: *The Revenues of the Kings of England*, 2 vols., 1925.

RS　Rolls Series (Chronicles and Memorials of Great Britain and Ireland).

RSG　H. Read: *English Stained Glass*, 1926.

S　*Speculum* (Mediæval Academy of America, Cambridge, Mass.).

SAC　*Surrey Archaeological Collections* (Surrey Archaeological Society).

SAP　J. D. Sedding: "The Architecture of the Perpendicular Period", in SPE, I, 1881–5, 31 ff.

SAW　J. T. Smith: *Antiquities of Westminster*, 1807.

SBL　E. L. Sabine: "Butchering in Mediæval London", in S, VIII, 1933, 335 ff.

SCA　J. Strzygowski: *Origin of Christian Church Art*, 1923.

SCC　E. L. Sabine: "City Cleaning in Mediæval London", in S, XII, 1937, 19 ff.

SCL　W. D. Simpson: "Castles of Livery and Maintenance", in BAA, 3 S., IV, 1939, 39 ff.

SCP　J. Skelton: *The Complete Poems*, ed. P. Henderson, 1931.

SCR　R. R. Sharpe: *Calendar of Coroners' Rolls*, 1300–78, 1913.

SDM　A. Stange: *Deutsche Malerei der Gotik*, 3 vols., Berlin, 1934–8.

SEA　O. E. Saunders: *A History of English Art in the Middle Ages*, 1932.

SEB　J. Stainer: *Early Bodleian Music*, 3 vols., 1901–13.

SEI　O. E. Saunders: *English Illumination*, 2 vols., 1928.

SEL　W. W. Skeat: *Specimens of English Literature*, 1394–1579, 1892.

SEM　L. F. Salzman: *English Industries of the Middle Ages*, 1923.

SEP　W. A. Shaw: "The Early English School of Portraiture", in BM, LXV, 1934, 171 ff.

SET L. F. Salzman: *English Trade in the Middle Ages*, 1931.

SHM A. P. Stanley: *Historical Memorials of Canterbury*, 1883.

SHT S. H. Steinberg: *Historical Tables*, 1939.

SIM *Sammelbände*, Internationale Musikgesellschaft.

SJS W. G. Searle: *The Chronicle of John Stone* (CAS, 8vo Publ., XXXIV), 1902.

SLB R. R. Sharpe: *Calendars of Letter-Books of the City of London*, 11 vols., 1899–1915.

SLC E. L. Sabine: "Latrines and Cesspools of Mediæval London", in S, IX, 1934, 303 ff.

SLI L. T. Smith: *The Itinerary of John Leland in or about the years 1535–1543*, 5 vols., 1906–10.

SLM L. F. Salzman: *English Life in the Middle Ages*, 1926.

SMC R. E. Swartwout: *The Monastic Craftsman*, 1932.

SMF *Songs and Madrigals of the . . . Fifteenth Century* (Plainsong and Mediæval Music Society), 1891.

SMM H. Saladin: *Manuel d'Art Musulman*, 2 vols., Paris, 1907.

SNE J. Strzygowski: *Early Church Art in Northern Europe*, 1928.

SNQ *Sussex Notes and Queries* (Sussex Archaeological Society).

SPA Somerset Archaeological Society *Proceedings*.

SPC W. W. Skeat: *Pierce the Ploughman's Crede* (EETS, O.S. 30), 1867.

SPE St. Paul's Ecclesiological Society *Transactions*.

SPM P. A. Scholes: *The Puritans and Music*, 1934.

SPN M. Symonds and L. Preece: *Needlework through the Ages*, 1928.

SPP W. W. Skeat: *The Vision of William concerning Piers the Plowman*, 1906.

SPW J. Skelton: *The Poetical Works*, ed. A. Dyce, 2 vols., 1843.

SRE F. M. Stenton: "The Road System of Medieval England", in ECR, VII, 1936, 1 ff.

SRS A. Steel: *Richard II*, 1941.

SS Surtees Society.

SSL J. Stow: *A Survey of London*, 1598, etc.

SSM L. F. Salzman: "A Sussex Merchant in London", in SNQ, IV, 1933, 193 ff.

SSP F. M. Salter: "Skelton's Speculum Principis", in S, IX, 1934, 25 ff.

STH G. Stretton: "The Travelling Household in the Middle Ages", in BAA, N.S. XL, 1935, 75 ff.

SWA A. P. Stanley: *Historical Memorials of Westminster Abbey*, 1st–3rd edns., 1868, etc.

SWH R. R. Sharpe: *Calendar of Wills enrolled in the Court of Husting, London*. 2 vols., 1889.

TBK U. Thieme and F. Becker: *Allgemeines Lexikon der bildenden Künstler*, 32 vols., Leipzig, 1907–.

TCG F. Thureau-Dangin: *Les Cylindres de Goudéa*, Paris, 1905.

TEH A. H. Thompson: *The English House* (Historical Association Pamphlet), 1936.

THD *The Three Historians of Durham, etc.* (SS, IX), 1839.

THT W. G. Thomson: *A History of Tapestry*, rev. ed., 1930.

TKI F. Thureau-Dangin: *Königsinschriften*, Leipzig, 1907.

TLL J. W. Thompson: *The Literacy of the Laity in the Middle Ages* (Univ. of California Publns. in Education, vol. IX), Berkeley, Cal., 1939.

TMA T. F. Tout: *Chapters in Mediæval Administrative History*, 6 vols., 1920–33.

TPD   T. H. Turner and J. H. Parker: *Domestic Architecture in England during the Middle Ages*, 3 vols. in 4, 1851–9.
TPM   A. H. Thomas: *Calendars of Pleas and Memoranda of the City of London*, 1323–1437, 4 vols., 1926–43.
TSM   L. Thorndike: "Sanitation Baths, and Street-Cleaning in the Middle Ages and Renaissance", in S, III, 1928, 192 ff.
TST   L. Thorndike: *Science and Thought in the Fifteenth Century*, Cambridge, Mass., 1929.

UEH   G. Unwin: *Studies in Economic History*, 1927.
UES   E. G. Underwood: *A Short History of English Sculpture*, 1933.
UGL   G. Unwin: *The Guilds and Companies of London*, 1938.

VES   A. Vallance: *English Church Screens*, 1936.
VHG   K. H. Vickers: *Humphrey, Duke of Gloucester*, 1907.
VM   *Vetusta Monumenta* (Society of Antiquaries of London).
VTM   E. Vinaver: *Malory*, 1929.

WAC   R. Warner: *Antiquitates Culinariae*, 1791.
WAH   R. Willis: *The Architectural History of Canterbury Cathedral*, 1845.
WAM   *Wiltshire Archaeological & Natural History Magazine* (Wiltshire), A. & N. H. Society).
WCC   R. Willis and J. W. Clark: *The Architectural History of the University of Cambridge*, 4 vols., 1886.
WDC   C. E. Woodruff and W. Danks: *Memorials of the Cathedral and Priory of Christ in Canterbury*, 1912.
WFB   F. Winkler: *Die Flämische Buchmalerei des XV und XVI Jahrhunderts*, Leipzig, 1925.
WGE   C. Woodforde: "Glass-Painters in England before the Reformation", in JMG, VI, 1935.
WHB   A. R. Wagner: *Historic Heraldry of Britain*, 1939.
WHP   J. G. Wedgwood: *History of Parliament*, 1936.
WIT   J. F. Willard: "Inland Transportation in England during the Fourteenth Century", in S, I, 1926, 361 ff.
WMB   R. A. Wilson: *The Miraculous Birth of Language*, 1937.
WOH   H. E. Wooldridge and others: *Oxford History of Music*, rev. ed., 8 vols., 1929–34.
WPE   T. Wright: *Political Poems and Songs . . . Edward III to Richard III* (RS), 2 vols., 1859–61.
WPJ   T. Wright: *The Political Songs of England . . . John to Edward II* (CS, VI), 1839.
WRS   H. Wallon: *Richard II*, 2 vols., Paris, 1864.
WS   Walpole Society.
WTB   C. Welch: *History of the Tower Bridge, etc.*, 1894.
WUC   J. F. Willard: "The Use of Carts in the Fourteenth Century", in H, N.S., XVII, 1932–3, 246 ff.
WVM   R. Willis: "Vaults of the Middle Ages", in RIT, I, 1842.

YAJ   Yorkshire Archaeological Society, Journal.
YTE   *Testamenta Eboracensia* (SS, IV, XXX, XLV, LIII, LXXIX, CVI), 1836–1903.

NOTES TO THE TEXT

INTRODUCTION

p. 1 Uruka-gina—KSA, 178 ff.; TKI, 47 ff.; CAH, I, 387.
"For the Heroes are dipped in Scarlet", LLP, 26; LCP, II, 439.

p. 2 Cf. HK. Gudea—TCG; CAH, I, 433 ff.

p. 3 Evolution—FSE; FWE; MSL; WMB.

p. 4 Red Book of Hergest—NMG, "Kilhwch and Olwen", 104. Russell—
FBB, 117 ff. Masons at table—cf. HHY, ix, 46, 53; HMC, Rep. II, 133.
Rise of civilization—PFP, 96. Imhotep—HIV.

p. 5 Sinan—cf. SMM. *Punch*—CMP, 103. Lawrence—LLP, 144; LCP,
III (*Pansies*), 731.

p. 6 Saxon Art—KAS; CRB.

p. 7 Mozart—MLM, vii, quoting HLM, 255.

p. 8 Dowson—FPD, "Against My Lady Burton", 163.
Arnold—ASP, quoted in DPC, 28–30.

p. 11 For the obviously indeterminable controversy between the Catholic and
Protestant schools of historians, see notably the works of H. Belloc and
G. G. Coulton, *passim*. Craftsmen—SMC. Paganism and Christianity—
cf. CMS; ACC; HVT, Chapter XXIII, 353 ff.

CHAPTER I

p. 18 Contacts with Mongol Asia—PRC in NTM, 124 ff.
Literary humanism—cf. AEC; LGM.

p. 21 Stereotype copying—cf. HCC in MM, XXIX, 40. Gervase—GCH;
annotated translation in WAH, 32 ff. St. Albans—GAS, II, 124–5.
Honnecourt—HVH. Pepysian sketch-book—JES.

p. 22 Graffiti—CMG.

p. 23 Vinsauf—FAP, 198.

p. 26 Harp Music—DAH.

p. 27 Elephant—One of Matthew Paris's drawings is reproduced in colour in
HMB, III. Crucks—IBC; AEH. cf. HPM, 71.

p. 31 Yeovil Church—GYC in SPA, LXXXIX, ii, 87.

p. 33 Sedding—SAP in SPE, I, 31 ff.

p. 36 Ranworth Screen—VES, 59–60.

p. 37 Salisbury Doom—HDS in WAM, L, 1944, 351 ff.

p. 42 Sedding—SAP in SPE, I, 31 ff.

CHAPTER II

p. 50 Ramsey—cf. HOW in BAA, 3 S., VI, esp. 40–2. St. Paul's—LSP in B,
CXXXIX, 1930. St. Stephen's—HSP in BM, LXXXVIII, 1946.

p. 51 Lyngwode—A. W. Goodman in AJ, LXXXIV, 125. Transoms—cf.
PCC in CST, 1915–16. Honnecourt—HVH, Pl. 34. Winchester,
Pilgrims' Hall—LEH, 358, Fig. 589–90; AHA in HFC, XV, pt. 2, 146.

p. 52 Lierne vaults—PGA, 359 ff.; PCB, 76 ff.; BGA, 340–2; BCA, I, 330–40.
Cf. WVM in RIT, I.

p. 53 Ars Nova—RMM, 336 ff.; PHM, 60–5. Cf. Aungervyle, Richard, in EB,
11–13th ed., II, 921–2; DNB. English Language—WPJ; WPE; ROL.
Editions: ARR; FRB; MPH; FME; HLC.

p. 54 The handiest complete editions of Chaucer's verse and prose in one
volume are those by W. W. Skeat, Oxford, 1895, etc., and the "Globe"
ed., 1898, etc. Piers Plowman—SPP; for Langland, see BPP, and
comment in LMH, 247 note. Other authors—MGW; MGE. Trevisa's
Higden in BLP. Somnour's Tale, ll. 391–8. SPC; the description
of a convent is included in SEL and modernized by Sir Alfred Clapham
in CGF, 256–7. Piers Plowman, C-text, Pass. xiv, ll.158–62; the more
commonly quoted version is from B-text, Pass. xi, ll.338–41. The music
of *Angelus ad Virginem* has been frequently printed, e.g. in EEH, II, 111.
CKN in S, VIII, 195; CPC in PBA, XXVII, 109 ff. For the immense
literature on the "Pearl Poet" see ROL, 289–92;, identity of the child
with the infant Margaret, cf. CSP in PMLA XLIII, 105–23.

p. 55 Farleigh—DSC, 151 note.

p. 56 Yevele, etc.—cf. HHY. John of Gaunt, Black Prince—JGR, 1372–6, II,
Nos. 1659, 1682. BPR. Gloucester school, etc.—cf. HOW in BAA,
3 S., VI; DMM in OAS, 84th Rep.

p. 57 Box—cf. WVM in RIT, I. Bradwardine—cf. DNB; his mathematical
treatises were printed at Paris between 1495 and 1530. Gyboun—CPR,
1338–40, 266.

p. 58 Ely—Cf. CSE. Page—EAS, N.S., II, 1884, 134; CSE, II, 29, 33, 45,
47, 61.

p. 59 Gloucester glazing—KPF in AJ, LXXIX, esp. 351. Thomas of Oxford—
cf. GGM, esp. 36–44, and authorities there quoted. Exeter glass—DEG,
26 and Pl. IIIA; WGE in JMG, VI. St. Stephen's Chapel accounts—
SAW. Brampton—SWH, II, 214. Lindsey—DIE, 187–8.

p. 60 Grasington—LWR, 150. Chuddere, *ibid.*, 151. Walton—DIE, 228.
Canterbury head—cf. HHY, 78 and Fig. 40. Winchester—CPW; G.
McN. Rushforth in DME, 504 and Fig. 318. GES, 272 and Figs. 332, 333.
Sluter—FPF, I, Pl. XXIII, XXIV. MHA, III. Gate tower—CGW,
77; antique statues—SEA, 113. St. Stephen's—SAW, 201–3, 210–16.

p. 61 Hugh of St. Albans—SWH, II, 106–7; PSP in A, LVIII, 286; SAW, 219.
BSM, esp. 162, 166, 169. John Prince—SCR, 263; SWH, I, 531, 592.
Gilbert Prince—SEP in BM, LXV, 171–84; JMP in BM, LXXXII, 77;
DIE, 184, 207, 251, 258; SAW, 202, 212; TMA, IV, 391; SWH, II,
319–20.

p. 62 SSL (Church of St. Giles, Cripplegate). Ashburnham and Mayfield—
SSM in SNQ, IV, 193. BTP, 26–8, Pl. 63–8; LKC, 278–83, Figs. 93,
94; W. R. Lethaby in *The Spectator*, 7 July 1923; reconstruction by
E. W. Tristram of Canterbury painting from Black Prince's tomb (in
colour) in ILN, 12 July 1930, at p. 72. CPP, 20; CWD in BM, LVIII,
reprinted in CFS; LWP in BM, LXV, 220–2.

p. 63 Beauneveu and Hesdin—FBH; FPF, I, Pl. VIII–XI, XIII, XIV; LGP,
24, 51–3; CFP, 16–17. Turin Hours—DHT; and in RA, 1910, pt. 2,
30 ff.; LHM; WFB, 15–23. Hubert van Eyck—cf. BAC, esp. 172–203.

Sherborne Missal—HSM. Pepysian sketchbook—JES in WS, XIII, 1–18. CWD—for theories of later date see SEP in BM, LXV; GLR in H, N.S., XXVI, esp. 237–8.

p. 64 Cologne school—AKM, esp. 380, 434, Pl. pts. 3, 4; RKM; SDM, III; GPA, 26–7. Herebrecht of Cologne—HMC, 9 Rep., I, 30, Nós. 7, 41. Meister Bertram—NWP in BM, LIV, 200ff.; NWA in BM, LXI, 146ff.; DBE in PKJ, LVIII, 40ff.; GPA, 21. Herman Scheere—RHI in BM, LXVI, 39ff.; RCM in S, XVI, 92ff.; KHS in AB, XXII, 1940, 138ff. Maelweel—TBK. FPF, I, Pl. XVIII, XX; LGP, esp. 48–9. Limbourgs —cf. DRH; FBH.

p. 65 Litlington—CCR, 1389–92, 158; DIE, 251; SWH, II, 319–20; SEP in BM, LXV; JMP in BM, LXXXII, 77; CPR, 1396–9, 573; CCR, 1399–1402, 282.

p. 66 Black Prince's tomb painting—ILN, 12 July 1930 at p. 72; BM, LV at p. 209. Martini—BMA in S, II, 471ff. Cologne—SEI, I, 112; BTP 24–6. English artists abroad—BCA, II, 619; THT, 82. Norwich— ERN; BTP, 39–40, Pl. 71; KMP, Pl. VI, VIII (colour); CGE, I, 120–4, Frontispiece (colour, of whole retable); Hope in NA, XIII, 1897, 293ff. Norfolk illumination—SEI, I, 113; MLP.

p. 67 Illuminators—MEI, esp. 28–36; RHI in BM, LXVI, 39ff.; RCM in S, XVI, 92ff.; KHS in AB, September 1940; HSM (includes colour frontispiece). Another illuminator at the end of the century was Alan Strayler, who produced the miniatures of the Golden Book of St. Albans Abbey. (British Museum, MS. Cotton Nero D. vii.) Siferwas's portrait of Lord Lovel—repr. in colour as frontispiece to MEI. Birds—cf. reproductions in HSM and FBH. Minor Arts—TMA, IV, 389–91; CPR, *passim*; SWH, II, 125, 272, 273, 434; SLC, in S, IX, 303ff., esp. 319.

p. 68 Impressment—CPR, 1396–9, 40; CPR, 1399–1401, 400. Tapicers— TMA, IV, 390; CPR, 1364–7, 421; SWH, II, 179. Embroideries— "Achievements of Edward, Prince of Wales, in the Cathedral of Canterbury", in VM, VII; SPN, 200–5, Pl. XXXII–III; CEE; LBL in BM, XXIX, 74ff. Roesia Burford—DIE, 133; SWH, I, 238, 609. Goldsmiths—DIE, esp. 122, 128, 133, 154, 159, 161, 163, 175, 177, 185, 201, 211, 221, 231, 242, 253, 272, 279, 288, 294, 305, 307, 339, 357–8, 382, 462–3, 466; KSE in AJ, XCVII.

p. 69 Bush—CPR, 1396–9, 319. Stage—CMS, esp. II, 380, 399; DIE, 244.

p. 70 Origins of Gothic architecture—cf. SCA; SNE. Folk polyphony—BFG in MQ, XIX, 417ff., quoted in RMM, 249. Old Hall MS.—transcriptions in OHM. Richard II as musician—HKM, 34. Leo, King of Armenia—DIE, 245–6; cf. E. Wellesz "Eastern Elements in English Ecclesiastical Music", in *Journal* of the Warburg Institute, V, 1942, 44ff. Ars Nova—RMM, 331–86; PHM, 60–72.

p. 71 Dunstable—BJD in PMA, LXV, 19ff., esp. 35; RMM, 411–24; WHB, 62; CPL, VIII, 1427–47, 516; CFR, 1452–61, 245; J. B. Bignell, "The Chirograph", No. 11, March 1940 (Catalogue), p. 4, No. 790: "Bradfield Herts, Copy of a deed of John Fraye in 5 Henry VI (1426–7) and of the will of John Dunstaple 7 July 1459, relating to Bradfield, in a sixteenth-century hand" (This document is now in the Hertford County Records Office); Corporation of London, Hustings Rolls 170 (44), 172 (55), 175 (15), 183 (28), 219 (9).

CHAPTER III

p. 72 For England in fifteenth century, see C. H. Williams and K. B. Mac-farlane in CMH, VIII, 1936; PFC in ECR, IX, 160 ff.; BYC in EHJ, I, 155 ff.; BWY in EHJ, III, 12 ff.; PWT; PPT. PFC in ECR, IX, esp. 163.

p. 73 Richard II—There is no satisfactory "life" of Richard II; the admirable biography by H. Wallon, 2 vols., Paris, 1864, has never been translated into English, and is now largely outdated by modern research; A. Steel: *Richard II*, 1941, is a scholarly guide through the maze of detailed material, but is "limited . . . to Richard in his political function". M. V. Clarke: *Fourteenth Century Studies*, 1937, is extremely valuable, but Froissart and Shakespeare are still the best guides: one because he was a man of culture personally acquainted with the King, the other as an artist of supreme genius. Villein education—RP, III, 294a; cf. LMH, 246. Revenue—RRK; TMA, IV, 208 ff. Royal Charity—JPR in S, IV, 149 ff.; HRR in RHS, N.S., X, 120 ff. Gower's attitude—MGE, I, xxi–xxviii.

p. 74 In visualizing the inter-relations of these distant series of events, assistance will be derived from the study of tables such as those in SHT.

p. 75 Offices—see, especially, CPR, *passim.*

p. 76 York glass—KYG. Editions (Hoccleve)—F. J. Furnivall: *The Regement of Princes* (EETS, E.S., LXXII), 1897; F. J. Furnivall and I. Gollancz: *Minor Poems* (EETS, E.S., LXI, LXXIII), 1892–7; (Lydgate)—H. Bergen: *The Fall of Princes* (EETS, E.S., CXXI–CXXIV), 1918–19; *The Troy Book* (EETS, E.S., XCVII, CIII, CVI, CXXVI), 1906–35; F. J. Furnivall and K. B. Locock: *The Pilgrimage of the Life of Man* (EETS, E.S., LXXVII, LXXXIII, XCII), 1899–1904; J. Schick: *The Temple of Glass* (EETS, E.S., LX), 1891; E. Sieper: *Reson and Sensuallyte* (EETS, E.S., LXXXIV, LXXXIX), 1901–3; A. Erdmann: *The Siege of Thebes* (EETS, E.S., CVIII, CXXV), 1911–30; R. Steele: *Secrees of old Philisoffres* (EETS, E.S., LXVI), 1894; H. N. MacCracken and M. Sherwood: *Minor Poems* (EETS, E.S., CVII and O.S. 192), 1910–34; (James I of Scotland)—W. W. Skeat: *The Kingis Quair* (Scottish Text Society, N.S. 1), 1911; (Charles of Orléans)—R. Steele: *The English Poems of Charles of Orleans* (EETS, O.S., 215), 1941; (Henryson)—G. G. Smith: *Works* . . ., 3 vols., 1906–14; H. W. Wood: *Works* . . ., 1933; (Dunbar)—W. M. Mackenzie: *The Poems of William Dunbar*, 1932.

p. 77 Lydgate—LMP, II, 411; "The Floure of Curtesy", ll. 8–14. Orleans—OEP, 83. Hoccleve—HRP, 71–2; ll. 1961–77.

p. 80 Rolleston and the inn-doors of Beverley—CPR, 1405–8, 482.

p. 81 For the Canterbury pulpitum the date of *c.* 1410 can be fixed from documents quoted by C. Cotton: "The Screen of the Six Kings in Canterbury Cathedral", in FCC, No. 20, April 1935. I owe this reference to the kindness of Mrs. Dorothy Gardiner. Wydmer—DIE, 326, 332; CPR, 1391–6, 363; CPR, 1396–9, 301; CPR, 1416–22, 66; CCR, 1413–19, 232; SET, 171 (facsimile).

p. 82 Broker—SWH, II, 440. Godeyer—DIE, 321. Broun—DIE, 338, 357.. Massingham—CCR, 1405–9, 455.

p. 83 St. Etheldreda—BTP, 41, Pl. 75. Chaucer and Hoccleve—JCC, I, 126–7; MEI, Pl. 94; SLM, 153, 163; SEA, 158.

p. 84 Norwich paintings—BTP, 40, Pl. 73, 74. Henry IV's tomb—colour reproduction in ILN, 14 November 1931, at p. 777. Wright and Kent— DIE, 296, 325; CCR, 1399–1402, 146, 282; CCR, 1405–9, 232, 250; SLB, "I", 255; TPM, 1413–37, 145, 149, 168, 176, 178; will of Thomas Wryght, P.C.C. 2 Luffenam, see App. V, i. Stone—DIE, 339; CCR, 1405–9, 122; CCR, 1409–13, 223. Richer—SLB, "I", "K"; BRB, 91; TPM, 1413–37, 121, 267; DKR, LXVIII, 266; Warwick Corporation, MS. Account Book of Richard Beauchamp, Earl of Warwick, for 1431, fo. xxi. Henry IV—DIE, 274–320. Norman—DIE, 276.

p. 85 Vyve—DIE, 285. Randolf and Melver—DIE, 339, 357.

p. 86 Agincourt Hymn—MEC, 14, 15, 42–3, 59–62. Carols—MEC. Songs— SEB, II; WOH, II, 132. Old Hall MS.—OHM. Dunstable, etc.—DTO, VII, XI, 1; XIX, 1; XXVII, 1; XXXI, XL (Bd. 14 and 15, 22, 38, 53, 61, 76); B.M. Add. MS. 36490; BLD in AM, VIII, 102ff. Damett— HNR, 48; HMW, 287; CPR, 1429–36, 106, 601; CPL, 1417–31, 226; will, P.C.C. 21 Luffenam, see App. V, ii.

p. 87 Sturgeon—DKR, XLII, 331; CPR, 1429–36, 264; HNR; NFA, II, 349, 404, 430; will, P.C.C. 10 Rous, printed in FEW, 131. Cook—CPR, 1413– 16, 289; CPR, 1416–22, 118, 123, 219; CCR, 1429–35, 49; CPR, 1452–61, 229. Forrest—NFA; will, P.C.C. 30 Luffenam. Pyamour, etc.—BJD in PMA, LXV, 19 ff. esp. 36; DKR, XLII, 328; DKR, XLVIII, 246; CCR, 1429–35; CPR, 1416–22, 272. Plummer—FPR in MA, IV 224ff.; CPR. cf. FCR in SIM, X, 563 ff.; RP. V, 473b.; ANJ, I, 52–3.

p. 88 Blithe, Gloucester—DKR, XLI, 739; XLII, 372. Wodehall, etc.—DIE, 361. Estcourt, Farley—DKR, XLVIII, 248, 251; will of Estcourt, Canterbury Register "Chichele" (Canterbury and York Soc.), pt. CIII, 1937, Pars Secunda 1414–43, 372. Kirketon—PMC, 35; DCP, IV, 471, 474–6, 540; DKR, XLVIII, 347, 355. Dunstable—see above, notes to p. 71.

p. 89 Power—CCR, 1441–7, 211.

CHAPTER IV

p. 90 Wolkenstein—PMC, 30; cf. RMM, 378 ff. Berneval—AJ, LXIV, 1907, 32–7; LXIX, 1913, 484; DKR, XLI, 756; of BDA..

p. 91 Caen, Shene—DKR, XLI, 686, 709. Stratford—DKR, XLVIII, 315, 396; CCR, 1435–41, 486; DIE, 458–9; CPR, 1461–7, 15. Protections, etc. —cf. Calendars of Norman Rolls (DKR, XLI, XLII) and French Rolls (DKR, XLVIII), *passim*. Calais works—DKR, XLVIII, 336, 343. Henry VI's marriage—cf. DIE, 452. King René—DEG, 2–3. Greeks in England—DKR, XLVIII, 364. Jacques Cordis—DKR, XLVIII, 373. Gosselyn, etc.—DKR, XLVIII, 394; cf. CPR, 1429–36, 537–9, 541–88.

p. 92 Claim to France—RHF in L, 4 S., XIII, 77ff. Lydgate—LMP, II, 613–24. ("The Title and Pedigree of Henry VI", "Roundel for the Coronation", "Soteltes at the Coronation Banquet".) Forme of Cury— printed in WAC, 1–35. Royal Cooks—CPR, under names John Goderich, Robert de la More, Thomas Beushef, William Hoghwyk.

p. 93 Earl of Warwick—see App. III. Journeys—to Paris, MS., fo. cxxxiv– cxlvd.; to London, MS., fo. cliii–clxviiid.; to Warwick, MS., fo. clxxviiid–clxxxiii. cf. STH in BAA, N.S., XL, 75 ff. Carriers—RHP, I, 660, quoted in SET, 205.

p. 94 Lydgate—LMP, II, "Mesure is Tresour", vv. 12, 13, pp. 778–9; "Every Thing to his Semblable", pp. 801–8; LAG, ll. 854–61, p. 26. LMP, II, "Tyed with a Lyne", ll. 54–6, p. 834; "That now is Hay some-tyme was Grase", pp. 809–13.

p. 95 Pre-Laureate official poets—BTL. Mapilton family—LTD; LDA, and information from unpublished Assize Rolls, temp. Edward I, kindly communicated by Mr. C. E. Lugard.

p. 98 Henry VI and Westminster—SWA, App. to Chapter II (in 1st–3rd editions only).

p. 99 All Souls College—JAS in HET. Massingham—WCC, I, 402; CSB in A, LXXVII, and CCM; Stratford-on-Avon, Shakespeare Birthplace Library, MS. Collections relating to Warwick by Captain Saunders.

p. 100 Porchalion—UES, 47–8; CPR, CCR.

p. 104 Daunte—DIE, 427. Stratford—see notes to p. 91, and SEP in BM, LXV, 184. Bee—EPL, 35; NPC, 1443–61 (VI), 129–140; CPR, 1461–7, 10. Essex—see notes above, p. 99 (Massingham).

CHAPTER V

p. 106 Towns—SET, 86–7; EHR, XLI, 1926, 170ff.; DHG, 251. Black Death and Fifteenth Century—LBD; LMH; PBD in H, III, 1918–19, 109; PFC in ECR, IX, 160ff.; KYG; cf. JHE in H, XI, 130, 211ff., esp. 136.

p. 107 For collections of wills and bequests to Church building, see N. H. Nicolas: *Testamenta Vetusta*, 1826; F. J. Furnivall: *The Fifty Earliest English Wills in the Court of Probate*, London (EETS, O.S. 78), 1882; R. R. Sharpe: *Calendar of Wills in the London Court of Husting*, 2 vols., 1888–9; L. L. Duncan and A. Hussey: *Testamenta Cantiana*, 1906–7; *Somerset Mediæval Wills* (Som. Record Soc., XVI, XIX, XXI), 1901–5; F. W. Weaver: *Wells Wills*; T. P. Wadley: *Wills in the Great Orphan Book and Book of Wills*, Bristol, 1886; *Testamenta Eboracensia* (Surtees Soc., IV, XXX, XLV, LIII, LXXIX, CVI); *North Country Wills*, 1383–1558 (Surtees Soc., CXVI), 1908; *Durham Wills and Inventories* (SS, II, XXXVIII, CXII), 1835–1906; A. R. Maddison: *Lincolnshire Wills*, 1500–1600, 1888; "Lincolnshire Wills in P.C.C.", in *Associated Architectural Societies' Reports*, XLI, 1932–3; J. F. Williams: "The Medieval Will as a Source of Local History" (East Anglia), in *The History Teacher's Miscellany*, II, 1923–4; cf. B. G. Bouwens: *Wills and their Whereabouts*, 1939; and lists of dated buildings in T. Rickman and J. H. Parker: *Gothic Architecture* (6th and 7th edns.), 1862, 1881. Bedford—cf. CJB in IHR, VII, 110ff. Gloucester—VHG.

p. 108 Castles—SCL in BAA, 3 S., IV, 39ff. Money—SET, 5, 8. Prices—BYC in EHJ, I, 155ff. Pecock—PRB; extracts in SEL, 48–56; cf. DNB. Chaundler—cf. DNB. His works are at Trinity College, Cambridge, Western MS. 881; and New College, Oxford, MS. 288—Burlington Fine Arts Club; (Catalogue of) *Exhibition of Illuminated Manuscripts*, 1908, p. 78, Pl. 109; KFD in A, LIII.

p. 109 Rous—E. M. Thompson in BM, I, 151ff.; A. G. B. Russell in BM, XXX, 23ff.; cf. DNB. Pageant—DHP. Puritans—SPM.

p. 110 Mediæval Building By-Laws—cf. London Assizes of Building of 1189 and 1212, printed in TPD, I, 275–83.

p. 111 Malory—VTM. Interludes—CMS, II, esp. 443–61. Clerk and Damsel—CMS, II, 324.

p. 112 York Fraternity of the Resurrection—York Corporation MS. B/Y, fo. 201b; for a transcript of this I have to thank the Rev. Angelo Raine. Drawings—BAH, 86–102; RDM; JES in WS, XIII.

p. 113 Higden—BLP, II, 165, quoted in CMP, 66. Portuguese exploration— PSR in NTM, 195 ff.; portrait of Dom Enrique in Plate at p. 200. Bristol voyage—NWW, 153; PPT; HEV in MM, XVI, 198 ff.; QEE in MM, XXI, 275 ff.

p. 114 Skelton—Editions: SPW; SCP; cf. SSP in S, IX, 25 ff. Musicians—FTC.

p. 115 Banaster's poem—SJS, 100. English singers abroad—NPC, 1436–43 (V), 218; LMC, 271–2. Echiquier—RMM, 383, 406; SHM, Note E, p. 277 (where "j. instrument appelle l'eschequier" is wrongly translated as "a chess-board").

p. 116 "Tied with a line"—SMF, 19. Mr. Hayes—HKM, 76.

p. 118 Wells Lady Chapel—BLW in SPA, XL, pt. ii, 32 ff. Baker—HWC; WCC, I, 412.

p. 119 Melrose—DDF in A, XXI, 346–9. Bruges—GEB, VI (Cart. de l'ancien Grand Tonlieu, II), 280, 369; GAB, III, 26. York and Dam—RFY, 72, 83; BFY, 19–20; GEB, II, p. 295, No. 1282.

p. 121 Hyndeley—RFY, 79–92, 208; BFY, 18, 19. Nicholl—WCC, I, 409, 596.

p. 122 Reredoses—AHA in HFC, XV; pt. 2, 149. Painted screens—BTP, 41–2, Pl. 77–82; VES, 57–62; cf. BCR; CGE. Saxon Kings—BTP, 47, Pl. 95, 96; FSC in SAC, XLVIII, 6 ff. Serle—CPR, 1467–76, 421; CPR, 1485–94, 48; DIE, 516.

CHAPTER VI

p. 123 S. Sitwell: *Mozart*, 1932.

p. 124 Skelton—see above, notes to p. 114. FAC, 25–6.

p. 125 Skelton—SCP, 263, 259, 311. I have used Mr. Henderson's revised text—see Preface. Skelton—SCP, 366.

p. 126 Julian, Epigram 1; JWW, III, 304–5. Wine—SET, 274, 376, 388. Ale, Beer, Tea—LAA.

p. 127 Guilds and Apprenticeship—KJM; CAR; SEM; KEG; UGL; UEH; SMC. Orchard—DNB; cf. DMM in OAS, 84th Rep.; LHP in NQ, CLXXXIX, 1945, 125. Divinity School—NWW, 281; see App. I, vi. Battlefield Church—RSG, 97, Fig. 18. Gatehouses—cf. AAC in CAS, *Proc.*, XL, esp. 50–1. Fan-vaults—HFV in AJ, LXVIII, 1–42.

p. 130 Virtue family—BRC, 61, 83, 99; BOC, 117, 125, 128, 130, 132, 135, 142, 157, 160; WHP, *Biographies of Members of the Commons House*, 1439–1509, 911; DRC, 200. See App. V, iii, iv.

p. 133 Skelton—SCP, "Against the Scots", p. 169.

p. 135 German Baroque—PEA, 98. Redman family—HLR, III, 68, 92, 271; MMC, 53, 69, 72, 73, 75, 76, 80, 81; ARA, 6, 27, 46, 66, 114, 116, 118, 129, 135, 142, 202, 204; FHB, 61.

p. 138 Coastal Forts—cf. OSH in A, XCI, 195—Kerb roof—AAC in CAS, *Proc.*, XL, 40–2.

p. 139 Bertie family—BLH; RPP, I, 1 ff.; BWB, 135; LPH, I, pt. i, No. 438 (3), p. 252; F. J. Baigent: MS. Abstracts of Hampshire Wills, Society of Genealogists Ac. 4088, p. 130.

p. 140 Painters—"The Serjeant Painters" in BM, LXXXIV, 81 ff.; LPH, I, i, No. 20, p. 16; I, ii, No. 2799; No. 1044 (8); EPL; NPP, 36. Players—CMS; GAL, 33. Musicians—FTC; HKM.

p. 141 Abyngdon at Bristol—NWW, 261.

p. 142 Sculptors—THD, 373; PRS in A, LXXXV; PCR in YAJ, XXIX, 157 ff.; RFY; YTE, V.

p. 143 Emler—LPH, I, pt. i, No. 307, p. 141; WTB, 67; CPR, 1494–1509, 473, 487. German sculptors—BGS in S, VIII, 165 ff.; BVS in S, X, 31 ff. Bellamy, etc.—LWR, 171; FRL. Winchester head—AFS in A LXXV, 165, Pl. LII.

CHAPTER VII

p. 145 Italian designs—cf. KAD in BM, LXXXII, 81 ff. English house— GST; GRE; GER; GEH; TEH.

p. 147 Warwick—for the Hiorne family, see *Country Life*, LIV (18 August 1923), 214 ff.

p. 148 Westminster, etc.—LKC; LWR; KYG; RSG.

p. 150 Literary bias—AMC, 145. Physiologus—BMC, 01; cf. DSM, 59.

p. 152 Mediæval index—MS. Rentals and Customs of Manors in Tottenham, Middlesex, in the possession of Messrs. Golding, Hargrove and Golding, London; cf. KWS. Gough Map—SRE in ECR, VII, 1 ff.; cf. PGM in GJ, LXXXI, 34 ff.

p. 153 Time-keeping—HSD; GSD; CUS; CDS; HCJ in A, LXXVII, 257 ff.

p. 154 Beushef—CPR, 1381–5, 237. Spices and strawberries—Warwick Accounts, MS., fo. cxcix, xlix.

p. 155 Perpendicular—LPC, 43; PMM, 58. Hammurabi—EEL, Law 229, p. 45.

p. 156 Pattern-books—HVH, 53–4. Literacy—ALE in L, 4 S., X, 163 ff.; cf. DLB; JHE in H, N.S., XI, 130 ff., 211 ff.; BEB; GLK in PBA, XXI, 201 ff.; TLL. Royal library—RKB in L, 4 S., XIII, 144 ff.; CPR, *passim*; NPP, 125.

p. 157 Travel—WIT in S, I, 361 ff.; WUC in H, N.S., XVII, 246 ff.; SRE in ECR, VII, 1 ff.; STH in BAA, N.S., XL, 75 ff.; cf. DHG, FWL. Travellers—NSS; NWW; SLI; cf. FLF, 113. Carriages—DIE, 263, 276; NPP, 123. See App. III. Hygiene—TSM, in S, III, 192 ff.; SBL in S., VIII, 335 ff.; SLC in S, IX, 303 ff.; SCC in S, XII, 19 ff.; DKR, XLVIII, 349; cf. TST.

p. 158 Villein marriage—LMH, esp. 246. Girls at school—ALE in L, 4 S., X, esp. 190. Edward III—HRP, 93, ll. 2556–62. Piracy—SET, 255; see App. II.

p. 160 Famine—LEF in S, V, 343 ff.

INDEX

SUBJECT INDEX

OF ENGLISH ARTISTS AND CRAFTSMEN

ACTORS and PLAYWRIGHTS: English; Gibson; Hamond; Maye; Medwall; Redford; Rutter; Scott.

ARMOURERS: Cologne; Stanlay.

BOOKS, Persons concerned with; Bauduyn; Burnham; Caxton; Depeden.

BRODERERS: Ashcombe; Burford; Carleton; Cologne; Glendale; Sauston; Strasbourg; Swan; Tiller; Vyve.

CARPENTERS, JOINERS, etc.: Alsebroke; Bird; Branche; Bytham; Coke; Cony; Crosse; Dobson; Foulford; Frankelyn; Geoffrey; Graveley; Hasill; Haynes; Herland; Howlett; Hurley; Karver; Lincoln; Lyngwode; More; Nedeham; Newhall; Norman; Page; Russell; Sam; Squyer; Toutmond; Walton; Wintringham; Wydmere.

COMPOSERS and MUSICIANS: Abingdon; Ashton; Banaster; Bramston; Bull; Byrd; Cook; Cornish; Damett; Dunstable; Fairfax; Farley; Farthing; Hawte; Hothby; Hygons; Lawes; Locke; Morley; Newark; Parsons; Pasche; Plummer; Power; Purcell; Pyamour; Redford; Squire; Sturgeon; Tallis; Taverner; Tye; Wodehall.

COOKS: Beauchef; Goodrich; Hoghwyk; More.

COPPERSMITHS, FOUNDERS, etc.: Austen; Broker; Ewen; Geyton; Godeyer; Hiltoft; Stephyns.

GLAZIERS and GLASS-PAINTERS: Attelard; Bee; Brampton; Chester; Geddyng; Lyen; Oxford; Prudde; Skynke; Thornton; Verrer.

GOLDSMITHS: Albright; Barentyn; Bottesham; Bush; Edmunds; Effomato; Gamenshede; Geyton; Grimsby; Harsey; Hessey; Hiltoft; Lamport; Melver; Randolf; Spalding; Theodore; Tildesley; Twyford.

MASONS, MARBLERS, etc.: Aldrych; Ampilforde; Attegrene; Atwodde; Aylmer; Barton; Battle; Beke; Bell; Bertie; Borde; Box; Burden; Cambridge; Canterbury; Carter; Cheney; Chevynton; Clarke; Clavyll; Clerk; Clifford; Clyve; Colchester; Cole; Couper; Cowper; Croxton; Croyland; Crundale; Danyell; Denys; Docheman; Dunkley; East; Elkins; Ely; Elys; Essex; Everard; Eyton; Farleigh; Fifelde; Forman; Garrett; Gloucester; Goldcliff; Gower; Growdon; Hashenperg; Helpston; Hobbs; Horewode; Horne; Hyndeley; Janyns; Joy; Jurdan; Lebons; Leget; Lesyngham; Lewyn; Lote; Lovell; Mapilton; Marwe; Marys; Maunsell; Mepsale; Molton; Orchard; Otes; Pak; Patrington; Pettyt; Playser; Pope; Porter; Powle; Ramsey; Redman; Richowe; Rodyngton; Roger; Rolston; Russell; Scune; Sens; Simon; Skillington; Smyth; Snelleston; Sponlee; Squyer; Stonhowse; Stow; Stowell; Studley; Swayne; Tempas; Thirsk; Titchmarsh; Turpyn; Vertue; Waleys; Walton; Wastell; Westerley; Winchcombe; Wolrich; Woodrofe; Wy; Wynford; Wynwik; Yevele.

PAINTERS and DRAUGHTSMEN: Attelard; Baker; Barneby; Beauneveu; Bee; Blithe; Bradewelle; Broun; Cambridge; Chaundler; Cologne; Coton; Daunte; Davy; Elham; Exeter; Frenge; Frensshe; Fyll; Godmered; Hilliard; Kent; Kyngeston; Leggard; Litlyngton; Maynard; Melton; Northfolk; Norwich; Ocle; Oxford; Paris; Pekele; Pokerich; Prince; Richer; Rous; Ruddok; St. Albans; Scheere; Serle; Siferwas; Somervill; Stone; Stratford; Strayler; Tassyn; Volpe; Walsingham; Whytyng; Wolfe; Worcestre; Wright.

POETS: Chaucer; Dunbar; Gower; Hawes; Henryson; Hoccleve; Langland; Lydgate; Minot; Rolle; Skelton; Strode; Surrey; Wyatt.

SCULPTORS and CARVERS: Baker; Belamy; Bolmone; Borde; Broun; Brownfleet; Chuddere; Dam; Drawswerd; Emler; Grasington; Hudd; Lindsey; Mapilton; Massingham; Nicholl; Nottingham; Patrington; Prentis; Reading; Reppys; Walton; Ymbar.

SMITHS: Johnson; Tresilian.

TAPICERS: Aghehe; Bullok; Lettreford; Underwood.

COUNTY KEY TO ILLUSTRATIONS

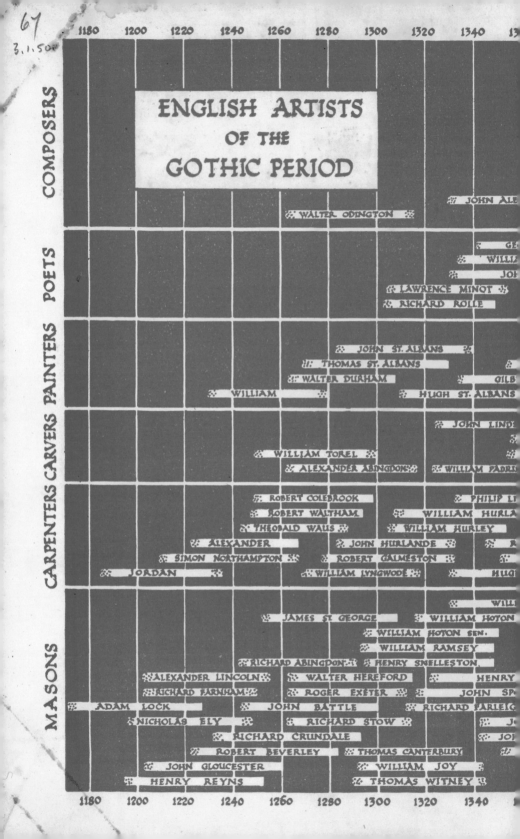

1180 1200 1220 1240 1260 1280 1300 1320 1340 13

ENGLISH ARTISTS
OF THE
GOTHIC PERIOD

COMPOSERS

JOHN ALE

WALTER ODINGTON

POETS

GE
WILLI
JO
LAWRENCE MINOT
RICHARD ROLLE

PAINTERS

JOHN ST. ALBANS
THOMAS ST. ALBANS
WALTER DURHAM   GILB
WILLIAM   HUGH ST. ALBANS

CARVERS

JOHN LIND
WILLIAM TOREL
ALEXANDER ABINGDON   WILLIAM PADRI

CARPENTERS

ROBERT COLEBROOK   PHILIP LI
ROBERT WALTHAM   WILLIAM HURLA
THEOBALD WAUS   WILLIAM HURLEY
ALEXANDER   JOHN HURLANDE   R
SIMON NORTHAMPTON   ROBERT GALMESTON
JORDAN   WILLIAM LYNGWODE   HUG

MASONS

WILL
JAMES ST GEORGE   WILLIAM HOTON
WILLIAM HOTON SEN.
WILLIAM RAMSEY
RICHARD ABINGDON   HENRY SNELLESTON.
ALEXANDER LINCOLN   WALTER HEREFORD   HENRY
RICHARD FARNHAM   ROGER EXETER   JOHN SP
ADAM LOCK   JOHN BATTLE   RICHARD FARLEIG
NICHOLAS ELY   RICHARD STOW   J
RICHARD CRUNDALE   JO
ROBERT BEVERLEY   THOMAS CANTERBURY
JOHN GLOUCESTER   WILLIAM JOY
HENRY REYNS   THOMAS WITNEY

1180 1200 1220 1240 1260 1280 1300 1320 1340